MESSIANIC PROPHECY

MESSIANIC PROPHECY

THE PREDICTION OF
THE FULFILLMENT OF REDEMPTION
THROUGH THE MESSIAH

BY

CHARLES A. BRIGGS, D.D.

HENDRICKSON
PUBLISHERS
PEABODY, MASSACHUSETTS 01961-3473

MESSIANIC PROPHECY
The Prediction of the Fulfillment of Redemption
Through the Messiah

Hendrickson Publishers, Inc. edition

ISBN: 0-913573-95-7

reprinted from the edition
originally published by Charles Scribner's Sons, New York, 1886

First printing — February, 1988

PREFACE.

———o———

MESSIANIC PROPHECY is the most important of all themes; for it is the ideal of redemption given by the Creator to our race at the beginning of its history, and it ever abides as the goal of humanity until the divine plan has been accomplished. There is no lack of works upon this subject. They are strewn along the Christian centuries in great abundance. And yet there are very few of them that have more than a transient value; for they either use Messianic Prophecy as a sword with which to smite the Jew or the infidel; or else as a crutch for a feeble faith in Christ and Christianity. There are very few of them that show any real interest in the theme for itself; there are still fewer that are animate with love and devotion to this greatest of all subjects. Messianic Prophecy has been too much dominated by the apologetical and the polemical interests, and the historical and the dogmatic bearings of the theme have been too much neglected.

This has given occasion to another common fault in the treatment of the subject. It has not been grasped as a whole and treated by a comprehensive method. Messianic Prophecy does not come to an end with the canon of the Scriptures of the Old Testament, as is commonly supposed. It assumes the same relative position in the Scriptures of the New Testament; and it

is the crown of the system of Christian doctrine. Hence
it divides itself into three great sections: the Messianic
Prophecy of the Old Testament, the Messianic idea of
the New Testament, and the Messianic ideal in the
history of Christian doctrine. No one can adequately
treat of any one of these sections until he has made a
comprehensive study of the whole subject.

The volume now given to the public is designed to be
the first of a series that will cover the whole ground.
It treats of Prophecy in general, of Messianic Prophecy
in particular, and then traces the development of the
Messianic idea in the Old Testament, concluding with a
summary of the ideal therein unfolded. It will remain
for a second volume to show how far this ideal has been
fulfilled by the first advent of the Messiah, and how far
it remained unfulfilled and was taken up into New
Testament Prophecy and carried on to a higher stage of
development. A third volume should trace the history
of the Messianic ideal in the Christian Church, and
show its importance in the development of Christian
doctrine.

Many of our readers will be surprised to find so little
reference to the fulfilment of the prophecies. This has
commonly been regarded as the most important thing.
Accordingly, the prophecies have been studied from the
point of view of their supposed fulfilment, and their
original meaning and their relation to the system of
Messianic Prophecy of the Old Testament have been
overlooked. Some prophecies have risen into dispro-
portionate prominence and have been exaggerated, while
other prophecies of equal and even greater importance
have been undervalued, and in some cases entirely
neglected. The Messianic ideal of the Old Testament
should be treated by itself and for itself, in order that
it may be understood as a system in its proportions and

in the inter-relations of its parts. I have not been able to escape altogether from the question of fulfilment. It is probable that a more rigid adherence to the plan that has been proposed would have excluded not a few references to the fulfilment that have found their way into the footnotes and even into the text. But it was not my purpose to undervalue the question of the fulfilment of the prophecies, and I did not care to be too strict in this matter. Furthermore, it was designed to treat the fulfilment in its proper place. I have given a summary of the Messianic ideal of the Old Testament at the close of this volume. It will be the work of the second volume to show how far that ideal has been realized in Christ and Christianity, and what still remains to be fulfilled.

I have not entered into the history of the interpretation of the passages, but have given the several interpretations, chiefly in footnotes, in order to explain those that have been adopted, and to discriminate them from others. The history of the interpretation of the Messianic ideal, according to the proposed scheme, comes into consideration in the third volume of the work.

The present volume traces the Messianic idea in its development in the Old Testament Scriptures. It does not enter into the Messianic idea of the apocryphal books, or of the Apocalypses, or of the Jewish sects of the four centuries, in the midst of which the first advent occurred, because the Messianic idea of the Old Testament is complete in the canon of the Old Testament. The Messianic ideas of the later Jews have their proper place as an external historical frame in which to set the Messianic idea of Christ and His apostles.

I have given the Messianic passages of the Old Testament in English translation, with a very few exceptions where they were of too great length. These translations

have been made from the original text. They have been
revised in order to conform with the Revised Version
whenever it seemed best so to do, partly because it
seemed desirable to recognise and take advantage of the
labours of those eminent scholars who have so recently
given it to the world; and partly because I am of the
opinion that any future revision must take its departure
from this vantage ground. In some cases the Revised
Version has been followed closely; but in the main it
has been used freely and has been departed from not
only when fidelity to the original text required it, but
also in many cases where I have preferred other renderings that have become familiar by long use. These
renderings are the product of the critical and historical
study of the original text, and are not proposed as sub-
stitutes for the renderings of the Revised Version or the
Authorized Version, which aim at a version for public
use.

The author has preferred to transliterate technical
words and explain them in footnotes, rather than to translate them inadequately or by uncertain renderings. The
divine names *Jahveh, 'El, 'Adonay, Shadday, 'Elyon, Jah,*
have not been translated, because they are proper names
of the Deity in most passages, and any translation misses
the sense. *'Elohim* has been translated God, except in a
few passages where it also is used as a divine name.
These names are unfamiliar to the English reader, but if
he will attend to their use in the successive passages
he will observe the importance of the discrimination.
Shades of meaning will attract his attention that he
could never discover in any version that translates them.
The neglect to distinguish between *'Elohim* and *'El* not
only obscures the difference in meaning, but also disregards the use of *'El* as a proper name in passages
where that use is of some importance. It is necessary

in a few words to explain my transliteration of יהוה by
Jahveh. I reaffirm what I have said elsewhere.[1] It
represents the Deity as an ever-living and acting person,
who enters into personal relations with His people, and
would have them address Him by a proper name in their
personal approaches unto Him in prayer and worship.
The later Jews, influenced by feelings of profound
reverence, which soon passed over into superstition,
abstained from pronouncing this name, and substituted
for it usually אדני, " Lord ; " or where יהוה אדני occurred,
אלהים, " God." Hence the Massoretes pointed יהוה with
the vowel-points which belong to אדני or אלהים, in order
to indicate that these other names of God were to be
used in place of יהוה ; and so the original pronunciation
of יהוה became lost. Hence in the LXX. and in most
translations " Lord," or its equivalent, is substituted for
יהוה. The word " Jehovah " is sometimes used in English
for this word. But it is a linguistic monstrosity.
Scholars are generally agreed that the original pronunciation was *Jahveh* (the *j* pronounced as *y*). There can be
little doubt that the substitution of " Lord " for *Jahveh*
in the translation of the Hebrew Scriptures and in the
Jewish Rabbinical Theology, has been associated with an
undue stress upon the sovereignty of God. The Old
Testament revelation in its use of יהוה emphasized rather
the activity of the ever-living personal God of revelation.
The doctrine of God needs to be enriched at the present
time by the enthronement of the idea of the living God
to its supreme place in Biblical theology, and the
dethronement of the idea of divine sovereignty from its
usurped position in dogmatic theology. Many English
scholars prefer the transliteration *Yahveh* or *Yahweh*.
I prefer *Jahveh*, because of its common use by foreign
scholars. I should have no objection to the other trans-

[1] *Presb. Review*, July 1885, p. 526.

literations if scholars would agree to any one of them. *Jahveh* is a brief, terse, and euphonious word, that has a wealth of meaning and of reminiscence of Biblical passages to all who are familiar with the Hebrew text. It is the name that God Himself gave to His people ; and if any name should be correctly pronounced and written, it would seem that it should be this one above all others.

The great majority of the passages are given in the lines and strophes of Hebrew Poetry. This part of the work has cost the author a large amount of severe labour. It has, however, opened up many new problems, and solved many perplexing questions. The author is well aware that there is a large amount of scepticism among Hebrew scholars as to the measurement of the lines and the strophical organization of Hebrew poetry, but this is due chiefly to the long-continued neglect of the subject, and to prejudices begotten partly by an ultra-conservative dislike of so-called novelties and by a timid clinging to the Massoretic system of accentuation. Those who are entitled to rank as authorities in the department of Hebrew Poetry have not doubted that there was some system of strophical arrangement, and some principles by which the lines were arranged ; for how else could Hebrew poetry be Poetry ? The principles that have been followed in the arrangement of the lines and strophes have been tried by some years of study and teaching, and have been applied with success to the greater part of the poetry of the Old Testament. These principles have enabled the author to discover several pieces of poetry in the Old Testament that have been previously unknown. I am assured of the correctness of these principles, and also of that arrangement of the great majority of the passages that is given in the book. But some of the passages are so difficult that the arrangement that I have given is tentative rather than final. The whole is submitted to the judgment of the candid scholar who has eyes to see the beauties of Hebrew Poetry. I have come to the conclusion that it would be no great task for an English poet to reproduce the entire body of Hebrew Poetry in corresponding English poetry of the same rhythm and strophical organization. If a real poet should perform this work he would confer an inestimable boon upon the English-speaking race, and give a version of the Old Testament that would be better adapted for popular use than any English version that translates Hebrew poetry into English prose.

The original text of all the passages has been studied in accordance with the principles of Textual Criticism. The Massoretic text not infrequently errs when compared with the ancient versions, and there are not a few passages where the principles of Hebrew Poetry aid us to a better text than that of any of the ancient authorities. No true scholar will despise critical conjecture in cases where the external evidence is unsatisfactory, and the text is manifestly corrupt. The author has taken great pains in this department of his work. The results are found in the translation, but the explanation of these results are given in the footnotes. These results will not please those who esteem the Massoretic text as well-nigh infallible. We have no hope of overcoming the prejudices of such scholars. We have done our work for those who have faith in the principles and methods of the Science of Textual Criticism.[1]

A most difficult task, that could not be avoided, was the arrangement of the passages in the order of their historical origin. A mechanical arrangement of the passages after the traditional method pursued by Hengstenberg, J. Pye-Smith, and most scholars who have written

[1] See my *Biblical Study*, p. 138 seq.

upon Messianic Prophecy would have been an easy task.
But this method gives us nothing better than a string of
exegetical papers without organic connection.   Messianic
Prophecy is a section of Biblical Theology.   It should
be treated in accordance with the principles and methods
of that branch of Biblical Science.   The development of
the Messianic idea is therefore of vast importance, and
all the passages must take their place in their historical
order, or that development cannot be traced to its full
extent.   The traditional position of many of these passages
will not bear serious examination.   It is impossible to
adhere to the traditional theories, and make anything of
a development of the Messianic ideal.   These theories
perish before the breath of Biblical Theology as well as
by the knife of the Higher Criticism.   The principles of
the Higher Criticism and of Biblical Theology have been
faithfully applied, and the author has reached much
greater satisfaction in the results of the investigation
than he deemed to be possible at the outset.   I shall not
deny that there are many cases of doubt, especially in
the arrangement of the Psalms.   But in all cases of
doubt it has seemed best to connect the doubtful passages
with other passages of similar import, where they seemed
to fit best in the development of the Messianic ideal.   In
general, the results correspond with those reached by the
great critics of the century; but in some cases I have
been compelled to depart from them, and in some
important passages to advance new theories which are
submitted to the judgment of all those who are in
earnest in the work of Biblical Criticism and Biblical
Theology.

This work is designed chiefly for theological students
and ministers of the gospel.   Accordingly I have carefully
summed up the Messianic idea of each passage or group
of passages in a compact and comprehensive statement.

These I have arranged in a series of sections that are numbered consecutively throughout the volume. Thus the student has an outline of the work for the purposes of review and as a preparation for an examination upon the subject. I have also furnished him with a critical apparatus in the footnotes for the study of the Messianic passages. These discuss all the important questions of textual criticism, higher criticism, philological explanation, and exegesis. The larger type of the book confines itself for the most part to the Messianic ideal as a part of Biblical Theology. All that is technical has been thrown into footnotes, and stands there by itself for the convenient use of the Hebrew student. The text is thus relieved of Hebrew words and critical discussions, so that any intelligent reader may use the book without being disturbed by anything that he cannot readily understand. For the author desires that his book may be of service to the thoughtful layman, and to Sabbath-school teachers, none of whom can be at all successful in their study of the Scriptures unless they know something about the Messianic idea that meets them everywhere in the sacred pages.

The author has devoted many years of study in preparation for the present work. It has cost him more labour than all other topics combined. It has been a labour of love and enthusiasm. And yet the theme is so great, so wonderful, so glorious, and so divine, that he has pursued it only to find that it escapes his grasp and transcends his efforts. He gives his work to the world, because he is convinced that a fresh study of the whole subject is greatly needed, and because he is assured that he has a contribution to make to its further discussion. At the same time he cordially invites the criticism of competent scholars. No one will be more ready than the author to welcome fresh light from any source. He prays

that whatever there may be of error in the book may
be detected and slain. The truth will take care of
itself. It cannot be resisted by the blind inertia of con-
servatism, or overcome by the mad rush of radicalism.
Truth is divine, and it will prevail over all obstacles
and enemies.

TABLE OF CONTENTS.

—o—

b

CHAPTER XIV.

THE MESSIANIC IDEA IN THE TIMES OF THE RESTORATION, p. 428.

CHAPTER XV.

THE MESSIANIC IDEAL, p. 476.

INDEXES.

MESSIANIC PROPHECY.

CHAPTER I.

HEBREW PROPHECY.

§ 1. *Prophecy is religious instruction. It is an essential feature of the religion of cultivated nations. It first appears as a function, then develops into an office, and at last organizes an order.*

Prophecy appears in any religion so soon as the need is felt of religious instruction, and therefore at a very early stage and among the most primitive peoples. It manifests itself at first in occasional and sporadic forms; but as the religion advances into higher stages, it develops into an office in order to give official guidance in religious knowledge and practice. In the patriarchal constitution of society the three functions of authority, prophecy, priesthood and royalty are ordinarily combined in the father of the family and the chief of the tribe; but at a very early stage the function of royalty is eliminated, and develops into the office of a monarch, and at a later stage into a dynasty: so the function of priesthood is eliminated and develops into an office and an order, which perpetuates itself by lineal descent or adoption. The prophetic function is ordinarily the last to develop into a separate order. It retains its closer relations with the

Deity, and therefore for a longer period maintains its independence of human relationships. In the highest religions the three orders exist side by side; but the prophetic order seldom develops beyond schools or guilds. This difference of the three functions in historical development originates from an essential difference in the functions themselves; for the function of royalty expresses the idea of government, the function of priesthood shapes the idea of worship, but the function of prophecy is the channel of religious instruction.

I. THE ESSENTIAL PRINCIPLE OF PROPHECY.

§ 2. *Prophecy as religious instruction claims to come from God and to possess divine authority. The prophet is an officer of the Deity, with a commission from the God whom he serves.*

Hebrew prophecy differs from other prophecy as the Hebrew religion differs from other religions. It has the common features which distinguish prophecy from priesthood and royalty. It has specific features which mark it off from the prophecy of all other religions. It is our purpose to rise from these common features to the specific features of Hebrew prophecy.

Prophecy as a special function of religion has the essential characteristics of religion itself. It involves some sort of union and communion between the Deity and man, whether it be real or ideal, traditional and fictitious, or historically evolved from divine communications, pretended, in order to power and influence, or presumed, owing to the deceptions of evil spirits, and abnormal personal conditions and circumstances. In any case, the prophet claims to come from God to impart religious instruction.

The Sacred Scriptures recognise the Hebrew prophets

as a species in the general class of prophets. The prophet of Jahveh speaks in the name of Jahveh, as the prophet of Baal speaks in the name of Baal.

Hebrew prophecy claims to be divine revelation. But other prophecy makes the same claim. Where then is the difference? On the one side it is urged that Hebrew prophecy is all true, and that the prophecy of all other religions is spurious and false. On the other side it is claimed that Hebrew prophecy, like all other prophecy, is a mixture of the true and the false.

It is in fashion with a certain sort of Christian apologists to ignore the science of religion, and insist upon the supernatural character of Biblical prophecy over against the purely human, natural or false prophecy of the other religions. They decline to recognise anything in common between Biblical prophecy and other prophecy. Such opinions may now be regarded as antiquated.[1]

The scholar observes that the same exclusive claims are put forth in the interest of the other great religions of the world, that their prophecy is the only genuine prophecy, and that Hebrew prophecy, in its present form at least, is spurious and false. Is the debate to be settled by the loudest and the longest dogmatism? Rather the inherent truth and reality of the prophecies are the determining factors and the final tests. The science of religion is in entire accord with Hebrew prophecy, in insisting upon the application of the supreme test, of veracity. Biblical prophecy claims to be true and real. It fears not the most searching criticism. Those silly Uzzahs who fear for the ark of God are guilty of pre-

---

[1] See Küper, *Das Prophetenthum des Alten Bundes*, p. 5, Leipzig 1870. Tholuck justly states, "Wie gross auch der Spielraum der dem Priesterbetrug und abergläubischer Selbsttäuschung zugeschrieben werden mag-dass eine Realität dabei zu Grunde gelegen, ist nun allgemein bei Philologen und Alterthumsforschern zur Anerkennung gekommen."—*Die Propheten*, p. 2, Gotha 1860.

sumption when they stretch forth impotent hands to prevent investigation. But real Christian scholars who are faithful to the word of God are not only willing that the tests should be applied by the doubtful and the inquiring; but they are determined to destroy doubt and to solicit faith by applying the tests themselves in the most thorough, comprehensive and exhaustive investigation. For the fires of criticism consume the hay, straw and stubble of human conceits and inventions which sprang from false methods of interpretation and preconceived theories of what prophecy ought to be. But all that is really valuable abides the test and rises in majesty above the ashes of human traditions.

Hebrew prophecy does not claim to be the only genuine prophecy. The Old Testament Scriptures represent prophecy as extending beyond the range of the chosen people in Melchizedek, Jethro, and Balaam.[1] It is not necessary, in the interests of the Christian religion, to insist that God left all other nations except Israel without religious guidance. The more the great historic religions of the world are studied in their genesis and their relations to the peoples who were influenced by them, the more truth, beauty and good are found in them. They had their appropriate task in preparing the nations of the world for the higher religion when it should come to them in the fulness of time.[2]

It was once the fashion to explain the good features of the other religions as relics of the primitive divine revelations recorded in the Bible, or as derived in some mysterious way from the Hebrews. But this fashion has passed away with the unscientific age. It has become evident that the facts are entirely different. The excellent features of the prophecy of the great historic religions of

---

[1] Gen. xiv. 18 ; Ex. xviii. ; Num. xxiii.-xxiv.
[2] See Cave, *Introduction to Theology*, p. 168 seq., Edin. 1886.

the world should be recognised and not resisted. If they are not as high in their order as the Biblical religions, they are still historic religions that have served multitudes of our race in their efforts to worship the Deity. It is unwise to explain them away by violent interpretations. Those who attack these religions by putting the worst constructions upon their prophecy ought to remember that they encourage the enemies of the Christian religion to treat Hebrew prophecy in the same arbitrary way. No argument can safely be used against heathen prophecy that may react to the damage of Hebrew prophecy. All prophecy must submit to the same tests. The tests will determine the extent of truth and falsehood in every prophecy of every religion. It is the Biblical and the scientific method to examine the phenomena and to abide by the results.[1]

II. THE PHASES OF PROPHECY.

§ 3. *There are three phases of prophecy which are common to the religions of the world — the dream, the vision, and the enlightened spiritual discernment.*

---

[1] We are entirely agreed with Dr. Maudsley, "If all visions, intuitions and other modes of communication with the supernatural, accredited now or at any time, have been no more than phenomena of psychology,—instances, that is, of subnormal, supernormal, or abnormal mental function,—and if all existing supernatural beliefs are survivals of a state of thought befitting lower stages of human development, the continuance of such beliefs cannot be helpful, it must be hurtful, to human progress."—*Natural Causes and Supernatural Seemings*, pp. 361–62, London 1886. But it is altogether unscientific to conclude from the fact that a very large number of supposed communications with the supernatural have been shown to be spurious, that therefore all others, even those of the Biblical religions, must be spurious likewise. A searching examination discriminates between true and false prophecy, just as clearly as it exposes every form of false science and philosophy. Men of science like Dr. Maudsley are as liable to slip in their hostility to the supernatural, as are theologians in their prejudices in favour of the supernatural.

These three phases of prophecy are familiar to the reader of the Scriptures. But he will find them also in the great religions of the world. The prophet Joel embraces them in his representation of the universal distribution of the prophetic gifts in the last age of the world, when the divine Spirit comes upon all classes and conditions of men.

> "Your sons and your daughters will prophesy,
>   Your old men will dream dreams,
>   Your young men will see visions." —Joel iii. 1.

§ 4. *The dream is the simplest phase of prophecy. It may arise from an abnormal condition of the body, or from the stimulation of a higher power. It may be genuine prophecy or spurious prophecy. There is need of discriminating tests.*

A dream has something of the wonderful about it, however it may originate. The man is so far passive to the impressions that are made upon him from without. Even when an excited organism or an abnormal condition of the body occasions the dream, it is beyond the control of the will of the subject; he is passive to the operations of his own higher powers, even though in some sense directing them. He is unable to resist the movement of his intellectual and emotional nature, which is hurried on by an impulse external to himself. It is not surprising that uncultivated persons and rude nations should ascribe this impulse to evil spirits or the heavenly powers. There is indeed in the spontaneous workings of the intellectual and emotional nature in dreams a facility which is unknown except in sleep. Unguided and unrestrained by external considerations and circumstances, or by the higher motives and principles of the reason and the will, the human spirit rushes on like a mountain torrent into the impending evil, or wings its flight like an eagle to the coming good. There is not infrequently in the dream an instinctive discernment of the issues of the present circumstances in which we or others may be involved.

The dream plays an important part in the prophecy of the Bible, in guiding the patriarchs of Israel and the human guardians of the Messiah, in the deliverance of Israel in Egypt and at Babylon. But the dream is a trouble to the monarchs of Egypt and Babylon without an interpreter. A Joseph and a Daniel were needed to voice their prophecies. But to the patriarchs and other sacred persons the dream was accompanied with its prophetic interpretation. The dream may or may not be prophetic. It may be instinctive prophecy or it may be divine prophecy. It may bear its interpretation with itself or it may need a prophetic interpreter. This prophetic interpreter may be a real prophet or he may be self-deceived or a deceiver. The dream is therefore simply a phase of prophecy, a test is needed to determine whether there be prophecy in it or not.

§ 5. *The most common phase of prophecy is the ecstatic state. This may be either natural, as in epileptics and persons who through nervous derangement have an abnormal intellectual and emotional development, or artificial, where the nervous organization is excited by external stimulants, or the agency of evil spirits, or the divine Spirit.*

In a rude and uncultivated age epileptic and deranged persons are regarded as possessed by evil spirits or the divine Spirit. Whether the spirit be good or evil, the Spirit of the one God or the influence of some one deity of a polytheistic system, depends more upon the religion of the people than upon the phenomenon itself. Such persons have strange experiences and utter marvellous sayings, which are regarded as coming from the Deity to warn

and guide mankind.   These are unnatural and beyond
experience, they are therefore regarded as supernatural.
The ecstatic state is commonly produced by artificial
means.   Those peculiarly inclined to it learn the art of
casting themselves into it, in order to enjoy the benefits
to be derived therefrom.   The prophets of Baal cut
themselves with knives, and cried out for hours in frenzy
for prophetic inspiration.   The 450 prophets of Baal

"called on the name of Baal from morning even until noon,
saying, O Baal, answer us.   But there was no voice, nor any that
answered.   And they leaped about the altar which was made.   And
it came to pass at noon, that Elijah mocked them, and said, Cry with
a loud voice, for he is god ; either he is musing, or he is gone aside,
or he has a journey, or peradventure he sleepeth, and he must be
awaked.   And they cried with a loud voice, and cut themselves
after their manner with swords and lances until the blood gushed
out upon them.   And it was so, when mid-day was past, that they
prophesied until the time of the offering up of the *Minchah.*" [1]

The necromancers are represented as chirping and
muttering in the practice of their art.[2]   The Shamans of
Eastern Asia use a tambourine and stimulants until they
cast themselves into an unconscious state, and then are
aroused to answer questions which are put to them.
Their answers are often surprisingly accurate, although
they know nothing that has transpired when they awake
into consciousness again.[3]   The Grecian prophetesses
were filled with the prophetic ecstasy by the foul gases

---

[1] 1 Kings xviii. 26 seq. פסח = leap, dance. על is at or about
the altar.   It is the sacred dance, the frenzied ecstatic whirling.   I
prefer to leave מנחה untranslated and transliterate it.   It is the
evening vegetable offering, probably consisting of grain or cakes.
There is danger of misconception in the rendering "oblation" given
in the R.V. as well as in the "sacrifice" of the A.V.   There is no
good reason for thinking that מנחה is here used for offering in
general, and there is lack of evidence as to the exact kind of vegetable offering used at this time.

[2] Isa. viii. 19.

[3] Tholuck, *Die Propheten*, p. 8 seq.

arising from clefts in the rocks. There the Grecian oracles were established and temples erected as at Delphi, Dodona and elsewhere.[1] At the present day the Dervishes of Mahometans cast themselves into the ecstatic state by whirling themselves in a circle or by howling for a long time. The Indian Fakirs cut themselves with knives as did the ancient prophets of Baal. There are also in the unconscious somnambulism and the gift of second sight kindred phenomena. In these ecstatic conditions involving unconsciousness to the external world the inner emotional and intellectual nature moves with great rapidity and freedom, and, as in the dream, reaches solutions of difficult problems and discerns the issues of events far and near. As in the dream so in the ecstatic state, there may be instinctive prediction and instinctive guidance through difficulties; or there may be entire failure. Biblical prophecy exhibits similar conditions of ecstasy. We have a picture of a band of prophets coming down from the high place with psaltery and timbrel and pipe and harp, and prophesying; and Saul meeting them, the Spirit of Jahveh came upon him and he prophesied with them.[2] Again Saul went to seek David and " the Spirit of God came upon him, and he went on and prophesied until he came to Naioth in Ramah. And he also stripped off his clothes, and he also prophesied before Samuel, and fell down naked all that day and all that night. Wherefore they say, Is Saul also among the prophets ? "[3]

As in the dream, so now in the ecstatic state. It is common to the religions of mankind. It is not absent from the Hebrew religion. It is not peculiar to the Hebrew religion. There is nothing in the ecstatic state as such to determine whether it results from divine

---

[1] Tholuck, *Die Propheten*, p. 6 seq.; Maudsley in *l.c.* p. 176 seq.
[2] 1 Sam. x. 5 seq.   [3] 1 Sam. xix. 23 seq.

influence or not. Every ecstatic state should be
tested ere it be accepted as the product of genuine
prophecy.[1]

§ 6. *There is also a higher order of prophets, who
through retirement and contemplation of the sacred mysteries*

[1] If we are not to assume, with the ignorant and barbarous races,
that the ecstatic state always has something of the supernatural
about it, we are also not to assume, with modern naturalistic
scholars, that the ecstatic state is never employed by supernatural
powers. For if the ecstatic state may be occasioned by disease or
by stimulants, why may it not be occasioned by the stimulation of
an evil spirit or a good spirit? True science will not close its eyes
to the question. There is no *à priori* objection to it that does not
arise beyond the domain of science, namely, in scepticism as to the
supernatural, or positive denial of the supernatural. Maudsley is
obliged to admit that the best work of the world has been done
under illusion (in *l.c.* p. 207), and that those who believe seriously
in the transcendent importance of human life, take it in tragical
earnest, and are ready to sacrifice strength and wealth and even life
in its service, are mainly or wholly dupes (p. 240). But most sober-
minded students will conclude that the serious, the devout, the self-
sacrificing reformers of the world are after all more likely to be
correct when they claim that they have been guided by a higher
power, and that the illusion and self-deception are rather with
those who cannot understand them, and who stubbornly close their
eyes to all the avenues that lead to the God of all grace. Kuenen
is more scientific when he says—
"A specific supernatural character can in no wise be ascribed to
the trance; its divine origin is not at all self-evident,—phenomena
of that nature were far from uncommon in ancient times and in the
Middle Ages, as it occurs even at the present day. It is true that for
a long time people had no hesitation in ascribing them to supernatural influence. They seemed so singular and extraordinary that
this explanation forced itself quite naturally on men's minds.
What could not be derived from God was therefore regarded as a
display of the power of the devil. But we now no longer occupy
that standpoint. Ecstasy is now accurately studied, compared with
other affections allied to it, and is explained from the human
organism itself, specifically from the nervous system. It may be—
on that point I determine nothing at present—that the trances of
the Israelitish prophets were of a nature altogether different; but
that must be proved separately, for ecstasy *in itself* is no supernatural phenomenon. It does not therefore advance us a step in
determining the origin of Old Testament prophecy."—Kuenen's
Prophets and Prophecy in Israel, p. 86, London 1871. See also
Ladd, *Doctrine of Sacred Scripture*, ii. p. 440 seq. 1883.

of religion have been spiritually enlightened to discern truths of a higher order than their fellows and to experience emotions of a deeper and more absorbing intensity. They have wondrous powers of insight and forecast. They read and interpret character and affairs. They are the masters of the past and the present, and they point the way confidently into the future.

Such prophets of a higher grade exist among the various religions of the world. Who can say that they are mere deceivers or enthusiasts ? Who can deny that some of them at least may have been guided by the divine Spirit in the ordinary influences of the divine Providence in their spiritual reflections and activities while they have been feeling after God ? If the Hebrew prophets were not only for Israel alone, but also in the end for the entire world, was there not a preparation needed by the other nations of the world to receive the prophecy of the Bible at the proper time ; and how could that preparation be so well accomplished as by prophetic voices in the midst of the other religions ?

Looking at these widespread phenomena of prophecy, we find that Hebrew prophecy exhibits similar phenomena. These are then the physical and psychological conditions of all prophecy, and are not peculiar features of Hebrew prophecy.[1]

Starting from these phases of prophecy which are common to the Hebrews and other nations, two con-

---

[1] Cicero already discriminated the higher order of prophecy from the lesser, " Duo genera divinationum esse dixerunt, unum quod particeps esset artis, alterum quod arte careret. Est enim ars in iis, qui novas res conjectura consequuntur, veteres observatione didicerunt. Carent autem arte ii, qui non ratione aut conjectura, observatis aut notatis signis, sed concitatione quadam animi aut soluto liberoque motu futura præsentiunt, quod et somniantibus persæpe contingit et non nunquam vaticinantibus per furorem."— Cicero, *de divin.* i. 18.

trasted positions are taken and erroneous theories are constructed by laying an undue emphasis upon one phase or another.

III. THE MONTANISTIC THEORY OF HEBREW PROPHECY.

§ 7. *The Montanistic theory represents the prophets as passive instruments of the divine Spirit. The ecstatic state with its vision is the essential feature of prophecy. The prophet sees or hears the revelation as something external to himself, and declares it is an external thing. He is taken possession of by the divine Spirit, so that his speech and writing are no longer his own, but the Spirit's, using him as an instrument.*

It should not be denied that this phase of prophecy does occur in the Bible. The hand of Jahveh is laid upon such men as Gideon, Jephtha and Samson, making them mere instruments or channels of divine influence. The prophetic mania comes upon a man like Saul. There is a dreaming of dreams by Pharaoh and Nebuchadnezzar; there is a seeing of visions by Balaam, and the hearing of a divine voice as by the child Samuel; and we find instruments of the most passive kind in the serpent of Eden and the ass of Balaam. But these are all of the lower phases of prophecy where the divine Spirit deals with incapable instruments ; rude men, heathen kings, coarser spirits, untutored boys, who had little susceptibility for communion with God, and with dumb beasts. It is not the appropriate method for spiritual and devout souls.

Balaam receives revelations in dreams. His ecstatic state is vividly described. He lies prostrate with closed eyes, seeing a vision and hearing words, which he is constrained to utter against his will:

> " Utterance of Balaam son of Beor,
>   Utterance of the man with closed eyes,
>   Utterance of the one hearing the sayings of *'El*,
>   And knowing the knowledge of *'Elyon*,
>   Who sees the vision of *Shadday*,
>   Lying prostrate and with eyes opened." [1]

But Moses the prophet of Jahveh is vastly higher than
this. God does not speak to him in visions, dreams, or
riddles, but face to face, shows him His form, and grants
him His communion.

> " If one is to be your prophet,
>   I, Jahveh, in the vision make myself known to him ;
>   In a dream I speak with him.
>   Not so my servant Moses,
>   With all my house he is entrusted,
>   Mouth to mouth I speak with him,
>   In an appearance without riddles ; [2]
>   And the form of Jahveh he beholds.
>   Why then do ye not fear
>   To speak against my servant Moses ?" [3]

Moses is the model of all subsequent prophecy. The
prophet who is to give divine instruction to Israel is like
him.[4] Hebrew prophecy is ordinarily of the highest
phase. It has its psychological basis in what we observe
in the highest order of prophets among the heathen.
Those isolated cases on which the modern Montanists

---

[1] Num. xxiv. 15, 16. We give the Hebrew divine names in
transliteration in order to show the differences which are obscured
by translation. אֵל, *'El*, is the Strong. By rendering God the difference between it and אֱלֹהִים is obscured. עֶלְיוֹן, *'Elyon*, is an archaic
intensive plural form with the meaning Most High. שַׁדַּי, *Shadday*,
has the meaning Almighty.

[2] The Massoretic text reads וּמַרְאֶה, and so does the Vulgate, but
the Vulgate renders *et palam*. The Samaritan codex and the LXX.
read בְּמַרְאֶה, and the LXX. renders ἐν εἴδει, which is better suited to
the context and the parallelism.

[3] Num. xii. 6–8. This little piece is poetry, and we present it
in the lines of parallelism.

[4] Deut. xviii. 18.

build their theory amount to nothing more than a lower
order of a more general class. They give at best a
mechanical, a magical sort of prophecy. The great mass
of Hebrew prophecy—compared with which the cases
referred to are trifling in number—exhibits a revelation
of a vastly higher character. It is not external, mechanical, or magical, but internal, spiritual and intelligent.
Hebrew prophecy is through the enlightenment of the
mind of the prophet, the stimulation of his moral nature,
the constraining of his will, under the most sublime
motives, the assurance of his soul that he is in possession
of divine truth, and that he is commissioned to declare it.[1]

The most primitive form of prophecy among the
Hebrews was doubtless of the lowest phases, external
revelations, through dreams or in ecstatic visions. From
this point of view the prophet was in the most ancient
times called a *seer*, and his prophecy a vision[2]—not seen

---

[1] See Riehm, *Messianische Weissagung*, 2 Aufl. p. 21 seq., Gotha
1885 ; *Messianic Prophecy*, p. 20, Edin. 1876. Hengstenberg in
modern times laid great stress upon the organ of sight in the ecstatic
state of Biblical prophecy. Few modern scholars have been able to
follow him. In more recent times König has emphasized the organ
of hearing and the divine communication through words and speech.
It is quite evident that divine communications are more frequent, in
the Old Testament representations, to the ear than to the eye.
Sometimes both organs are open to divine revelation. But it seems
to us that König has failed in his emphasis upon hearing, no
less than Hengstenberg in his emphasis upon seeing. The criticism of Riehm upon his theory is quite just. It is sufficient that
we recognise the divine origin of the communication as external
to the soul of man. There are no sufficient reasons for extending
this external origin to the form and the mode of the communication.
The stimulation of the higher nature of man by a divine impulse is
all that can be proven with reference to the mass of Hebrew
prophecy. The mode of the stimulation seems to be ordinarily
within the man, when his powers are active and not passive, when
the divine ideal springs up in the forms of the prophet's own thinking and expression. See Riehm in *l.c.* p. 22 seq., and König in *l.c.*
ii. pp. 142 seq., 360 seq.

[2] רָאָה = seer, and its synonymous חֹזֶה, gazer, beholder. That
which is seen is also called מַרְאָה or מַחֲזֶה or חִזָּיוֹן = vision. There

indeed with the physical eyes, for these were closed in slumber or in unconsciousness to the external world— but seen by the inner eye. But even here in this lowest sphere of Hebrew prophecy, where the prophet was merely passive and the vision or dream an object of internal sight, there is the presence of God in a distinguished manner, as in the theophanies of the heavenly ladder in Jacob's dream, the fiery furnace in Abraham's vision, and the cherubic chariot in the vision of Ezekiel.[1] There is also an interpreting voice which guides the inner eye to see and to understand what it could not otherwise observe. For unless the dream and the vision of Hebrew prophecy were something more than mere dream or vision, unless they have with them the peculiar marks of the Deity, we could not accept them as divine. It is in these lower grades of prophecy that we find the specific features of Hebrew prophecy as well as in the higher.

But the later, higher and more common name of the Hebrew prophet is *Nabi*,[2] which means speaker, or preacher. From this point of view the prophetic word is called suggestion, communication, or utterance of

is no such distinction between these terms as König finds (*Offen-barungsbegriff*, ii. p. 29 seq., Leipzig 1882. See Riehm in *l.c.* p. 45).

[1] Gen. xxviii. 12 seq. ; Gen. xv. 12 seq. ; Ezek. i.

[2] נביא is an intransitive noun from the stem נבא. It is not found in the active or passive species, but only in the reflexive, either the *Niphal* or *Hithpael*. It is kindred with נוב, which is used of the coming forth of fruit. So in Prov. x. 31, "The mouth of the righteous *putteth forth* wisdom." It is like the Arabic *naba'a* = to rise up, become audible, to proclaim, and the Assyrian *nabû* = to call, proclaim, name. נביא is therefore the spokesman, preacher. This is essentially the view of most recent interpreters, Ewald, Fleischer, Delitzsch, König, Mülau, and Volck, *et al.* Kuenen objects that the Arabic verb is more likely a denominative, and that the Arabic noun was derived from the Hebrew, and that furthermore the verb is used in Hebrew only in the reflexive species (*Prophets*, p. 42). But this does not explain the Assyrian verb, and the reflexive species properly mean to act as spokesman or preacher. Kuenen agrees with Tholuck, Gesenius, *et al.*, that נביא is a passive noun, from נבא, kindred with נבע = to boil up, pour forth, and that

God; or "word of Jahveh;"[1] or message,[2] which the prophet was to lift up in song or preaching.

So from this higher point of view the prophet is called servant of God, involving a close relationship to the Deity as His own servant—a man of God, and also a man of the Spirit.[3]

Indeed, so close is the intimacy between Jahveh and His prophets that

"Surely 'Adonay Jahveh doeth nothing,
Unless he hath revealed his secret plan to his servants the prophets.
Hath a lion roared, who will not hear?
Hath 'Adonay Jahveh spoken, who will not prophesy?"[4]

These prophets are therefore like Moses, in close union and constant communion with their God. They ordinarily depend upon a subjective and internal communication through the stimulation of their higher nature to perception, conception, comprehension and expressive utter-

---

the prophet is one who is caused to boil over with the divine word. They refer to רחש in Ps. xlv. 2 for the idea. Hupfeld, Riehm, Schultz, *et al.*, compare נבא with נאם, and take them both as passive forms with kindred meaning. But most scholars regard נאם as meaning, breathe, whisper. It is found in the verbal form only in Jer. xxiii. 31. It is elsewhere used as a passive part. construct before God or the prophet, or a personification of evil (Ps. xxxv. 12). It seems to us that the stems are similar, and they must have synonymous meaning. *Namu* is found in late Babylonian with the meaning *proclaim.* We prefer to regard נביא as preacher and נאם as utterance.

[1] דבר יהוה is used but once in the Pentateuch, in Gen. xv. 1, where it differs from the mode of revelation in the context, and seems to be the generalization of a later editor. It is a frequent term in the prophets.

[2] משא is a noun formed by מ from נשא = to lift up. It is the *message* that the prophet lifts up in song or preaching. It is usually found in connection with predictions of judgment or warnings, and is commonly rendered *burden.*

[3] איש הרוח (Hos. ix. 7) indicates that the prophet is a man acting with divine authority and under the influence of the divine Spirit.

[4] Amos iii. 7, 8. אדני, *'Adonay*, the Lord.

ance of the mysterious counsels of divine revelation, by the voice and the pen.[1]

IV. THE NATURALISTIC THEORY OF PROPHECY.

§ 8. *The naturalistic theory starts from the highest phase of prophecy which exists among the heathen. It brings into view the wondrous insight and foresight of men of genius. It points to the great religious teachers of the world outside of the Hebrew nation. It claims that the Hebrew prophets were men of the same kind, though of a higher and nobler grade, in the measure that their religious conceptions were higher and nobler.*

We admit that the productions of human genius and the religious teachings of the prophets of the religions of the world may be explained sufficiently by the ordinary operations of divine providence upon the souls of men, without extraordinary divine influence. But we claim that Hebrew prophecy cannot be explained in this way. We recognise common features in Hebrew prophecy and other prophecy so far as these have been traced. But after all that is common has been eliminated, that which is peculiar to Hebrew prophecy is of such a character as to prove its divine origin and guidance.

A careful discrimination of the elements found in the prophecy of all other religions and in the Hebrew religion, and the comparison of the results, brings the vastly higher and grander features of Hebrew prophecy

---

[1] See Delitzsch, *Messianic Prophecies*, p. 17, Edinburgh 1880, who aptly cites Chrysostom Hom. xxix. *in ep. ad corinthios :* "This is the peculiarity of the mantis ; to be beside oneself, to suffer constraint, to be struck, to be stretched, to be dragged like a madman. The prophet, however, is not so, but he speaks everything with calm understanding and with sound self-possession, and knowing what he proclaims, so that before the result we can even from these things distinguish between the mantis and the prophet."

to scientific statement and invincible position.[1] This will be manifest both in the differences in form and the differences in content, and above all in the entire conformity to truth and fact, in such sublime heights of conception and such vast reaches of comprehension, that it transcends the powers of human origination and guidance, and compels resort to the divine mind and the divine power to explain its origin and its development into such a sublime organism.

V. THE DISTINGUISHING FEATURES OF HEBREW PROPHECY.

§ 9. *The prophet of Jahveh is personally called and endowed by Jahveh with the prophetic spirit. He speaks in the name of Jahveh and in his name alone. He is one of a series of prophets who guide in the development of the Hebrew religion. He absorbs and reproduces previous prophecy. He transmits prophecy with confidence to his successors. Hebrew prophecy is an organism of redemption.*

We have seen that Hebrew prophecy has the same three phases that are found in all great religions, but that it cannot be explained by theories which build on any of these phases. It claims to be a divine revelation, resting upon higher and more substantial grounds than these. Indeed we not only have to distinguish between Hebrew prophecy and all other prophecy; but in Hebrew prophecy itself it is necessary to eliminate the genuine from the spurious: for there are those who speak in the name of Jahveh and are prophets of lies.[2] There are those who mistake their conceits and fancies for divine communica-

---

[1] Müller, *Science of Religion*, p. 37, 1873, "I make no secret that true Christianity, I mean the religion of Christ, seems to me to become more and more exalted the more we know and the more we appreciate the treasures of truth hidden in the despised religions of the world."

[2] Jer. xxiii.

tions. There are those who are deceived by lying spirits.[1] There are professional prophets in Israel who prophesy for gain and for political influence. The faithful prophet of Jahveh has to contend against these false prophets of Jahveh as well as against the prophets of Baal. He does it through the divine assurance that he is in possession of the truth of God, and that he is called to proclaim it. For the true prophet of Jahveh differs from other prophets not in those phases of human experience and expression which are essential to prophecy and common to mankind, but as the Hebrew religion differs from all other religions. For an extraordinary divine influence which is called supernatural, to distinguish it from the ordinary influences of the divine Providence which are called natural, used the psychological and physical conditions of human nature to determine through them that religion and so that prophecy in its origin and through its organic development towards the accomplishment of a divine plan of redemption.[2]

Without denying to other religions an occasional divine influence in their prophecy, springing from the ordinary working of the divine Providence in the affairs of mankind, without excluding altogether the prophecy of the great religions of the earth from occasional extraordinary divine influences such as are called supernatural, we claim that these extraordinary divine influences give Hebrew prophecy its characteristic features; for we find them extending through a long period of historical development, increasing in intensity, complexity and comprehensiveness as they accumulate upon one another, combining so as to constitute Hebrew prophecy an organic whole, a sublime ideal of redemption.

[1] 2 Chron. xviii.
[2] Simon, *The Bible an Outgrowth of Theocratic Life*, chap. viii. Edin. 1886.

VI. THE PROPHETIC CALL AND ENDOWMENT.

§ 10. *Hebrew prophecy originates in a personal revelation of God to man in theophany. It is communicated to successive prophets by the influence of the Spirit of God. The divine Spirit assures the prophet of his possession of the truth of God and of his commission to declare it; endows him with the gifts and spiritual energy to proclaim it without fear or favour, and despite every obstacle; guides him in the form of its delivery, and directs him to give it its appropriate place in the prophetic system.*

The Hebrew religion is a religion of union and communion with God, a living, growing, everlasting religion. The Hebrew prophets present us with an immortal religion. They derive it by direct communication with the ever-living God. It is the theophanic manifestation of God in forms of time and space and the sphere of physical nature, to call and endow the master spirits of Hebrew prophecy, that constitute one of its most distinctive features. Hebrew prophecy as Hebrew miracle-working springs from theophanies. These were the sources of every new advance. They constitute a series leading on to the incarnation as their culmination. They were the divine seals to the roll of Hebrew prophecy, sealing every new page with an objective divine verification and authentication. They bind the prophets into an organic whole. They come in the great crisis of the development of prophecy, and shed their glorious light over the prophecies that precede and those that follow. We have not only therefore the calling and endowment of particular prophets by these theophanies, but the calling and the endowment of prophetic chiefs to originate and perpetuate a succession of prophets with an organic system of prophecy.[1]

[1] "The case admits of no doubt—the canonical prophets are mutually allied and are closely connected with one another. The

We do not find these theophanies in connection with every prophet, but only with the greatest prophets, the reformers of their age. It is possible that other prophets were also called by theophanies which they have not described to us. But this is improbable. It was indeed unnecessary. Theophanies are to initiate religious movements and mark the stages of their development, but are not the constant feature of prophecy. Ordinarily Hebrew prophecy comes from prophets who have the internal subjective assurance of the truth of God and their commission to declare it. But in all cases of objective as well as subjective assurance the prophet's powers are taxed to the utmost to give expression, in the human forms of his own nature and surroundings, to the divine ideas that have taken possession of him.

In order to explain this internal communication we would refer to the witness of the Holy Spirit giving the Christian assurance of salvation, the assurance of sonship to God, and the gratification of knowing that prayer is accepted and answered. This testimony of the Spirit is a divine assurance imparted by a supernatural energy to the believer's soul.[1]

The difference in the operation of the Holy Spirit in these cases is not in mode. The divine energy is the same—the Spirit of God. The subjects of the influence are the same — pious men. The same supernatural impartation of the divine Spirit to the human spirit is made in all these cases. The difference consists in the

one may stand more by himself, the other may be more dependent upon his predecessors; collectively they all form, as it were, one school, or they may be likened to the links of one chain."—Kuenen, *Prophets*, p. 74.

[1] See Oehler, *Theology of the Old Test.* ii. p. 336 seq., Edin. 1883, and Riehm in *l.c.* p. 35 seq. The polemic of König (in *l.c.* ii. p. 194 seq.) against this position seems to us without force. See also Ladd, *Doctrine of Sacred Scripture*, ii. p. 369 seq., and *Presbyterian Review*, v. p. 384.

contents of this influence—and in the measure of the energy. The contents in the other cases mentioned are: sense of sonship, of the love and favour of a heavenly Father, of communion with Him, of conformity to His will, of receiving the benefits desired in prayer. The contents of the influence that inspires the prophet are: the revelation of truth in its relation to the particular prophet and in its relation to the organism of prophecy, and the obligation to declare that truth in the form in which it is conveyed, and to give it its place in the prophetic system.

There is also a difference in the extent and degree of the energy, for the prophet is empowered to deliver the truth of God without fear or favour despite obstacles and resistance of every kind. The intensity of this energy differs greatly in different prophets. In Moses and Elijah, in Isaiah, Jeremiah and Ezekiel, the heroes of prophecy, who were called in theophanies, it was so intense as to enable them to stand alone with God against their own nation and the world, and to overcome by its divine energy all opposing forces and circumstances. And yet never was the individuality of these heroes of prophecy so marked, never their humanity more apparent, never the peculiar features of their own character so distinct, as in those great crises when the fires of God within them were burning with the most intense light and heat. The divine imparted its energy to the human and merged its objectivity in the subjectivity of the prophet, in this infallible assurance of having and holding and declaring the invincible truth of God.

VII. THE TEST OF PROPHECY.

§ 11. *The infallible test of the genuine prophecy of Jahveh is its entire conformity to truth and fact.*

The infallible assurance of the soul of the prophet may be difficult to distinguish from the false assurance of enthusiasts and the confident self-assertion of prophets of lies, and yet here is the place where the distinction must be made.

The possibility, yes, the probability of mistakes is recognized in the Scriptures and provided for in the warning of Moses.

"For these nations, which thou art about to dispossess, are accustomed to hearken unto sorcerers and unto diviners ; but as for thee, Jahveh thy God hath not suffered thee so to do. A prophet from thy midst, of thy brethren, like me, will Jahveh thy God raise up unto thee ; unto him shall ye hearken ; according to all that thou didst ask from Jahveh thy God in Horeb, in the day of the assembly, saying, 'I cannot again hear the voice of Jahveh my God, and this great fire I cannot see any more, lest I die.' And Jahveh said unto me, 'They have done well in what they have spoken. A prophet will I raise up for them from the midst of their brethren, like thee, and will give my words in his mouth, and he will speak unto them all that I charge him. And it will come to pass, that whosoever will not hearken unto my words which he will speak in my name, I will require it of him. Only the prophet who shall presume to speak a thing in my name, which I have not charged him to speak, and who shall speak in the name of other gods, that prophet shall die. And if thou say in thy heart, How can we know the thing which Jahveh hath not spoken ? What the prophet speaketh in the name of Jahveh, and the thing transpire not and come not, that is the thing which Jahveh hath not spoken. In presumption the prophet hath spoken. Thou shalt not be afraid of him.'"[1]

Here then is a divine test of prophecy given at the very foundation of the Hebrew system. Not the signs and wonders and external forms of prophecy are to be the test, for as Jesus said, "There will arise false Messiahs and false prophets, and will show great signs and wonders: insomuch that if possible they will deceive the very elect,"[2] but the internal character, the

[1] Deut. xviii. 14–22. [2] Matt. xxiv. 24.

essence of the prophecy, whether it be in the name of Jahveh, whether it be true and real, whether it be to the honour of God, whether it conform with the prophetic system. This is the absolute test to which every Hebrew prophet submits, and which every pious man is bound to apply. This test of divine truth gives a mutual obligation. It gives a divine sanction to the prophet himself to declare the truth of God, and it also gives the most sacred obligation to the people to yield obedience to the word of truth.

Any such slavish adhesion to à priori claims as the scholastic theory requires is unscriptural and it is immoral. It is the sign-seeking condemned by our Saviour as so characteristic of the Pharisees of his time. Every divine revelation demands the most searching criticism and inquiry as to its truth. The more earnest and searching the inquiry, the more complete will be the mastery that the divine truth will gain over the soul, and the more sincere and faithful will be the adhesion to it.

VIII. THE DEVELOPMENT OF PROPHECY.

§ 12. *Prophecy first appears as an occasional function of the antediluvians and patriarchs. Moses was the first official prophet, and the model of all that followed. Samuel was the first to make it a distinct office and to found prophetical schools. The prophets are the counsellors of the monarchs and the reformers of the nation, and as such reach a sublime height in Nathan, Elijah and Elisha. They instruct the nation in its history and its covenants, its institutions and its worship, and give birth to schools of psalmody and wisdom. Prophecy attains its height in a series of prophets who deliver oral prophecies as the divinely appointed national reformers, and subsequently record their prophecies as the several successive sections of an organic system of divine revelation to mankind.*

Prophecy was first developed into an office in Moses, who became the model of all subsequent Hebrew prophets. Prior to Moses the prophetic function is displayed at times in Enoch and Noah, in Abraham and Jacob, but it is sporadic. Moses predicts a prophet like himself over against the sorcerers and diviners of the Canaanites, but knows nothing of an order or succession of prophets. Prophecy remains sporadic until Samuel, who is called to the office of prophet, and who like Moses at first combines the prophetic and regal functions, but after the resignation of his civil authority establishes the prophetic office apart by itself, and becomes the founder of prophetical schools. With Samuel the prophetic office takes its place as an independent office alongside of the royal and priestly orders, and enters upon centuries of development.

The prophets at first appear like Samuel with some of the functions of the judges. They suddenly appear at the court of the king or before a national assembly. They execute their commission of exhortation, promise or warning, and disappear. Their religious instruction has a political cast. The schools of the prophets are frequently mentioned in the historical books at various places and in considerable numbers. They seem to have been engaged in the study of the instruction of Jahveh and in His worship with songs and dances. To them we may attribute the earlier historical poems and poetic narratives embedded in the historical books. They were being prepared through many generations from Samuel to Joash for the peculiar work the prophetic order was ordained to do. They gave birth to the schools of psalmody and the schools of wisdom, and prepared the way for the greatest prophets. They combined the history and the poetry, the laws and the wisdom, to reproduce them at the appointed time in higher and grander forms.

After the division of the kingdom it was in the northern realm that the prophetic activity had the fullest development. This was in order to lead Israel through the severe crises in her history. And thus the prophetic order rises rapidly to a sublime elevation and grandeur in Elijah and Elisha as they appear endowed with miraculous power, and boldly confront kings and princes as if they would single-handed turn the heart of princes and bend the nation to the will of Jahveh.

But these functions of the prophetic office, making history as great religious heroes, and recording the history of redemption with its covenants and institutions, were preparatory to the highest function of giving the divine revelation in historical development and in a living, growing and ever consolidating organism. Combining the sum-total of the divine revelation of the patriarchs and judges, and especially of Abraham and Moses and of Samuel, they rolled it along with immense and ever increasing weight, power and sublimity, hasting on to the latter days. The prophets as an order of preachers and teachers constitute a grand stairway, advancing prophet after prophet in linked succession until the organism of prophecy is completed and the revelation of the Messiah is at hand.

As the prophetic office was rising to its highest functions, it developed into four schools or tendencies, three of which, the school of psalmody, the school of wisdom, and the school of the ritual, moved in the ordinary planes of prophecy, while the prophetic function of the schools of the prophets moving in narrower lines rose to its towering heights of guiding the nation through the perplexities of the present, towards a realization of the grander ideals of the future. The whole Old Testament is prophecy

in the broader sense of the term, and yet when we
distinguish the law from prophecy we are halting on the
threshold of a still more thorough discrimination which
eliminates from prophecy in general, the Law and the
Wisdom and the Psalter, in order to rise at once to a
conception of prophecy which is at the same time narrower
and higher. For the Hebrew prophets grasp the great
essential principles of the Hebrew religion. They trace
them in their most characteristic features in historical
development. They apprehend the exact issues of their
own times. They realize the eternal ideals of the
prophetic system. They raise these on the banners of
reform. The Hebrew prophets are thus essentially a
series of reformers. Their office is to hold up the ideal
of reform and urge to its realization. They are the true
successors of Moses—they lead on to Christ. They
marshal the religious forces of Israel, and from age
to age advance the lines of the faithful in closer conformity to the divine ideal, which lies at the basis of the
Hebrew religion, and which dominates its history. This,
then, is the great feature of Hebrew prophecy, its grand
march forward in spite of every obstacle from triumph to
triumph. The author of the Epistle to the Hebrews [1]
begins the roll-call of the heroes, but stops almost at the
beginning for want of time and space to complete them.
No such names are to be found in the history of any
other nation,—or in the history of all the other religions
combined,—heroes of battles the most sublime the world
has ever seen; battles not for the religion of Israel alone,
but for the religious progress of humanity, for the everlasting religion of mankind.

[1] Heb. xi.

IX. THE PROPHETIC IDEAL.

§ 13. *Hebrew prophecy combines in a remarkable manner the real and the ideal. If the real is in exact conformity to truth, still more is the ideal a mirror of the divine mind. The ideal of Hebrew prophecy is the regulative factor of the entire Old Covenant revelation. It is at once the goal and the impulse of the entire historical development. It comprehends the essential principles of religion, doctrine and morals. It combines the circumstantial and the variable with the essential and invariable to be ultimately attained by all. Above all, it is an ideal of the complete redemption of mankind.*

In the marvellous progress of Hebrew prophecy the most significant factor is the combination of the real and the ideal. In the midst of the circumstantial and the variable, adapted to particular persons and occasions, the determining influence is ever the essential ideal which abides, amidst all the vast variety and intricate complexity of detail, the permanent, the everlasting and the ultimate —not a stereotyped ideal in forms to which everything must be conformed, but a living ideal adapting itself with ease and grace to every circumstance and every occasion and every person, and yet so exalted above the temporal and the local and the purely formal, that these are incapable of limiting its growth or checking its progress. It is indeed a living, an eternal, an absolute, an infinite ideal—what else can it be than the product of the divine mind ?

This ideal is readily discernible throughout Hebrew prophecy. We see it not only in the ten commandments, the quintessence of Mosaism, but it pervades the entire legislation and all the codes, as the regulative element giving shape and organization to the whole. It is this ideal that makes the Psalter the psalm book of the uni-

versal Church, that gives the Wisdom literature its
ethical influence upon all times and lands, that makes
Hebrew history the mirror of humanity, that constitutes
the Hebrew prophets the teachers of the world. Call
this ideal what we please, supernatural or natural, it
matters not. It is higher and grander than any other
natural known to man; it is so much higher and grander
that it separates Hebrew prophecy from all other prophecy. It gives it a unique position and importance.
It is an ideal ever realizing itself, and yet as high above
reality as ever. If it be not divine in origin and direction, whence did it originate? It lifts us to the higher
powers—it has the attributes of the Infinite One. It is
divine revelation.

If we look at the doctrines of the Hebrew prophets
and compare them with the doctrines of other prophets,
the divine features of these doctrines are manifest. Thus
the doctrine of the unity and personality of God, as the
God of creation and of redemption, was grandly conceived
and stated in uniform and ever advancing clearness and
consistency by the Hebrew prophets alone. Compare
with this idea of God, the Polytheism, Pantheism, and
Deism of other religions, and we are forced to the inquiry,
whence could this idea have come save from God Himself?
We do not claim that such an idea could not be evolved
by the human mind. But, in fact, such an idea has not
been evolved in any other religion. Such an idea is not
readily accepted by those who are not in sympathy with
the Christian religion. The human mind drifts to Pantheism or Deism rather than to the Biblical doctrine of
God. It seems impossible truly to apprehend the Biblical
doctrine of God save by personal union with God through
the grace which the Bible itself offers. The union of the
finite with the infinite can be effected only by the Infinite;
the personal knowledge of the Infinite can be afforded

only by the advent of the Infinite Himself.   The human soul is capable of this divine knowledge, and Hebrew prophecy gives the divine knowledge that satisfies the soul.   This is an evidence that that prophecy has a divine source.

The Hebrew doctrine of man is no less divine.   The unity of the race is a unique conception of the Bible.   It is above the prejudices of the other religions against other races.   The Hebrew prophets were Hebrew patriots, but their prophecies grasped humanity and embraced the world.   This original unity of mankind lost by sin is to be restored by grace, and the Hebrew doctrine of the ideal man—holy and perfect as God is holy and perfect— is so grand and inspiring that the philosophy and theology of our times has as yet failed to apprehend it.   Where do we find such an intense and realistic conception of sin ?   How dark and dread the representation, and yet how true to fact and human consciousness !   The Hebrew prophets were faithful men—they saw human sin through divine eyes, and they portrayed it in its guilty colours. The natural man was incapable of such true and noble anthropology without divine instruction.

But prophetic theology culminates in its doctrine of redemption.   This is the golden thread of Hebrew history and of the Hebrew religion.   The union of God and man by redemption, that is the noble ideal that inspires Hebrew prophecy throughout : steadily and unfalteringly the prophets lead the nation to the apprehension and realization of that ideal.   It has none of that miserable pessimism that characterizes so many of the lower religions and even the lower philosophies of our day. It has none of that spurious optimism which the human reason yearns for and pantheistic systems present.   It represents the good and the evil in everlasting conflict ; but this conflict is a conflict which is a development of redemption into higher stages and grander achievements. The doctrine of redemption given by the Hebrew prophets is a divine idea, and cannot be explained as an evolution of human hopes and fears and aspirations.

The theology of the Hebrew prophets throughout is such a wondrous combination of reality and truth, of the temporal and the eternal, the actual and the ideal, that it evinces the conception of a mind that grasps the ages in faithful and vivid realization, and that has the power of representing that conception in terms that stand the test of time and circumstance. The doctrines of the Hebrew prophets transcend the powers of human apprehension and conception, and like the sublime ideas of the reason—form and time and space—circumscribe human knowledge, and invoke the Deity to explain them as conceptions of the divine mind.

In the sphere of doctrine the ideal is most easily detected and presented. It is in the sphere of religion and of morals that Hebrew prophecy is ordinarily attacked. But it is just in these departments where the necessity of adaptation to time and place and circumstance is most apparent. No prophecy could be true prophecy that would not meet the practical issues of life. Hebrew prophecy in its historic development adapts itself to the needs of the day and the person and the affair. Hence we must eliminate the circumstantial and the variable from the essential and the permanent in these departments. But it is this very power of adaptation that proves the original vitality and wondrous efficacy of the Hebrew religion and the prophetic ethics. We are not dismayed at the lowest stages of religion when we see it advancing through the centuries to higher and higher stages towards the realization of a perfect ideal. We are not surprised at a low grade of morals tolerated in a rude and untutored people, when we see that grade rising higher and higher in the divine discipline of a nation. The imperfection and the grossness of the earlier Hebrew religion, and the morals of the earlier stages of Hebrew prophecy, are patent to all, but these do not disprove the divinity of the grand religious and ethical ideals of prophecy. There is this strife between the divine ideal and the historical reality which makes the history of Israel seem like a series of apostasies, and which has so coloured the stream with sin and evil that theologians have been too often forgetful that it is in fact a stream ever flowing onward. The divine ideals are indeed ever constraining the people of Israel to conformity with them; and the prophets are the standard-bearers in this religious and ethical progress of the nation. These ideal elements are essential to the system of Hebrew prophecy, they are in religion and in morals the constitutive parts —they are the primitive, the permanent, the advancing, yes, the ultimate and eternal elements. They are absolutely true and everlastingly real. They cannot be explained save by a conjunction of divine forces with human agencies. They involve a union of God and man in the prophetic heroes of redemption.

These phenomena, these essential features of the Hebrew prophecy, imply an extraordinary divine influence, continued from age to age, giving unity to the prophecy of a great number of different prophets. Hebrew prophecy presents us a system of instruction which cannot be explained from the reflections of the human mind. It gives us a view of redemption as the final goal of the world's history, which is heaven-born, and not a human invention. It accomplishes a work in advancing the redemption that overcomes all human resistance as by a divine force. Its holy character—its spotless purity—its absolute truth—its implicit confidence in the ultimate accomplishment of the most beautiful, elevating and sublime hopes—all combine in showing that one supreme, superhuman energy inspired it all.

Demanding the most searching criticism from the start, it has endured that criticism in all ages—such a criticism as no other prophecy has been able to endure—such as has, in fact, beaten into ruins all other prophecy. A still more searching criticism it is passing through to-day, that abiding the test, its truth and reality may conquer and sway mankind.

The Hebrew prophets therefore were prophets not merely in the sense of the oracles and sibyls and prophets of other religions, but in that holy men of God spake as they were moved by the Holy Spirit of Jahveh.

CHAPTER II.

PREDICTIVE PROPHECY.

§ 14. *Prediction is a common feature of the religions of mankind, but it is comparatively a small section of Hebrew prophecy. Hebrew prediction gains its vast significance from its content, the central nucleus of the prophetic ideal; the completion of redemption through the Messiah.*

It is a common habit so to identify prophecy with prediction that the terms to many minds become practically identical. But prophecy is properly far more extensive. Prediction constitutes but one feature of genuine prophecy, and that not the common, but the extraordinary feature. It is only one section, and that the smallest, of the range of prophetic instruction. It is a weakness rather than an excellence to exalt the predictive element as such. It is one of the evil fruits of an unwholesome apologetic that has been transmitted to us from the previous century, when there was a greedy grasping after anything and everything in the form of prediction that might in any way serve to exalt the supernatural character of the Bible.[1] Prediction is not a

[1] "We can here proceed on an observation which has already forced itself upon us, while we were discussing the prophecies regarding the judgment upon Israel. To the question, 'fulfilled or not fulfilled,' we received from time to time no clear or unambiguous answer. Nay, what is of greater significance, more than one paragraph of the prophetical writings, which yet treats of the future, scarcely admits of being regarded as *prediction*. This would be

peculiar feature of Hebrew prophecy. It is found in other domains than religion, and occurs in all religions. The human mind is endowed with certain faculties which may be trained to prediction. A statesman who understands the constitutional history of his country, and is master of the political forces at work in the present, may be able to predict the combinations that these will assume, and their issues in the future. A theologian may be able to discern the coming conflicts in the Church and predict in a measure the results. The laws that govern human action are as exact and certain in their operation as the laws of the physical universe. It only needs a knowledge sufficiently extensive, an insight sufficiently profound, a foresight sufficiently clear, to predict the future of an individual, a family, or a nation. There is moreover among men an anxiety respecting the future which is so widespread as to be natural. And when the issue of present events and present action is important, it is natural, and it is common to seek the counsel of the higher powers. A Christian under such circumstances resorts to prayer. A heathen under the same circumstances resorts to prophets of various kinds.

Prediction as a phase of Hebrew prophecy can only be understood from the general conception of religious instruction. Prediction is the instruction that prophecy gives as it looks forth from the present into the future. Prediction is the most important section of Hebrew

---

wholly inexplicable, if prediction had been the chief object of the prophets. On the other hand, such a phenomenon is in the highest degree natural, if they had another task, a different aim. But such is indeed the case. Their business is not to communicate what *shall* happen, but to insist upon that which *ought* to happen. The maintenance of the Jahveh-worship as they comprehended it— that is what they had in view in the whole course of their activity."
—Kuenen's *Prophets and Prophecy in Israel*, p. 344, London 1877.

prophecy, simply because it presents the essential ideal of the completion of redemption through the Messiah.

I. THE SOURCES OF PREDICTION.

§ 15. *There are many sources of prediction to which the heathen resort, such as, necromancy, magic, divination, augury, astrology, palmistry, the use of Teraphim ; all of which are forbidden in the Old Testament under penalty of death. The only source of prediction to which the Hebrews were allowed to resort was the sacred lot, whose decision was an expression of the will of Jahveh. Jahveh was the sole source of prediction. He gave it and withheld it as He pleased.*

Heathen prediction is almost exclusively of a lower grade than the instruction given in the religious systems of the world. It is of a coarse, sensuous and superstitious type, and prediction constitutes a much greater proportion of heathen prophecy than it does of Hebrew prophecy.

The lowest form is probably necromancy. This was a favourite resort of the religion of Baal—consulting the dead by means of necromancers who were supposed to hold communications with them. We have a curious case of this in the bringing up of Samuel for Saul by the witch of Endor.[1] Necromancy is supposed to have been connected with some form of ventriloquism, and to have been usually associated with the assuming of the ecstatic state through the use of drugs and stimulating exercises. These necromancers are in the Old Testament associated with wizards [2] and magicians [3] who used magic

---

[1] Such a necromancer is called an אוֹב, and such a woman is called mistress of an אוֹב. See 1 Sam. xxviii.

[2] יִדְּעֹנִים.　　　[3] מְכַשְּׁפִים.

arts of various kinds, and are represented [1] as " muttering and chirping," using strange ejaculations and frenzied exhortation and warning.

There is another class of these heathen prophets called diviners,[2] who seek for direction in the future by the investigation of combinations in various objects of nature. The most common of these is in the use of the entrails of animals and the observation of the flight of birds, the rustling of leaves or the movement of sacred animals or unusual occurrences. This is called augury, and was extensively practised by the Greeks and Romans. Divining by observing the movements of liquids in a vessel or hydromantic is referred to by Joseph.[3] There is a divining by shooting arrows and noting their flight, as in the case of the king of Babylon.[4] Teraphim, little images of household deities, are also employed for this purpose.[5] There is still another class of heathen prophets called astrologers, who seek in the movements of the stars and the appearances of the heavenly bodies and the phenomena of the skies guidance for the affairs of earth. Then there is the most inveterate of all these forms of heathen prophecy, witchcraft and palmistry. Indeed there are scarcely any phenomena of nature which have not been resorted to by men in their anxiety to determine the future of themselves or others.[6]

It is characteristic of Biblical prophecy that it denounces all these forms of heathen superstition. It puts them under the ban, and regards them as sins against the divine majesty, incurring the penalty of death. The idea at the bottom of all this heathen prediction is that the Deity will manifest His will for the guidance of His

---

[1] Isa. viii. 19. [2] קסמים. [3] Gen. xliv. 5.
[4] Ezek. xxi. 21–23. [5] Ezek. xxi. 21 ; Zech. x. 2.
[6] Küper, *Das Prophetenthum das Alten Bundes*, p. 1 seq., Leipzig 1870.

worshippers. The custom of the religion determines the methods to be used.

The only use of natural objects that is lawful in Biblical prophecy is the casting of lots. In the ancient times of Israel we have a number of examples of the use of the sacred lot. It detects the criminal Achan[1] and the innocent Jonathan.[2] It divides the Holy Land among the tribes.[3] It determines the time and the circumstances of battles. The *Urim and Thummim* is ordinarily regarded as a sacred lot to be cast by the priest; but it is properly a sacred stone in the sacred bag[4] of the high priest, which assured him that he would have the divine illumination and complete knowledge necessary to enable him to decide on the religious questions submitted to him. It is the priest who is thereby guided to speak the predictive and decisive word. To this *Urim and Thummim* of the priest's ephod, Saul and David frequently resort for guidance.[5]

Saul is represented as in a desperate condition when he is abandoned by God, who answers him " neither by dream nor by *Urim* nor by prophet."[6] He resorts to the unlawful necromancy only to hear the bitter tragedy that awaited his rebellious career. The prophet Isaiah rebukes Israel for restoring to the necromancers rather than to God:

" When they say unto you, Seek unto the necromancers and unto the wizards;—

Ye chirpers and mutterers, should not a people seek unto their God ?

On behalf of the living will they seek unto the dead for instruction and for testimony ?"[7]

---

[1] Josh. vii. 14 seq.   [2] 1 Sam. xiv. 43.
[3] Josh. xiv.–xix.
[4] האורים והתמים (Lev. viii. 8). These are abstract intensive plurals, meaning, enlightenment, and completion or perfection.
[5] 1 Sam. xxx. 7 seq.   [6] 1 Sam. xxviii. 6.
[7] Isa. viii. 19. We disregard the Massoretic accents here,

II. DIVINE SOURCE OF HEBREW PREDICTION.

§ 16. *Hebrew prediction uses the several phases of Hebrew prophecy. It is distinguished by its contents from all other prediction. These contents are of such a character as to imply divine origination and direction. They are gathered into an organism that presents a divine ideal of redemption which transcends human powers of construction.*

Hebrew predictive prophecy rises up in sublime majesty above every form of divination, and uses all the varied forms of prophecy, especially the higher, to present its instruction. The prediction is sometimes given in dreams or visions in the ecstatic state. In these cases the future is represented in dramatic forms in the imagination and fancy. The conditions for such prediction are in the constructive power of the imagination, in sleep and the ecstatic state. These creatures of the imagination are ordinarily occasioned by strong recollections, by intense interest in particular things, by great anxiety with reference to certain events. It is not uncommon for the imagination under such circumstances to leap into the future experience by foreboding or ardent anticipation. The imagination may discern the issues in which we are interested more clearly and accurately than the reasoning powers. These predictions, not uncommon to the dream and the vision, present us phenomena kindred with Biblical prophecy. They present us the psychological conditions which show such predictions to be not only possible but probable. How then does Biblical pre-

because the poetry has here the hexameter movement (see chap. vii. 7). הַמְצַפְצְפִים. The article is here for the vocative case, as often in Hebrew. The absence of the preposition is against taking it as in apposition to אֶל הַיִּדְּעֹנִים. לַתּוֹרָה is ordinarily taken as exhortation to the people. "To the law and to the testimony!" But we should expect in this case the preposition אֶל, as in the previous context.

diction differ from these predictions of the imagination?
An attentive examination of the phenomena ought to
convince any scientific observer that the predictions that
occur in the dreams and visions of Hebrew prophecy
transcend the native energies of the imagination. The
imagination can only reconstruct the material given to it.
The predictions of Hebrew prophecy present us material
as well as combinations of material that must have had
another origin than the previous experience of the prophet. The vision of Abraham, as to the 400 years'
pilgrimage of his seed in Canaan and in Egypt, not only
gives the pilgrimage of his seed in Canaan and in Egypt,
which was a natural product of his imagination; but
also the long duration of an affliction through many
generations before the ultimate conquest of Canaan and
the realization of the covenant promises, which was the
reverse of the natural operation of his imagination under
the circumstances.[1] The dreams of Pharaoh as to the
years of plenty and famine, while they sprang out of the
natural circumstances of the land of Egypt and the
position of Pharaoh, yet in their elaboration they transcend any possible combinations of the imagination without external guidance, which could hardly have been
other than superhuman.[2] The necessity of interpretation
and the exactness of the interpretation when the secret
clue was given, show that the adjustment was that of a
higher power which had made the dream to correspond
with the predetermined reality. The same is true of the
dreams of Nebuchadnezzar, the visions of Daniel and
others.[3] The natural conditions and features of the
person who dreams and is in ecstasy are there, but the
prediction itself is so extraordinary, so comprehensive, so
exact, so unerring, that it implies an infallible divine
influence. Passing from the prediction of the dream and

[1] Gen. xv.   [2] Gen. xli.   [3] Dan. ii., vii.

the vision to the prediction in the song of the ecstatic state, we observe that Balaam's predictions [1] were the reverse of his wishes, his hopes and his wilful determination and effort that they should be otherwise. His imagination was constrained by an overpowering influence to bless in the harmonies of sacred song the people whom he anxiously strove to curse in odes of triumph of their enemies. Such prediction cannot be explained by purely natural influences.

But ordinarily the predictions of the Hebrew prophets issue from men who are in entire sympathy with their utterances. They are expressed with an intensity of emotion and a rhetorical vigour which assume the forms of poetry and song, and sometimes are accompanied with bodily action and symbolical illustration.

Predictive prophecy is ordinarily of the highest kind, in the forms of human language spoken or written. As such it expresses the insight and the foresight of the prophet, where the reasoning powers co-operate with the imagination and the fancy in the construction of the grandest conception of prophecy.

It is necessary to discriminate the natural from the supernatural features. No one should deny that the Hebrew prophets were men of extraordinary genius. It is not necessary to degrade the Hebrew prophets as men in order to exalt the divine influence that employed them. They exhibit a wonderful familiarity with the history of their nation. They were patriots in the best sense. They show a wide acquaintance with the religious and political affairs of neighbouring nations. They were statesmen. But above all they were pious men, whose religious experience was intense, whose devotion was profound, and whose ethical character was exalted. We expect such men to have wondrous insight and foresight.

[1] Num. xxiii.–xxiv.

Their intimate acquaintance with the past, and their familiarity with the present, urged them to a keen apprehension and a vivid realization of the future.

We are not surprised to find prediction mingled with historical instruction and direct practical guidance of the people in the affairs of the present. We should not think it necessary to explain all of the predictions of the prophets from an extraordinary divine influence. As men who were pre-eminently wise, and gifted with the highest religious endowments, living in communion with God, their wisdom was capable of prediction such as transcended that of other men.

But when we have eliminated all that can fairly be demanded in this regard, it should be acknowledged by the careful student that there is a great body of Hebrew prediction which cannot be so explained. The insight of the Hebrew prophet is so profound that it transcends the native energies of human perception, the comprehension is so vast that the conception trained to its highest capacity could not grasp it,—the foresight is so far-reaching that no human imagination could spring to its goal. Hebrew predictive prophecy, while it arises in accordance with the psychological condition of the human soul, so transcends its normal powers that we are constrained to think of the divine mind as its source and inspiration.

This is true if we measure Hebrew prophecy merely by the consciousness of the individual prophet; but when we consider that the prophets were linked in a chain, and that their predictions are combined in a system, —an organic whole which no individual prophet could possibly comprehend, which now stands before the scholarly world in marvellous unity and variety as the object of the study of the ages of the past, which absorbs the energies of the present, and which arches the future even to the end of the world,—we are forced to the conviction that the one master of the Hebrew prophets was the Spirit of God ; and that the organic system of prophecy is a product of the mind and will of God.

III. THE SYMBOLICAL FORM OF HEBREW PREDICTION.

§ 17. *Prediction from its very nature presents the future in the forms of the present and the past. These forms are not real and literal representations of the future, but ideal and symbolical. The interpreter finds the ideal prediction in the form of the symbol. Symbolism rises in several grades from the use of external objects of sense to the more internal and higher ideals of the imagination and fancy.*

We are met on the threshold of Hebrew prediction with the bold statements of Kuenen, that Hebrew prediction has been proved false by history in so many particulars that the system cannot be regarded as true and divine. Its predictions have not been fulfilled in the time allotted them, and the fulfilment is no longer possible. The reverse of the predicted has often happened. Hebrew prediction has been disproved by events, and it must take its place with all other prophecy as a compound of truth and error, of blasted hopes and disappointed expectations.[1] These charges will not bear serious examination. They really concern only the scholastic theory of prophecy and misinterpretations of predictions.

The scholastic theory of prophecy, which was essentially Montanistic, failed to distinguish between the form and the substance of prophecy. It sought above all verbal accuracy and circumstantial and detailed fulfilment. It sought by strained interpretations to identify prophecy and history. The efforts to show the literal fulfilment

[1] Kuenen in *l.c.* chap. v.

of the predictions of Daniel in the history of Israel from the exile to the advent, in its dreadful inconsistencies of interpretation, have so disgraced the science of Biblical Interpretation that it is a marvel that the book has survived such cruel manipulation. The vain efforts to find Christian history depicted in the Apocalypse of John has so damaged the book that we are not surprised that even Christian scholars should have abstained from its study as unprofitable. Predictive prophecy has been made a burden to apologetics by the abuse that has been made of it by self-constituted defenders of the faith and presumptuous champions of orthodoxy. It is necessary that evangelical critics should rescue predictive prophecy from the hands of those who have made such sad mistakes.

Kuenen has taken advantage of the errors of the scholastic theory and interpretation of predictive prophecy, and has dealt Hebrew prediction the severest blows it has ever received. We shall parry these blows of Kuenen by showing that they have destroyed the scholastic theory, but they have not in the slightest degree injured Hebrew prediction as such.

Predictive prophecy has its necessary forms and limitations, which we should carefully study in order to understand it. We shall first distinguish the form from the substance of the prediction, and then present the necessary limits of Hebrew prediction; for we would unfold the truth which Tholuck has so well expressed when he says, "It is not prediction of the accidental, but of that which is of religious necessity, which is the essential thing in Hebrew prophecy." [1]

Kuenen has the right of it over against the scholastic apologists when he says: "When they assert that the prophecies have been fulfilled exactly and literally, and thence deduce far-reaching consequences, we cannot rest

[1] *Die Propheten*, p. 77.

satisfied with the general agreement between the prediction and the historical fact, but must note also along with that the deviation in details, as often as such a deviation is actually apparent." [1] But Kuenen and the Scholastics are here alike in error, for the prophecies are predictive only as to the essential and the ideal elements. The purely formal elements belong to the point of view and colouring of the individual prophets. We are not to find exact and literal fulfilments in detail or in general, but the fulfilment is limited, as the prediction is limited, to the essential ideal contents of the prophecy. We start therefore from the point of view of the prediction, and thence rise through several forms of prediction.

The future judgment and redemption, the two poles of predictive prophecy, are necessarily based on present experience of discipline and upon the history of redemption and judicial acts of Jahveh in the past. Looking forth into the future, prophetic prediction clothes and represents that which is to come in the scenery and language familiar to it in the present and in the past. The most suitable events, persons, and things of the past and the present are employed. Hence the type or the symbol lies at the basis of all genuine prediction. The particular type chosen depends partly upon the experience of the prophet and the circumstances of the times; partly upon divine command or the enlightenment of the prophetic Spirit.

§ 18. *The lowest form of symbolic prophecy is the use of external things like cords, sticks, yokes, vessels and the like, to represent in a rude but graphic way the impending event.*

The historical books of the Old Testament contain a large number of examples of the use of rude symbols;

[1] In *l.c.* p. 132.

and the prophetical books give not a few of them. Thus Ahijah the Shilonite "laid hold of the new garment which was on him, and rent it in twelve pieces. And he said to Jeroboam, Take thee ten pieces; for thus saith Jahveh, the God of Israel, Behold, I will rend the kingdom out of the hand of Solomon, and will give ten tribes unto thee." [1] The pieces of garment here symbolize the tribes of Israel, and the rending of the cloth, the division of the tribes into two kingdoms, with ten tribes to one kingdom and two to the other kingdom. Sometimes we cannot be sure whether the symbolic thing was actually used or was simply put into the discourse of the prophet. Thus Ezekiel uses two sticks with the names of Judah and Israel, which he joins to make one stick in his hand in order to represent the ultimate reunion of the kingdoms.[2] Jeremiah uses two baskets of figs, the one very good, the other very bad, to represent the good and the evil classes in Israel and the ultimate ruin of the one and redemption of the other.[3]

These are sufficient examples of a large number of symbolic things used by the Hebrew prophets. No one would look for exact and literal fulfilment of these symbols. All agree in seeking the ideal content.

§ 19. *The Hebrew prophets ordinarily use higher symbols, which are called types, such as historic persons or events, great institutions, or experiences in real life. The exact correspondence of type and antitype is impossible. The antitype transcends the type as the ideal transcends the form which is inadequate to present it.*

The doctrine of typology has been greatly abused in the Christian Church, by seeking and finding types everywhere in Scripture. There is indeed no limit to the use of types. Almost every person, thing, circumstance or

[1] 1 Kings xi. 30, 31.   [2] Ezek. xxxvii. 15 seq.   [3] Jer. xxiv.

event may be used to represent an antitype in some
respect. There is a proper use of typology in the
practical interpretation of the historical books. But we
have here only to do with the types which the prophets
themselves use. These are in sufficient variety as they
are gathered from the past or the present, from persons
or things, from circumstances or events, from experiences
of everyday life, and from the great objects of nature.

The type may be a person like Moses, David, or
Solomon. What more natural than that the Messiah
should be represented as a second Moses, a prophet like
him and yet his superior; a warlike monarch, victorious
as David; a prince of peace like Solomon? There have
been those who have argued from the prediction of a
second Elijah, that the original Elijah was to rise from
the dead; but Jesus gave the true interpretation when
He saw this second Elijah in John the Baptist.[1] The
nature of the type is such that it enables us to understand in general what the character of the person so
represented is to be, but exact identification or literal
correspondence between the type and the antitype would
be no less absurd than if we were to suppose that the
prophet conceived of the resurrection of every person he
used as a type,—such a conception would indeed destroy
typology altogether. The person is a type used to
represent another person in the particulars of the prediction. The person used as a type belongs to the form of
the prediction and not to its substance. He is illustrative,
descriptive and representative, but nothing more. He no
more corresponds with the exact reality of the future
than the ten pieces of the garment of Ahijah corresponded
with the ten tribes of Israel.

When now instead of a person we use an institution
like the passover, or the ark of the covenant, or the tiara

[1] Matt. xi. 14; Mal. iv. 5.

of the high priest as symbols of the institutions of the new dispensation, the laws of symbolism forbid that we should expect exact and literal correspondence. They require that with a certain formal correspondence the antitype should be vastly higher and grander in form than the type. Transcendence is essential to the idea of the type. So in the use of a great historic event like the exodus, or the conquest of Canaan, or the captivity in Egypt, or the wanderings in the wilderness to represent the future experience of redemption, to expect exact correspondence and literal fulfilment destroys the very nature of typology.

The higher we ascend in symbolism the more difficult the discrimination between the essential ideal of the symbol and the unimportant clothing, but this does not justify the interpreter in insisting upon exact and literal conformity in the one case any more than in the other. It rather urges to a closer study of the symbol in order to make those discriminations upon which the meaning of the prediction depends. For the Hebrew prophets rise to the most intricate themes in their symbolism. They not only use the external history of the past with its great persons, institutions and events, but they freely employ the great persons and institutions and events of their own times, and even enter into the deep and sacred experiences of their own souls, in order to represent the innermost experience of future persons and generations. To expect exact and literal fulfilment of such types is unnatural and unscientific. It transgresses the nature of the type, which requires that the symbol or type should represent the prediction only in certain given features. The type is the clothing of the predicted ideal. It is the duty of the interpreter to determine the essential idea, and to decline to allow himself to be absorbed either in the general features or in the minute details of the type.

It is the one aim of the interpreter to find the key to the symbol, and by it unlock the mystery of the representation. For predictive prophecy is and must be a higher parabolic teaching. If the Hebrew moralists used ancient stories and legends, and clothed them with familiar scenery in order to point a lesson (and the Hebrew Haggada is full of this method of instruction)—if our Saviour used the parable to enforce an ideal that was to be of everlasting importance and we find it a delightful task to search for the key, why should any one deem it essential to find exact correspondence in the prophetic symbol? Why should he not rather use every effort to find the door to its mysteries? Indeed, predictive prophecy from its very nature not only assumes the symbolic form, but it hides its solution. For the peril to prediction is in efforts on the part of false prophets and impostors to realize it. The clue is a secret clue, often so carefully hidden that centuries of study have not found it. Prophecy is its own interpreter, and it is often designed by the infinite mind that its solution should remain unknown until the event itself occurred. Like the predictive dreams of Pharaoh and Nebuchadnezzar, they need a Joseph or a Daniel to find the golden thread to guide through their labyrinthine mysteries. The great symbols of Hebrew predictive prophecy remained riddles of comfort and warning—all the more dread and inspiring from their profound and awful mystery—until they were resolved by the events predicted. The first advent is the great resolver of all Old Testament prophecy. Jesus opened the understanding of His apostles that they might understand the Scriptures. The second advent will give the key to New Testament prophecy. It is the Lamb that has been slain, the everlasting and blessed One who alone opens the sealed book, solves the riddles of time, and resolves the symbols of prophecy.

D

§ 20. *The Hebrew prophets rise to a higher use of symbolism in the constructions of the imagination and the fancy. They employ the parable, the allegory and the tale. In these forms of prediction there is a contrast between the real and the ideal, which is sometimes expressed in the extravagance and grotesqueness of the representation. The fulfilment is the reverse of literal and exact correspondence.*

Hebrew prophecy rises above the simple use of the type to a higher form which has been called *typicoprophetic.* Sometimes the type remains by itself as if by simple index, without explanation, it would point out in a graphic symbol as a sign the impending future; but often the type is found inadequate in itself for the work of prediction. The prophet works with it, strains and stretches it beyond any possible proportions, so that it becomes extravagant and even grotesque. This use of the type is in order to emphasize the contrast between the type and the antitype, and shows that exact, literal correspondence is impossible. Thus the poet uses a gigantic vine to illustrate the marvellous growth of the kingdom of God. It was transplanted from Egypt to Canaan, covered the whole land, reached with its branches from the Mediterranean to the Euphrates, cast the cedars of Lebanon in shade of its gigantic boughs.[1] Thus Daniel uses the stone cut out of the mountain without hands growing to become a vast mountain filling the whole earth.[2] The mountain of the house of Jahveh rises above the highest mountains.[3] Ezekiel represents the New Jerusalem and the holy land in impossible proportions and situations.[4] Some of these cases are so grotesque and extravagant that no one could for a moment think of an exact and literal fulfilment. And

[1] Ps. lxxx.
[3] Micah iv.   Isa ii.
[2] Dan. ii.
[4] Ezek. xl. seq.

yet there are a large number of predictions which in their proper interpretation are no less impossible. These have been so interpreted by Scholastics as to find exact fulfilment, and by Rationalists as to show that they have not been fulfilled. A striking example of this is the new temple and holy land and institutions of Ezekiel, and under this head may be brought all that large class relating to Israel's future which Kuenen argues to be unfulfilled and to be impossible of fulfilment. He classifies them thus: (1) the return of Israel out of captivity; (2) the reunion of Ephraim and Judah; (3) the supremacy of the house of David; (4) the spiritual and material welfare of the restored Israel; (5) the relation between Israel and the Gentiles; (6) Israel's undisturbed continuance in the land of their habitation.[1]

If exact and literal fulfilment of these prophecies was designed in the predictions, then we must agree with Kuenen that they have been disproved by history; but it is against the laws of prophetic prediction so to interpret them. These predictions are not only impossible now, but in form many of them always were impossible. Israel in predictive prophecy is not Israel after the flesh but Israel after the spirit, as the Apostle Paul explains.[2] The true children of Abraham are the faithful.[3] The Christian Church is the legitimate successor of the Israel of old and the heir of its promises.[4] The essential contents of these predictions when eliminated from their formal elements are spiritual and not carnal.[5] The type was made extravagant and impossible so as to show that the ideal contents were in contrast with their formal presentation. It is thus essential to this form of prediction that the realization should be the reverse of literal and exact correspondence.

[1] In *l.c.* p. 189 seq. [2] Rom. ix. seq. [3] Rom. iv.
[4] 1 Pet. ii. 4 seq. [5] König in *l.c.* ii p. 396 seq.

§ 21. *The highest form of Hebrew prophecy is called direct prophecy. But even here the symbolical form is not abandoned. There is a more subtile use of symbolical language. This is especially true in the combinations of sacred numbers. The secret clue is to be discovered as the only safe guide to interpretation.*

The highest form attained by Hebrew prediction is ordinarily called direct prophecy. It seldom is found alone, but usually accompanies the type as its explanation. Sometimes the type is abandoned as inadequate, and symbolical language assumes its place for the higher stage of the prediction. Then again the prediction rises in three stages. Beginning with the type, the prophet advances to such a use of it that it becomes extravagant in his hands. It is then cast aside and he springs to his climax in direct prophecy. Even in this highest form of prediction the symbolical form is not abandoned, it is only changed to the use of figurative, illustrative, descriptive language, and the interpretation instead of becoming easier has become more difficult. This is especially the case in the use of numbers. It is just here that the Apologists have made the greatest blunders which the Rationalists have not been slow to utilize for the destruction of Hebrew prophecy.

Thus Kuenen insists that because the prophets expected that their predictions would soon be realized[1] and that the events predicted were close at hand,[2] they were mistaken, and their predictions were not fulfilled even when they happened at a long time subsequently or may yet be capable of realization. So it is represented that because Jesus and His apostles expected the second advent very soon after the first that they were mistaken. But all these objections rest upon a mistaken conception of predictive prophecy. The times of prophecy are as

[1] In *l.c.* p. 103.   [2] In *l.c.* p. 110.

symbolical as the objects themselves. We claim that all prophetical numbers are symbolical, and that none of them are to be taken as exact or literal. The efforts of interpreters to determine from the numbers of Daniel the intervals to the first advent have ignominiously failed. The efforts of interpreters to measure the times of the Apocalypse and indicate the times of the second advent are worse than ridiculous. Those who indulge in such follies are blindly labouring to undermine and destroy Hebrew prophecy and the Bible itself, of which it is an essential part.

The prophets all share in this characteristic feature of presenting their predictions as near of realization.[1] If the prophetic numbers are taken as exact and literal, consistency of interpretation forces us to regard these terms also as exact and literal. But if we take this position, then we cannot escape the conclusion that all of the prophets were in error as to the element of time, and that their predictions were in so far false. But we claim that the prophetic temporal terminology is symbolical as prophetic prediction is throughout symbolical, and that exact and literal numbers are against the essential principle of prediction. It would reduce predictive prophecy to a system of chronology. The prophetic numbers are riddles and enigmas to be solved after the key is found. The meaning is not on the surface. This is true also of the terms *near* and *at hand*. The prophets ever continue to use these expressions as the technical language of prophecy. How could they go on doing so if these terms had a strict and exact meaning? Every prophet would appear to his successors as in error in this particular. Nearness to Joel would prove a long historical distance to Isaiah. Isaiah's nearness would be

---

[1] The Hebrew term קרוב and the Greek ἐγγύς are essential prophetic terminology.

long past to Jeremiah, and Jeremiah's to Malachi, and yet they go on representing the day of Jahveh as at hand—His judgments and His redemption as near, without any indications of a lack of confidence in their predecessors, but with a full reliance upon the integrity of prophecy. And Jesus and His apostles use these identical terms in the same way, although all the prophetic predictions of the Old Testament were remote to them.

Still further, while Jesus uses this prophetic terminology, He expressly teaches that the times and seasons are reserved to God, that no man, or angel, or even the Son of man can define them.[1] These terms must therefore have a technical prophetic sense, and this is not difficult to determine.   The *nearness* and the *at hand* of prophetic prediction - indicate the certainty of the events.   They are as vivid to the mind and as ardently desired or anxiously dreaded as the events of to-morrow.   They are on the to-morrow of prophecy—those latter days in view of which every intervening time is of infinitesimal importance and overlooked as of trifling moment.   The *nearness* and *at hand* of prophetic prediction indicate also the uncertainty of the time.   The interval between the to-day of prophecy and the to-morrow of prophecy is but a night-time of uncertain duration, so uncertain that to-day is and must ever be of supreme importance.   For to-day is a preparation, not for the interval until the last days, but for the last day itself, which is at hand in the sense that it is ever impending.

Thus in every form of prediction the laws of prediction preclude exact and literal fulfilment.   They require us to find the key or clue, and only by the key or clue can we find those essential ideal elements, originally designed in the prediction, embodied in it, stereotyped therein, and waiting for the time when the event will

[1] Matt. xxiv. 42 seq. ; Mark xiii. 32 seq. ; Acts i. 7.

justify them and prove their reality and their divine origin. When Hebrew prophecy is regarded from this point of view, we observe that its fulfilment has been raised above the designs of impostors and deceivers. False Messiahs have presented themselves as fulfillers of Hebrew prophecy, and these have ever pointed to some trivial details, and urged literal and exact correspondence ; but when the true Messiah came, His correspondence with prophecy was not distinctly recognized. It was not exact and literal. It was not on the surface. It was not until the death on the cross, the resurrection and ascension of the Messiah that the key to Old Testament prophecy was given, and its solution found in part. The risen Saviour opened the understanding of His apostles that they might understand the Scriptures. It will not be until the second advent that the ultimate solution of the prophetic system will be given. The first advent resolved all Hebrew prophecy into two great parts, and in giving us the fulfilment of the one part it guarantees the fulfilment of the other part.

IV. THE LIMITS OF PREDICTION.

§ 22. *The prophets are human beings, and although they become the instruments of conveying divine ideas to their fellow-men, yet these divine ideas assume the forms and the clothing of the human medium through which they pass. They cannot transcend the psychological and physical features of human nature.*

The prophets being men of intellectual and moral worth, influenced by the divine Spirit to think, feel and act with reference to the divine ideas imparted to them, they speak and write and act under the physical and psychological laws of their own being. The prophets, looking into the future, follow the lines of the move-

ments of their own times, tracing them to their results.
Their insight and foresight are intensified by the energy
of the divine Spirit which enlarges their native intellectual and moral powers to the extent that may be
necessary for the purposes of the prediction.

§ 23. *It is a law of predictive prophecy that the pro-*
phet foresees the final goal to which the movements of his
time are tending, and which they will inevitably reach; but
he does not foresee all the conditions and circumstances
that intervene or modify the approaches to that end.

He predicts in a few broad outlines and graphic
touches, but he is not and he cannot be an annalist or a
historian. He sees the final end of redemption or of
judgment upon the individual, the nation or the world;
but he cannot grasp in his conception or delineate in his
representation all the forces converging to that end, or
the various curvings of the historical movements in their
approaches to the ideal. He sees the end to be attained,
and the relation to that end of the persons or things or
events in which he is more immediately concerned; but
he cannot see the intervening objects and events, and the
forces constantly increasing in complexity as they converge towards it.[1] The prophet stands as it were
upon a lofty mountain. Far in the distance, beyond
the range that bounds the horizon of his generation,
he sees the goal of the journey. But he cannot see
all the hills and valleys, the rocks and streams and
the lesser mountain ranges which intervene between
him and the predicted goal. It seems but a short
journey, and it would be short if it were possible to
move on directly to the goal. But this is not possible,
for events must take their course in accordance with

---

[1] Riehm in *l.c.* 2 Aufl. p. 104 seq.; Edinburgh edition, p. 84 seq.;
also König in *l.c.* ii. p. 307 seq.

human conditions and circumstances. The prophet
cannot emancipate himself from his human nature and
surroundings. He cannot divest himself of his historic
position and circumstances. He cannot ignore or escape
his point of view. God has given him his position as a
religious teacher in a particular generation and in a
certain epoch of the world's history and in a certain
geographical locality. Hence his prediction clothes itself
with the local, the temporal and the circumstantial dress.
The future events cannot be presented in prediction in
the circumstances of the future and from the point of
view of the future. If that were so it would no longer
be prediction, but history.

§ 24. *Prediction rises above temporal measurements and
chronological distinctions. The end in view ever seems near
as the object of hope and ardent longing, or the object of
dread and anxious foreboding, the central theme of the
message of comfort or of warning; and yet the prophet
knows not the times or seasons which God hath reserved to
Himself.*

The prophet may be able to measure the distance in
time in symbolical numbers having in the proportions of
prophecy a relative importance; but he cannot count in
measures of human time, or enable his interpreters in
subsequent ages to calculate better than himself.[1] The
times of prophecy are enigmatical and in the highest
degree uncertain. If they show, on the one hand, the
great deliberation of God, that He prepares the way for
the fulfilment of His promises as if a thousand years were
but a day or the fraction of a night, and that He waits
for the completion of the appointed time when the ages
have became full and ripe for the event; they yet show,
on the other hand, the swift and inevitable movement of

[1] Riehm in *l.c.* 2 Aufl. p. 109 seq.

the divine purpose, as if a thousand years' labour were to be accomplished in a day or an hour or a moment; for when that moment approaches, which is the final goal of all prophecy, that supreme hour of the world, that day of doom, which is ever presented as near and at hand, events will move with the rapidity of the lightning flash and surprise the whole creation with that most wonderful transformation, which is the ripe fruit of the entire development of the earth, the birth for which the creation has been travailing through the centuries.

This then is the ringing lesson of all predictive prophecy. Be patient in suffering, for redemption is surely coming—we know not how quickly. Repent immediately, for the day of judgment may come at any moment. This is the constant attitude of Biblical prophecy—this is the lesson of its symbolical *near* and *at hand.*

§ 25. *There is an uncertain factor in all prediction which depends upon the ever varying relations of God and man in the interplay of human freedom and divine law. The variation of motives in the divine mind and in human experience, and the corresponding variation of forces in history, shorten or prolong, simplify or make complex and uncertain all preparatory times and events.*

This is the most difficult and the most neglected of all the limitations of Hebrew prediction. It springs out of the divine constitution of the individual man, and the complex organization of human society and national life. Kuenen very properly emphasizes this point, but in such a way as to make Hebrew prediction altogether human and altogether uncertain.[1] We should use great caution here so as not to do violence either to the divine or the human element. The representations of Scripture show very clearly that there is a divine motive for

[1] In *l.c.* p. 346 seq.

hastening the time of prediction, namely, in order to the redemption of the elect. And there is a divine motive for lengthening the interval, to increase their number. And so men must sometimes pray for the coming of the Redeemer, and then again for the progress of redemption. This interplay of motives in the divine mind and in human petition, and of forces in history, shorten and prolong and render uncertain all preparatory times and institutions. In the predictions of judgment there are limitations in the warning to repentance and the possibility of redemption. In the predictions of redemption there are ever limitations in warnings against sin and apostasy and the possibility of judgment. Thus in the larger frame of the prediction there are conflicting forces and movements which cannot prevent its ultimate realization, but which lengthen or shorten the interval and modify the circumstances and conditions.

Hebrew prophecy is not ashamed of occasional re-calling of circumstantial threatenings and promises. God is the Sovereign and Father of His people.[1] He has not wound up human events like a clock and left it to unwind itself in the remorseless swing of its pendulum. He watches over the destinies of the world with patient love and providential care. In the general drift of His purpose and the immense sweep of His design He has provided for occasional modifications and adaptations to time and place and circumstances. God and man are united in the working out of the purpose of redemption, and that working gives opportunity to repentance unto salvation. The conditional element does not destroy the essential prediction any more than it destroys the workings of God in the past and the present. It rather enhances the glory of Hebrew predictive prophecy that it has room for the free play of the conditional factor,

[1] König in *l.c.* p. 390 seq.

without permitting it to modify the determinative and essential factor.

Ever bounding the prophetic range of insight and foresight is the horizon of a complete redemption. It is the same with each prophet as he comes with a fresh message and sees farther and wider and deeper than his predecessors; and so along the whole line of prophets even into the New Testament and in the prophetic utterances of Jesus and His apostles. This does not show any incorrectness in the earlier prophecies, but rather that they were what they must be from the very nature of the case, partial and incomplete. The prophetic inspiration is all the grander, that these partial revelations coming from so many different persons, in widely different intervals of time, yet fit into each other with the utmost nicety, adjusting themselves to the harmonious proportions of one complete and perfect system of divine revelation; as so many folds of a developing germ, unfolding slowly yet grandly in majestic proportions into the historical Messiah, Christian salvation, the second advent hope and the *Dies irae.*

V. MESSIANIC PROPHECY.

§ 26. *The central theme and the culmination of Hebrew prophecy is the Messianic ideal. Messianic prophecy is the prediction of the completion of redemption through the Messiah.*

Hebrew prophecy rises in higher and higher stages until it culminates in Messianic prophecy. This is the central theme about which all its lessons cluster. This is the fountain whence all its streams of blessing and of cursing flow in never-ending succession. Messianic prophecy is the prediction of the fulfilment of redemption through the Messiah. This prediction is not confined to

official prophets—it is not limited to any form of Old
Testament literature. It is found in the history and in
the poetry as well as in the prophetic books. It is
indeed spread all over the literature of the Bible as the
thread of light that binds its writings into an organism
of redemption.

Messianic prophecy is in some respects not an adequate
term, for we do not limit ourselves to those predictions
which point evidently to a personal Messiah. The
material of Messianic prophecy embraces the work as
well as the person of the Messiah; and indeed all those
benefits that result to the kingdom of God through Him;
in other words, everything that has to do with the future
redemption. Hence von Orelli prefers the term "completion of the kingdom of God." [1] But the kingdom of
God is in some respects too wide a term and in other
respects too narrow. The completion of redemption is
the proper idea rather than the completion of the kingdom of God. But inasmuch as this completion is
accomplished only through the Messiah,—as His person is
the central theme to which the fulfilment of redemption ever points,—it seems better to embrace Him in the
definition and make His name the characteristic one in
the general terminology. This we do sufficiently well if
we embrace all the elements under the term Messianic
prophecy and define it as the completion of redemption
through the Messiah.

We have then to determine the relation of the completion of redemption through the Messiah to the general
doctrine of redemption in Hebrew prophecy. The
doctrines of Hebrew prophecy may be embraced under
the three divisions: God, Man, and Redemption. The
doctrine of redemption may be presented—(1) As a pre-

---

[1] C. von Orelli, *The Old Testament Prophecy of the Consummation
of God's Kingdom traced in its Historical Development*, Edin. 1885.

sent possession of the people of God; (2) as an acquisition in a future state; (3) as completed in the times of the Messiah. The first is the doctrine of redemption proper, the second is the doctrine of the future state, the third is Messianic prophecy. Indeed the three develop necessarily out of the prophetic doctrine of redemption.

The Biblical doctrine of redemption as a divine revelation has the characteristic of completeness. It is ever unfolding to perfection. It contains in its earliest statements the whole doctrine of redemption in germ. It comprehends at once the past, the present and the future. It covers this life, the coming life in this world and the future life beyond the grave. It is essentially progressive redemption. The present redemption kindles the hope of a more complete redemption in the future. As the past leads on to the present, so the present advances into the future, and the attention is fixed upon the ultimate goal of glory.

To the individual and the succeeding generation this must be beyond the gateway of death; but to the chosen people as a people, and to the race of man which is conceived as an everlasting unit, there is a steady and constant advance to the Messianic goal. Hebrew predictive prophecy, in its view of redemption in the future, springs from past and present experience of redemption. The Old Testament redemption advances in a long line of historic and predictive succession towards the New Testament redemption, and the New Testament redemption marches onward towards the redemption of the Messianic end, and in this end it is the privilege of the living and the departed alike to share. Thus the two systems of present advancing redemption and future completed redemption are related as substance and shadow, as type and antitype, as the building in course of erection to the finished building, as the elementary and preparatory studies to the perfected wisdom. In the redemptive system of the Old Testament we see the unfolding germ whose flower and fruit appear under the New Covenant. The child Israel is trained by the pedagogy of prophecy for the manhood of Messianic times. The redemption of the Law and the Prophets is realized in Him who came to fulfil the Law and the Prophets. And thus the Messianic prophecy of the Old Testament may be regarded as the New Testament in the Old—the ever living and developing ideal which inspired the faith, hope and love of the Old Testament saints, and gave their elementary redemption its sole efficacy and grace. And so with still greater intensity of meaning the New Testament Messianic idea has as its mission the edification of the Church of Christ and its preparation for the grander and ultimate glories of the perfect redemption of the second advent and the end of the world.

VI. THE FULFILMENT OF MESSIANIC PROPHECY.

§ 27. *Messianic prophecy is an advancing organism expressing in ever richer and fuller representations the ideal of complete redemption through the Messiah. History advances with prophecy toward the same goal, but prediction points the way. History constantly approximates to the Messianic ideal. It seems to fulfil the prediction as it advances, and to give ground for the theory of a double sense or a progressive fulfilment; but this is only the preparation of history for the real fulfilment which awaits it at the end of the course in the Messiah of history, the suffering, reigning and glorified Redeemer.*

The essential ideal of Messianic prophecy determines the principles by which it is to be interpreted. It is the highest and the essential phase of predictive prophecy. It is yet an ideal in constant development. There is no section of Biblical doctrine which has been so little understood and so much abused as Messianic prophecy. The Scholastics have interpreted the Messianic passages in accordance with the Christian doctrine of the person and work of Christ, from the point of view of a logical system of theology derived from the Bible, and they have ignored the organic system of Messianic prophecy in the Bible itself. They have overlooked the stages of development of the Messianic idea. They have neglected its varied phases. They have seen neither the unity nor the variety of the organism. They have sought above all things an Old Testament Christology. On the other hand, Rationalists have ignored the ideal element, and, in limiting the Messianic prediction to the local, temporal and circumstantial elements, determine the substance of the prediction by its external form, seeking in every way to exclude references to the Messiah and the redemption brought to the world through Him. If predictive prophecy in general can be interpreted only by finding the key, much more is this the case with Messianic prophecy, the culmination of predictive prophecy. For this we need the Master's key—that will unlock the mysteries of each prediction, and pass us through the entire system of predictions. We hesitate not therefore to state that the key of Old Testament prophecy is the first advent of the Messiah which unlocks a large number of its chambers. But the key of the entire system will not be given until the second advent. But this does not justify us in forcing New Testament meaning into Old Testament passages. If the Messiah gives us the key, He does not transform the predictions into histories. It is still necessary for us to see the connection between the Messiah as the central object of the prediction and the mind of the predicting prophet and the stage of redemption present to his experience. There is but one legitimate method for the interpretation of Messianic prophecy, and that is, (1) to study each prediction by itself with the most patient criticism and painstaking exegesis in all the details; (2) to study it in relation to other predictions in the series and note the organic connection; (3) to study it in relation to Christ and His redemption. Such a method will discern that Messianic prophecy of the Old Testament is an organic whole—an advancing organism culminating in the Christ of the incarnation, of the cross and of the throne.

This enables us to test the theory of the double sense. There is no double sense to Hebrew prediction. The prediction has but one sense. But inasmuch as the prediction advances from the temporal redemption of its circumstances to the eternal redemption of the Messiah, and it is part of a system of predictions in which the experience of redemption is advancing, it cannot be otherwise than that some of the elements of the predicted redemption should be realized in historical experience ere the essential element of the Messianic redemption is attained. This has induced some interpreters to speak of a successive fulfilment, or of a fulfilment in gradual approximation to the end. This is not a true representation of the facts of the case. There is but one fulfilment in the Messianic times. But all history is preparing the way and advancing toward that fulfilment. As prediction is rising in successive stages to higher and broader and more extensive views of the Messianic redemption, the history of redemption is advancing with it towards the same end. Thus we ought to expect that the Messianic ideal should be realized in some of its phases ere the ideal itself is attained, and that the later predictions should base themselves on these partial realizations. But we should

E

not be willing to acknowledge that the predictions find their fulfilment in these historic and predictive approximations. The Messianic ideal is the one essential thing to be determined in its relation to the Messianic end.

The Messianic idea, in its historic development, will separate itself more and more from the temporal, the local and the circumstantial, in order to rise to greater heights. We shall take care therefore in tracing its development to note this gradual differentiation, and to observe at the same time the historic process of redemption in its preparation for and advance toward this ideal, which, like the city of God and the enthroned Redeemer, ever rises in greater glory before it.

CHAPTER III.

THERE are several Messianic prophecies in the Pentateuch,—that unique collection of material relating to the
origin of Israel and mankind. These prophecies are
separated by wide intervals of time,—they mark the
great epochs of the world from the origin of our race
until the settlement of Israel in the land of Canaan.

These prophecies are contained chiefly in ancient
pieces of poetry, which the several authors of the narratives of the Pentateuch inserted in their histories. They
received their present order from the hands of an inspired
editor, who combined these ancient stories into a match-
less organism to constitute for all time the fundamental
divine Word to mankind.[1]

[1] The analysis of the Pentateuch into four distinct narratives,
with their distinct codes of legislation, is the result of a century of
study by the most famous critics of the age. There are slight
differences of opinion in the analysis at some points ; but these are
chiefly at the seams which bind the narratives together, and are
due to the editor's work, who in his efforts to make the entire composition as harmonious and symmetrical as possible, sometimes
obscured the signs of difference. But the concord of critics in the
work of analysis as a whole is wonderful, in view of the difficulties
that beset the work of higher criticism. The few objectors among
Hebrew scholars display their own unfamiliarity with the practical
work of criticism, when they overlook these solid results and point
to the difficulties as evidences that the problem has not been solved.
The differences of opinion among practical critics, and the difficulties
in the analysis, are where they ought to be from the very nature of
the case. Instead of disproving the work of criticism, they are
therefore an indirect evidence of its correctness. The differences
and difficulties disappear one after another as the investigation

The priestly narrator, in the first chapter of Genesis, gives an ancient poem of the creation.[1]   In the sixth strophe we have a description of the endowment of mankind as the last, the highest and the best of the host of God.

§ 28. *Mankind was created in the divine image, and endowed with dominion over the creatures.   His destiny was to assume sovereignty, and take possession of the earth by a numerous posterity.*

" And God said, Let us make mankind in our image and according
     to our figure,
That they may have dominion over the fish of the sea and the birds
     of heaven and the cattle,
And over all the earth, and over all that creep upon the earth.
And God created mankind in his image,
In the image of God he created him,
Male and female he created them.

---

advances.   The evidences for the analysis into four narratives are— (1) Differences in use of words and phrases ; (2) differences in style and methods of composition ; (3) differences in point of view and representations of religious institutions, doctrines and morals.   We have given this latter subject a thorough investigation.   We have by careful induction gathered the theology of each of the documents by itself and then compared them, and have found such a thorough-going difference, that it is simply impossible that they should have come from the same original author.   We hope at some future time to present the theology of the Pentateuch to the public.   In the meanwhile we refer to Dillmann, *Genesis*, 4th Aufl. 1882 ; Reuss, *Gesch. der Heiligen Schriften A. T.* 1881 ; Kuenen, *Hist. crit. Onderzoek*, i. 1885 ; Wellhausen, *Die Composition des Hexateuchs*, in his *Skizzen u. Vorarbeiten*, ii. 1885 ; also my "Critical Study of the History of the Higher Criticism," *Presbyterian Review*, 1883, p. 69 seq.

Scholars are not agreed in the names that they give to the four documents.   The priestly narrator is the Q. of Wellhausen, the A. or first Elohist of Dillmann.   The prophetic narrator is the Jahvist. The theocratic narrator is the second Elohist.   The Deuteronomist is agreed to by all.

[1] See my article on "The Poem of the Creation," in the *Old Testament Student*, April 1884.

And God blessed them and said unto them,
Be fruitful and multiply, and fill the earth and subdue it,
And have dominion over the fish of the sea and the birds of heaven,
And over all the animals which creep upon the earth.
And God said, Lo ! I do give you all herbage,
The seed scatterer which is on the face of the earth,
And all the trees in which is the fruit of the tree scattering seed ;
For you shall it become food, and for all the animals of the earth,
And for all the birds of the heaven, and for everything creeping
    upon the earth,
In whatever there is breath of life—all the greenness of herbage I
    do give for food.
And it became so ; and God saw all that he had made, and it was
    very excellent."   —Gen. i. 26–30.

The poet represents that mankind was endowed with
the image and figure of the heavenly intelligences with
whom God consulted in making our race.[1] That image
is the essential form, the mode of manifestation of
heavenly beings. It is not merely physical, it is not
merely moral, it is the form in which the essential nature
manifests itself, the inner form, the mode of being which
distinguishes man and his archetypes from all other
beings,—that form which shapes the physical in the
world of sense into the graceful and majestic body which
distinguishes man from all other creatures, and which in

---

[1] The plurals נעשה and צלמנו are referred by the older interpreters to the Trinity; but this overlooks the several stages in the
divine revelation. The doctrine of the Trinity is a Christian doctrine,
and it was first revealed in the New Testament. Some have thought
of a co-operation of God and nature in the production of man, but
this is against the usage of the poem, which represents God as commanding His host, and nature as obedient to His commands. Dillmann and Orelli explain the plural of the verb and suffix after the
analogy of the emphatic plural of the noun, so that God speaks out
of the fulness of His own being. But such a usage of the verb and
suffix is elsewhere unknown. It is best to think of God as associat-
ing with Himself, in the creation of man, the heavenly intelligences
whose form, as well as that of God Himself, man shares. This is
the view of Philo, Targum Jonathan, Raschi, Aben Ezra, Gabler
and Delitzsch, and is in accordance with Ps. viii. 6, which is based
on our passage. (See § 49 of this volume.)

the spirit world is the mode of manifestation by which individuals are distinguished from one another and recognise one another. The image of God with which man is endowed covers his entire nature—it is the form of his essential being.[1] In this image of God the destiny of man is involved. This is presented in our poem as having dominion over the other creatures of God, the earth itself, and the animal and vegetable species upon it. This dominion is to be obtained not by an individual man, or a pair, but by a human race. Man was created in sexes, was blessed with fruitfulness, and commanded to fill the earth and subdue it. All things without restriction were given into his hands—all animals and the entire vegetable world. The entire earth and its wealth are to be subdued by his godlike majesty and power. Man is the lord of nature. He is very excellent, and all things that are given by the Creator into his care are likewise very excellent as an organized host of God. There were no sin and no evil. Man was supreme over all, and his destiny was to assert his supremacy over all

---

[1] צלם and דמות are synonymous. They both refer to the form or figure of man, and not to the pictorial likeness. Some theologians refer the form to the higher nature of man. But there is nothing in the text or context to suggest such an interpretation. The context urges us to think of the entire man as distinguished from the lower forms of creation,—that which is essential to man and may be communicated by descent to his seed. The bodily form cannot be excluded from the representation. Indeed it is this form which is assumed by angels and the theophanic Malakh and the Son of God Himself. The bodily form is only the physical expression of a spiritual form which continues with man in Sheol after death, in which also God reveals Himself to disembodied spirits in the future life (Ps. xvii. 15). This form is indeed the mode of expression of the heavenly intelligences in their relations to each other. It involves all the higher endowments of man, his reason, conscience, intelligence, power of speech, all by which, as a higher being, he acts in the world of spirits and the world of matter. Physical matter is not the form of man, it is shaped and used by the form, which is essentially spiritual, and it disappears with the decay of the material substance.

the earth. This is conceived as a task before him to be accomplished only through a numerous posterity. It is through the multiplication of the children of men that the earth is to be subdued and the sovereignty of mankind accomplished. This is not the reduction to submission of a series of hostile provinces and rebellious creatures; but the gradual taking possession of a kingdom given to mankind by God, and which he assumes in province after province of his vast domain by divine right.

This blessing and original endowment of mankind is not specifically a Messianic prophecy, and yet it is the condition and framework of all prophecy, for it is the divine plan for mankind—the divinely-appointed goal of his history.

I. THE PROTEVANGELIUM.

§ 29. *The protevangelium is a divine blessing wrapt in judgments. It predicts the ultimate victory of the seed of the woman over the serpent, after a conflict in which both parties will be wounded.*

Messianic prophecy begins with the dawn of human history. The history of mankind opens with a sublime tragedy—the original sin of our first parents, and their expulsion from the garden in Eden. They bear with them from Paradise the Magna Charta of human history; they enter into the world to engage in a life-long struggle whose issue is death and victory. From their Creator's hands they received the protevangelium, the glad tidings of redemption. It was wrapt about with curses and sorrows; thereby they recognise God as their Redeemer. The protevangelium is contained in the poem of the Fall of Mankind, with which the prophetic narrator begins his story. The human pair had been

formed by the hands of God, and the breath of His
nostrils had imparted to them life and intelligence.
God entered into the sphere of his own creation in
theophany, in order to endow mankind with godlike
faculties and train them in their exercise. The garden,
with its trees and animals, was for the education of our
race. There can be no religious training without trial.
The temptation was necessary for the ethical culture of
Adam and Eve. The tree of life and the tree of death
set before them in simple, graphic and impressive forms
the good and the evil. The enjoyment of the permissible
good gave them an increasing experimental knowledge
of the good. The abstinence from the prohibited evil
gave them an increasing theoretic knowledge of the
evil; and thus the discrimination between the good and
the evil became sharper as they advanced in ethical
culture. The trees had accomplished their purpose, the
time had come for a higher temptation, the animal
tempter is added to the tree. An evil spirit assumes
the form of the serpent, and tempts the woman to transgression.

The serpent is evidently something more than the
animal serpent. There is intelligence, conception, speech,
and knowledge higher than that of the man or the
woman. The woman knew that she had to deal, not
with a mere serpent, one of the animals under her
dominion, but with a higher power, a spiritual intelligence, who had entered the garden in hostility to her
Creator, with the avowed purpose of delivering man from
bondage. As the Creator assumed human form in order
to the creation and training of the human pair in the
garden of Eden, so now a hostile spirit assumed the form
of the serpent in order to deceive and ruin them. There
is nothing in this primitive poem to indicate that the
author attributed to the animals of Eden powers of

reasoning and speech. The author would rather, by attributing the naming of animals to man, and by showing that man could find no companion among them, imply that the powers of reasoning and speech were endowments of man which the animals did not possess.

The tempter assails all the avenues of human nature. The woman's physical appetite is excited by the fruit of the tree; her æsthetic sense is attracted by its beauty; her intellectual powers are stimulated by the promise of godlike knowledge; she ought to have resisted and to have overcome this temptation, and thereby advanced to a higher state of godlikeness in the possession and enjoyment of the good; but she was seduced and she was overpowered; she yielded and she fell. She seduced her husband and he fell with her. The human pair fell from godlikeness and became like evil spirits. But there was a difference between the tempter and his victims, and in that difference there was the possibility of redemption. There was a threefold gradation in guilt and a threefold gradation in punishment. For the evil spirit, the tempter, there was no excuse. He was altogether a tempter and blasphemer. The woman was tempted, and sinned, and became a tempter. The man was tempted and transgressed. God appears in theophany as Judge and as Redeemer. He presents our race with the protevangelium wrapt in the severe sentences of judgment pronounced upon the three transgressors. Herein is the germ of promise which unfolds in the history of redemption. Out of the despair of the first fall, in the experience of the first sin and shame, sorrow and pain, the heart of man rebounds with hope into the future which was opened by the divine prediction. It was the voice of the theophanic God which said unto the serpent—

> " Because thou hast done this, cursed be thou,
>   Away from all beasts and from all animals of the field ;
>   Upon thy belly shalt thou go,
>   And dust shalt thou eat all the days of thy life.
>   And enmity will I put between thee and the woman,
>   And between thy seed and her seed ;
>   He shall bruise thee on the head,
>   And thou shalt bruise him on the heel." [1]
>
> —Gen. iii. 14, 15.

The animal serpent is degraded from the position to which he was entitled by his grace and beauty and his intelligence, and reduced to a wretched condition as a fugitive from the presence of man and animals, condemned to hide from them and flee from their presence and their wrath.[2]

The strophe rises to the punishment of the evil spirit, which used the animal as his instrument.   There is a prediction of a perpetual enmity not only between the woman and the serpent, but between the entire race and descendants of the woman and the serpent.   This enmity involves a perpetual conflict, in which injury is wrought on both sides.   The wounds inflicted by the serpent are in secret and in treachery, behind the back of man and beneath his heel.   But the wounds inflicted by man upon the serpent are openly upon his head, crushing him to death in the dust.

The term seed is a generic term for the entire race of

---

[1] See my article, "The Poem of the Fall of Mankind," in the *Reformed Quarterly Review*, April 1866.

[2] עַל נְחֹנְךָ תֵלֵךְ is thought by Keil and Delitzsch, after the older interpreters, to imply that the form of the serpent was changed ; that previously he had walked in the garden among the other animals, and now for the first was condemned to crawl in the dust. The phrase אָכַל עָפָר has also been interpreted to the effect that the serpent's food was the dust. But eating the dust is similar to the phrase biting the dust, and implies nothing more than living in the dust of the ground.   The curse denounces a change of condition rather than of form.

descendants of the woman on the one hand and the serpent on the other. The seed of the serpent embraces all the evil race derived from him. This prediction points not merely to the whole family of snakes, but to the serpents of the higher world, the evil spirits, and to the serpents among mankind, the evil men, and seducers, called by Jesus the children of the devil,[1] indeed all the forces of evil which array themselves against the children of God. The seed of the woman embraces the human race as such, that is, all who take part in the conflicts of the race with the forces of evil. There are those who by birthright belong to the seed of the woman who become by apostasy the children of the serpent. There are also those who are won as trophies of grace from the seed of the serpent and are adopted into the seed of redemption. These two great forces are in conflict throughout history.

This enmity and conflict are to result in an eventual and final victory of man over the serpent. It is something more than a mere dislike and hostility to snakes; it is a conflict in which man is to bear a brave and hazardous part; and the victory is one which is to overcome the vast injury wrought by the serpent in the temptation and fall of man. It is a victory which is a redemption from evil and sin, as the fall was a fall into sin and evil. We have then a blessing to the human race involved in this curse of the serpent; a promise of redemption to be accomplished not by the woman, but by her seed. Her seed is the entire race of her descendants. But inasmuch as the serpent is represented as bruising the heel of the man, and is distinguished from his seed in God's direct address to him as *thou*, and the original tempter himself is thus to be the finally crushed and conquered foe, it seems to be necessary to think of the

[1] John viii. 44.

seed of the woman as culminating in an individual victor
who is to be the champion of his race and gain the final
victory over the serpent.[1] This last conflict is to be a
conflict in which there will be no more deception of the
woman ; but the son of the woman, a second Adam, will
avenge his mother's shame and his father's dishonour, and
retrieve the fortunes of his race by transforming death
into victory.[2]

Thus we have in this fundamental prophecy explicitly
a struggling, suffering, but finally victorious human race,

---

[1] The unity of the seed is maintained in the demonstrative הוא and
the suffix ־נו. The individuality of the serpent is also emphasized in
the final conflict by the אתה, which shows that the serpent of the
temptation and the serpent of the final conflict are the same
individual. The אתה is contrasted with the הוא, and as the אתה is
discriminated from the seed of the serpent, so we must see in the
final conflict an individual son of man arising out of the seed of
the woman to become the serpent bruiser. The Roman Catholic
reference of הוא to the Virgin Mary is supported by the neglect to
distinguish between the masculine and feminine of the demonstrative.
It is also favoured by the contrast between the serpent and the woman
which runs through the strophe. But the suffix ־נו cannot be
feminine, and the reference to the woman would require the re-
appearance of Eve in order to the final victory, and not a second Eve,
one of her descendants. Eve is punished by the sorrows of child-
birth. In child-birth is her hope of redemption. The Redeemer is
to be born of the woman, and to lead His race to the ultimate victory.

[2] There is some difficulty in the verb שׁוּף, which occurs but thrice
in the Old Testament. But in Ps. cxxxix. 11 the best critics correct
the text to ישׁוכני, so that we have but one passage (Job ix. 7) to
bring into comparison. The parallelism of Job ix. 7 urges the meaning, crush or bruise ; and that is best suited to our passage. The
Syr., Vulgate, Arab., Targum of Jonathan and Samaritan Targum
favour this. But the LXX. and the Targum of Onkelos favour the
meaning, watch, guard ; and these latter are followed by Gesenius
and Dillmann. The weight of authority is in favour of wound. The
wound on the head is a crushing, a mortal wound ; a trampling under
foot, a victory. The wound on the heel might also be regarded as
mortal, if we think of the venom of the serpent's sting. But this is
inappropriate to the Messianic idea. There is a contrast between
head and heel which suggests a contrast between a crushing defeat
and a slight injury to the victor. If any one should prefer to think
that the victory is gained by the death of the victor, he will not
cause any other difficulty to the Messianic fulfilment than that it
seems unlikely that the first rediction should be so precise.

and implicitly a struggling, suffering and finally victorious son of the woman, a second Adam, the head of the race. The seed of the woman expands through the ages into a race of multitudes of individuals, but in that expanding seed there is a central nucleus in which the original unity is maintained. In the fulness of time this gives birth to the second Adam, the Redeemer. The protevangelium is a faithful miniature of the entire history of humanity, a struggling seed ever battling for the ultimate victory. Here is the germinal idea which unfolds in the sufferings and sorrows, the hopes and joys of our race until it is realized in the sublime victories of redemption.

The protevangelium is the only Messianic prophecy which has been preserved from the revelations made by God to the antediluvian world. Centuries roll on without any further light on the future redemption. The sentences of judgment realize themselves in the death of our first parents and their posterity. The sorrows of woman and the toils of man come upon generation after generation of mankind. Sin develops in the descendants of Adam until they become totally corrupt and ripe for the judgment which comes upon them in the great catastrophe of the deluge, blotting them out from the face of the earth, with the exception of a single family which is redeemed in the ark owing to the righteousness of a single man. The protevangelium is the star of promise in the night of the deluge, but there was no sign of daybreak. The going forth from the ark into the renovated earth begins a new era of mankind, and this era is opened with the second Messianic prophecy.

II. THE BLESSING OF SHEM.

The family of Noah was redeemed in the ark from the judgment of the deluge. The original destiny of

mankind to subdue the earth to his dominion, and the
promise of the protevangelium that the seed of the woman
would gain the victory over the serpent, were the inheritance of Noah pressing on to realization through his
children.   Immediately on going forth from the ark to
take possession of the renovated earth, he expresses his
faith and gratitude by a sublime act of worship.   This
is described in that ancient poem of the deluge which is
preserved in the story of the prophetic narrator.

§ 30. *Immediately after the deluge a divine promise
assures the posterity of Noah of the stability of the earth,
and the uniformity of the seasons.*

> And Noah built an altar to Jahveh,
> And took some of all the clean beasts,
> And some of all the clean birds,
> And offered a whole burnt-offering on the altar.
> And when Jahveh smelled the odour of gratification,[1]
> Jahveh said to his very soul,
> I will not again any more curse
> The ground for man's sake,
> Though the structure of the heart of man be evil from his youth ;
> And I will not again any more smite
> All living things as I have done.
> During all the days of the earth,
> Seed-time and harvest, and cold and heat, and summer and winter,
> And day and night will not cease."   —Gen. viii. 20–22.

This strophe of the poem of the deluge contains a
sublime promise of God, which though not strictly a
Messianic promise, yet affords the conditions for the
further development of the Messianic idea.   The earth
to be subdued by man is to remain essentially the same
throughout its history.   The regular course of the seasons

---

[1] ריח ניחח.   This is an odour or scent that gives gratification or
satisfaction to God.   It is the odour of the whole burnt-offering,
which is accepted by God as pleasing and gratifying to Him.

will continue until the period of the earth is completed. The sin of mankind is recognised as a factor in the conflict,—sin not only in the tempter and the outer world, but sin which is in the very structure of the innermost man. And yet no great catastrophe will change the form and condition of the earth until the destiny of man has been accomplished.

Sin survived the deluge and soon manifested itself in the children of Noah. An act of sin is the occasion of the second great Messianic prophecy which opens the second epoch of the world's history.

§ 31. *In the prediction of Noah the curse of Canaan is servitude, while Ham and his other sons are ominously passed by. The blessing of Japhet is enlargement. The blessing of Shem is the dwelling of God in his tents.*

The second Messianic prophecy, like the first, is a blessing which springs up in contrast to a curse. Sin and shame are the occasion of the prediction. The sin is against the second father of our race, the patriarch Noah. The shame is in the evil conduct of his youngest son Ham. The sentence and the blessing are pronounced not directly by God, but by the patriarch, who in the spirit of prophecy speaks not only his own determinations but also the divine decree. The blessing and the curse give a fresh glance into the history of mankind,—a history which is not only a struggle against evil spirits with the assurance of an eventual victory, but is also a struggle between three great races of mankind.

There are three parties in this prediction of the patriarch. There are again three degrees of virtue and sin represented in the three children. The sin and shame are confined to one son, Ham, but the virtue of Japhet is transcended by the piety of Shem. These three degrees of moral character in the three children of

the patriarch receive their interpretation in the history
of the races which were to spring from them and people
the earth.

> " He said, Cursed be Canaan ;
> A servant of servants will he become to his brethren.
> And he said, Blessed be [1] the God of Shem,
> And let Canaan be servant to him.
> May God spread out Japhet,
> And may He dwell in the tents of Shem,
> And let Canaan be servant to him."　　—Gen. ix. 26–27.

The aged patriarch, inspired by the spirit of prophecy,
reads in the faces and souls of his sons the lines of
passion and of character that will distinguish the races
of their descendants and determine their history.　The
shameful conduct of Ham in dishonouring his aged father
was an index of the sensual nature of the man which
would perpetuate itself in his children and give character
to his race.　It is singular that the glance of the patriarch
should pass over the guilty Ham to the grandson Canaan.
It was in accordance with retributive justice that Ham
should receive in his own experience the same dishonour
through his son that he himself had been guilty of to
his father Noah.　It was also to sharpen the curse by
distinguishing one of the sons of Ham, upon whom it
would pour itself out to the full, while the father and
his other sons are passed by in ominous silence.　The
curse of Canaan is servitude to his brethren—the hard
toil of mankind is intensified in the sorrows and bitterness of human bondage.

The patriarch turns from Ham to his brothers.　He
sees in their respectful conduct in hiding their father's
nakedness the manly reverence and virtue of their
characters.　Shem, the first-born, the heir of his father's

---

[1] The prophetic narrator here inserts the divine name Jahveh
in the ancient poem.

religious nature, first receives the blessing. Reflecting upon all that God had done for him, the patriarch invokes the divine blessing upon his son. The first revulsion of feeling recalls the shameful conduct of his youngest son, and the curse the second time bursts from his lips—

"Let Canaan be servant to him."

The soul of the patriarch now expands under the inspiration of prophecy, and he utters the full and final prediction in which all the members appear. His soul bounds within him as he beholds the manly virtue of his second son, and taking his inspiration from his name he said:[1] "May God enlarge Japhet," spread him, and give him a large place, a large portion for his inheritance. Then turning to Shem, he continued, and "may He (that is, God) dwell in the tents of Shem." Let God be his portion and his inheritance. May God grant His presence and take up His abode with him. Once more recurring to the wicked son, the curse for the third time came forth—

"Let Canaan be servant to him."

Shem is the central figure of the prophecy, Canaan its dark background, and Japhet its distant perspective. The curse of Canaan is servitude, while Ham and his other sons are ominously passed by. This corresponds with his nature, which was sensual. The blessing of Japhet is enlargement, in accordance with his nature, which was ideal. The blessing of Shem is the presence and the indwelling of God, in accordance with his character, which was spiritual.

Leaving Canaan and Japhet, we shall consider more closely the blessing of Shem, in which the Messianic prophecy is contained.

[1] יֶפֶת, the name, and יַפְתְּ, the verb, are both from פתה.

F

The blessing of Shem is the presence and indwelling
of God.[1] The Shemites have God for their portion.
The divine presence is ever in their tents—they are the
bearers of the true religion. The law the prophets and
Christianity came through them. Religious contemplation
is the chief characteristic of the face. The central
idea of the prophecy is the advent of God to dwell in
the tents of Shem ; the divine advent being the germ of
a Messianic idea at the opposite pole from the seed of
the woman of the protevangelium.

In the former prophecy we have the human side of
Messianic redemption brought out in the victory of the
seed of the woman over the serpent. Here, on the other
hand, we have the divine side of Messianic redemption
in the prediction of the advent of God as a blessing in
the tents of Shem. These two lines of Messianic

---

[1] Authorities greatly differ as to the subject of ישכן. The Targum
of Onkelos, Philo, Maimonides, Rashi, Aben Ezra, Baumgarten,
Delitzsch, Conant, Lewis, et al., take אלהים as the subject ; but
the ancient Fathers and Reformers and the great body of modern
interpreters, even Dillmann, regard Japhet as the subject. It is
better to take אלהים as the subject for the following reasons :—(1)
The presumption is that the subject of the previous clause, especially
in a parallel line of Hebrew poetry, should be the subject of the
following clause, where no subject is given. It is possible that the
unexpressed subject should be found in the indirect object of the
previous clause ; but it should require a strong reason from the
context. (2) The Heptastich containing the blessings and the curse
is subdivided into three parts by the curse of Canaan as a refrain.
In the first part, a distich, only Canaan appears. In the second
part, also a distich, Canaan and Shem appear. In the third part, a
tristich, the three sons appear. We might suppose that Japhet is
the central figure of the tristich, as Shem had been of the previous
distich. This would justify our making him the subject of ישכן ;
but it would place Shem in subordination to him, and represent
Japhet as the hero of the prophecy. But, on the other hand, the
trend of the poetic movement seems rather to bring the three sons
in co-ordination in the tristich as two sons are co-ordinated in the
previous distich. (3) In the narrative of the honourable conduct of
the two brothers, the name of Shem comes first, as if he were more
prominent, and indeed the leader in that which was done. It

prophecy, the human and the divine, henceforth develop side by side in Messianic prophecy; they approximate at times, but never converge till they unite in the person of Jesus Christ, the God-man, at His first advent, and still more at His second advent.

III. THE BLESSING OF ABRAHAM.

Another long interval occurs in the history of the development of the Messianic idea. The sons of Noah multiply until they become families, tribes and nations, and crowd the original home of the race.

In chastisement for their ungodliness they are dispersed from Babel, and proceed to the fulfilment of their respective destinies. From among the Shemite tribes which remained on the Euphrates, rapidly degenerating from the pure religion, God chose a single pair, Abram and

---

seems singular, therefore, that he should be placed in subordination to Japhet in the blessing. (4) The patriarch blessed the God of Shem in the previous distich. God is thus in a peculiar sense the God of Shem. It is entirely in keeping with this blessing that the God of Shem should dwell in the tents of Shem. (5) The peculiar blessing of Japhet is expansion. There is slight connection between that blessing and the dwelling in the tents of Shem. The most natural interpretation of dwelling in the tents of Shem would be, that he was to conquer Shem and occupy his territory. But this would be a humiliation to Shem, which would be little better than the curse of Canaan, and not at all in keeping with the story on which the prophecy is founded. (6) There is another interpretation of שֵׁם, which seems more appropriate if the verb is to have Japhet as subject, namely, "tents of name," or "tents of renown," representing that the expansion of Japhet would be accompanied with world-wide fame and renown. But this would so greatly emphasize the blessing of Japhet as to cast Shem into shadow. (7) The context of the narration and the previous distich would lead us to expect that Shem should be the prominent figure in the prophecy. This is also in accordance with the subsequent history and with the development of the Messianic idea. If Japhet be the subject, we have more of a political than a religious prophecy, which seems to me unnatural to the experience of the patriarch under the circumstances.

his wife, to go forth from their native land into a far
country to be the parents of a chosen people, and be a
blessing to the world.   The call of Abram begins a new
era in history, and as such, like the previous eras, opens
with a Messianic prophecy.

§ 32. *The covenant with Abraham established a blessed
relationship between the seed of Abraham and God, and
between the seed of Abraham and mankind, and also
assigned the seed of Abraham a land of blessing.*

The original prediction is given by the prophetic
narrator.   It is a prediction in the form of a blessing.
It is contained in a direct address of Jahveh to Abraham.
We are not informed whether it was through a theophanic
appearance as is usual in this author, or by an internal
communication to the soul of the patriarch.

"And Jahveh said unto Abram,
   Go thou from thy land,
   And from thy kindred, and from thy father's house,
   Unto the land which I will show thee :
   And I will make thee a great nation,
   And I will bless thee, and I will make thy name great ;
   Therefore be thou a blessing,
   And I will bless those blessing thee ;
   But those making light of thee shall I curse ;
   And all the clans of the earth [1] will bless themselves with thee."
                                                —Gen. xii. 1–3.

Abram is called to separate himself from his kindred
in order to become the father of a chosen seed of blessing.
He is summoned to leave his native land and go forth
into a land which Jahveh will give him for an inheritance.
He is assured that in this land his name will become a
blessing to all the clans of the earth.   Abram obeys the

___

[1] The important technical terms in this prediction are גוי גדול
and כל משפחת האדמה.   These we reserve for consideration farther
on.   See p. 89.

call, and thereby gains the blessing as an inheritance; and secures for himself and mankind advancement in the Messianic promise. He goes forth into the land of Canaan; and in the midst of that land, at Shechem, by the oak of Moreh, he is assured that he is in the promised land; and there he erects an altar to Jahveh, as the sacred pledge that he had taken the divine promise to himself and recognized Jahveh as the God of the promised land.

We notice first of all a narrowing of the elective grace of God from the seed of the woman, through the race of Shem to the seed of Abraham. And yet this limitation does not destroy the universality of the previous promises —rather this limitation itself is in order to intensify the chosen nucleus for the benefit of the whole. What is lost in extension is gained in intension. The thoughts are concentrated on the seed of Abraham, and his seed is made the channel of blessing to all. And thus the previous Messianic ideas of a suffering and victorious human race, and the advent of God to the tents of Shem, have an important development, especially the former,— that is, the human side of Messianic redemption,—in that there is a more exact specification as to form and place in the indication of a special seed of blessing and a particular place of blessing; and thereby also of a blessed relationship of the particular seed of Abraham to the whole seed of the woman.

There is striking contrast between the reality and the ideal promise. Abraham was an old man and childless, yet Jahveh promised to make of him a great and innumerable seed. He went forth from his native land not knowing whither, yet he was a pilgrim to a holy, blessed land. He went, separating himself from his race and kindred, and yet he was the chosen means of uniting the kindreds and races in a common blessing.

The original promise is unfolded still further in the story of the prophetic narrator.

"Lift up now thine eyes and see, from the place where thou art, northward and southward, and eastward and westward : for the whole land which thou art seeing, to thee will I give it, and to thy seed for ever, and will set thy seed as the dust of the land, that if a man be able to number the dust of the land, thy seed also may be numbered. Arise, walk about in the land to its length and to its breadth, for to thee will I give it."—Gen. xiii. 14–18.

The promised land is enlarged from the "this land," as seen at Shechem, to "the whole land" which he could see from the hill country of Judah, "northward and southward, and eastward and westward"—"its length and its breadth." The promise, "I will make thee a great nation," is enlarged by the comparison of the promised seed with the innumerable "dust of the land."

We have still another Jahvistic reference to the promise in the form of a divine reflection upon it in view of His purpose to destroy Sodom and the cities of the plain.

"Shall I go on concealing from Abraham what I am about to do, seeing that Abraham will altogether become a nation, strong and mighty,[1] and all the nations of the earth will bless themselves with him ?"—Gen. xviii. 17–19.

The theocratic narrator gives the blessing of Abraham in another form. Abram was anxious lest he should remain childless, and lest his inheritance should fall into the hands of his chief steward Eliezer. His anxiety was removed by the prediction of God Himself.

"This one will not be thine heir : on the contrary, he who will come forth from thy bowels, he will be thine heir. And he led him forth without, and said, O look heavenward, and count the stars, if thou art able to count them ; and he said to him, Thus will thy seed become."—Gen. xv. 4, 5.

---

[1] גוי גדול of xii. 2 has become גוי גדול ועצום. The כל משפחות האדמה of xii. 3 appears in the variant כל גויי הארץ.

In accordance with this prediction, the seed of Abram is not merely to be derived from his household,—his dependants,—but from his own son who is yet to be born. And his seed is to be as innumerable as the stars. The prediction then enlarges upon the promised land, and declares that it is not immediately to pass into the possession of the seed of Abraham. There is to be a period of four hundred years of bondage in Egypt. A fourth generation will return from bondage and take possession of the promised land. This prediction is precise in describing the extent of the land. It is to embrace the territory from the river of Egypt to the Euphrates. The lands of the eleven nations are specified, including the aboriginal population, the tribes of the Canaanites, the Syrian Hittites, and their associate nations. A vast territory is assigned as an inheritance to the posterity of Abram.[1]

The priestly narrator gives the blessing of Abram in connection with the establishment of the Abrahamic covenant, which is sealed by the sign of circumcision, and accompanied by an expressive change of name.

" It is I, '*El Shadday*,[2] walk about before me, and be thou perfect ; and I will make my covenant between me and thee, and I will multiply thee very greatly. And Abram fell upon his face. And God spake with him, saying, I,—lo ! my covenant will be with thee, and thou wilt become father of a multitude of nations, and thy name will no more be called Abram ; but thy name will be Abraham : for a father of a multitude of nations do I make thee. And I will cause thee to be very very fruitful, and make thee into nations ; and kings from thee will issue. And I will establish my covenant between me and thee, and thy seed after thee for generations, for an everlasting

---

[1] Gen. xv. 18–21.

[2] The divine name אל שדי is the characteristic name of the God of the patriarchs according to the priestly narrator. It is a combination of אל, the Strong, and שדי, the Mighty. אל is commonly used with predicates such as שדי.

covenant, to become God to thee and to thy seed after thee ; and I
will give to thee and to thy seed after thee the land of thy sojourning, the whole land of Canaan, for an everlasting possession ; and I
shall become God to them."—Gen. xvii. 1–8.

The promised land is the " land of thy sojourning," the
" whole land of Canaan." This is to be an "everlasting
possession " of his seed. The promised seed is expanded
into " a multitude of nations," which takes the place
of the "great nation" of the blessing in the poem of
the prophetic narrator. Accordingly the name Abram,
" exalted father," is changed into Abraham, "father of a
multitude," and nations and kings are to issue from him.
He is to be the father of a race, and not merely of a
single tribe or nation.

The last form of the Abrahamic blessing is given by
the editor of the Pentateuch in the combination of the
representations of the prophetic and theocratic narrators
with some additional features of enlargement and of
explanation. The trial of Abraham and his faithfulness
in the severest strain upon his faith, were the occasion for
the final advancement of his blessing.

" And the Malakh Jahveh [1] called unto Abraham a second time
from heaven, and said : By myself I swear, is the utterance of
Jahveh, that because thou hast done this thing and hast not withheld thy son, thine only one, that I will richly bless thee, and I will
greatly multiply thy seed as the stars of heaven and as the sand
which is upon the shore of the sea, that thy seed may inherit the gate
of their enemies ; and all the nations of the earth will bless themselves in thy seed, because that thou hast hearkened to my voice."—
Gen. xxii. 15–18.

This blessing is more than a blessing or a covenant, it

---

[1] מלאך יהוה. This is not an angel commissioned by Jahveh, but
a theophany of Jahveh Himself in the form of an angel. Hence the
constant identification of Jahveh and the Malakh Jahveh, the
transition from one to the other, and the recognition of the Malakh
as God on the part of those to whom the theophanies were made.

is in the form of a divine oath. There is no advancement in the promised land beyond the whole land of Canaan of the covenant which is given in the priestly narrative. The promised seed is to become as innumerable as the stars of heaven (as in the theocratic narrative) and as the sand of the sea-shore, which is a third comparison differing from the dust of the land of the prophetic narrator. But the third feature of the original promise is that which receives amplification here. " All the clans of the earth will bless themselves in thee," and " all the nations of the earth " of chap. xviii. of the prophetic narrator become " all the nations of the earth will bless themselves in thy seed." [1] And "I shall curse those making light of thee " of the original promise is enlarged into " thy seed will inherit the gate of their enemies." This is an unfolding of the curse upon those making light of Abram. They are reduced to submission by war.

The blessing of Abraham becomes the inheritance of Isaac. The children of Abraham by Hagar and Keturah, his concubines, separate themselves and become heads of

---

[1] The chief difficulty in the blessing of Abraham is in the ונברכו בך כל משפחת האדמה (xii. 3), which appears in xxii. 18 as והתברכו בזרעך כל גויי הארץ. The parallelism in thought is manifest, and yet every word except כל is different. The latter passage is clearer and later, and should be regarded as an interpretation of the former by the Redactor, who had the advantage of both the prophetic and theocratic narrators in his final representation. The extent of the blessing in the latter passage is " all nations," which takes the place of " all clans." This is like xviii. 18 of the prophetic narrator. The greater divisions are substituted for the lesser, for according to the constitution of Israel the nation was divided into tribes, and these tribes into clans. The nations are limited by הארץ, which takes the place of the האדמה. The אדמה is used in the first passage probably to distinguish it from the ארץ in the limited sense of land. But in the second passage there is no need of distinction. It is possible to think of ארץ in the latter passage as used in the limited sense, referring to the land of Canaan, and think of the nations of Canaan. But in the development of the Messianic idea it is sub-

tribes and nations. The prophetic narrative gives an account of a theophany to Isaac when he went up to Beersheba, in which the Abrahamic blessing is assigned to him without enlargement.

"It is I, the God of Abraham thy father, fear not, for I shall be with thee, and bless thee, and multiply thy seed, for the sake of Abraham my servant."—Gen. xxvi. 24.

The blessing is transmitted to Isaac, and first of all by divine assignment prior to the birth of the twins.

"Two nations are in thy womb,
And two peoples will separate themselves from thy bowels;
And people will be stronger than people,
And the greater will serve the lesser."   —Gen. xxv. 23, 24.

This prediction breaks up the seed of Isaac into two nations, assigns the headship with the blessing to Jacob, and makes Edom subject to him, as Canaan had been made subject to Shem in the blessing of Shem. The favouritism of the father sought to overcome the divine assignment, but the craft of Rachel and Jacob secured

---

sequent to the protevangelium and the blessing of Shem, and it seems altogether inappropriate to give it such a limited reference. And when we consider the subsequent development of the Messianic idea in the history, this is still more inappropriate. The nations of Canaan were rather the enemies whose gates the seed of Abraham possessed, than nations who congratulated themselves upon the presence of Israel in their land, and participated in their blessing. The blessing in the last form comes upon the nations through the seed of Abraham, which is more specific than the original promise that it was to come through Abraham himself. The verb gives the chief difficulty. The Hithpael of the second passage must be taken as reflexive. This favours the view that the Niphal of the same verb, in the first passage, should be reflexive also. The Niphal may be passive, but the passive meaning should never be adopted unless there is evidence against the usual reflexive meaning of the form. We do not hesitate, therefore, to adopt the view of most recent interpreters, De Wette, Gesenius, Ewald, Knobel, Delitzsch, Dillmann, *et al.*, that the form is reflexive, and we render, "bless themselves with thee."

the birthright for the divinely-appointed heir. The prophetic narrative gives the patriarchal blessing—

> "May God give to thee of the dew of heaven
> And of the fatness of the earth,
> And abundance of corn and new wine.
> May peoples bless thee,
> And nations do thee homage;
> Be thou a mighty one to thy brethren,
> And let the sons of thy mother do thee homage.
> Cursed be those cursing thee,
> And blessed be those blessing thee." —Gen. xxvii. 27–29.

The promised land is here emphasized as to its fertility and fruitfulness. The nations are to be subdued, and are to recognize the supremacy of Jacob. The blessing is enlarged in a theophany granted to Jacob on his way to Haran.

> "And he said, It is I, Jahveh, the God of Abraham thy father and the God of Isaac. The land upon which thou art abiding, to thee will I give it and to thy seed. And thy seed will become as the dust of the land, and thou wilt break out westward and eastward, and northward and southward; and all the clans of the land will bless themselves with thee.[1] And lo I shall be with thee, and keep thee in every place whither thou goest, and bring thee back to this land. Yea, I shall not forsake thee until that I have done that which I have spoken to thee."—Gen. xxviii. 13–16.

This prediction is a reiteration of xii. 1–5 and xiii. 14–17. The only advance is in the enlargement of the promise, "I shall be with thee," of xxvi. 24, into "I shall be with thee and keep thee, and bring thee back—

---

[1] בזרעך is an addition by the editor, who combined the prophetic and theocratic narratives. Otherwise the language of the original promise recurs, ונברכו בך כל משפחות האדמה, and xiii. 14–17 reappears in עפר הארץ. And "the land upon which thou art abiding, westward and eastward, and northward and southward," is a slight variation of "the place where thou art, northward and southward, and eastward and westward." "To thee shall I give it" is an exact verbal repetition.

will not forsake thee." The personal care and presence
of Jahveh are greatly emphasized. The priestly narrative
gives the same blessing in different forms. It is first
mentioned in connection with the sending of Jacob to
Padan Aram.

> "Thou shalt not take a wife of the daughters of Canaan.
> Arise, go to Padan Aram,
> To the house of Bethuel the father of thy mother,
> And take thee a wife from thence
> Of the daughters of Laban thy mother's brother.
> And may 'El Shadday bless thee,
> And may he make thee fruitful, and may he multiply thee,
> So that thou may become a congregation of people.
> And may he give to thee the blessing of Abraham,
> To thee and to thy seed with thee,
> To inherit the land of thy sojourning,
> Which God gave to Abraham." [1]   —Gen. xxviii. 1–4.

This is simply the repetition of the Abrahamic
covenant of Gen. xvii. The priestly narrative gives a
reiteration of the blessing on the return from Padan
Aram, which is accompanied with a change of the name
of Jacob into Israel, as Abram's name had been changed
into Abraham.

> "Thy name will not be called any more Jacob, but, on the contrary,
> Israel will thy name become. And he called his name Israel. And
> God said to him, It is I, 'El Shadday, be fruitful and multiply.
> A nation and a congregation of nations will come from thee; and
> kings will issue from thy loins. And the land which I gave to
> Abraham and to Isaac, to thee will I give it; and to thy seed after
> thee shall I give the land." [2]—Gen. xxxv. 9–12.

---

[1] אל שדי is the divine name, as in xvii. 1–8. המון גוים appears in
the synonymous קהל עמים. The verb פרה and the phrase ארץ
מגריך also recur.

[2] This piece closely resembles xxviii. 1–4 and xvii. 1–5. קהל עמים
is here קהל גוים. "Kings from *thy loins* issue" takes the place of
"Kings *from thee* issue" of xvii. 6.

IV. THE BLESSING OF JUDAH.

The family of Jacob has increased to twelve sons, with numerous grandchildren and dependants. They have descended into Egypt to sojourn for a while under the protection of the wise and great Joseph. The aged patriarch upon his dying bed, in accordance with the traditions of his family, is about to pronounce his blessing, and the spirit of prophecy comes upon him, and he utters the fourth Messianic prophecy. All temporal possessions fade from his view in the contemplation of those covenant promises, to attain which in early youth he had outwitted his brother who undervalued them, and to which he had clung through weakness and varied fortunes even to the last hour of his existence. Sublime act of faith, guided by the spirit of prophecy, he divides the promised land as if it were already in his possession.

§ 33. *Jacob divides the promised land among his sons, excluding none from the inheritance, but assigning the headship to Judah. Judah is promised the attainment of his portion,—the pre-eminence in Israel, the obedience of the nations, and the enjoyment of the manifold blessings of the land. The other sons share in these blessings in a measure, but Ephraim is to enjoy them to an extraordinary degree.*

The prophecy takes up the covenant blessing of Abraham, and unfolds it, bringing out new and important features. Thus the leading thought to Abraham had ever been the promised seed, about which his faith, hope, aspirations and trials ever centred. With reference to this element of the covenant, there is an important difference from the previous testaments of the promise. Abraham and Isaac have each excluded all but one son from the covenant relation. Jacob, however, excludes none of his children. For although he denounces his three eldest sons, and deprives them of their rank, assigning them a subordinate position on account of their passionate character, which boiled over in incest and wanton cruelty, he does not deprive them of a share in the promised land, which he divides up among all his sons in accordance with their respective characters and the relative part they have to play in history. And when he comes to Judah he singles out this tribe as a nucleus in the midst of the tribes. As Israel had been set apart as a nation of blessing in the midst of the nations, so Judah is now set apart as the leading, conquering tribe in the midst of the tribes.

> "O thou, Judah, thy brethren will praise thee;
> Thy hand will be on the neck of thine enemies.
> The sons of thy father will do homage to thee.
> O lion's whelp, Judah!
> From the prey, my son, thou dost go up.
> He doth bow down. He doth lie down as a lion,
> And as a lioness. Who will rouse him?
> The sceptre will not depart from Judah,
> Nor the ruler's rod from between his feet,
> Until that which belongs to him come,
> And he have the obedience of the peoples;
> Binding to the vine his ass,
> And to the choice vine the foal of his ass,
> He doth wash with wine his garment,
> And with the blood of grapes his clothing;
> Dark flashing his eyes with wine,
> And white his teeth with milk." —Gen. xlix. 8–12.

The essential idea which Jacob found in the Abrahamic covenant was the promised land. His whole life and experience as an exile and a wanderer had caused him to lay hold of this feature with all the strength of his soul.

It is this element of the promise that has the highest development in his prophecy. The promised land is to be conquered from the original inhabitants. Judah in lion-like heroism and power leads the van of his warlike children. The patriarch's glance follows the fortunes of this victorious march, and discerns its goal of conquest. The interpretation of the prediction depends upon the meaning of *Shiloh*. The English versions regard this as a name of the Messiah. But this view was not introduced to the Christian Church till the sixteenth century, and has slight exegetical support. All the ancient versions and interpreters take a different view of the form. We follow the LXX. version in our rendering.[1]

---

[1] שִׁילֹה is the term that contains the clue to the meaning of the prediction. In the discussion that follows we have been greatly indebted to the admirable critical study of Prof. Driver upon this word in the *Journal of Philology*, 1885.

I. The Massoretic pointing seems to rest upon either of two interpretations—(1) It is *Shiloh*, the place of the tabernacle and the ark, before Jerusalem was chosen as the holy city. This is a favourite view of modern critics. It is favoured by the name of the place, גִּילֹה. From this point of view Shiloh is the goal of the march of the tribes, the place in the promised land whose occupation would give the assurance that the conquest had been made. The resting of Judah there at the head of the tribes would imply the taking possession of the inheritance. I formerly held this opinion, but have been constrained to abandon it. For there is no early authority in its favour. It is a modern opinion, and the ancient view is better supported by text and context. (2) It would seem that the Massoretic pointing originated from the opinion that שִׁילֹה was the noun, שִׁיל with the suffix ה meaning *his son*, for we find this in the Targum of Pseudo-Jonathan, and in several leading Jewish scholars from the tenth century onwards. There is no such Hebrew word in the Old Testament; but the Mishna uses שָׁלִיל, with the meaning, embryo. Calvin adopted this opinion, and was followed by others in the sixteenth century. This interpretation has no Biblical authority, and is not in accordance with the context. It has been abandoned in recent times. (3) שִׁילֹה has been taken as the name of the Messiah. The first appearance of this opinion is in the Talmud, *Sanh.* 98*b*. But here we have no interpretation of the passage or the word, but simply an appropriation of the word for a name of the Messiah, just as we have *Yinnon* from Ps. lxxii. 17, *Channiah* from Jer. xvi. 13, *Menachem* from Lam. i. 16, and the *Leprous one* from Isa. liii. 4, and so on. See § 45. On such a slender basis the name was introduced to Christians by Sebastian Münster in 1534, and through his influence passed over into the Great Bible in 1539, and has been retained in all the subsequent English versions. We shall give sufficient reasons to show that it is an untenable

The idea of the patriarch is, that Judah will assume
the headship of Israel, and lead the nation in its march
until they attain possession of their inheritance, namely,
the promised land, and especially the submission and
obedience of the peoples.   Having attained this goal of
the promise, Judah abides in everlasting peace and
prosperity.

The patriarch, after assigning the headship to Judah,
enlarges upon the fertility of the land which Judah is to
enjoy and in which the other sons are to share.   Joseph

opinion, but first we shall present the other interpretations.   (4)
Rosenmüller, Gesenius and others have taken the form as shortened
from שִׁילֹן or שִׁילוֹם.   But such a reduction of the form is inadequately supported, and we should certainly expect the *older* form
in such an archaic piece of poetry.   It matters little whether it be
taken as the name of a person, *e.g.* rest-bringer, or of a place, place
of rest.   This class of opinions has no proper support in etymology
or in the text or context.

II. The Massoretic pointing is an interpretation, and it is not
sustained by the Samaritan Codex or the ancient Versions.   The
Samaritan Codex has שלה; and the versions, with the exception of
the late Pseudo-Jonathan, go back on the same form.   The LXX.,
Aquilla, Symmachus, Peshitto, Targum Onkelos, Targ. Jerusalem,
and even Saadia read שֶׁלֹּה, and Ezek. xxi. 32 seems to favour
this form in its המשפט עַד בֹּא אֲשֶׁר לֹו, which seems to be a reminiscence of our passage.   (See § 77.)   The Targums of Onkelos and
Jerusalem render "whose is the kingdom."   The Peshitto renders
"whose it is," which is explained by Aphraates and Ephraim as
"whose is the kingdom."   Saadia renders "whose it is."   The LXX.
and Theodotion render ἕως ἄν ἔλθῃ τὰ ἀποκείμενα αὐτῷ.   This is
favoured by von Orelli and Driver, and seems to me to be the true
interpretation.   Judah is to retain the sceptre until he gain
possession of *his own*, the inheritance assigned him.

III. There are several other opinions that seem to me unsatis-
factory.   (1) Jerome reads שֶׁלֹח = one sent.   (2) Lagarde and
Bickel amend the text by reading שָׁאִילֹה "his desired one."   (3)
Cheyne would read עַד כִּי יָבוֹא יֻשַׁת לֹו.

The present weight of critical opinion is so decidedly against taking
this as a personal name of the Messiah, that it would not be worth
while to discuss it further were it not that the English versions
have deeply impressed this error on the minds of multitudes.
Besides the arguments which we have adduced from the form itself,

is the son who is to enjoy prosperity in the greatest measure.

> " A fruitful bough is Joseph,
> A fruitful bough by a fountain,
> With branches it doth mount upon the wall,
> When they were bitter against him they went on shooting ;
> When the bowmen were hostile to him,
> His bow abode in perennial strength ;
> And the arms of his hands were active,
> Because of the hands of the Mighty One of Jacob,
> Because of the name of the Shepherd of the stone of Israel,[1]
> Because of the 'El of thy father.

---

and the authority of all the ancient versions, which, however they may differ in other respects, all agree in not taking it as the name of the Messiah, we shall give some general arguments — (1) All previous Messianic prophecies, and all those that follow for many centuries, with the single exception probably of the prophecy of Moses, are generic, and do not refer specifically to an individual Messiah. To make this prophecy not only specific, but *so* specific as to give the name of the Messiah, disturbs the course of development of the Messianic idea, and is without example until a very late period of Biblical prophecy. (2) The historical and psychological experience of Jacob was such as to induce him to lay great stress upon the promised land and victory over his enemies. He is dividing his inheritance among his children, and he thinks of their conquering that inheritance from its present possessors and dispossessing them. If, now, we regard Shiloh as the name of a person, we are compelled to suppose that the stress was for him still more than for Abraham upon the promised *seed*. For he would not only designate a tribe, *Judah* in the midst of the tribes, but still further, name a *Shiloh* of the tribe of Judah, which would be a double leap in prophecy without any psychological preparation, and without a parallel in the development of the Messianic idea. (3) We have furthermore the fact that no such name as *Shiloh* is given to the Messiah elsewhere in the Old Testament. In the development of the Messianic idea, such a name has no subsequent unfolding. The New Testament does not know of it. A Jewish rabbinical conceit gave birth to the notion, and it was introduced to the modern Christian world by scholars who were too much influenced by such conceits without altogether understanding them in their origin and significance.

[1] This is a difficult line, and is variously interpreted. The LXX. and Vulgate lead in pointing מִשָּׁם = thence, the Syriac and Targum of Onkelos point מִשֵּׁם = because of the name. This is more in accordance with the parallelism, which requires that the preposition מִן

Now may '*El Shadday* help thee,[1]
And bless thee with the blessings of heaven above,
With the blessings of the deep crouching beneath,
With the blessings of the breasts and womb.
The blessings of thy father do prevail
Over the blessings of the ancient mountains,[2]
The desirable things of the everlasting hills ;
Let them come on the head of Joseph,
Upon the crown of the prince of his brethren."—Gen. xlix. 22–26.

The blessings of the tribes are inherited in the course of the history of Israel. They reach beyond the conquest of Canaan by Joshua and Caleb. They transcend the victories of David and the wealth of Solomon. They point to the last days which bounded the vision of the last of the patriarchs as he was about to depart to his fathers. They will find their realization only in the fruition of Messianic prophecy at the end of the world,

should have the same force in the three parallel lines. It is best, with Herder, Ewald and Dillmann, to regard רעה as construct before אבן, and to find a reference to the stone of Bethel (xxviii. 18 seq., xxxv. 14). Jacob uses the name Shepherd for God in xlviii. 15.

[1] The Massoretic וְאֵת is not supported by the LXX., Sam., Syriac, Saadia, and some Hebrew MSS., which read וְאֵל, which are then followed by Bleek, Hitzig, Tuch, Ewald, and Dillmann. The rendering of the Revised Version, "And by the Almighty, who shall bless thee," is unjustifiable. For the force of the preposition מִן cannot be carried over into the clause וְאֵת, and it is against the laws of Hebrew syntax to translate a weak Vav with an imperfect as a relative clause. The principles of textual criticism, both internal and external, require אֵל.

[2] The Massoretic pointing הוֹרַי, and the attachment of עד to the next clause, are incorrect. The Samaritan Codex reads הרי עד, which may be best pointed as הַרְרֵי עַד. The fully written הו for ה belongs to the earlier stages of vocalizing the text, and is of the nature of interpretation. This pointing interprets the form as from הרה, to conceive, and hence "those who conceived me," my parents. But הרה belongs to the mother and not the father. The parallelism "everlasting hills" strongly supports "ancient mountains." So most modern critics and the margin of the Revised Version.

for He who reigns until all things are put under His feet will first gain for Judah and Israel all that belongs to them: the obedience of the nations of the world, the supremacy over mankind. The Lion of the tribe of Judah, who opens the seals of the book of heaven (Rev. v. 5, xxii. 16), is He who goes on conquering and to conquer until His enemies are made His footstool, and universal peace and prosperity prevail. There is in this prophecy explicitly only the victorious Judah, the submissive nations, and the occupation of the promised land by the tribes of Israel; but implicitly there is also the lion of Judah, the praise of Israel, the conqueror of the nations, the Messiah, who is to bring all these promises to their fruition.

And thus the primitive promises of redemption have risen in several stages through the seed of the woman, the race of Shem, the seed of Abraham, Isaac and Jacob, to the tribe of Judah. The redemption is a victory over the serpent, a subjugation of the Canaanites, the Edomites, and the nations of the land and the earth. All nations will bless themselves with the blessings of this redemption. The fruits of the victory are in a land of blessing. God dwells among the Shemites—He is the God of Shem, and especially of Abraham, Isaac and Jacob, and their seed for ever. He gives them a land as an inheritance, which is rich and fertile and filled with every blessing. These Messianic promises of the patriarchs constitute the most precious inheritance, which they transmit to the tribes of Israel as the bearers of redemption for mankind.

CHAPTER IV.

MESSIANIC PROPHECY OF THE MOSAIC AGE.

THE blessing of Jacob was the comfortable hope and ideal inheritance of the Hebrews during the dark years of Egyptian bondage. It began to realize itself when Jahveh, with mighty hand and outstretched arm led forth His people through the sea and the wilderness, to His own august presence at Mount Sinai.

I. ISRAEL THE SON OF JAHVEH.

§ 34. *Jahveh adopts Israel as his first-born son, assigns him an inheritance in the midst of the nations, and guides him with paternal care until he takes possession of it.*

Moses was commissioned by Jahveh to deliver Israel from Egypt. The prophetic narrative gives an account of the message he bears to Pharaoh king of Egypt.

"And thou shalt say unto Pharaoh, Thus saith Jahveh, Israel is my son, my first-born. And I say unto you, Dismiss my son that he may serve me. If thou dost refuse to dismiss him, I shall go on to slay thy son, thy first-born."—Ex. iv. 22, 23.

In this commission Israel as a nation was adopted into the sonship relation, as the first-born of the nations; and was thereby taken under the special protection and guidance of God, who assumes the personal name Jahveh as the Father of Israel. This relation is more fully explained in the song of Moses, which has been preserved in the prophetic narrative.

100

"Is he not thy father who begat thee?
Did he not make thee, and prepare thee?
Remember the days of old,
Consider the years of generation after generation;
Ask thy fathers to tell thee,
Thine elders to say to thee.
When 'Elyon would give the nations an inheritance;
When he would disperse the sons of mankind,
Establish the bounds of the nations,
According to the number of the sons of Israel;
For the portion of Jahveh is his people,
Jacob the line of his inheritance,—
He finds him in a grazing land,
In a waste, howling wilderness,
He encompasses him about, he attentively considers him,
He guards him as the pupil of his eye."—Deut. xxxii. 6–10.

II. THE KINGDOM OF GOD.

§ 35. *God redeems Israel from Egypt as His own choice property, and constitutes him a kingdom of priests and a holy nation.*

After the safe arrival of Israel at the mountain of God, the first word was a promise unfolding the Messianic idea with reference to Israel as a nation. Moses was the mediator of this promise. He receives it from a theophany, and bears it to the people whom he has led from Egypt unto the mountain of God. The theocratic narrative gives it in the poetic form.

"Thus shalt thou say to the house of Jacob,
And thou shalt announce to the sons of Israel,
Ye have seen what I did to the Egyptians,
And that I bore you on eagles' wings,
And brought you unto myself;
And now if you will attentively hearken to my voice,
And keep my covenant,
You will become to me a choice possession beyond all peoples,
Though the whole earth is mine;
Yea, you will become unto me a kingdom of priests and a holy
    nation."   —Ex. xix. 3–6.

This promise was fundamental to the Mosaic covenant relations prior to the Sinaitic legislation. All the world belongs to God, and yet in the midst of the world He has chosen a nation whom He has redeemed from bondage and taken to Himself as a purchased possession, a valued property.[1] God is sovereign of the whole earth, and yet He has elected a nation over whom He is to reign in a special and peculiar manner. Thus we have a further unfolding of the second Messianic prophecy, in that the dwelling of God in the tents of Shem becomes the reign of God as the King of the kingdom of Israel. And thus the foundation of the idea of the kingdom of God was laid, which henceforth constitutes one of the most essential Messianic ideas.

The kingdom of God is a kingdom of priests, a holy nation. It has a sacred ministry of priesthood, as well as sovereignty with reference to the nations of the world. As holy, the Israelites are the subjects of their holy King, and as priests they represent Him, and mediate for Him with the nations. Thus the third feature of the Abrahamic covenant is unfolded. As the essential thing to Abraham had been the promised seed, and as the essential thing to Jacob had been the promised land, so now, when Israel had become a nation, separating itself from the Egyptians, and entering into independent national relations to the various nations of the world, the essential thing became the relation which they were to assume on the one side to God their king, and on the other to the nations, and indeed first of all the positive side of that relation. This is represented in our promise: as a ministry of royalty and priesthood. They are a kingdom of priests, a kingdom and a priesthood combined in the unity of the conception, royal priests or priest kings.[2]

[1] סְגֻלָּה.

[2] מַמְלֶכֶת כֹּהֲנִים. The construct relation combines the two terms

This is the way in which the seed of Abraham is to be a blessing to the world.   They have priestly and royal functions to fulfil.   As the redeemed of God, they are His priests, and are to mediate the redemption of the world.   As kings they are to be the armed host of God, to subdue the nations to His sceptre.

Thus Israel was called to a universal priesthood. This priesthood was prior to the establishment of any priestly office in Israel, and is not to be interpreted in any technical sense.   This universality in the calling of Israel as a nation is at the basis of all the Mosaic institutions, and was not abrogated by any subsequent legislation.   The selection of an order of priesthood in Israel, at a subsequent time, did not do away with the universal priesthood of the nation.   The establishment of a royal dynasty did not supersede the royalty of the nation.   The promise maintained its validity in all the subsequent history of Israel.   It was reassumed by the Christian Church, which in a peculiar sense became the property of God, a kingdom of priests and a holy nation,[1] owing to its union with the priest king after the order of Melchizedek.   In the priesthood of the nation there is the generic priesthood which advances through the Levitical, Aaronic, and Zadokite lines, until it culminates in the Messianic priest.   In the royalty of the nation there is the generic divine kingdom on earth, which advances through the dynasty of David until it culminates in the King of glory, who at the head

in one conception.   It is a closer relation than the genitive case. It is nearer the compound noun.   The second term is something more than a closer definition or qualification of the first.   The conception of priesthood and royalty are so combined that, in their unity, the one is as important as the other.   They are priest-kings and also royal priests, both in one.   And this is ascribed to the nation as a whole, just as sonship is ascribed to the nation as a whole, in the prophetic narrative.

[1] 1 Pet. ii. 9; comp. Eph. i. 14; Tit. ii. 4; Col. i. 12, 13.

of an army of priest-kings conquers in the last battle of the world.[1]

III. THE CONQUERING STAR.

§ 36. *Balaam represents that the kingdom of God is apart from the nations of the world. God is its king. It is composed of vast numbers, and is irresistible. It will subdue all nations to its sceptre.*

Under the inspiration of the promise at Horeb the ten words and the book of the covenant were given; and the organized kingdom of God set out on the march to Canaan. After forty years' wanderings under the leadership and discipline of their heavenly King, they arrive on the banks of the Jordan and prepare to cross to the conquest of the promised land. Here they at once enter into conflict with many strong nations, who try their energies to the utmost. Some of them are conquered; others are hostile, but are prevented by fear from engaging them; the whole land of Canaan is preparing to resist their advance over the Jordan. Out of these circumstances the next Messianic prophecy arises. This prophecy is not like the previous ones, either from the voice of God in theophany to the patriarch or nation, or through the inspired patriarch to his children. It is through a prophetic voice of one outside the fold of Israel. And it was eminently fitting that the darker side of the relation of Israel to the world should be unfolded in this way. Balaam was one of the wise men of the East, dwelling in a land where religion has ever been of a purer and nobler type than on the banks of the Nile or the Indus. He had doubtless been inclined to seek the God of Israel by the fame of His mighty works, which had been noised abroad among the nations. He was an inquirer after the true God with the spirit of

[1] Rev. v. 10, xix. 11 seq.

a heathen magician, like Simon Magus and Judas of New Testament times, a child of the devil, influenced by the love of money to make the true religion a means of gain. Balaam seems to have been widely known as a prophet whose blessings and curses were alike effective.

The king of Moab, fearing the Israelites who had passed him by, and coveting the rich land which the Amorites had conquered from him, now in the possession of the Israelites, thought that if he could gain the God of Israel to his side, he might overthrow them. So he sends to Balaam to come and curse them. Balaam, coveting the large rewards offered, desires to go, but is warned by God—

> "Thou shalt not go with them,
> Thou shalt not curse the people ;
> For blessed be they."   —Num. xxii. 12.

The king of Moab continues to urge him with pressing invitations, and at last God permits him to go, with a warning that he should obey the word of God. He goes to Balak, and three times the king takes him to as many different mountain peaks that he may curse Israel. Three times the prophet goes with Balak, hoping that God may change, and that he may be permitted to curse Israel. But each time the curse is transformed into a blessing of increasing significance, until the fourth attempt ends in the complete discomfiture of Balak and a grand Messianic prophecy. At first he ascends the high place of Baal, and from the midst of seven heathen altars reiterates the blessing of Abraham.

> "Lo, a people alone, he dwelleth,
> And he reckons himself not among the nations.
> Who hath numbered the dust of Jacob ?
> Or who hath counted [1] the fourth of Israel ?

---

[1] In accordance with the parallelism, we read, after von Orelli, מִי סְפַר instead of מִסְפַּר.

Let me,[1] myself, die the death of the upright,
And let my last end be like his."   —Num. xxiii. 7–10.

He next ascends to the summit of Pisgah, and the blessings of Judah and of the covenant of Horeb combine.

"Lo, to bless I have received (commandment);
And if he bless I cannot reverse it.
He doth not behold trouble in Jacob,
And he doth not see misery in Israel.
Jahveh his God is with him,
And the shout of a king is in him.
'*El* has been bringing him out of Egypt,
As the swiftness of the yore-ox has he,
For there is no magic in Jacob,
And no divination in Israel ;
At the due time it will be said of Jacob
And of Israel, what hath '*El* wrought ?
Behold, the people rises up as a lioness,
And as a lion lifts himself up :
He will not lie down until he devour prey,
And drink the blood of the slain."

—Num. **xxiii.** 20–24.

The third time he ascends Peor, and the blessings of Abraham and Jacob combine.

"How excellent are thy tents, Jacob,
Thy tabernacles, Israel, as vales,[2]
Spread forth as gardens by a river,
As lign-aloes which Jahveh planted,
As cedars beside waters.
May water flow from his buckets,
And his seed be on many waters,
And may his king be higher than Agag,
And may his kingdom exalt itself.

---

[1] נפשׁי is not "my soul" or "my life," but is reflexive, "myself," as frequently in Hebrew.

[2] The Massoretic accents of vers. 6, 7 are incorrect. The parallelism is rather—

משכנתיך ישראל כנחלים
נטיו כגנות צל־נהר

> 'El has been bringing him forth from Egypt,
> Yea, as the swiftness of the yore-ox has he.
> He eateth up the nations, his adversaries,
> And their bones gnaweth and crusheth.[1]
> He doth couch, doth lie down as the lion,
> And as a lioness ; who would stir him up ?
> Blessed be those blessing thee,
> And cursed be those cursing thee."   —Num. xxiv. 5–9.

In these blessings Balaam unites the lines drawn by previous predictions, in order to advance from them to a further unfolding of the Messianic idea in his last prediction.

> "I see it, but it is not now ;
> I observe it, but it is not near.
> A star doth advance out of Jacob,
> Yea, a sceptre doth arise out of Israel,
> And it doth smite through the corners of Moab,
> And it doth break down all the sons of tumult.
> And Edom has become a possession,
> Yea, Israel is a doer of valiant deeds ;
> Yea, let one out of Jacob have dominion over his enemies,
> And destroy the remnant of Seir."[2]   —Num. xxiv. 17–19.

After predicting the triumph of the kingdom of God over Edom and Moab, the prophet turns to the other hostile nations near and far—Amalekites, Kenites and Assyrians.

> "First of the nations was Amalek,
> But his last end (extends) unto one ready to perish.

---

[1] The Massoretic חֵץ = arrow, is against the context, which refers to the yore-ox and the lion, and the use of arrows is inappropriate to these animals. It seems to us that the original reading was ועצמתיהם יגרם ומחץ. The Massoretic וחציו ימחץ has arisen by repetition of similar letters.

[2] We change the text by transferring איביו from the line where it is inappropriate to the sense and the structure of the line, to the line where it is really needed to supply the verb with an object and complete the line. We also change the meaningless מעיר into שעיר, which seems to be needed by the context. We also think that והיה ירשה שעיר is a mistaken repetition of והיה אדום ירשה.

> Strong is thy dwelling-place,
> And set in the rock thy nest :
> Nevertheless Kain will be for wasting ;
> How long ere Asshur carry thee away captive ?
>
> Alas ! who can live when *'El* establishes it ?
> But ships will come from the coast of Kittim
> And afflict Asshur and afflict Eber ;
> But he also will go on unto one ready to perish."
>   —Num. xxiv. 20–24.

Balaam unfolds the royal side of the relation of Israel
to the nations, as the previous prophecy had unfolded
rather the priestly side.   The term sceptre is generic,
and does not point to a monarch, but to Israel as the
kingdom of God.   The term star is synonymous with
sceptre, and is fitting in the mouth of the semi-heathen
prophet from the East, who was accustomed to find in
the stars indications of future events, as his predecessors
and successors in the Orient from the most ancient
times.   Thus the prophecy predicts that Israel, as the
kingdom of God, will subdue the nations and destroy all
enemies.   The prominent nations of the prophet's time
represent the hostile nations of all time, who are subdued
in turn by the kingdom of God.   The nations mentioned
here are representative ones : those far and near in the
range of the prophet's vision.   They are the types and
forerunners of all those nations who war against the
Israel of God, as they are presented to us in later prophecy ; the enemies of this stadium of history being the
advanced guard, the front line of an innumerable host,
advancing in every epoch of history, until the final
conflict with Gog and Magog at the end of the world
(Rev. xx. 8 sq.).   Explicitly the prophecy is generic,
and refers to the kingdom of God as thus triumphant ;
but implicitly it involves in the subsequent development
of the idea the royal house of David, and his subjugation

of the nations, and still further, the royal sceptre of David's greater son.

IV. THE EVERLASTING PRIESTHOOD.

§ 37. *Phinehas receives the covenant of the everlasting priesthood of his seed as a reward of fidelity.*

When Israel appeared before Jahveh at Mount Horeb they received their Messianic calling with reference to the nations of the world, and a divine instruction to enable them to fulfil this calling and to mark them off from the other nations as a royal, priestly, consecrated people, the inheritance of God. This instruction was given in successive revelations from the theophany of the pillar of cloud and fire, unfolding and enlarging more and more as the people were able to comprehend it. The fundamental instruction, according to the four narratives, was the ten words of the tables of stone, the tables of the covenant, the tables of the testimony, as they are variously called by the writers of the Pentateuch. This fundamental instruction was enlarged into a decalogue of worship, called the Little Book of the Covenant, by the prophetic narrative;[1] into the twelve decalogues, which constitute the Greater Book of the Covenant of the theocratic narrator;[2] into the Book of Instruction of the Deuteronomist, and the sanctity code and priest code of the priestly narrator.[3] These several codes all have passed through a series of later editings, which have enlarged and modified them in some respects, but they

---

[1] Ex. xxxiv. 12–28. See my article, "Little Book of the Covenant," in *The Hebrew Student*, Chicago, May 1883.

[2] Ex. xx. 22–xxiii. See my article, "Greater Book of the Covenant," in *The Hebrew Student*, June 1883.

[3] The sanctity code is in a body in Leviticus ; but the priest code is scattered through Exodus, Leviticus, and Numbers, accompanied with historical introductory statements.

give us essentially the divine instruction through the mediator Moses in varied modes of representation and forms of codification.[4]

The priestly narrator lays great stress upon the priesthood and the sanctity of the religious institutions of Israel. God was enthroned in the most holy place, to which there was graded access by several ranks of priesthood, culminating in the great high priest. The single Messianic prophecy of the priestly narrator has the priesthood as its theme. The fortitude and fidelity of Phinehas earns him the promise.

"Therefore say, Lo, I am going to give to him my covenant of peace ; and he and his seed after him will have the covenant of an everlasting priesthood, because that he was zealous for his God and made an atonement for the children of Israel."—Num. xxv. 12, 13.

The priestly succession is here assigned to the line of Phinehas for ever. The Messianic feature is in the establishment of an *everlasting* priesthood. This is a generic prophecy which culminates in the everlasting priesthood of the Messiah, the great High Priest after the order of Melchizedek. And thus the priesthood of the nation has advanced to an everlasting order of priests in the nation.

V. THE PROPHET LIKE MOSES.

§ 38. *Moses predicts a prophet like himself, divinely authorized to speak, who will complete the divine instruction and demand obedience under penalty of judgment.*

The four Messianic prophecies last considered are of one group, all unfolding some phase of the Abrahamic covenant.

The stress for Abraham and Isaac was upon the

[1] See my article, " A Critical Study of the History of the Higher Criticism, with Special Reference to the Pentateuch," *Presbyterian Review,* iv. p. 74 seq.

promised seed, for Jacob upon the promised land, for Israel as a whole upon their relation to the nations of the world; at Sinai, when alone with their King and God, upon their priestly ministry of blessing; on the mountains of Moab, when in conflict with the nations, upon their royal work of subjugating and reigning over them. The everlasting priesthood of Phinehas springs from the necessity of priestly mediation for Israel himself. These, with the protevangelium relating to the seed of the woman, are all of one common type; they are all generic in character; they represent the future redemption as coming through the seed of the woman, the race of Shem, the seed of Abraham, the tribe of Judah, the kingdom of Israel, the priesthood of Phinehas. They do not explicitly point to an individual, although the individual Messiah is ever implicitly involved. The Messianic prophecy upon which we are now to reflect is of a different character and type.

The Deuteronomist emphasizes the relation of love between Jahveh and His people. Jahveh has chosen Israel out from the nations to be His own people. He is Jahveh their God. As Moses said unto Israel—

"Only to your fathers Jahveh did cleave, to love them, and chose their seed after them, even you above all the peoples "—Deut. x. 16.

The Deuteronomist represents Moses as saying in the midst of his discourse—

"According to all that thou didst ask from Jahveh thy God in Horeb, in the day of the assembly, saying, 'I cannot again hear the voice of Jahveh, my God, and this great fire I cannot see again, lest I die.' And Jahveh said unto me, 'They have done well in what they have spoken. A prophet will I raise up for them, from the midst of their brethren, like thee; and will give my words in his mouth, and he will speak unto them all that I charge him. And it will come to pass that whosoever will not hearken unto my words which he will speak in my name, I will require it of him.'"
—Deut. xviii. 16–19.

Moses humbly recognizes the incompleteness of his work, while he projects the divine instruction into the future, and sees its completion in another prophet like him, yet his superior in authority and dignity, who is to be the prophetic mediator between Jahveh and His royal people, who is to take up the instruction as Moses left it, and unfold it in still more significant relations.[1]

The work of this prophet is to declare the whole word of God with authority, demanding obedience under the penalty of the divine judgment. The very fact that the prophet is like Moses involves in that resemblance a ministry like that of Moses, and, indeed, a ministry of instruction and revelation of the word of God. And in

[1] The interpretation depends primarily upon the signification of נביא. Is it a collective or a simple singular? Does it refer to the prophetic order, or an individual prophet? The Jewish commentators and most recent interpreters regard it as a collective and generic term. There is much in favour of this view. The context speaks of the priests and Levites as a class, and the false prophets and heathen magicians as classes. Again, unless this passage be interpreted as referring to the order of prophets, there is no passage in the Pentateuch that recognizes or authorizes later prophecy. Furthermore, all previous Messianic prophecy is generic, and the first prophecy of the next period is also generic. We should expect such an one here. But there is insufficient authority for taking נביא as collective. The Samaritans base their Messianic hopes on this passage, rejecting all later prophecy, and interpret it as referring to a Messianic prophet. The context is also in favour of an individual prophet; for the prophet is not only represented as coming forth from Israel, but is also compared with Moses, and thus presumptively he is an individual likewise. It is true that the Mosaic instruction makes no provision for an order of prophets. But it is not necessary that it should do so. Later prophecy does not depend on the Pentateuch for its authority, but upon God Himself, who called the prophets immediately and sent them forth as He did Moses. The reign of Jahveh, the King of Israel, was immediate and continuous over His people. The priest code prescribed an order of priests, but nothing further. Jahveh, the theocratic King, reigned over the people, and He commissioned whom He would to speak and act for Him; and herein was the guarantee for the perpetuity and unfolding of divine revelation. It was necessary that the priestly organization of the people should be always complete; for their communion with their God must be

that the instruction and revelation of Moses is the word
of God that liveth and abideth for ever, it is involved
that the instruction and revelation of that prophet will
not be in antagonism with that of Moses, but a further
unfolding and completing of it. We have already re-
marked that the instruction of Moses was not delivered once
for all in a complete and organized form ; but successively
in the unfolding of the primitive germ in the tables ; and
that presumptively it had not reached its end and goal,
but was still in an incomplete condition. The prophecy
that we are studying predicts the prophet who is to carry
that development on to its end, and bring the revelation
to its completion. Indeed, the entire legislation of the

continuous and unbroken. But it was not necessary that there
should be an unbroken and continuous unfolding of divine revelation. God made new revelations of His will as the people were
trained by the older revelation to receive them ; so that in some
cases development was rapid, in other cases tardy. It was not even
necessary that the royal organization of the people should be always
complete and unbroken. The princes of the tribes as the representatives of Jahveh communed with their King through the *Urim
and Thummim ;* only on critical occasions was a princely mediator
required, and he was always called forth by Jahveh when needed.
The divine Spirit came upon such men as Joshua and Gideon, and
they led the people and delivered them from their enemies. The
prophetic ministry was fulfilled as a rule through the instructions,
written or unwritten, in the hands of the people. It was only
when these needed unfolding that Jahveh summoned a prophet to
reveal His will, to increase and enlarge the material of the divine
revelation. And hence no official prophet appeared in Israel until
Samuel, the last of the שֹׁפְטִים, and the father of a new era. The
prophetic office of Moses was not transmitted to his successors.
And hence there was nothing in the historical or psychological
experience of Moses to incline him to predict an order of prophets.
The very fact of the distinction between his own ministry and that
of the Levitical priesthood in this particular would incline him to
look for one summoned directly by Jahveh like himself, without
predecessors or successors. Thus, in accordance with the general
principle of prophecy, he sees the Messianic end in which the divine
instruction left incomplete by himself will be completed by a
prophet greater than himself ; but he does not see all the intervening steps to that end. He sees only that first stadium in which
false prophets and magicians appear to mislead the people.

Pentateuch is predictive in character, looking forward with Moses to its completion and fulfilment in the prophet greater than Moses. The ten words of the tables are the germ, the fundamental instruction; but even these are capable of improvement, and do improve in the ethical development of the religion of Israel. And the same is true of the Little Book of the Covenant of the prophetic narrator and the Greater Book of the Covenant of the theocratic narrator, the Deuteronomic code, and the sanctity code and priest code of the priestly narrator; for the subsequent revelation of the psalmists and prophets give the worship of the people and their civil and social life an ever advancing development—all tending to their completion in the prophet who was to come, the second Moses.

The characteristics of the prophet predicted are thus: (1) that he is to be an Israelite, (2) that he is to be like Moses, (3) that he is to be authorized to declare the whole word of God with authority. There is no prophet in Jewish history who at all satisfies these conditions. None can compare with Moses, or be said to stand as his superior in completing his revelation; none in the history of Israel until the advent of Jesus Christ.[1]

---

[1] This John the Baptist recognized when he cried, saying, "This was He of whom I said, He that cometh after me is preferred before me: for He was before me. . . . For the law was given through Moses, but grace and truth came through Jesus Christ. No one hath seen God at any time; the only-begotten Son, which is in the bosom of the Father, He hath declared Him" (John i. 15–18). Philip after he had found Jesus said to Nathanael, "We have found Him of whom Moses in the law and the prophets did write" (John i. 45). The Samaritan woman recognized Jesus as the Messiah, the prophet (John iv. 29). The multitude on the sea of Galilee exclaimed, "This is truly the prophet that should come into the world" (John vi. 14). Jesus tells the Pharisee, "For had ye believed Moses, ye would have believed me; for he wrote of me. But if ye believe not his writings, how shall ye believe my words?" (John v. 46, 47). The Pharisees accused Jesus of violating the law and wishing to do away with the religion of Moses, but He said, "I came not to destroy the law or

VI. THE BLESSING AND THE CURSE.

§ 39. *The doctrine of divine judgment springs from the divine instruction in the several codes, and the blessings and curses attached thereto as their sanction.*

The four narrators of the Pentateuch give us four different representations of the divine judgment, each in accordance with the nature of his code. The simplest representation is appended to the greater book of the covenant.[1] The representation of the prophetic narrator is not connected with his code,—the little book of the covenant,[2]—but is in the song of Moses.[3] The Deuteronomist gives a solemn enumeration of the blessings and curses in connection with his code.[4] The priest code gives its sanction at the close of the sanctity code.[5] We shall first consider the blessings beginning with the covenant code.

"If ye will serve Jahveh your God, he will bless thy bread and thy water, and I will remove sickness from thy midst. There shall

---

the prophets, but to fulfil" (Matt. v. 12). The apostles likewise represent Jesus as the prophet like Moses. Thus Peter in his address in the temple quotes our prophecy, and applies it to Jesus (Acts iii. 22–26); Stephen also (Acts vii. 37). Paul represents Christ as the end of the law for righteousness, that is, its culminating end (Rom. x. 4); so also the law as the pedagogue leading to Christ (Gal. iii. 24). The Epistle to the Hebrews represents Jesus as the Mediator of the New Covenant of which the Old Covenant through Moses was the shadow and type. The resemblance to His brethren was that they might not be brought face to face with God. Hence Jesus was made like His brethren (Heb. ii. 17), in order that He might sympathize with them and save them. The resemblance of Jesus to Moses, and His superiority, is well carried out in Heb. iii. Jesus is compared with Moses in faithfulness in all his house, and yet is counted worthy of more glory than Moses, inasmuch as he who hath built the house, the Church, hath more honour than the house, to which even Moses belonged, Moses being but a servant, Christ being the Son. Hence the application of the third thought of our prophecy in the warning not to harden the heart against Christ, as Israel had hardened their hearts against Moses.

[1] Ex. xxiii. 20–33. [2] Ex. xxxiv. 12–28. [3] Deut. xxxii.
[4] Deut. xxvii.–xxviii. [5] Lev. xxvi.

not be one failing of her young or barren in thy land ; the number of thy days will I fulfil. My terror will I send before thee, and I will discomfit all the people among whom you will come. . . . And I will make thy boundary from the Red Sea even to the sea of the Philistines, and from the wilderness unto the River ; for I will give into your hand the inhabitants of the land, and thou wilt drive them from thy presence."—Ex. xxiii. 25–31.

The song of Moses describes the blessings of the land of promise, and expresses regret that they could not be fulfilled.

> "If they were wise, they would understand this,
> They would discern their end :
> How would one pursue a thousand,
> And two put a myriad to flight."   —Deut. xxxii. 29, 30.

The Deuteronomist enlarges upon the blessings of obedience.

" Blessed wilt thou be in the city, and blessed wilt thou be in the field. Blessed will be the fruit of thy body, and the fruit of thy ground, and the fruit of thy cattle, the increase of thy kine, and the young of thy flock. Blessed will be thy basket and thy kneading trough. Blessed wilt thou be when thou comest in, and blessed wilt thou be when thou goest out. Jahveh will cause thine enemies that rise up against thee to be smitten before thee ; they will come out against thee by one way, and will flee before thee by seven ways. . . . Jahveh will open unto thee his good treasure, the heaven, to give the rain of thy land in its season, and to bless all the work of thine hand : and thou wilt lend unto many nations, and thou wilt not borrow. And Jahveh will make thee the head and not the tail; and thou wilt be above only, and thou wilt not be beneath."—Deut. xxviii. 3–13.

The blessing of the sanctity code is not so elaborate as the rhetorical form in Deuteronomy, but it is more comprehensive.

" If in my statutes ye walk, and my commandments ye keep and do them, I will give your rains in their season, and the land will give its produce, and the trees of the field will yield their fruit. And the threshing will reach for you the vintage, and the vintage will reach the planting, and ye will eat your bread to the full and dwell in confidence in your land.   And I will give peace in the land, and ye will lie down and there will be none to affright ; and I will cause the evil animal to cease from the land, and the sword will not pass through your land ; and ye will pursue your enemies, and they will fall before you by the sword, and five of you will pursue a hundred, and a hundred of you will pursue a myriad ; and your enemies will fall before you by the sword.   And I will turn unto you, and make you fruitful, and multiply you, and establish my covenant with you, and ye will eat old store, and bring forth the old because of the new. And I will put my tabernacle in your midst, and my soul will not abhor you, and I will walk about in your midst, and become your God, and ye will become my people."—Lev. xxvi. 3–12.

These blessings of the covenant are the ideals of the prophets, and they recur one after another in the later prophecies of the Psalter and the prophets.   They are based upon the blessings of the patriarch Jacob.[1]

The curses of the Mosaic codes are also the basis of the predictions of divine judgment that constitute one of the most significant features of prophecy.   The book of the covenant is meagre here.   The people are warned not to rebel against the theophanic Malakh, lest he should not forgive their transgression.[2]   The song of Moses is elaborate here, and lays the basis of the doctrine of the divine judgment.

"And he said, I will hide my face from them,
I will see what their end will be :
For they are a very froward generation,
Children in whom there is no faith.
They have moved me to jealousy with that which is not God ;
They have provoked me to anger with their vanities ;
And I will move them to jealousy with those which are not a people ;
I will provoke them to anger with a foolish nation.
When a fire is kindled in mine anger,
It doth burn unto Sheol beneath ;
And devour the earth with her increase,
And lick up the foundations of the mountains.

Gen. xlix.   [2] Ex. xxiii. 21.

I will heap mischiefs upon them ;
I will spend mine arrows against them ;
They will be wasted with hunger, and devoured with burning heat
And bitter destruction ;
And the teeth of beasts will I send upon them,
With the poison of crawling things of the dust.
Without the sword will bereave,
And within the chambers terror ;
Both young men and virgins,
The suckling with the man of grey hairs.

.   .   .   .   .   .

Verily I lift up my hand to heaven,
And say, as I live for ever ;
If I have whetted my sword, the lightning,
That mine hand may take hold on judgment ;
I will render vengeance to my adversaries,
And recompense them that hate me ;
I will make mine arrows drunk with blood,
And my sword will devour flesh ;
Of the blood of the slain and the captives,
Of the chief of the leaders of the enemy."   —Deut. xxxii. 20-42.

The Deuteronomist enlarges upon the curses, both in
the specification of the transgressions that are cursed
and of the curses themselves, concluding with the general
prediction.

"And it will come to pass, that as Jahveh rejoiced over you to
do you good, and to multiply you, so Jahveh will rejoice over you
to cause you to perish, and to destroy you ; and you will be plucked
from off the land whither thou goest in to possess it.   And
Jahveh will scatter thee among all peoples, from the one end of
the earth even unto the other end of the earth ; and there
thou wilt serve other gods, which thou hast not known, thou
nor thy fathers, even wood and stone.   And among these nations
wilt thou find no ease, and there will be no rest for the sole
of thy foot ; but Jahveh will give thee there a trembling heart,
and failing of eyes, and pining of soul : and thy life will hang
in doubt before thee ; and thou wilt fear night and day, and wilt
have none assurance of thy life : in the morning thou wilt say,
Would God it were even ! and at even thou wilt say, Would God
it were morning ! for the fear of thine heart which thou wilt fear,

and for the sight of thine eyes which thou wilt see. And Jahveh will bring thee into Egypt again with ships, by the way whereof I said unto thee, Thou shalt see it no more again: and there ye will sell yourselves unto your enemies for bondmen and for bondwomen, and no man will buy you."—Deut. xxviii. 63–68.

The curses of the sanctity code are given in Leviticus. We give the most significant of them, omitting the protases of the conditional clauses, all of which imply transgression of the code.

"I also will do this unto you, and appoint terror over you, consumption and fever that will consume the eyes, and make the soul to pine away : and ye will sow your seed in vain, and your enemies will eat it ; and I will set my face against you, and ye will be smitten before your enemies : and they that hate you will rule over you ; and ye will flee when none pursueth you. . . . And I will break the pride of your power ; and make your heaven as iron, and your earth as brass : and your strength will be spent in vain ; and your land will not yield her increase, and the trees of the land will not yield their fruit. . . . And I will send the animal of the field against you, and it will rob you of your children, and destroy your cattle, and make you few in number ; and your ways will become desolate. . . . And I will bring a sword upon you that will execute the vengeance of the covenant ; and ye will be gathered together unto your cities. And I will send pestilence among you ; and ye will be delivered into the hand of the enemy. . . . And ye will eat the flesh of your sons, and the flesh of your daughters will ye eat. . . . And I will make your cities a waste, and bring your sanctuaries unto desolation, and I will not smell your odour of gratification. And I will bring the land into desolation : and your enemies which dwell therein will be astonished at it. And you will I scatter among the nations, and draw out the sword after you : and your land will be a desolation, and your cities will be a waste. Then will the land enjoy her Sabbaths, as long as it lieth desolate, and ye be in your enemies' land. . . . And yet for all that, when they be in the land of their enemies, I will not reject them, neither will I abhor them, to destroy them utterly, and to break my covenant with them : for I am Jahveh their God ; but I will for their sakes remember the covenant of their ancestors, whom I brought forth out of the land of Egypt in the sight of the nations, that I might be their God : I am Jahveh."—Lev. xxvi. 16–45.

Before entering upon another period it is requisite that we should gather into a higher generalization the results thus far attained. There are several Messianic prophecies in the Pentateuch which may be grouped under four heads: the Adamic, Noachic, Abrahamic, and Mosaic, for the fourth, fifth, and sixth are but the further unfolding of the third. There are two lines of Messianic prophecy, the human and the divine; the human, the culminating head of the woman's seed, who gains the victory over the serpent; the divine, the descent of Jahveh to dwell in the tents of Shem, to bestow blessings upon the faithful and judgments upon His enemies. There are two channels of blessing, the seed of Abraham and the land of Canaan; the seed of Abraham through the lion of the tribe of Judah, the land of Canaan as the inheritance of the tribes of Israel. The universal inheritance of mankind is mediated by the central inheritance of Israel. There are two phases of blessing, the ministry of a holy, priestly, and royal people, the son of God; and the sovereignty of a victorious kingdom of God. There is a second Moses, whose prophetic ministry will complete the revelation of God, and an everlasting faithful priesthood for the people of God.

Now these are the great outlines of Messianic prophecy, the broad foundations upon which all later prophecy is built. These are separated for the most part widely from one another; they do not harmonize as yet, but they unfold each by itself, approximating to its fellows, developing new lines into which they depart; but all centre at last in the Messiah at His first or second advent. Like the stars, they relieve the darkness of the olden time, receiving constant additions to their number until they all at last are absorbed in the dawning sun of redemption.

CHAPTER V.

THE period of the Judges was ill adapted for the development of the Messianic idea. The conquest of the Holy Land and the settlement of the tribes in the midst of the conquered Canaanites whom they had failed to drive out, resulted in breaking up the national unity, in lowering the spiritual tone through the influence of the people of the land, and in decay of the religious life of the nation. It had been impossible to observe any of the Mosaic codes during the wandering in the wilderness. It was also impossible to realize the Mosaic ideal during the period of the Judges. An effort was made after crossing the Jordan to advance in religious life by observance of circumcision and the passover; but little progress was made beyond the simplest requirements of the code of the covenant. For several centuries Israel remained in a disorganized condition. But Jahveh did not forsake them. He sent His Spirit upon heroic men to deliver His people from their enemies and bring them back to their allegiance to Himself. There was a long succession of disastrous defeats and of marvellous victories. The enemies of Israel were gradually worn out, and Israel was more firmly established in the land. The period of the Judges closes with no important enemy save the Philistines, who had attained a pre-eminence in Palestine greater than that of any of the hostile nations which preceded them in the oppression of Israel. At this time

Eli was the presiding priest at Shiloh, and his two sons, Hophni and Phinehas, ministered as his assistants ; but with such impiety, that they dishonoured the worship of Jahveh and brought ruin on their father's house.   The deep-seated corruption of the sons of Eli is the occasion of a prediction which, while it concerns chiefly the house of Eli and the succession in the priesthood, also points to the Messianic end, as it gives direction to the prediction of the everlasting priesthood in the line of the faithful Phinehas.

I. THE FAITHFUL PRIESTHOOD.

§ 40. *A faithful priesthood will take the place of the unfaithful line of Eli, and minister before an anointed king for ever.*

An unnamed man of God comes to Eli with the following prophecy.

" And I will raise me up a faithful priest.
  According to that which is in my heart and in my soul[1] will he do.
  And I will build him a faithful [2] house,
  And he will walk before mine anointed [3] always.
  And it will come to pass, that all that are left in thine house
  Will come to bow down to him for a piece of silver,[4]
  And will say, Put me, I pray thee, into one of the priest's offices,
  That I may eat a morsel of bread."   —1 Sam. ii. 35, 36.

---

[1] בלבבי ובנפשי are rendered by the Revised Version, "in my heart and in my mind."   But לבב, in usage, is associated with the mind, and נפש is more closely connected with the emotional nature.

[2] The Revised Version renders בית נאמן, a sure house.   But it is more consistent to give the same meaning to נאמן here as with כהן נאמן above.

[3] This is one of a number of passages that indicate that a king was in the mind of Israel as an ideal longing from the beginning. The disorganization of the nation, the independence and rivalries of the tribes, prevented the realization of the ideal of Deut. xvii. 14–20 until the time of Saul and David.

[4] The Massoretic text adds וככר לחם, but this is not in the LXX. ;

This prediction removes the eldership and presidency in the priesthood from the line of Eli to another line which is not here designated. It is a narrowing of the elective grace of God with reference to the everlasting priesthood promised to Phinehas.[1] A faithful priest and a faithful house will be raised up instead of the unfaithful Eli and his house. To this faithful priesthood the family of Eli will do homage, as the brother of Jacob did homage to him.[2] The chief difficulty in this piece is the statement that this faithful priest will " walk before mine anointed." The anointed cannot then be the anointed priest, but must be another anointed one, namely a king. This then involves the conception of a royal dynasty with whom the Messianic priest would be in faithful association. There is a transition from priest to priestly house, so that the prediction is generic.

II. THE ALL-KNOWING JUDGE.

§ 41. *Jahveh is the all-knowing Judge. He espouses the cause of the weak and executes justice. He judges the whole earth, and will exalt the king of Israel.*

Jahveh was preparing Israel for a new era in his history. The pious Hannah was chosen as the mother of the prophet who was to introduce the Davidic age. Hannah, like Sarah of old, bursts forth in a song of praise inspired by the prophetic spirit in view of the gift of her son to her by God and her devotion of her son to God. She rises to the conception of the all-knowing Judge, and sings the praise of Jahveh in a song which is re-echoed through all subsequent prophecy, and especially in the

it disturbs the rhythm, makes the line too long, and is a premature statement of that which comes appropriately in the climax of the last line.

[1] Num. xxv. 12, 13. [2] Gen. xxvii. 29.

song of the blessed Virgin, the mother of the Messiah.
The song is a vivid description of the new era, in which
the all-knowing Jahveh weighs the actions of men, and
equitably readjusts the inequalities of human life.

I. "Then Hannah prayed and said,
　　My heart doth exult in Jahveh,
　　My horn [1] is exalted in Jahveh,
　　My mouth is enlarged [2] over mine enemies,
　　Yea, I rejoice in thy salvation.
　　There is none holy like Jahveh,
　　Yea, there is none beside thee,
　　And there is no rock like our God.

II. Speak no more proudly, [3]
　　Let not bold words issue from your mouth ;
　　For an all-knowing [4] God is Jahveh,
　　And by him [5] are deeds weighed.
　　Heroes of the bow are broken, [6]
　　But stumblers gird on valour ;
　　The full for bread hire themselves,
　　But the hungry keep holiday for ever ; [7]
　　The barren doth bear seven,
　　But the one having many children doth languish.

---

[1] The horn is the symbol of strength and dignity (Pss. lxxxix. 24,
cxii. 9, cxxxii. 17).

[2] The widening of the mouth is a gesture of laughter and joy
(Ps. cxxvi. 2 ; Isa. lx. 5).

[3] The Massoretic text repeats נבחה ; but it is without force, and
destroys the rhythm.

[4] אל דעות. The abstract plural should be rendered " all-knowing."

[5] The *Qeri* לו is better than the *Kethibh* לא.

[6] קשת גברים. The construct has the force of combining the two
nouns into a compound like the English *bowmen*.

[7] The Massoretic text connects עד with the next line. But it gives
no good sense there, and it leaves the one line too short, and makes
the other too long. The LXX. has another reading which does not
satisfy. Böttcher and Thenius would read עצבן, and render " cease
from labour." This gives an appropriate thought. But it is easier
to render עד " for ever," and attach it to the previous line. This
gives an appropriate contrast.

III. Jahveh kills, and he quickens,
He brings down to Sheol, and he doth bring up ; [1]
Jahveh disinherits, and he enriches,
He humbles, yea, he lifts up on high ;
He raiseth up from the dust the weak,
From the dunghill he exalts the poor,
To enthrone [2] him with nobles,
That he may give him a throne of glory as an inheritance ;
For Jahveh's are the pillars of earth,
And he set upon them the world.

IV. The feet of his favoured ones he guards,
But the wicked in darkness are silenced ;
For not by power can a man prevail. [3]
Let Jahveh's adversaries be frightened,
Over them in heaven may he thunder, [4]
Jahveh judgeth the ends of earth,
In order to give strength [5] to his king,
In order to exalt the horn of his anointed."

—1 Sam. ii. 1–10.

The reign of Jahveh in judgment has in view the
exaltation of a king in Israel.   These predictions of a
royal dynasty in Israel advanced toward realization
through Samuel, who becomes at first a prophet like
Moses, and the founder of the prophetic order, then is
called to the judgeship, and finally transfers his political
authority to the king, in order to be above all things
and alone the prophet of Jahveh.   The children of
Israel were impelled by the circumstances in which they
were placed to yearn for a king and a dynasty, and the
national unity which this involved.   The capture of the

---

[1] There is an abrupt change by the ו consec. which may be
expressed by the English emphatic present.

[2] יְנַחֲלֵם is a final clause.

[3] There is a play upon the noun גבר in the verb יִגְבָּר.

[4] The text of the LXX. reads יַרְעֵם for יֵחַתּוּ and עָלָיו for עָלוֹ, and
in many MSS. inserts several lines from the text of Jer. ix. 23, 24.
These have crept in from the margin.   The rhythm and strophical
organization are to be found only in the Hebrew text.

[5] וְיִתֶּן and וְיָרֶם are final clauses.

ark and the destruction of Shiloh brought this to the focus of a popular demand. The demand assumed the form of rebellion against Samuel and against Jahveh, whom Samuel represented ; because it was really the demand for a permanent dynasty which would prevent the direct calling of the individual by God ; but it was in the line of the Mosaic ideal and of the divine purpose, although it was premature on the part of the people. The reign of Saul was a temporary provision, which showed how premature the establishment of the kingdom had been. The reign of Saul was a transition from the old order of things to the new. Though Saul was the king, Samuel remained the master of political as well as religious affairs.

First with the anointing of David and his establishment on the throne of Zion, first after the removal of the ark thither, and the establishment of the religious and political unity of the nation in Jerusalem, did Messianic prophecy make a new advance.

III. THE COVENANT WITH DAVID.

§ 42. *Jahveh adopts the seed of David as His Son, whom He will chastise by human agents for sin, but will never forsake. He promises to build David's seed into an everlasting dynasty, and that He will dwell in the house to be erected by it in His honour.*

The occasion of the covenant with David was the desire of David to build a house to Jahveh in Jerusalem. This desire was rewarded with a promise which transcends all previous predictions in its unfolding of the Messianic idea. Nathan the prophet came to David with the prediction which in its Messianic part is as follows :[1]—

[1] There are two versions of the prediction, the one in 2 Sam. vii. 11–16, the other in 1 Chron. xvii. 10–14. We give what seems

"Therefore Jahveh doth tell thee,[1]
That Jahveh will make [2] thee a house,
And it will come to pass when thy days will be fulfilled,[3]
And thou wilt lie down [4] with thy fathers,
I will raise up thy seed after thee,
Him who will issue from thy bowels.[5]
I will establish his kingdom.
He will build a house to my name,[6]
And I will establish his throne for ever.[7]
I will become a father to him,
And he will become a son to me ;
Whom when he acts perversely I will chastise [8]
With rods of men and with blows of the sons of men ;
But my mercy I will not remove from him,[9]
According as I removed it from him who was before thee,[10]

---

to us to be the original text, so far as we can determine it from a comparison of these versions. The prediction is a poem with the trimeter movement.

[1] The chronicler omits יהוה, and changes והגיד into ואניד. The rhythm is preserved in Samuel.

[2] The chronicler uses יבנה for יעשה, and כי for ו. The less precise text of Samuel is to be preferred.

[3] The chronicler reads והיה כי מלאו for כי ימלאו. Here the LXX. of Samuel agrees with the chronicler, and his text is better save that the imperfect tense is to be preferred.

[4] The chronicler has ללכת עם for ושכבת את. The syntactical construction and the archaic expression of Samuel are to be preferred.

[5] The chronicler has יהיה מכניך for יצא ממעיך. The LXX. of Samuel reads יהיה. This is less precise, and is better ; but ממעיך is simpler and more archaic.

[6] The chronicler has לי for לשמי. The text of Samuel is more archaic.

[7] The text of Samuel omits the suffix of כסאו and inserts ממלכתו. But this insertion is not in the LXX. of Samuel, and it makes the line too long. The chronicler is to be preferred.

[8] Lines 11 and 12 are not given by the chronicler. But there is no sufficient reason to doubt their originality.

[9] The chronicler reads אסיר מעמי, which is supported by the LXX. of Samuel, and is better than יסור ממנו.

[10] The chronicler is better here. The mention of Saul by name in Samuel is too close for the original poem, and is more like subsequent reflection and explanation.

And thy house will be made firm for ever,[1]
Thy [2] throne will be established for ever."

—2 Sam. vii. 11–16 ; 1 Chron. xvii. 10–14

There are three elements in this prediction—(1) The
everlasting reign of the house of David ; (2) the erection
of the house of Jahveh by the seed of David ; (3) the
exaltation of the seed of David to the rank of sonship
with God, with paternal discipline on account of sin, and
with everlasting mercy. These three elements are the basis
of the Messianic idea throughout subsequent prophecy.
They unfold the previous predictions of redemption.

1. The prediction of Balaam, of a sceptre and star
arising out of Jacob, is now to be unfolded in the sceptre
of David's line. Jacob's prediction of the lion of the
tribe of Judah, who conquers peace and prosperity and
gains possession of all that belongs to him, is advanced
in the lion of Bethlehem, and prefigured in the victories
of his brilliant reign. The throne of David rises higher
than the sceptre of Jacob and the conquering chieftain
of Judah—it enlarges the scope of the prediction, and
fills it with grander conceptions. The prophecy is still
generic. The kingdom of Israel, the tribe of Judah, is
narrowed into the seed of David. The seed of David
assumes the place and significance of the seed of the
woman and the seed of Abraham.

2. The erection of the house of Jahveh is the further
unfolding of the blessing of Shem. Jahveh is not only
to dwell in the tents of Shem, in the midst of the tribes
of Israel, as their King and their God, but He is to take

---

[1] The text of Samuel וְנֶאְמַן בֵּיתְךָ is to be preferred to the chronicler's וְעֲמַדְתִּיהוּ בְּבֵיתִי. But both texts insert מַמְלֶכֶת without sufficient reasons. It seems to be explanatory. Samuel appends לְפָנֶיךָ,
which is not in the chronicler, and seems to have arisen by repetition
from the previous line.

[2] The chronicler incorrectly uses the third person of the suffix
for the second person.

up His abode in Jerusalem, in a temple to be erected by the seed of David. There is no explicit reference to Solomon as the builder of the temple, but to the seed of David in general. The temple of Jahveh is to be an everlasting temple, and the seed of David as a whole is to have the care of that temple, which is conceived of in the prediction in its culmination, and not merely in the temple erected by Solomon. The temple of Solomon was the historical movement toward a realization of the prediction; it was not the accomplishment of the ideal of the prediction, for that ideal was something higher and more glorious than the temple of Solomon.

3. The highest feature of the prediction of Nathan is, however, in the relation of sonship thereby established. Israel at the exodus had been taken up into the relation of sonship to Jahveh. Israel was His son, His first-born. Now this relation of sonship is applied to David and his seed in a peculiar and higher sense. This relation of sonship involves two special phases—chastisement and mercy. The chastisement is on account of sin, and in order to its removal. This feature is omitted by the chronicler. It is chastisement by paternal love,—it is by the use of men of high and low degree. But it is a chastisement of redemption. The mercy of God, His paternal mercy, is everlasting; it will never depart from David and his seed as it had departed from Saul. The conception of the suffering seed of the prot-evangelium is now advanced to a higher stage—the suffering is not here through the temptations and assaults of the evil one, the serpent, but through the chastisement of paternal love. The affliction comes through evil men who render the supremacy and the victory difficult and hazardous, but cannot stay it or prevent its ultimate realization. For over above all this affliction is

I

the hand of the Father God who uses these wicked men as the rods of His chastening love.

The prediction has been rashly interpreted as referring to Solomon. But Solomon is only the herald of its realization, like David himself. Solomon by his historical transactions points the way to the ultimate realization in the Messiah, who pursued the way of suffering to gain the glories of redemption, who suffered the chastisements of His Father God for the redemption of the race. It is true we cannot refer the committing iniquity, the acting perversely, to Him as a person. But none of the features of the prediction refer to Him directly as a person. The prediction throughout is generic. It finds its realization in him as the culmination of David's line. The dynasty of David is an everlasting dynasty. It continues from David onward to reign over Israel, but it is only in Jesus Christ that it really becomes an eternal throne. The dynasty of David is the builder of the house of Jahveh, beginning with Solomon and continuing through the noble monarchs of that line to care for the temple of their God; they rebuild it under Zerubbabel, but it is not until Jesus Christ erected the temple of humanity in heaven at the right hand of God that the prediction attained its ideal. The paternal mercy and chastisement were realized in the history of the Davidic dynasty, but that mercy was first made sure for ever in the suffering of Jesus Christ when He was chastised, not for His own sins, but for the sins of the Davidic dynasty, of Israel and the world. In the prophecy of Nathan the predictions of the Pentateuch are transformed into new ideals to constitute the basis of Messianic predictions in the future.

The Davidic covenant is the embodiment of the hope of David and the theme of his last meditations. The prophetic historian, the author of the Books of Samuel,

has preserved the last words of the sweet singer of Israel
in the following beautiful poem :—

I. " Utterance [1] of the man whom the Most High [2] has raised up.
The Spirit of Jahveh speaks in me,
And his word is upon my tongue.
The God of Israel doth say to me,
The Rock of Israel doth speak.

II. A ruler over men—righteous :
A ruler in the fear of God,
Yea, he is like the morning light when the sun rises,
A morning without clouds,
From shining, from rain, tender grass sprouts from the earth.

III. Is not thus my house with 'El ?
For an everlasting covenant hath he made with me,
Arranged in all things, and secured,
Yea, all my salvation and every delight,
Will he not cause it to sprout ?

IV. But the worthless, all of them are thrust away [3] like thorns ;
For they cannot be taken with the hand ;
The man touching them
Must be armed with iron and the spear's staff ;
And they will be utterly [4] consumed with fire."
                                —2 Sam. xxiii. 1–7.

---

[1] The editor has enlarged the first strophe by dwelling upon the
character of David as the anointed of God ; thus—
    " Anointed of the God of Jacob,
        Sweet in the songs of Israel."
[2] עַל, according to Gesenius, is an adverb = on high, highly, but
it is only here in this sense. The Vulgate renders עַל as a preposition, de Christo. It is better to take עַל as a shortened form of
עֶלְיוֹן, as in Hos. ii. 7, vii. 16, and to follow the LXX. ὃν ἀνέστησεν
ὁ θεός, and point the verb הֻקַם.

[3] מֻנַּד is Hoph. part. : only here from נוד = shake out, thrust
away, or from נדד = flap wings and flee, and thus chased away.
מֻנַּד is used in Job xx. 8.

[4] בַּשֶּׁבֶת = in their dwelling, from ישׁב. But the LXX. reads בְּבֹשֶׁת
by transposition of letters, and the Vulgate usque ad nihilum,
reading שֶׁבֶת, cessation, from שׁבת.

In this swan - song David clings to the Messianic promise as his greatest delight. He pictures the righteous, God-fearing ruler shining forth like the dawn and springing up like the tender grass after a shower. He expresses his confidence in the firm, sure and everlasting covenant of God, that He will cause all his salvation and delight to spring up in due time, and that He will utterly destroy all the wicked adversaries.

The life and experience of David and Solomon his son become the typical frames of the Messianic idea, as they fill up the outlines of the prediction of Nathan. It matters little whether these are presented to us in the words of David or Solomon, or of some other poet of their circle or age. That David or Solomon is their theme, and their experience the Messianic type, justifies us in treating them together.

IV. THE CONQUERING KING.

§ 43. *Psalm CX. cites an utterance and oath of Jahveh to the Messiah, enthroning him at his right hand as the priest-king after the order of Melchizedek.   He then stands at his right hand as he goes forth at the head of a priestly army to the conquest of the nations.*

The 110th Psalm is in the form of an utterance from Jahveh respecting the son of David. It is therefore a prediction that unfolds the prediction of Nathan. It is composed of two strophes of six pentameter lines each.

I. " Utterance of Jahveh to my Lord ;[1] 'sit enthroned at my right hand
    Till I make thine enemies a stool for thy feet ;'

---

[1] לַאדֹנִי. The Psalmist recognizes the recipient of the utterance of Jahveh as his Lord and Sovereign. The utterance was made directly to him ; as in Ps. ii., the Messiah himself cites a decree of Jahveh.

The rod of thy strength Jahveh sendeth out of Zion :
Rule in the midst of thine enemies.[1]
Thy people are volunteers[2] in the day of thy host, in beauty of
holiness.
From the womb of the morning thou hast the dew of thy young
men.[3]

II. Jahveh hath sworn, and he will not be sorry,
  'Thou art a priest for ever after the order of Melchizedek.'
  The Lord on thy right hand doth smite kings in the day of his
  wrath.
  He judgeth among the nations. It is filled with dead bodies;[4]
  He doth smite the chiefs[5] [going] over[6] a wide land.
  Of the brook on the way he drinketh,[7] therefore he lifteth his
  head."

The first strophe cites an utterance exalting the
Messiah to the right hand of God, to a throne of supremacy over all his enemies.   He is then represented as
riding forth from Zion in his chariot, at the head of an
army of youthful volunteers, a multitude vast as the
dew-drops of the morn, in fulness and freshness of
youth, and in holy and beautiful attire.

The second strophe cites an oath of Jahveh making

---

[1] Line 4 is a half line in order to a metrical pause.

[2] נדבות is used, as in Judg. v. 2, to indicate the heroic courage of
the people.   They volunteer to follow their king into the battle.
There is no sufficient reason for thinking of the free-will offerings of
the priest code.

[3] טל ילדתך = dew of thy youth.   The youth does not refer to the
age of the king, as some have supposed, but to the age of the volunteers.   They are young men in holy attire.   They spring forth at
his call as fresh and numerous as the dew-drops at the break of day.

[4] מלא גויות.   The verb is intransitive.   Its subject is the battle-
field, which is sufficiently plain from the context.

[5] ראש is collective, and parallel with מלכים.

[6] על is pregnant, implying the verb הלך.   It indicates the wide
extent of the battlefield and the victory.

[7] This is a reminiscence of the victory of Gideon and his men at
the spring Harod (Judg. vii.).   The king presses on in pursuit of his
foes, and drinks of the brook while in movement, without halting.
He is eager to gain a complete victory.   He lifts up his head in the
proud consciousness that it has been gained.

the Messiah a priest-king after the order of Melchizedek. It represents Jahveh on his right hand in the conflict. We see him dashing in pieces the kings and the chiefs of the enemy in order to exalt the Messiah to be chief over all. The victorious march extends over a wide country; the battlefield is filled with the slain. The Messiah is wearied with the struggle, but he halts not in his march of victory, drinking of the brook on the way like the warriors of Gideon, and tarries not until his exaltation over all has been accomplished.

This prediction combines priesthood and royalty in the Messiah. It is thus an unfolding of the covenant of Sinai. As the nation of Israel had then been constituted a kingdom of priests, a holy nation, so now by a divine oath the Davidic monarch is constituted the priest-king at the head of a kingdom of priests. Melchizedek is the model for such a priest-king coming down from primitive times. The prediction of Balaam is resumed, and the conquering sceptre which dashes in pieces all enemies is now in the hands of this priest-king, the second David. Zion is the seat of his dominion over the nations. The intimate relationship is represented as an enthronement at the right hand of Jahveh, and also as the presence of Jahveh at his right hand in the battle. This idea was never realized in the history of Israel. It belongs to the great High Priest after the order of Melchizedek, who reigns on the heights of the heavenly Zion until all things are subdued to His heavenly sceptre.

V. THE ENTHRONED MESSIAH.

§ 44. *Psalm II. represents the Messiah enthroned on Zion at the right hand of Jahveh as His son, citing a divine decree entitling him to the position, with all its prerogatives, of universal and everlasting sovereignty.*

" Why do nations rage,[1]
And peoples meditate a vain thing ?
Kings of earth set themselves,
And rulers do take counsel together :
Against Jahveh, and against his anointed,

Saying, 'Let us break their bands asunder,
And let us cast away their cords from us.'

II. He that is throned in heaven laugheth :
The Lord derides them :
Then he speaks unto them in his anger,
And in his hot wrath troubles them,

. . . . . [2]

Saying, 'Verily, I, even I, have set my king
On Zion, my holy mountain.'

III. Let me tell of a decree of Jahveh,[3]
He said unto me, 'Thou art my son,
I, to-day,[4] have begotten thee.
Ask of me and I will give nations,[5]
Thine inheritance and possession will be the ends of earth ;
Thou shalt break them with an iron sceptre,
As a potter's vessel dash them in pieces.'

---

[1] רגש is an Aramaic word only used here in Hebrew. It is kindred with רעש = to quake. It indicates the noisy demonstrations, the tumult that precedes rebellion.

[2] The second strophe is an antistrophe to the first, so arranged that every line is in antithesis to its fellow, with the single exception of the fifth. We should expect the object of the wrath of God to be mentioned here to correspond with the previous strophe. In view of the symmetry of the psalm in other respects, I cannot escape the feeling that a line has been omitted by a later editor or copyist.

[3] אֶל חֹק יהוה. We disregard the Massoretic accents, and regard חֹק as construct before יהוה, and thus we avoid the awkward placing of יהוה before the verb, which seems to be without force here, and it also make the lines more symmetrical.

[4] The day is the day of the installation. The begetting is the establishment in the official sonship relation, as in the prediction of Nathan (2 Sam. vii. 11–16) and the covenant with Israel (Ex. iv. 22).

[5] We follow the rhythm and disregard the Massoretic accents in this line and the following.

IV. And now, ye kings, act wisely,
Be instructed, judges of earth.
Serve Jahveh with fear,
And reverence with trembling, render[1] sincere[2] homage,
Lest he be angry, and ye perish in the way;
For soon his anger may be kindled.
Blessed are all who seek refuge in him."

The first strophe represents the nations as plotting to throw off the yoke of the recently installed monarch, the anointed son of Jahveh. In the antistrophe Jahveh is seen quietly laughing at their uneasiness, deriding their vain devices, speaking in anger to those who are rising up in rebellion, and terrifying with his wrath the plotting assembly, all culminating in the decisive word that God had already installed the Messiah.

The second part of the psalm introduces the Messiah himself as speaking; telling of a decree of Jahveh which

[1] We disregard the accents of lines 4 and 5, and attach נשקו־בר to the previous line, and thus make a better rhythm.

[2] בר is rendered "son" in the Peshitto and modern Versions. But the R.V. in the margin rightly calls attention to the renderings of the ancient Versions. The Targum renders, "receive instruction;" the LXX. δράξασθε παιδείας; the Vulgate, apprehendite disciplinam. They take בר as the Aramaic noun, meaning "instruction," "piety." Aquilla, Symmachus and Jerome render, "worship in purity," and take בר as meaning "pure," "clear." The rendering "son" has only the Peshitto in its favour. The word is only found once in Hebrew, in Prov. xxxi. 2, which is distinguished by other Aramaisms. The Peshitto's authority is weakened by the fact that it follows its own dialect. Our psalm uses the Hebrew בן for son in ii. 2. Moreover, the absence of the article is hard to explain with this meaning. The previous line exhorts to reverence Jahveh, and the following context is referred more naturally to Him. The context urges that we should have here some expression of reverence and submission to Jahveh. Moreover, we should expect "kiss the sceptre," rather than "kiss the son." The ancient Versions, with the exception of the Peshitto, give strong external authority in favour of the rendering to which the context tends. This is best given by taking בר as a proper Hebrew word, with the meaning "pure," "sincere," and by translating "render sincere homage;" for the kiss is the kiss of homage and not of affection. The rhythmical arrangement that we have given favours this view.

entitled him to the rank of sonship and dominion over the nations. The antistrophe of this part is a warning to those inclined to rebellion, that they submit themselves with sincere homage to the divinely-enthroned monarch.

The cited decree reminds us of the oracle of Ps. cx. and the promise, 2 Sam. vii.; but the contents of the decree are somewhat different from either of these predictions. We have therefore another and an independent divine communication. There is an advance upon the conception of Ps. cx. There the Messiah was called to the right hand of Jahveh, and rides forth to the battle at the head of an army of priest - kings to the victory over the nations. Here the Messiah is calmly seated at the right hand of Jahveh in the relation of sonship, enthroned on Mount Zion, and rebuking his enemies with a divine decree, which entitles him to his position, with all its prerogatives of sovereignty. The relation of sonship is emphasized. The subjugation of the rebellious is represented as the inevitable result of his irresistible power. The conquest of Ps. cx. is presupposed.[1]

VI. THE RIGHTEOUS KING.

§ 45. *Psalm LXXII. represents the Messianic king ruling in righteousness, mercy and peace, receiving the homage of the nations, the source and object of universal blessing.*

The psalm presents the aspirations of Israel for the Messianic king, and, with a prayer for divine endow-

---

[1] The decree is cited by Paul in Acts xiii. 33 and Rom. i. 4, and rightly applied to the enthronement of Jesus the Messiah at the right hand of God in heaven at His ascension. In the Epistle to the Hebrews (i. 5) it is combined with 2 Sam. vii., and referred to the enthroned Jesus. In Acts (iv. 25) the fruitless rebellion of the nations is applied to the gathering together of Herod and Pilate, the Gentiles and the people of Israel against the crown rights of Jesus. These New Testament writers clearly discern the essential features of the prediction as fulfilled in the antitype of Solomon.

ments, predicts the character of the monarch and his
reign. None but Solomon could present the type for
such an ideal. Each of the three strophes begins with a
prayer. They correspond with the prayer of Solomon
for wisdom at Gibeon and at the dedication of the
temple. Never before or subsequently has there been
such a reign of peace and glory in Israel. The predictions of the Messianic king were pointed in a more
peaceful direction by the reign of Solomon. We observe
in this psalm a further unfolding of the blessings of the
nations, which have been presented already in the
Abrahamic promise, but have assumed in the subsequent
predictions of Jacob, Balaam and the previous psalms the
form of subjugation and crushing. Here the sceptre of
iron is transformed into a sceptre of reconciliation and
peace.

I. "O God, give thy judgments [1] to a king, and thy righteous-
       ness to a king's son.
   He will judge thy people with righteousness, and thine
       afflicted with judgment.
   The mountains will bear peace for the people, and the hills
       in righteousness.
   He will judge the afflicted of the people, save the sons of the
       poor, and he will crush oppressors.
   They will fear thee as long as the sun, and before the moon
       through all generations.
   He will come down like rain upon the mown grass : as
       showers will he water the land.
   In his days will the righteous flourish ; and abundance of
       peace till the moon be no more.

---

[1] The Revised Version neglects the jussives of vers. 8 and 15
and renders them as futures. The margin renders them and the
common forms of the imperfect that follow, all alike as jussives.
Both are wrong in neglecting the differences in form and meaning.
The strophes begin with the jussives of petition and then change
into the imperfects of prediction. The Revised Version entirely
misses the rhythm. The psalm is a hexameter with occasional
pentameters and tetrameters.

II. Yea, let him rule from sea to sea; and from the river unto
    the ends of the earth.

Before him they that dwell in the wilderness [1] will bow;
    his enemies will lick the dust.

Kings of Tarshish and the isles will render tribute,[2]

Kings of Sheba and Seba will bring gifts,

Yea, all kings will do obeisance to him: all nations will
    serve him.[3]

He will have pity upon the weak and poor; and the persons
    of the poor will he save;

From oppression and from violence he will redeem their life;
    and precious will their blood be in his eyes.

III. Yea, let him live; and let them give him of the gold of Sheba:

And let them pray for him continually; all the day bless him.

Let there be abundance of grain in the land,[4]—

On the top of the mountains it will rustle with its fruit like
    Lebanon,

Yea, they will bloom out of the city as the grass of the earth.

Let his name be for ever; before the sun let his name sprout
    forth.[5]

And all nations will bless themselves [6] with him; they will
    pronounce him happy."

---

[1] צִיִּים = the animals or tribes of the dry and waterless wastes.

[2] אֶשְׁכָּר, a noun, only used here and Ez. xxvii. 15, is formed by
prefix א from שׁכר. It means *gift, hire, tribute.*

[3] There is an interpolation between the fifth and sixth lines, as
we can see by comparing Job xxix. 12—

כִּי יַצִּיל אֶבְיוֹן מְשַׁוֵּעַ וְעָנִי וְאֵין עֹזֵר לוֹ

כִּי אֲמַלֵּט עָנִי מְשַׁוֵּעַ וִיתוֹם וְלֹא עֹזֵר לוֹ

The clause with כִּי is different from all the other clauses of the
previous and subsequent context, which are all clauses of direct
statement in future indicatives in the progressive parallelism.

[4] Line 3 of strophe III. is a broken line in order to gain a
metrical pause. The Revised Version follows the accents and misses
the movement here and in the following line.

[5] יָנִין, *Hiph.* of נון. The *Qeri* has יִנּוֹן, *Niph.* The word is only
found here. It means to *sprout, produce fruit. Jinnon* is a
Talmudic name for the Messiah, based on this passage (Schöttgen,
de Messia, p. 4) and Talmud, *Synhed.* 98b.

[6] יִתְבָּרְכוּ בוֹ כָּל גּוֹיִם is based on the Abrahamic promise, Gen. **xxii.**
18, xxvi. 4. (See p. 89.)

The reign of Solomon was marked by a multitude of tributary gifts and voluntary presents sent by many nations and presented by their princes to the wise and great monarch. Egypt, Phœnicia, Sheba, Tarshish, and possibly India honoured him with gifts. This made it possible to see in him the reflection of the Messiah receiving the grateful offerings of the nations. The universality of the blessing is well brought out. It attains a climax in the closing reiteration of the Abrahamic blessing. There is also an unfolding of the blessing of the holy land in the line of the prediction of Jacob.

VII. THE BRIDAL OF THE MESSIAH.

§ 46. *Psalm XLV. represents the Messianic king in Godlike majesty' as a bridegroom espousing and rejoicing over the nations as his brides.*

The occasion for the composition of this psalm was probably the marriage of Joram of Judah with Athalia of Israel.[1] But it matters little if some other monarch be regarded as the type. The Psalmist contemplates the glories of the bridegroom, the splendours of the bridal ceremony, and the joys of the marriage. These mirror to him the bridal of the Messiah with the nations. There is an advance from Ps. ii., which presents the absolute authority and permanence of the reign of the Messiah over the nations, through Ps. lxxii., which describes the blessings of that reign, to Ps. xlv., which represents the relation of the Messiah to the nations as a marriage relation. The psalm is composed of three rapidly increasing strophes with refrains; the external form corresponds with the swell of the description.

[1] See Delitzsch, *Psalmen*, 4 Aufl. p. 359, Leipzig 1883.

I. "My heart swells with a goodly matter :
I am saying my work respecting a king :
My tongue is the pen of a ready writer,
Thou art fairer than the children of men ;
Grace has been poured out on thy lips ;
    Therefore God hath blessed thee for ever.

II. Gird thy sword upon thy thigh,
O hero,[1] thy glory and thy majesty ;
In thy majesty prosper, ride on,
In behalf of faithfulness and meekness,—righteousness ;[2]
That thy right hand may show thee wonders.
Thine arrows are sharp ;
Peoples fall under thee ;
Thou art in the midst[3] of the king's enemies.
Thy throne, O divine one,[4] is for ever and ever :
A sceptre of equity is the sceptre of thy kingdom ;
Thou dost love righteousness and hate wickedness :
    Therefore God, thy God, hath anointed thee.

---

[1] The Massoretic accents are wrong. The rhythm, parallelism, and assonance favour the arrangement

חגור חרבך על־ירך
גבור הודך והדרך

[2] עֲנָה־צֶדֶק is anomalous. עֲנָה is not a construct, but an absolute shortened because of the *Makkeph*. צדק is therefore in apposition with it. The LXX. inserts καί.

[3] בלב is not to be connected with arrows, but with the monarch, who is represented as pressing into the midst of his enemies, as in Ps. cx. 2, בקרב איביך. Comp. Ex. xv. 8, בלב־ים.

[4] כסאך אלהים. The most natural interpretation is to take אלהים as vocative, and conclude that the monarch is addressed as divine. This is not strange to ancient poetry. The great kings reflect the divine majesty, and in a sense partake of the divine nature. Comp. Ps. viii. 5, lxxxii. 6, John x. 35, where אלהים is used for the exalted monarchs and heavenly intelligences. The Messianic king is pre-eminently the son of God, and as such might with propriety be addressed as אלהים, without any thought of confounding him with the one God of Jewish faith. Hupfeld, Moll, *et al.*, take כסאך as construct before אלהים, notwithstanding the suffix, and refer to several passages where they find a corresponding usage. But these may all be explained in another way, so that this usage is not sufficiently sustained. Ewald, Hitzig, *et al.*, regard אלהים as predicate, the substantive being used as an adjective, and render, "My throne is divine ; " but this lacks justification in Hebrew usage.

III. O, oil of joy [1] above thy fellows,—
Myrrh and aloes,—cassia—
All thy garments are from ivory palaces,
Whence [2] kings' daughters make thee glad.
In thy precious things the queen doth stand,
At thy right hand in gold of Ophir.
Hearken, daughter, consider and incline thine ear,
And forget thy people and thy father's house;
And let the king desire thy beauty:
Since he is thy lord, do homage to him;
And the daughter of Tyre will come with a gift,
The richest nations will court thy face.
All glorious is the king's daughter;
The inner palace [3] is of tissue of gold:

---

[1] We divide the strophe here (a) because the refrain seems to be but a single line at the close of the three strophes; (b) the strophes thus gain the proper number of lines to make a regular proportion in the increase, each strophe in turn doubling its predecessor in the swell of the song; (c) the anointing of the refrain is weakened by the limitation of it to joy, for it was the anointing of the installation; (d) the strophe appropriately begins with the theme that characterizes it, namely, the joy of the bridegroom. Accordingly the king is represented as himself the oil of joy. He is surrounded with all the delightful odours and plants, so that he himself concentrates them and embodies them (see Song of Songs i. 3, iv. 13 seq.).

[2] מני is explained (a) as an incorrect form of ממנה or ממנו, and thus parallel with the previous מי. The LXX. renders ἐξ ὧν ηὔφρανάν σε. This would favour a reading מש־, for this song, like the Song of Songs, belongs to the dialect of Samaria, where ש־ is used for אשר. This by mistake would be reduced to מני. This gives the proper sense. The ivory palaces are then the boxes that contained the precious garments of the bridegroom, possibly made by the hands of the princesses to gratify him. (b) A favourite interpretation in recent times is to take מני as a defective form of מנים = stringed instruments, and to think of the music of the marriage. So R.V. after Ewald, Hupfeld, Delitzsch, Riehm, Perowne, et al. But this is nothing more than an attractive and fashionable theory. (c) The Targum takes it as Minni = Armenia; but there is nothing to sustain this conjecture.

[3] The R.V. attaches פְּנִימָה to the king's daughter, and renders it "within the palace," thinking that she had already entered. But this is against the following context, which represents her as being

Her clothing is of embroidery : [1]
She is conducted to the king :
The virgins follow after her,
Her companions are conducted to thee,
They are conducted with joy and exultation,
They are brought into the king's palace.
Instead of thy fathers may thy children be,
Whom thou wilt set as princes in all the earth,
Let me celebrate thy name in all generations.
Therefore peoples will praise thee for ever." [2]

The Messianic bridegroom is Godlike, but he is not
identified with God in this psalm.   As the son of
God, the anointed, he bears the divine majesty and
reflects the divine glory. [2]

VIII. THE ADVENT OF JAHVEH AS DELIVERER.

§ 47. *Jahveh comes in theophany for the deliverance
of his anointed, the subjugation of his enemies, and the
extension of his dominion.*

Ps. xviii. is one of the choicest hymns in the
Psalter.   It is of eight strophes, of fourteen trimeter
lines each.   It is probably Davidic in origin, as it seems
to reflect his historic experience.   But his experience
is idealized, and therein the Messianic element appears.

conducted to the king.   It is best therefore to discard the accents
and connect this word with the next line.   The poet then describes
the interior of the palace as decorated with tissue of gold.
[1] The lines now become dimeters to increase the vigour of the
description and make the movement more rapid and abrupt.

לבושה לרקמות
תובל למלך
בתולות אחריה
רעותיה מובאות־לך

[2] This is cited in Heb. i. 9, together with extracts from Ps. ii., cx.,
and 2 Sam. vii., to show the exalted nature of Christ's sonship and
His elevation above angels.   The marriage of the son of David with
the daughter of the nations, represents the marriage of the Messiah
with His Church (John iii. 29 ; Eph. v. 25 ; Rev. xix. 7–9).

The psalm is given in another text with some important variations in 2 Sam. xxii. By a careful examination of these two texts and their versions, we have adopted the text that lies at the basis of the translation that follows.

The adoption of David and his seed into the relation of divine sonship secures them the favour, the everlasting mercy, and occasional interpositions of God in their behalf. The psalm described such an interposition in the coming of God in theophany to deliver the Psalmist from great trouble. It then describes the exaltation of David, the subjugation of his enemies, the extension of his rule to distant nations, and the praise of God among them for the wonders He has wrought.

> "Thou hast delivered me [1] from the strivings of my people;
> Thou wilt set me [2] at the head of the nations:
> A people I know not will serve me,
> At the hearing of the ear will they obey me; [3]
> Strangers will fawn [4] upon me,
> Strangers will fade away from their strongholds. [5]
> Jahveh liveth, and blessed be my rock; [6]
> Yea, exalted be the God of my salvation:
> The 'El who taketh vengeance for me,

---

[1] The readings ותפלטני and עמי of Samuel are to be preferred on account of their closer historical application.

[2] The reading תשימני of the psalm is to be preferred to תשמרני, because it is more consistent with the context.

[3] This line is transposed with the following in Samuel: the parallelism of the psalm is simpler.

[4] The Hithpael יתכחשו of Samuel is to be preferred to the Piel of the psalm.

[5] The text of Samuel inserts ויחגרו by repetition from the kindred letters (ממסגרותם)(מ) that follow. It gives no good sense, and makes the line too long. The psalm by transposition of two radicals reads ויחרגו, and gives a good sense. The line in both cases is too long. The R.V. breaks up the line into two short lines, and spoils the strophe. Both are alike insertions, and should be stricken out.

[6] Samuel inserts צור, which is possibly original.

And who bringeth down peoples under me,[1]
Who bringeth me out from my enemies,[2]
Yea, he will lift me up above those rising against me :
From the violent [3] thou wilt deliver me ;
Therefore I shall give thee thanks among the nations,
To thy name will I sing praises, Jahveh ; [4]
Who magnifies the great salvation of his king,
And shows mercy to his anointed,
To David and to his seed for ever."

—2 Sam. xxii. 44–51 ; Ps. xviii. 43–50.

IX. JAHVEH THE VICTORIOUS KING.

§ 48. *Psalm XXIV. represents Jahveh Sabaoth entering
the holy city as the triumphant King of Israel.*

The removal of the ark of the covenant from the
house of Obed - Edom to Jerusalem [5] by David, in a
festival procession of great magnificence, was a turning-
point in the history of Israel.   It united the residence
of Jahveh, the great King of Israel, to the residence of
the dynasty of David, which had been selected by him
for the Messianic king.   There can be little doubt that
the second half of the 24th psalm was composed with
this event in view, whether it belong to the first part of
the psalm or not.   The psalm is antiphonal, with
responsive voices and a chorus.

---

[1] The psalm reads וידבר, but it is an Aramaism, and is difficult
to explain with its ו consec.   The clause appears in Ps. xlvii. 4,
and may have been unconsciously assimilated by a copyist owing
to the similar letters of the original participle which is preserved in
מריד of Samuel.   The context requires a participle.

[2] The מוציאי of Samuel is better suited to the context.

[3] איש חמס is not violent man, as if an individual were thought
of.   But איש is a noun of relation, and the phrase means, *violent
fellow*, or the *violent*.

[4] יהוה makes the previous line too long.   By transposing it the
lines become correct trimeters.

[5] 2 Sam. vi. ; 1 Chron. xv.

K

Chorus.	{ "Lift up your heads, O ye gates ; Yea, lift yourselves,[1] ye everlasting doors : That the King of Glory may come in.
Inquiry.	Who, then,[2] is the King of Glory ?
Response.	{ Jahveh, strong and mighty, Jahveh, mighty in battle.
Chorus.	{ Lift up your heads, O ye gates, Yea, lift them, ye everlasting doors ; That the King of Glory may come in.
Inquiry.	Who is he,[2] the King of Glory ?
Response.	{ Jahveh Sabaoth, He is the King of Glory."

Jahveh the triumphant King of Israel enters the city that He has selected as His residence and everlasting capital. He has conquered all His enemies, and is to reign from thence over all, and manifest His glory to the nations.[3]

X. THE IDEAL MAN.

§ 49. *The ideal man in his humility is a little below the heavenly intelligences in dignity, but is exalted to dominion over all creatures.*

[1] הנשאו is Niphal, and is reflexive rather than passive. The gates are personified, and called upon to rise up and extend themselves in every way, so as to give worthy entrance to a monarch of such majesty and glory.

[2] זה is used to emphasize the interrogative, as frequently in Hebrew. It is incorrectly rendered "*this* king" in A.V., and is altogether ignored in R.V. In ver. 10 it is enlarged to מי הוא זה. This is incorrectly rendered by R.V. and A.V., as if it were מי מלך הכבוד הזה. The inquiry is, Who is this one ? namely, the King of Glory, the one you are praising so greatly.

[3] The triumphant entrance of Jahveh into Zion is the type of the ascension of the Messiah, Jesus, to the heavenly Zion after His triumphant resurrection.

I.   "*Jahveh, our Lord,*
       How excellent is thy name in all the earth !
   Thou whose glory doth extend [1] over the heavens,
   Out of the mouth of little children and sucklings,
   Thou dost establish strength because of thine adversaries,
   To silence the enemy and the avenger.
   When I see thy heavens, the work of thy fingers,
   Moon and stars which thou hast prepared,
   What is frail man, that thou shouldest be mindful of him ?
   Or the son of man, that thou visitest him ?

II. When thou didst make him a little lower [2] than the divine beings,[3]
    With glory and honour crowning him ;
    Thou madest him to have dominion over the works of thine hands,
    All things thou didst put under his feet ;
    Sheep and oxen all of them,
    And also beasts of the field,

---

[1] תנה is in form a cohortative imperative of נתן. Böttcher regards
it as a permissive imperative, and renders, "mayest thou thyself set
thy glory in the heaven." Gesenius renders, "which glory of thine
set thou above the heavens." But this is against the context, which
is a praise of God's glory as manifest, and not a petition that it
may be displayed. Kimchi, Delitzsch, and others take it as infin.
const. for the usual תנת = תנת = תנה, like רדה for רדת (Gen. xlvi.
3). The R.V. follows the Peshitto and Jerome, Hupfeld and
Perowne, in rendering "who hast set ;" as if the form were נתתּה.
But it is better to follow the LXX. ἐπήρθη, with Ewald, Riehm,
Hitzig, and read תְּנָה, as a cognate stem with תנת = stretch out,
extend.

[2] וַתְּחַסְּרֵהוּ. The ו consec. imperf. cannot be rendered as in R.V.,
"*For* thou hast." It begins a new strophe, and is preceded by
imperfects, to which it cannot be in consecution. We regard it as
the protasis of a temporal clause with the historic imperfect in the
apodosis.

[3] מאלהים is rendered by the ancient Versions and New Testament
citation (Heb. ii. 7), so also A.V. : "*angels.*" This is not strictly
correct, because it would exclude the divine Being Himself. But it
is incorrect to think of the divine Being alone as in the R.V.
אלהים refers to the divine beings, the godlike ones, the heavenly
intelligences, who reflect the divine majesty. Hupfeld and Hengstenberg render by the abstract "*divinity ;*" so Perowne, "little
lower than God, or little less than divine." But this lacks sufficient
justification.

> Birds of heaven and fishes of the sea,
> Those that pass through the paths of the seas.
> *Jahveh, our Lord,*
> *How excellent is thy name in all the earth!"*

This beautiful little psalm may be regarded as a reminiscence of the original endowment of mankind as given in the Poem of the Creation.[1] First, the humility of man is presented over against the glory of God. In dignity he was made to fall a little short of those divine beings who are associated with God as heavenly intelligences, or, as we would now say, the angels. He is yet crowned with glory and honour, and with dominion over all creatures. This dominion of man is his original endowment, the ideal after which he is to strive all his life. It is the ideal of the human race as such. The psalm presents that ideal manhood which is first realized in the second Adam, who achieved the ideal for Himself and the race.[2]

XI. THE IDEAL MAN TRIUMPHANT IN DEATH.

§ 50. *Psalm XVI. is a typical Messianic psalm, presenting the ideal man enjoying the favour of God in a happy lot in life, and in communion with God after departing from life.*

Psalm xvi. is composed of three strophes of eight trimeter lines each.

---

[1] See § 28.

[2] The Messiah at His advent seems to have kept this ideal in mind in His favourite term for Himself, ὁ υἱὸς τοῦ ἀνθρώπου, used no less than fifty different times in the Gospels (seventy-eight if we count the parallel passages ; Keim, *Jesu von Nazara*, ii. 66). For this term indicates in the usage of Jesus at once His humility and His destiny as the second Adam.

I. "Preserve me, *'El*, for I seek refuge in thee.
   I say [1] to Jahveh, 'Thou art my Lord : [2]
   Is not my good dependent on [3] thee ?'
   (I say) to the saints [4] which are in the land,
   'My nobles,[5] in whom is all my delight.'
   Their sorrows will be multiplied who exchange for another.

---

[1] אָמַרְתְּ is pointed as 2 fem. perf. We must then supply the subject נַפְשִׁי, as the Targum and margin of R.V. But this is awkward, and is thought of only as the easiest way of explaining the Massoretic points. Disregarding them, we may take the form as the 1st pers. perf., with final י elided, like the Aramaic אָמְרֵת. So LXX., Vulgate, and R.V. Gesenius, Hupfeld, Ewald, Perowne. Indeed ת occurs in two MSS., De Rossi, and also in Ps. cxl. 13; Job xlii. 2; 1 Kings viii. 48 ; Ezek. vi. 59.

[2] אֲדֹנָי is the divine name *Lord*. But the ancient Versions render "My Lord;" so R.V. The pointing should then be changed to אֲדֹנִי. Hupfeld thinks that the י— is to distinguish the form from אֲדֹנַי, "my lords ;" but such a change is no more likely in this case than in other emphatic plurals, and it runs the greater risk of being mistaken for the divine name itself.

[3] עַל is variously explained—(a) by Ewald, Delitzsch and R.V., "*over beyond ;*" (b) by Riehm and Moll, "*in addition to ;*" (c) by Kimchi and Rashi, "*incumbent upon.*" Hupfeld gives בל the meaning "only,"—but without sufficient authority in usage, and renders, "my happiness rests *only* upon thee." Perowne changes בל into בֹּל, and renders, "my happiness rests *wholly* upon thee." The LXX. and Vulgate render, "since thou hast no need of my goods ;" giving עַל the meaning of "for," "for the profit of," as if it were אֶל. The Peshitto renders, "my good is from thee ;" and Jerome, "*non est sine te.*" We prefer to regard the clause as interrogative.

[4] לִקְדוֹשִׁים. Ewald gives לְ the force of "*as for,*" "*as regards ;*" Hupfeld, Moll, and Perowne, "*belonging to.*" It is best to regard it as parallel with לַיהוה, and thus the indirect object of אמרת.

[5] אַדִּירֵי is regarded by Gesenius (*Lehrg.* § 176*d*) as a construct for the absolute. But this is bad grammar. It is a construct before the relative clause that follows, if we retain the Massoretic points. But it is better to point אַדִּירֵי ="*my nobles.*" The LXX., Vulgate and Arabic Versions take the form as a verb, and are followed by Schürer, Diestel and Kamphausen, who read אַדִּיר. The chief difficulty remains in the וְ and the הֵמָה. The וְ is taken by De

I shall not offer their drink-offerings of blood,[1]
And I shall not take their names upon my lips.

II. Jahveh is my portion,[2] my inheritance and my cup:
Thou maintainest[3] my lot.
The lines have fallen to me in pleasantness;[4]
Yea, I have a goodly heritage.
I shall bless Jahveh who doth counsel me:
Yea, in the dark night[4] my reins will teach me.
I have set Jahveh before me continually:
Since he is on my right hand, I shall not be moved.

III. Therefore my heart doth rejoice,
And my glory[5] exult,
Yea, my flesh dwells in trust;
For thou wilt not abandon me myself to Sheol,

Wette and R.V. as introducing the apodosis; but it involves **a**
transfer of the המה, and if this is to be done it is still better **to**
transfer the ו to לקדושים. However, we may take the ן as intensive, "yea," "verily." The המה is best taken as the representative
of the copula, if the present text is preserved.

[1] מדם. מן is the preposition expressing the source or material.
The drink-offerings are regarded as consisting of blood, because they
were offered with hands stained with bloodshed.

[2] מנת is probably an Aramaism for מְנָתִי, as נחלת for נחלתי. It
is explained by Ewald as a construct of מנוה; so Hupfeld (see Ps.
xi. 6, lxiii. 11; 2 Chron. xxx. 4).

[3] תומיך is usually taken as Hiph. of ימך, like the Arabic root,
meaning "*full, ample.*" But Hupfeld, Perowne, Delitzsch and
R.V. regard it as an irregular participle of תמך=*held fast, maintain.*
Böttcher thinks that it is a diminutive of תמך = *dear little possession.* The LXX. favours the participle. But in this case the
pointing should be changed. Ewald takes it as a noun, with the
meaning *possession.* This is best, if the Massoretic points are
followed.

[4] נעמים is rendered by R.V., after Ewald, Delitzsch, Perowne
and others, as *lovely places.* But it is more properly, with Hupfeld,
Böttcher and Moll, an abstract plural, meaning *loveliness, sweetness.*
So לילית is not *night seasons,* but *dark night,* as in Song iii. 1.

[5] כבוד is a synonym of נפש (comp. Ps. vii. 6), with reference **to**
personal honour.

Thou wilt not suffer thy favoured one [1] to see destruction ; [2]
Thou wilt make known to me the path to life,
Fulness of joys is in thy [3] presence,
Pleasures on thy right hand for evermore."

The Psalmist bases his hopes on having sought and
found refuge with God, from whom comes all his good.
His delight is in the pious of the land, and he will not
compromise himself with other gods or with the offerings
of the wicked. His happy lot has been assigned him by
God, and he looks confidently into the future. He does
not expect to escape death, but he is assured that God
will not forsake him when he departs to Sheol. He will
not see destruction there, but will find a path of life and
will enjoy the presence of God, and will be placed at
His right hand for evermore. The Psalmist has no
thought of a resurrection, but of a blessed experience of
communion with God after death. This ideal is a Messianic ideal, first to be attained by the man in whom alone
God is entirely well pleased. It was first through the
resurrection of Jesus Christ that the attainment of this
hope became possible and actual for the human race.[4]

---

[1] חֲסִידְךָ. The *Qeri* is to be preferred in accordance with the
ancient Versions, the N. T. citations (Acts ii. 27, xiii. 35) and ancient
interpreters ; so Delitzsch, Perowne and others. It is also most in
accordance with the context. The *Kethibh* חֲסִידֶיךָ is the more difficult
reading, and on that account is preferred by Ewald, Hupfeld and
others. But this is the only reason in its favour. The external
and internal evidence outweighs this.

[2] שַׁחַת is rendered by the ancient Versions except the Targum,
and by the N. T. citation, Acts ii. 27, *destruction, corruption*, as a
segholate noun from שָׁחַת = to *corrupt, destroy*. But Gesenius,
Ewald, Hupfeld, Delitzsch and Perowne render *pit*, as if it were a
noun from שׁוּחַ = to sink down, and so parallel with שְׁאוֹל ; but this
derivation is not so easy, and the ancient authorities are to be
followed.

[3] אֶת = μετά = in association with the face or *presence* of Jahveh.

[4] Accordingly Peter applies the passage directly to Jesus Christ,
Acts ii. 27, and Paul in Acts xiii. 35, and rightly ; for although there
is no thought of a resurrection from Sheol in the psalm, yet the

The Messianic idea in the Davidic period made a marked advance both on the human and on the divine sides. The ideal of the race is presented in the dignity of man as falling a little short of heavenly intelligences, and exalted to dominion over the creatures. The pious man enjoys the special favour of God in this life, and is assured of the continuance of that favour after death. The Davidic king has become the especial channel of the Messianic ideal. He has been exalted to the position of divine sonship, has been enthroned on Mount Zion as a priest-king, and has received authority to reign over Israel and the nations. He conquers all enemies, espouses them as his brides, and reigns in peace and righteousness over them for ever. He is scourged by his divine Father on account of sin, but will never be forsaken by the divine mercy. He builds the temple of Jahveh, and enjoys the divine presence in his capital. He has a faithful priesthood associated with him.

The divine side of the Messianic idea has unfolded in parallelism with the human side. Jahveh comes in theophany to deliver His anointed and subdue his enemies. He is a great conqueror, a King of Glory, who battles at the right hand of the Messiah, and triumphs over all foes. He ascends to Mount Zion to reign there for ever. He is the all-knowing Judge who rights all wrongs, and is especially gracious to the weak, the afflicted, and the oppressed.

resurrection of Jesus Christ for the first time revealed to man what was that blessful experience that the pious might expect to enjoy with God after death. There is no thought of a personal Messiah in the psalm; yet in that David and none of his successors attained the realization of this blessed hope, it led on to the Messiah who first was able to attain it for Himself and His people.

CHAPTER VI.

MESSIANIC IDEAS OF THE EARLIER PROPHETS.

THE Hebrew Scriptures contain a collection of sacred writings named by the Rabbins, the later prophets, to distinguish them from the earlier prophets, the historical narratives of Joshua, Judges, Samuel and Kings. These are prophets in the higher sense.

JOEL.

The earliest of these prophets was Joel, who prophesied during the first part of the reign of Joash.[1] Many recent critics of the school of Graf think that the prophecy is post-exilic and the representation apocalyptic, on account of the ritualistic tendencies of the prophet; but his intense yet classic style, the reference to the Philistines and Arabians as the chief enemies, the general and indefinite representation of the Messianic idea, as well as his entire theological attitude, point to the earlier times. The occasion of his prophecy was a fearful plague of locusts which had come upon the land and laid it waste. This was followed by a distressing drought, consuming all that the locusts had left. The prophet interprets these events as divine chastisements, heralding still severer afflictions in the great and terrible day of Jahveh. Hence he exhorts the people to turn to Jahveh with all their hearts, to call a solemn assembly by the

[1] So Credner, Hitzig, Ewald, Keil, Delitzsch, Wünsche.

sound of the trumpet, and to fast and weep and pray, saying—

> "Spare thy people, Jahveh,
> And give not thine heritage to reproach,
> That the nations should rule over them ;
> Wherefore should they say among the peoples,
> Where is their God ? "
> —Joel ii. 17.

The prophet then assures them that Jahveh is jealous for His land, that He pities His people, and that He will do great things for them. The former prosperity will return with the removal of the chastisements. He will pour out His Spirit on all flesh, judge the nations in the vale of judgment in the great and terrible day, and give everlasting peace and prosperity to His people.

The style of Joel is classic and highly poetical. His discourse " is like a rapid sprightly stream flowing into a delightful plain." [1]

I. THE DAY OF JAHVEH.

§ 51. *Joel describes the advent of Jahveh by His Spirit in the outpouring of the manifold gifts of prophecy upon all classes and conditions of men ; in the display of wonders on earth and in heaven heralding the approach of the great and terrible day ; and in the deliverance in Jerusalem for all who call upon Jahveh, and are called by Him. All nations are assembled in the vale of Jehoshaphat for judgment. This is represented as a great harvest accompanied with convulsions of nature. The people of God become a fertile land, their enemies a desolate wilderness.*

> "And it will come to pass afterward,
> I will pour out my Spirit upon all flesh ;
> And your sons and your daughters will prophesy,
> Your old men will dream dreams,
> Your young men will see visions :

---

[1] Wünsche, *Joel*, p. 38, Leipzig 1872.

And also upon the bondmen and upon the bondwomen,
In those days I will pour out my Spirit,
And I will put wonders in heaven,
And on earth [1] blood and fire and pillars of smoke,
The sun will change itself into darkness, and the moon into blood,
Before the coming of the great and the terrible [2] day of Jahveh,
And it will come to pass that whosoever will call on the name of
    Jahveh will be delivered ;
For in Mount Zion and in Jerusalem will be rescue,
According as Jahveh doth say,
And among the survivors [3] whom Jahveh is going to call." [4]

                                         —Joel iii.

Joel vividly describes the advent of Jahveh in the outpouring of His Spirit on all flesh, and in providing salvation for His people in the great and terrible day of His wrath. Joel dwells on the former part of his theme in the third chapter, the latter part being the dark background from which, after presenting it, he returns to the scenes of the past and the present. He recalls the sad features of the invasion of Judah by the Arabs and the Philistines in the reign of Jehoram, when they carried into captivity the children of Judah, and spoiled the land of its riches.[5] From this sad scene he rises in the assurance of divine retribution to his theme of the divine judgment. He proclaims it at first with reference to these nations individually, as an exact recompense ; and then from these as types he rises in prophetic thought to

---

[1] הָאָרֶץ is usually attached to the previous line ; but the parallelism and rhythm are against it. There may be a reference to war in the expressions of this line ; but if this be so, it is, in accordance with iv. 9 seq., a reference to the war of Jahveh, in which the theophany and convulsions of nature constitute the principal features.

[2] The LXX. read נִרְאָה, and rendered by ἐπιφανῆ, and is followed by the New Testament in Acts ii. 20.

[3] The LXX. read בְשָׂרִים = evangelized ; but this is a later usage, and is not well sustained.

[4] The קְרָא of Jahveh is antithetical to the קְרָא of the people.

[5] 2 Chron. xxi. 16.

the judgment-seat of the world, and beholds all nations assembled for judgment.

We have seen that Messianic prophecy has two lines of development which run parallel with each other, and never coincide under the Old Testament,—the advent of Jahveh, and the advent of the seed of the woman, who is also the seed of Abraham and the seed of David. The advent of Jahveh is now represented in two distinct phrases : first, as an advent of grace and revival through the outpouring of His Spirit, and then as an advent of judgment in the outpouring of His wrath. In subsequent prophecy these two phases generally appear apart, but sometimes blend together, as in Chapter III., in sublime mystery. Under the New Testament fulfilment, however, the divine advent is resolved into two advents, the one at Pentecost, the other at the judgment day at the end of the world.[1]

In the interpretation of this prophecy we are not to limit its range to the era of the first advent, for the advent of grace is an advent which continues until the advent of judgment. The time between the advents is the last day of Old Testament prophecy. Hence the mingling of the two in the predictions.[2]

[1] Peter (Acts ii.) claims that this prophecy was fulfilled in the outpouring of the Holy Spirit on the day of Pentecost. And Paul (Rom. x. 12, 13) applies our passage to the universal gospel call and the calling upon God through faith in Jesus Christ and the confession of His name. The description of the wonders reappears in Matt. xxiv. 29, *e.g.* in the discourse of Jesus as premonitions of the destruction of the world.

[2] Thus the gifts of the Holy Spirit were striking and marvellous on the day of Pentecost, when He descended in theophany to abide with men ; and His gifts, the χαρίσματα of Rom. xii. 6, 1 Cor. xii., were peculiar to that age. Yet notwithstanding these gifts of the Holy Spirit have disappeared for eighteen centuries as to their more striking and miraculous forms, they are none the less present, and have ever been present with increasing and not diminishing fulness and efficacy, as to their substance and real intrinsic worth. They are the more in accordance with the promise itself, that they

The prediction of the great judgment is in the form of a proclamation of Jahveh, the King of Israel, to the nations, calling them to the last conflict, which is to decide the destiny of all. It is composed of three strophes.

I. " Proclaim ye this among the nations;
　　Consecrate war ; [1] arouse the heroes ;
　　Let all the men of war draw near, come up.
　　Beat your ploughshares into swords, and your pruning-knives
　　　　into spears :
　　Let the weak [2] say I am a hero.
　　Assemble [3] and come all nations,

---

have become so common and universal in their form as well as in their substance ; for the Holy Spirit is the abiding Paraclete, as the Saviour promised (John xiv. 16). Like the meek and lowly Jesus, He prefers the quiet and unostentatious impartation of His gifts and graces, as He distributes appropriately to each individual of the millions of Christian souls, marshals the forces of the Church in her conflicts with Antichrist, and steadily and constantly advances towards the completion of the work of grace for the world.

In the same way we are to interpret the wonders of heaven and earth. We may think of the marvels of the theophanies at the crucifixion, the resurrection and Pentecost, but guided by our Saviour's interpretation of the fall of the tower of Siloam (Luke xiii. 4, 5), and His reference to the destruction of Jerusalem (Matt. xxiv.), we are to regard the great and the little convulsions of the heavens and the earth as individually and collectively heralds of the approaching convulsions of the judgment day. And thus guided by St. Paul (Rom. x. 12), we see the deliverance on Mount Zion in the redemption of Jesus, and think of the gospel call going forth through the Spirit and Bride to the ends of the earth ; and of that constantly increasing number from all parts of the world who confess the name of Jesus, and find salvation through faith and the communion of prayer.

[1] War was consecrated by sacrifices; see 1 Sam. vii. 8; Isa. xiii. 3; Jer. li. 27.

[2] חלש is found only here in the nominal form. Job xiv. 10 has the verbal form. These are the only two examples of the use of this stem in Hebrew in the sense that is common to it in Aramaic.

[3] עוש is found only here. It is rendered by the LXX., Peshitto and Targum, assemble, come together. This is favoured by the parallelism. Most interpreters prefer to regard it as kindred with חוש, and render, hasten.

From round about gather[1] thither,
Lead down,[2] Jahveh, thy heroes.
Let the nations arouse themselves to come up
Unto the valley of Jehoshaphat ; for there shall I sit enthroned
To judge all nations from round about.
Put forth the sickle, for harvest is ripe :
Come, tread ye ; for the winepress is full,
The fats overflow ; for their wickedness is great.

II.   Multitudes, multitudes in the valley of decision,
For near is the day of Jahveh in the valley of decision.
The sun and moon put on mourning,
And the stars withdraw their brightness,
And Jahveh roareth from Zion,
And from Jerusalem giveth his voice ;
So that heaven and earth quake :
But Jahveh is a refuge for his people,
And a stronghold for the sons of Israel.
Then will ye know that it is I,
Jahveh, your God,
Dweller in Zion my holy mountain.
And Jerusalem will be a holy place,
And strangers will no more pass through her.

III.   And it will come to pass in that day,
The mountains will drip with new wine,
And the hills will flow with milk,
And all the brooks of Judah will flow with water.[3]
And a fountain will issue from the house of Jahveh,[4]
And water the vale of Shittim.[5]

---

[1] וְנִקְבְּצוּ is Niphal perfect with Vav consec. But it is rendered by the Versions as an imperative. This is favoured by the context and the rhythm. Kimchi, Ewald and Wünsche take the form as an anomalous imperative. But it is better to read an imperative at once, הַקְבְּצוּ without the וֹ.

[2] הַנְחַת is Hiph. imper. of נחת. The LXX. renders, ὁ πραὺς ἔστω μαχητής.

[3] This representation of the wonderful fertility of the land is based upon the earlier promises, Gen. xlix. ; Ex. iii. 8 ; Lev. xxvi.

[4] The stream from the house of God is a familiar conception of later prophecy, where it is more elaborate ; see Ps. xlvi. 4 ; Ezek. xlvii. ; Zech. xiv. 8 ; Rev. xxii. 3.

[5] הַשִּׁטִּים, the acacias. This was the name of the waste section

Egypt will become a desolation,
And Edom will become a desolate wilderness,
Because of violence [1] toward the children of Judah,
When they shed innocent [2] blood in their land.
But Judah will abide for ever,
And Jerusalem for generation after generation.
And I will cleanse [3] their blood that I have not cleansed,
For Jahveh is a dweller in Zion. " [4]   —Joel iv. 9–21.

This is the classic passage referring to the divine judgment which reappears in all subsequent Old Testament prophecy, and in the New Testament in the words of our Saviour and John.   We see first the assembly of armed hosts of all nations before the throne in the valley of decision.   On the one side stand the armies of the enemies.   On the other side stand the armies of God, the weakest of its warriors a hero.   The judgment is not so much a conflict of armies as a great harvest.   There is a reaping with the sickle of judgment, a treading of grapes in the winepress.   Multitudes are in great terror and confusion, for all nature is in commotion.   The sun, moon and stars put on mourning.   Heaven and earth quake, and a terrible voice causes all nature to tremble.   Finally, we observe the result of this judgment. The enemies have become a desolation, a desolate wilder-

---

on the east of the Jordan where the Israelites were seduced by the Moabites, Num. xxv. 1. The prophet represents this stream as crossing the Jordan in its influence. This is impossible in fact. It is thus an evidence of the symbolical character of the representation (see p. 50).

[1] חֲמַס. The construct is here the construct of the object—violence towards.

[2] נָקִיא, for the usual נָקִי, only here and Jonah i. 4, an Aramaism.

[3] נִקֵּיתִי, Piel of נקה = to be pure ; Niph., to be innocent ; Piel, to make pure, cleanse, and so to pronounce clean, acquit. The cleansing away may be by ceremonies of atonement or by punishment. The context is in favour of the latter.

[4] שֹׁכֵן בְּצִיּוֹן, an appropriate close to the prophecy, to emphasize this as the great central fact of consolation and confidence. Comp. יְהוָה שָׁמָּה, Ezek. xlviii. 35.

ness, while the condition of the people of God is as an exceedingly fertile land. Jahveh dwells in Zion, Jerusalem is holy, the land flows with wine and milk. A fountain of living waters goes forth from the house of God and quickens the most barren portions of the land, so that there is everywhere life and prosperity, for God dwells in Zion, the fountain source of every blessing to His land and people.[1]

AMOS.

The second Messianic prophet is Amos the herdsman of Tekoa. Amos prophesied during the reign of Jeroboam II. of Israel and Uzziah of Judah. Jeroboam II. was the greatest of all the kings of the northern kingdom. He conquered Damascus and all Syria to the Euphrates, although he did evil in the sight of Jahveh, as did his namesake the founder of the monarchy.[2] Uzziah of Judah served Jahveh and prospered. He conquered Edom and Arabia Petræa to the gulf of Elah and the river of Egypt.[3]

During these reigns the kingdoms of Israel and Judah enjoyed a wider dominion than that of David. Israel was never more prosperous; but, alas! this prosperity was all external. The house of David was still bereaved of the northern tribes, who were corrupt and hostile; so much so, that during the previous reign of Amaziah of Judah they had broken down the wall of Jerusalem and spoiled the temple and the king's palace.[4] The breaches had not been healed, but were growing wider and wider,

---

[1] We are guided by our Saviour (Matt. xxiv.), in His prophecy of the destruction of Jerusalem and the world, to refer the prophecy to the final judgment of the last great day (see also Rev. vi. 12, xiv. 14–20, xvi. 16, xx. 11–15, xxii. 13).

[2] 2 Kings xiv. 24, 25.   [3] 2 Chron. xxvi.

[4] 2 Kings xiv. 12–14 ; 2 Chron. xxv. 17–24.

more and more incurable. Israel and Judah both feel
secure in their prosperity; but the prophet sees the
internal corruption, and warns of the impending wrath of
Jahveh,[1] who will scourge them as Damascus, Gaza, Tyre,
Edom, Ammon, Moab, "for three transgressions and for
four."[2] Judah, and still more Israel, will be involved
in no less severe ruin. Fire will kindle in their walls
and devour their palaces. They have been warned by
famine, by drought, by locusts and mildew, by pestilence
and war, by earthquake and fire. The several charges
of the fourth chapter conclude with the warning, " Prepare to meet thy God, O Israel." In chap. vii. the
prophet sees a vision of locusts, then a terrible fire
devouring all before it. These are not to be. Jahveh
stands with plumb-line over the wall. All the high
places and sanctuaries of Israel are to be made desolate.

Finally, in chap. ix. the prophet sees Jahveh standing over the altar of the temple court and commanding
His destroying angel to smite the altar and temple and
dash them in pieces upon the head of all the people.
None will escape the judgment, wherever they may hide,
in Sheol or heaven, in the bottom of the sea or woody
Carmel; for before Him all nature trembles, the earth
melts, and becomes like Egypt in the overflow of the
Nile. There is to be a sifting as of corn in a sieve, but
not one grain of wheat will perish.

II. THE REBUILDING OF THE RUINED HOUSE OF DAVID.

§ 52. *Amos predicts that Israel will be sifted among
the nations, but not a grain will be lost. The ruined house
of David will be restored to its former prosperity. It will*

[1] W. R. Smith, *The Prophets of Israel*, Lecture III., Edinburgh
1882.
[2] The terrible refrain of the first and second chapters

L

take possession of the nations as its inheritance.   The land
will become rich and fruitful as the everlasting abode of
the people of God.

I. " For, lo ! I am going to give charge,
    And sift the house of Israel among all nations,
    As grain is sifted in a sieve,
    And not a grain falls to the ground.
    All the sinners of my people will die by the sword,
    Who are saying it will not come nigh,
    The evil will not overtake us.
    In that day I will raise up the fallen hut of David,[1]
    And wall up its breaches,[2] and raise up its ruins,[3]
    And build it as in days of old ;
    In order that they may seek Jahveh,[4]
    The remnant of Edom and all nations,
    Upon whom my name is called,
    Is the utterance of Jahveh, doer of this.

II. Lo, days are coming, is the utterance of Jahveh,
    When the ploughman will overtake the reaper,
    And the treader of grapes, the sower of seed,[5]
    And the mountains will drip with new wine,
    And all the hills will melt ;[6]

---

[1] סֻכַּת דָּוִיד, booth or hut, indicating graphically the reduced condition of the בֵּית דָּוִיד of the prediction in 2 Sam. vii. (see § 42).

[2] פִּרְצֵיהֶן. The fem. plural suffix is from the resolution of the house into its walls.   It may contain a reference to the division of the kingdoms.

[3] הֲרִיסָה, fem. noun, only here, from הָרַם, *tear down*.

[4] The Hebrew text has יִרְשׁוּ אֶת שְׁאֵרִית אֱדוֹם. The LXX. (Alex. codex), New Testament, Acts xv. 17, and Arabic Version read יִדְרְשׁוּ אֶת יהוה שְׁאֵרִית אָדָם.   Some MSS. of LXX. read אֹתִי.   The Vulgate, Peshitto and Targum support the Massoretic text.   The rhythm favours the LXX. so far as יִדְרְשׁוּ אֶת יהוה are concerned.   The pointing אֱדוֹם seems to us better suited to the context and the dependence on previous predictions. The Messiah is called *Bar Naphli* (Talmud, *Sanhed.* fol. 96. 2) on the basis of this passage.

[5] This is the same blessing as that attached to the sanctity code, Lev. xxvi. 5.

[6] Compare Joel iv. 18.

And I will restore the prosperity [1] of my people Israel,
And they will build waste cities, and inhabit them ;
And plant vineyards, and drink their wine ;
And make gardens, and eat their fruit ;
And I will plant them upon their land,
And they will not again be thrust out from upon their land
Which I have given them ;
Jahveh thy God doth say."

The prophet takes up the human side of Messianic prophecy, and views the Messianic blessings as resulting from the restoration of the prosperity of the house of David. The house of David appears to the prophet as reduced from a palace to a hut, and then as in ruins ; so far below the Davidic glory had his seed fallen. But this condition is not to continue, the breaches are to be walled up, the ruins are to be re-erected, they will be rebuilt as in former times. The promises made to Abraham, Israel and David are to be fulfilled. The remnant of Edom, and all the heathen upon whom Jahveh's name shall have been called, will seek Jahveh. The blessings of the promised land, especially as presented in the blessing of Jacob [2] and connected with the reign of the Messianic king, [3] are to be fulfilled. Harvests will follow one another in rapid succession, the land will overflow with fruit, and the hillsides will be covered with flocks and herds. The land becomes the abiding habitation of the people under the protection of God. Thus the same blessings are here ascribed to the restoration of the house of David as in Joel accompany the advent of Jahveh. [4]

The person of the Messiah does not appear in this prophecy, but there is the generic reference to the house of David and the people of Israel. [5]

---

[1] שוב שבות =restore prosperity ; שבות is from שוב, and not from שבה.
[2] Gen. xlix.   [3] Ps. lxxii.   [4] Joel iv.   See p. 158.
[5] James in his discourse, Acts xv. 16, guides us to find the fulfil-

HOSEA.

The third Messianic prophet is Hosea, who prophesied during the latter part of the reign of Jeroboam II. of Israel and Uzziah of Judah, and also during the reign of their immediate successors.[1]

The brilliant period of Jeroboam II. was followed by a sad decline into political and social ruin. There was no truth, no mercy, no knowledge of God in the land of Israel; and so utterly had they apostatized that they were abandoned by Jahveh to ruin. In this spirit Hosea prophesied, being the Jeremiah of the northern kingdom.

Hosea is really one of the greatest of the prophets of Israel. Rated as such by the ancient synagogue, he stands first in the order of the twelve lesser prophets. His style differs greatly from that of the classic Joel. He is rude and rough, original in thought and expression, obscure and difficult. Unusual words, constructions and metaphors are frequent. He is bold and impetuous as a mountain torrent, sublime in denunciation as a thunderstorm, and yet tender and affectionate in his consolations as the dew of the morning and the light of dawn. He is fond of imagery, especially from the forest, mountain and field; and lives as a warm-hearted patriot in the earliest scenes of Hebrew history, from which he draws frequent illustrations of future blessedness.[2] "The address of the prophet is like a wreath woven of the most different flowers, comparisons entwined with comparisons, meta-

ment of this prophecy in the erection of the kingdom of Christ on the day of Pentecost, and in the gathering in of the Gentiles by apostolic labours.

[1] The later title is apparently incorrect in extending his prophetic activity into the reign of Ahaz and Hezekiah. There is no internal evidence for it. See W. R. Smith in *l.c.*, Lecture IV.

[2] Comp. Wünsche's *Hosea*, p. xxvii. seq.

phors joined to metaphors.   He breaks a flower, and
throws it away in order again at once to break another.
As a bee he flies from one bed of flowers to another in
order to suck honey from the most different kinds of
sap." [1]

III. THE RESTORATION OF ISRAEL.

§ 53. *Hosea predicts the restoration of Israel after discipline.*   (a) *The children of Israel are guilty of whoredom
with Baal ; they receive the names, Jezreel ('El scattereth),
Lo-ruhamah (uncompassioned) and Lo-ammi (no people of
mine).   They are to unite under one head, the second
David, to receive compassion, to be the children of the living
God, and to be planted in their land for ever.   (b) Mother
Israel, guilty of adultery with Baal, is rejected by her
husband Jahveh.   But after faithful discipline in the
wilderness she is restored to the land, where she is remarried.
The divine attributes become the bonds of union.   All nature
responds to His will, and war is brought to an end.   (c)
Jahveh is faithful in love to unfaithful Israel.   After
depriving her for a while of the benefits of civil and religious
institutions, she returns with penitence to Jahveh and the
second David.   (d) Israel is to go into captivity, but will not
be abandoned.   Jahveh will roar like a lion, and the people
will flock like birds from the lands of their exile and inhabit
their own land again.   (e) Israel is to die of plague and
pestilence, and descend into Sheol ; but Jahveh will ransom
him from thence.   (f) Israel is to become a very fruitful
land, blessed with the dew of the love of Jahveh.*

The human and the divine lines of the Messianic
idea are in the prophecy of Hosea, yet they are distinct.
Hosea takes up the familiar Oriental idea that Israel is the
wife of Jahveh, and that all forsaking of Him and going

---

[1] Eichhorn's *Einleitung*, 4 Aufl. iv. p. 286.

after idols is adultery.[1] This idea he carries out under three symbolic transactions, the deep fall of the adulterous wife being described in order to set forth in the end the grandeur of her restoration.

I. "And Jahveh said unto Hosea, Go take thee a woman of whoredom[2] and children of whoredom : for the land is committing great whoredom in departing from[3] Jahveh. So he went and took Gomer, daughter of Diblaim ; and she conceived, and bare him a son. And Jahveh said unto him, Call his name *Jezreel;* for in a little while I will visit the blood of Jezreel upon the house of Jehu, and will cause the kingdom of the house of Israel to cease. And it will come to pass in that day,[4] I will break the bow of Israel in the vale of Jezreel. And she conceived again, and bare a daughter. And He said to him, Call her name *Lo-ruhamah:*[5] for I will no more have compassion on the house of Israel; for I will entirely take them away.[6] And I will have compassion on the house of Judah, and save them by Jahveh their God, and I will not save them by bow, nor by sword, nor by battle, by horses, nor by riders. And she weaned *Lo-ruhamah,* and conceived, and bare a son. And He said, Call his name *Lo-ammi:* for ye are not my people, and I will not be yours.

And the number of the children of Israel will be as the sand of the sea, which cannot be measured nor numbered ; and it will come to pass, in the place where it will be said to them, Ye are not my people, it will be said to them, Sons of the living God. And

---

[1] See W. R. Smith in *l.c.* p. 170 seq., for a fine explanation of the origin of this representation.

[2] זנונים. The abstract plural indicates that the whole bent of the woman was harlotry.

[3] מאחרי is pregnant, implying the verb הלך.

[4] ביום ההוא. The day of battle on which the fate of the kingdom was decided in the plain of Jezreel, the historic battlefield of Israel. We have no historic account of a battle with the Assyrians here ; but such an one is not improbable.

[5] לא רחמה may be taken as Pual part. with מ elided, or as 3 fem. sing. of the perf.

[6] נשא אשא. This verb is rendered by R.V. and many interpreters in the technical sense "pardon," "that I should in any wise pardon them ;" but the context favours the more common meaning, "take away," which is followed by most interpreters.

the children of Judah and the children of Israel will gather themselves together, and appoint them one head, and go up from the land : for great will be the day of Jezreel."—Hos. i.–ii. 2.

The prophet is commanded to take a wife whose whole bent is harlotry, and whose children inherit their mother's evil propensities. It is doubtful whether the command was designed to be actually obeyed. It seems altogether unnecessary that the symbol should have taken form in real life. The graphic representation in the language of the prophet was sufficient. The representation is realistic and intense with passion ; but this only shows the powerful imagination of the prophet and his descriptive power under the influence of the prophetic spirit.[1] Whether real or ideal, the symbol is plain enough. Israel is the adulterous wife, and the people are her impure children. This section of the prophecy plays upon the names of the three children, thereby contrasting the chastisement with the restoration.

Jezreel, the first and most prominent name, means, *'El* scattereth and *'El* planteth. Thus Israel is to be scattered in defeat and slaughter upon the battlefield of the plain of Jezreel. Here the plain of Jezreel is the scene of the judgment, as the vale of Jehoshaphat in Joel. And the prophecy derives great force from the play upon the names of these well - known localities.

But *Jezreel* also means God soweth ; so in this place He will gather them together again under one head. Judah and Israel will march forth from the land of their captivity in the days of Jezreel, will be planted or

---

[1] W. R. Smith in *l.c.* p. 180, is not sufficiently considerate when he says : "It is difficult to understand how any sound judgment can doubt that Hosea's account of his married life is literal history." The representation of Dr. Smith is eloquent and persuasive, but it is not altogether convincing.

sowed in Jezreel, and become multitudinous as the sand of the sea-shore in fulfilment of the Abrahamic promise.

Lo-ruhamah means uncompassioned—or she is not compassioned. This was the condition of Israel when abandoned by Jahveh, when His tender mercies gathered about Judah alone. But in the Messianic time *Lo-ruhamah* becomes *Ruhamah*, the compassioned. Israel and Judah mutually recognize one another as sisters. The sure mercies of David[1] flow upon them through the one head, the Messiah of David's line, whom Israel and Judah will jointly recognize and follow in marching up from the land of their captivity.

Lo-ammi means no people of mine, because Israel had been rejected by God, who refused any longer to be theirs. But in the Messianic time they become *Ammi*—my people. Israel and Judah will mutually recognize their brotherhood, and that each alike is the people of God. Yes in the very place, that is Jezreel, where it was said to them, Ye are no people of mine, it will be said to them, "My people;" "The sons of the living God."

This portion of the prediction brings into view a second David as the monarch under whom the restoration is to take place.[2]

II. There is another variation of the symbol in chap. ii. In the first representation the stress was laid upon the punishment of the children and their restoration. The stress is now laid upon the mother herself.

> I. "Say ye to your brethren, *Ammi*;
> And to your sisters, *Ruhamah*.
> Plead with your mother, plead;

---

[1] 2 Sam. vii. See p. 129.
[2] The fulfilment of the prediction is found, according to Rom. ix. 25, 1 Pet. ii. 10, in the gathering together of the children of God by adoption under the one head, Jesus Christ.

If she will not be my wife,
I will not be her husband.
Then let her remove her whoredoms from her face,
And her adulteries from between her breasts ;
Lest I strip her naked,
And set her as the day when she was born,[1]
And make her as a wilderness,
And set her like a dry land,
And slay her with thirst ;
And upon her children have no compassion ;
For they are children of whoredom.

II. Verily their mother played the harlot :
She that conceived them acted shamefully when she said,
I will [2] go after my lovers,
The givers of my bread and my water,
My wool and my flax, mine oil and my drinks.
Therefore, behold, I am going to hedge her [3] way with thorns,
And wall up her wall,
That she may not find her paths.
When she would pursue her lovers,
She will not overtake them ;
When she would seek them, she will not find.
Then she will say, I will [2] go,
And I will return unto my former husband ;
For it was better for me then than now.

III. Indeed she did not know
That it was I who gave to her
The corn, and the new wine, and the new oil,
And silver I multiplied to her,
And gold which was used [4] for Baal.
Therefore I shall take again
My corn in its time and my new wine in its season,

---

[1] הולדה, rare use of infin. Niph. with suffix.   It is passive.
[2] אלכה, cohort, expresses resolution.
[3] The Massoretic text has דרכך, but this has nothing in its favour except difficulty.   LXX. Arabic, Peshitto read דרכה, her way.
[4] עשו, a relative clause.   There is a transition from the mother to the people, in order to bring out the universality of the guilt.

And pluck away my wool and my flax,
Used for covering [1] her nakedness.
And now I will reveal her shame
In the eyes of her lovers,
Seeing that no one [2] can deliver her from my hand,
And I will cause all her mirth to cease in her feasts,
Her new moons, and her sabbaths, and all her festivals.

IV. And I will lay waste her vine and her fig-tree,
Whereof she said,
They are a hire [3] for me
That my lovers gave to me ;
And I will make them a forest,
And the wild beasts of the field will devour them.
And I will visit upon her the days of Baalim,
When she used [4] to burn incense to them ;
When [5] she decked herself with her nose-rings and her jewels,
And went after her lovers ;
And me she forgat, is the utterance of Jahveh.
Therefore, behold, I am going to allure her,
And bring her unto the wilderness,
And speak unto her heart. [6]

V. And I will give to her her vineyards from thence,
And the vale of 'Akhor for a door of hope.
And she will respond [7] there as in the days of her youth, [8]
As in the day of her going up from the land of Egypt.
And it will come to pass in that day, is the utterance of Jahveh,
Thou wilt call me my husband,

---

[1] לכסות is pregnant, implying a verb, therefore we render, "used
to cover."

[2] אישׁ is here indefinite, "one," τίς.

[3] אתנה is only found here. It is a noun, from נתן, with the meaning, hire.

[4] תקטיר is a frequentative imperf.

[5] וַתַּעַד is an emphatic change of tense to emphasize and give
direction to the specific charge.

[6] על־לבה = unto her heart, to her very soul, or inner nature.

[7] ענה may have either of the two meanings, to *sing*, as Jerome,
Saadia, De Wette, Umbreit, Wünsche, *et al.*; or to *respond*, as
Ewald, Hitzig, Hengst., Keil, Nowack. The latter is more suited
to the context.

[8] נעורים is abstract plural, *youth*.

And thou wilt not call me any more my Baal,[1]
And I will remove the names of Baalim from her mouth,
And they will not be remembered any more by their name ;
And I will conclude for them a covenant in that day,
With the wild beast of the field and with the bird of heaven,
And the creeping thing of the ground, and the bow and the
    sword,
And the battle will I break from the land,
And I will cause them to dwell in confidence.

VI. Verily,[2] I will espouse thee to me for ever;
Verily,[2] I will espouse thee to me in righteousness,
And in justice, and in mercy, and in compassion ;
Verily,[2] I will espouse thee to me in faithfulness.
And thou wilt know that I am Jahveh ;[3]
And it will come to pass in that day I will respond ;
I will respond to the heavens, is the utterance of Jahveh.
And they will respond to the earth ;
And the earth will respond to the corn,
And the new wine and the new oil,
And these will respond to *Jezreel*,
And I will sow her to me in the land,
And I will have compassion upon *Lo-ruhamah*,
And I will say to *Lo-ammi*, Thou art my people,
And he will say, My God."

—Hos. ii. 3–20.

This section brings before us mother Israel guilty of
adultery with Baal. Her children are exhorted to plead
with her to forsake her adulteries. Yet she does not

---

[1] בַעְלִי. There is here a play upon words. בַעַל was an ancient
divine name, meaning Lord, and synonymous with אָדוֹן. It was in
early times used of the true God, Jahveh ; but in the time of Hosea
it had become so associated with the sun-god of the Canaanites,
that it must be no longer used for the true God. It is probable
that אָדוֹן was used in Judah as בַעַל in Israel. בַעְלִי = my lord, is used
over against אִישִׁי, my man, my husband.

[2] The weak Vavs with the imperfects are intensive. It seems
difficult to give them any other meaning here.

[3] The Massoretic text of the Western Jews is יָדַעְתִּי אֶת יְהוָה, and
this is supported by the LXX. But the Babylonian codex reads
כִּי אֲנִי יְהוָה, and this is supported by the Vulgate, and seems best
suited to the contrast between בַעְלִי and אִישִׁי above.

repent, and therefore is stripped of her gifts that she had received of her husband Jahveh, and had attributed to Baal. Jahveh hedges up her way and walls her in, so that she cannot attain unto Baal. Then she repents and returns unto her husband. He receives her again, but first subjects her to discipline, as with Israel in the wilderness. Here the prophet uses the exodus from Egypt and the entrance into Canaan as the symbolic framework for his Messianic prophecy. As at the early marriage Jahveh led her forth from Egypt into the wilderness, so now at the restoration she goes forth into the wilderness. There her husband comforts her, and gives her the vineyard of which he had stripped her. From the wilderness he leads her back into her land by the vale of Akhor. This vale had been the vale of tribulation to ancient Israel through the sin of Achan, but had become a door of hope, being the vale through which they ascended to the capture of Ai, and thus obtained a permanent lodgment in the midst of the land.[1] Thus restored Israel will pass through the vale of tribulation, and even there find a door of hope through which she will enter into possession of her inheritance. She is then reunited to her husband for ever. A covenant with the animal kingdom is made, and the instruments of war are destroyed. The covenant with the animal kingdom, in accordance with Gen. i. and Ps. viii., is to bestow upon Israel the original endowment and ideal inheritance of mankind. The instruments of war are destroyed in order to permanent peace. The divine attributes are the holy bands which bind together in indissoluble union.

" All nature responds to the advent of Jahveh. It is as if we heard the sublime harmonies of the powers of nature as they act upon one another, sustained and moved by the fundamental tone of the creating and

[1] Josh. vii.-viii.

shaping spirit." [1]   The marriage of Jahveh to Israel is somewhat different from the marriage of the Messianic king to the nations as we have observed it in Ps. xlv. The marriage is a remarriage of an unfaithful wife.[2]

III. The prophet, in the third section of his symbol, lays stress upon the great love of Jahveh to His unfaithful wife.

"And Jahveh said unto me, Go again, love a woman, beloved of a friend and an adulteress, according to the love of Jahveh toward the children of Israel ; though they are turning unto other gods, and are lovers of raisin cakes.[3] And so I bought[4] her to me, for fifteen pieces of silver and a homer and a half of barley, and said unto her, Many days thou shalt abide for me ; thou shalt not commit whoredom, and thou shalt not belong to any one. And I also will (abide) for thee. For during many days the children of Israel will abide, without a king and without a prince, and without a peace-offering and without a pillar, and without an ephod or teraphim.[5]

---

[1] Umbreit, *Commentar ü. d. Kleinen Propheten*, Hamburg 1877.

[2] We are then to think not of the bridal of the Messiah of the New Testament, which is from another point of view like that of Ps. xlv., but of the Church as the mother (Rev. xii.), as the woman clothed with the sun, and with the moon under her feet, and having upon her head a crown of twelve stars, who is persecuted by the dragon and driven into the wilderness, yet is preserved by God for eventual restoration ; for as Hengstenberg says : "The three stations—Egypt, the wilderness, and Canaan—are ever present ; but we go from the one to the other only with the feet of the spirit, and not as under the Old Covenant, at the same time with the feet of the body."

[3] אשישה = grape or raisin cake, used as מנחה by the worshippers of Baal, and eaten in the sacrificial meals (comp. 1 Sam. xxv. 18).

[4] אכרה. The meaning "buy" is generally given to this form כרה in accordance with the context. The price is the price of a slave (Ex. xxi. 32), half in money and half in barley. The wife of Jahveh had become the slave concubine of Baal. There is here, as in chap. ii., a reference to deliverance from bondage in which Egypt is the basis of representation.

[5] These things of which Israel would be deprived are arranged in three pairs, the one referring to the service of Baal, the other to the service of Jahveh. During her period of discipline, civil and religious institutions would not be in her possession.

Afterwards the children of Israel will return, and seek Jahveh their God and David their king ; and come trembling [1] unto Jahveh and unto his goodness in the latter days."—Hos. iii.

This passage emphasizes the love of Jahveh towards Israel notwithstanding her unfaithfulness, a love which is punitive and yet restorative.   She is to abide many days alone as a widow away from her husband and away from her lover Baal.   This is interpreted to mean that Israel will abide many days without a government and without a worship of their own, without the king of David's line and without a prince of any other line, without the worship of Jahveh and without the worship of Baal. Afterwards they will seek Jahveh their God and David the Messianic king, and come trembling to Jahveh in the latter days.   It is evident that the prophet does not identify the human Messiah, the second David, with Jahveh, although they are closely united so that a returning to the one is a returning to the other.[2]

Hosea gives several fine pictures of the restoration, and uses symbols of great strength and beauty.   Chapter xi. represents the deliverance from Egypt under the figure of a father teaching his son to walk and drawing him on with cords of love.   But the son becomes rebellious notwithstanding loving care, healing words, and tender provisions for his support.   On this account he is delivered over to the Assyrian.   The prophet then graphically depicts the grief of the father and the resulting restoration.

> " How can I give thee up, Ephraim ;
> Deliver thee over, Israel ?
> How can I make thee as Admah,[3]
> Set thee as Zeboim ?

---

[1] פחד אל is pregnant, so that בוא is to be supplied.

[2] Compare Ps. ii. and cx.   See pp. 132–137.

[3] These are the cities destroyed with Sodom (Gen. xiv. 8).

> Mine heart is turned within me,
> My compassions are kindled together.
> I will not execute the heat of my anger,
> I will not again destroy Ephraim :
> For I am 'El, and not man ;
> A Holy One in the midst of thee :
> And I will not come to consume,[1]
> After Jahveh they will go,
> As a lion will he roar :
> When he roareth,
> Then let[2] children come trembling from the seaward,
> Come trembling like a bird from Egypt,
> And as a dove from the land of Asshur ;
> And I will cause them to dwell in their houses,
> Is the utterance of Jahveh."   —Hos. xi. 8–11.

This prediction looks forward to a second deliverance from captivity after the model of the Egyptian. But the captivity is viewed as extending to Egypt, Assyria and the seaward.

Chap. xiii. gives another representation of the punishment and of the restoration. Israel has destroyed himself by his iniquity. The kings, given by God to the people reluctantly in accordance with their cravings, can no longer save them. The time for punishment has come, Israel is to die and be restored after he has descended into Sheol.

[1] בְּעִיר might be brute, cattle, beast. It would heighten the contrast of the previous line—God and no man ; a holy God, and not a beast to devour. A.V. and R.V. render " *in the city;* " but this would require the article and does not give good sense. עִיר is taken by many, De Wette, Henderson, Gesenius, and Ewald, as from עיר = to be hot, and so they get the meaning *anger;* but this is questionable, and is not in accordance with the parallelism. Many recent interpreters, Steiner, Cheyne, *et al.*, think of בער, to consume, destroy, and point it as infin. or participle. This is suited to the context and seems to be best.

[2] The weak ו with the imperf. cannot be taken as the apodosis, for that would require ו consec. of the perfect. We might take it as in emphatic parallelism ; but we would rather expect that the trembling would be the result of the roaring, and not co-ordinate with it. It is better therefore to take it as jussive.

"From the power of Sheol I will redeem thee,
From death I will ransom thee.
Where are thy plagues, Death?
Where is thy pestilence, Sheol?
Compassions will be hid from mine eyes."—Hos. xiii. 14.

Jahveh here summons death and Sheol to do their worst,—bring on their plagues and pestilences, and put Israel to death. He will not interpose in His compassion to save the nation. But after the nation has died and has gone into the Sheol of the nations, then Jahveh will redeem them by bringing them up from Sheol and by imparting to them new life. The prophet thus predicts a national resurrection. This is the first appearance of the conception of a resurrection in the Old Testament theology. It first emerges as a Messianic idea, in connection with the restoration of the nation as a nation.[1]

Chap. xiv. 2–10 represents the restoration in language of tenderness and beauty. The Assyrian captivity is coming. Nevertheless it will not totally destroy the nation. The people are called to repentance and obedience, and receive the promise of divine love and revival. The poem is dramatic. We have first an exhortation of the prophet, then Ephraim addressing Jahveh in penitence, and Jahveh responding with promises of blessing. This is then continued in a conversation between Ephraim and Jahveh. The prophet concludes with an exhortation.

(*Prophet*) "O return, Israel,
            Unto [2] Jahveh thy God;
            For thou hast stumbled by thy iniquity.

---

[1] The R.V. correctly renders this passage and removes the errors of the A.V. The passage is quoted by Paul in 1 Cor. xv. 55 and applied to the triumph of the individual believer over death. The application was a proper one. It is not, however, an interpretation of our passage, for it has in mind only the resurrection of Israel as a nation, and has no reference to the resurrection of the body. The same idea of a national resurrection recurs in Ezek. xxxvii.

[2] עַד for the usual אֶל.

> Take with you words,
> And return unto Jahveh ;
> Say unto him everything.[1]

(*Israel*) Forgive iniquity and accept good [2] things ;
> And we will render the fruit [3] of our lips.
> Asshur cannot save us,
> Upon horses we will not ride,
> And we will not say any more our god
> To the work of our hands ;
> Thou by whom the orphan receives compassion.

(*Jahveh*) I will heal their apostasy,
> I will love them freely ;
> For my anger hath turned from him.
> I will be as the dew to Israel ;
> Let him bloom as the wild flower,[4]
> And let him strike his roots like Lebanon,
> Let [5] his shoots grow,
> And let his majesty be as the olive,
> And let him have scent like Lebanon ;

---

[1] כל is regarded by many interpreters as a rare use of the word as an adverb = *altogether ;* but Hebrew idiom would use the infin. absolute for this purpose. It is taken by Vulgate, R.V., Henderson, Gesenius, etc., as a rare example of the separation of this adjective from its noun = *all iniquity ;* but this is bad syntax, and it also makes the line too long and the previous line too short. The LXX. seems to have read instead of it the negative לא with כי. It is best to attach it to the previous line, after Houbigant, Newcome, *et al.* These make it qualify the subject of the verb, "*all of you ;*" but it is better to take it as the object, "*all, everything,*" make a complete confession. Compare עשה כל, Isa. xliv. 24.

[2] טוב is also taken as an adverb by A.V., Henderson, and many others, "*graciously.*" But it is better, with LXX. Vulg. R.V., and most interpreters, to take it as an object of the verb. We should then refer it to the *good things* to be offered as a sacrifice.

[3] פרים. Thus pointed it is bullock, as the lips are represented as taking the place of bullocks, the latter being in explanatory apposition ; so Vulgate, Ewald, R.V. But the margin of the R.V. follows the LXX. and Syriac. Newcome and Steiner rightly prefer it.

[4] שושנה. The wild flower of Sharon, the anemone, the brilliant scarlet. See Song of Songs ii. 1, 2.

[5] יך is a jussive form, and this forces us to render it as jussive, and make the context conform thereto.

M

> Let those who abide in his shadow return,
> Let them quicken [1] the corn,
> And let them bloom like the vine,
> And their memory be as the wine of Lebanon.

Ephraim [2]　What have I to do any more with idols?

　(*Jahveh*)　I have responded, and I shall [3] regard him.

(*Ephraim*)　I am like a green cypress.

　(*Jahveh*)　Of me is thy fruit found.

　(*Prophet*)　Whoso is wise, let him understand these things;
> Understanding, let him know them:
> That the ways of Jahveh are upright,
> And the righteous walk therein,
> But transgressors stumble therein."

The restoration of Israel is here conceived as accompanied with great prosperity, as in Joel and Amos.[4] The land becomes exceedingly fertile like the slopes of Lebanon. Corn and wine, the olive tree, aromatic plants, and wild flowers abound. The people rejoice under the love and blessing of Jahveh, all the more that they have been restored to favour after a season of discipline on account of sin, and that in the experience of heartfelt repentance they have found forgiveness.

Messianic prophecy in this period has advanced under the experience of suffering on the part of Israel, and in

---

[1] Quicken the corn, to make it live and grow, or cultivate it; a strange expression, justified by the symbolism of the passage.

[2] Ephraim is here introduced into the text by mistake. It really belongs to the margin or the thought. So the Jewish interpreters Raschi, Aben Ezra, and Kimchi supply יאמר. Cheyne, Nowack, *et al.* follow the LXX., and regard all but the third member of the verse as the words of Jahveh, and accordingly read לֹו for לִי. But these first lines are as we have given them, the first and third words of Ephraim, the second and fourth words of Jahveh.

[3] וַאֲשׁוּרֶנּוּ. The tense changes to contrast the response already given with the promise of future watchful care.

[4] See pp. 158 and 162.

view of the impending exile of the northern kingdom.
Both lines of the Messianic idea assume a new form in
view of these circumstances.   The advent of Jahveh has
two sides.   It is on the one hand for the revival of
Israel, and on the other hand for the judgment of all the
nations that are hostile to His kingdom.   It is especially
the restoration of Israel that is emphasized.   The restoration is represented as the remarriage of an adulterous
wife after a period of discipline ; as the recall from exile
of a rebellious son ; as the resurrection from the dead of
one upon whom the plagues of death have been heaped
by divine punishment ; as the bestowal of blessings upon
a repenting people ; as a revival through the outpouring
of the divine Spirit upon all classes and conditions of
men ; and as the bestowal of wonderful fertility and
peace upon the holy land.

The house of David is to fall into ruins and then be
rebuilt, and gain its supremacy over Israel and the
nations.   The returning exiles are to return in allegiance
to David as well as to Jahveh, and are to unite under
His headship.

CHAPTER VII.

ISAIAH AND HIS CONTEMPORARIES.

THE earlier prophets, whose predictions we have considered in the previous chapter, had the rival kingdoms of Israel and Judah more or less in view. They accompanied the northern kingdom in its failures with their expostulations, rebukes, exhortations and promises. The Assyrian period came, and this great world-power, after conquering Syria, the earlier foe of Israel, finally overthrew Israel herself and removed considerable numbers of the people into captivity. The age of Hezekiah introduces a new era of revival and prosperity for Judah, after severe struggles and conflicts. Judah is now alone the kingdom of God without a rival. Jerusalem becomes the centre of the kingdom of God as never before. The Assyrian is the rod of chastisement. He strives to reduce Judah to the same condition as Israel, but in vain. For the struggle is now a struggle about the holy standard itself, and Jahveh espouses the cause of His suffering people. He raises up His greatest prophets. He pours forth divine instruction in richness and fulness transcending every previous period. Jahveh Himself comes down in theophany as in days of old, and works stupendous miracles in the destruction of the host of Sennacherib and in the healing of Hezekiah.[1] A new era began for Judah. A great revival took place. Sacred psalmody and wisdom were revived. Collections

[1] 2 Kings xix.–xx.; Isa. xxxvii.–xxxviii.

of psalms and sentences were made, and several great prophets uttered prophecies which emphasized as never before the spirituality of the true religion, and urged the nation to move forward toward the realization of the prophetic ideal.

The earliest of the prophecies of this period is probably that little piece which was quoted by Isaiah and Micah from an older prophet.[1] These two prophets use the older prediction, and set it in the midst of other predictions. The variations between the two texts are slight. We give the original text so far as we can from a careful criticism of the two passages.

I. THE EXALTATION OF THE HOUSE OF JAHVEH.

§ 54. *The temple mount is to be exalted above all mountains as the throne of Jahveh, the goal of the pilgrimage of the nations, the source of instruction and judgment. The reign of Jahveh will result in the destruction of the weapons of war, and in universal peace and prosperity.*

> "And in the latter days it will come to pass,
> That the mountain of the house of Jahveh will appear,
> Established [2] on the top of the mountains,[3]
> And it will be exalted above the hills;

---

[1] Isa. ii. 1–4; Micah iv. 1–5.

[2] Isa. ii. 2 destroys the rhythm by transposing נכון to the beginning of the sentence, before יהיה. יהיה means, to become, to come forth, to appear.

[3] בראש = on the head or top of the mountains, that is, exalted above them all, so that all mountains radiate from it to the several parts of the earth. It is thus rendered visible to all that they may direct their pilgrimages thither. This physical transformation is in the mind of Ezek. xl. 2 and Zech. xiv. 10. It is impossible in fact, but this makes it all the more evident that the prediction is in the symbolical form (see p. 50 seq.). It is against the context to render, with Kleinert and others, "as the chief of the mountains," as pre-eminent in estimation.

And peoples will flow unto it.[1]
And many nations will go and say,
Come and let us go up unto the mount of Jahveh,
Unto the house of the God of Jacob ;
That he may teach us of his ways,
And that we may walk in his paths ;
For out of Zion will go forth instruction,
And the word of Jahveh from Jerusalem.
And he will judge between the nations,[2]
And admonish many peoples ;
And they will beat their swords into ploughshares,
And their spears into pruning-hooks ;[3]
Nation will not lift up sword against nation,
And they will not learn war any more.
And they will dwell each under his vine
And under his fig-tree, and none will make them afraid.[4]
    For the mouth of Jahveh Sabaoth hath spoken it."

The prophet beholds the temple mount, which had
been highly exalted by the erection of the temple of
Solomon, despised and scorned by the proud hills of the
earth upon which the temples of other gods were situated.[5]
He sees this temple mount rising from its degraded con-

---

[1] Isaiah reads וְנָהֲרוּ אֵלָיו כָּל הַגּוֹיִם ; Micah, וְנָהֲרוּ עָלָיו עַמִּים. The
text of Micah is to be preferred. The preposition עַל is more suited
to the idea of the mountain ascent. There is a variation in the
terms עַמִּים and גּוֹיִם throughout, and this variation is not uniform,
but seemingly capricious. Thus Isaiah uses גּוֹיִם in lines 5 and 13
for the עַמִּים of Micah, but the reverse is the case in lines 6 and 14.
But the LXX. of Isaiah in line 6 reads גּוֹיִם, and this is doubtless
correct.

[2] This line and the following are lengthened in Micah by the
addition of רַבִּים in the former and עַד־רָחוֹק in the latter. The
shorter lines of Isaiah are more suited to the rhythm. Isaiah uses
עַמִּים רַבִּים for גּוֹיִם עֲצֻמִים of Micah. These seem to be intentional
variations. But the simplicity of the text of Isaiah commends itself
as more likely to be that of the original author.

[3] There are several slight variations, e.g. אֶל in Isaiah ; וְאֶל in
Micah (l. 8) ; חֲרֻבוֹתָם in Isaiah for חַרְבֹתֵיהֶם in Micah (l. 15) ;
יִשָּׂא in Isaiah for יִשְׂאוּ in Micah (l. 17) ; יִלְמְדוּ in Isaiah for יִלְמְדוּן
in Micah (l. 18).

[4] Lines 19, 20 and 21 are only given by Micah.

[5] Comp. Ps. lxviii. 15, 16.

dition, until it towers above the mountains as the central mountain of the world, visible and accessible to all nations who flow in streams of pilgrimage unto it. From the presence of Jahveh goes forth instruction to guide them so that they walk in the light of it. At the same time judgment goes forth to destroy the instruments of war, so that every one may abide in peace and safety. Universal and everlasting peace is the goal of the prediction.

It is vain to seek for any physical fulfilment of the prediction. The sublime description transcends anything that is physical or historical, and from this very fact points to the ideal content which is realized in the exaltation of Jesus Christ to be the heavenly temple, the source of instruction, judgment and everlasting peace to the world.

The higher criticism of Zechariah has shown that the section chaps. ix.-xi. belongs to the age of Hezekiah. It differs from the other parts of Zechariah (1) in historical situation, which is in the last days of the northern kingdom; (2) in style and language, especially in its poetical structure and spirit; (3) in its theological conception. There are several important Messianic ideas in this beautiful trimeter poem. These are in many respects presupposed in the corresponding predictions of Isaiah and Micah.[1] It would seem that this section, together with the section chaps. xii.-xiv., by a post-exilic

---

[1] C. H. H. Wright, in his *Zechariah and his Prophecies considered in relation to Modern Criticism*, London 1879, does not succeed in removing the objections to the traditional view. Stade in *Zeitschrift f. alttest. Wissenschaft*, 1882, rightly sees that Zech. xii.-xiv. is post-exilic, but does not sufficiently estimate the differences between this section and the one now under consideration. We cannot enter on the discussion here; see Orelli in *l.c.* p. 251 seq. We put the Messianic predictions in their historical order, and this presents one line of argument for the proper historic situation.

author other than Zechariah, were appended to Zechariah in order to make the four books of the prophets symmetrical in length. The same was the case with the additions to Isaiah.[1] It should always be remembered that the twelve lesser prophets were in ancient times treated as a single book.

II. THE KING OF PEACE.

§ 55. *Zion rejoices at the advent of her king, who comes meek and yet victorious, riding upon the foal of an ass. He has destroyed the weapons of war, and reigns in peace over the earth.*

> " Exult greatly, O daughter of Zion ;
> Shout for joy, O daughter of Jerusalem :
> Lo, thy king cometh to thee :
> Righteous and victorious [2] is he ;
> Lowly, and riding upon an ass,
> Even upon a colt, the foal of an ass.
> And I will cut off the chariot from Ephraim,
> And the horse from Jerusalem,
> And the battle bow will be cut off ;
> And he will speak peace to the nations ;
> And his rule will be from sea to sea,
> And from the River unto the ends of earth."
> —Zech. ix. 9, 10.

This prediction presents the same essential idea as the prophecy just considered, Micah iv. 1–5. The establishment of universal peace is there attributed to the exaltation of the temple, and here it is attributed to the victory of the Messianic king ; but the theme of both predictions

---

[1] See p. 192.

[2] נוֹשָׁע is Niph. part. of ישׁע, save, and is " one saved," *e.g.* by God and hence triumphant, victorious, Isa. xlv. 17 ; Deut. xxxiii. 29. "Having salvation" of the R.V. is hardly correct. The margin, "having victory," is better.

is universal and everlasting peace. It is probable that both pieces came from the same unknown prophet. The king is here presented in somewhat different features from the king of the Psalter.[1] There the glory and power of the king were emphasized. Here the king's humility and righteousness. He rides upon the ass, the animal of peace, because the war - horses have been destroyed. The representation is nearest to that of Ps. lxxii. We have here the original of the representations of Isaiah and Micah.[2]

III. RESTORATION THROUGH THE SEA TROUBLE.

§ 56. *Israel and Judah will be restored from exile to their own land. Jahveh will bring them from Egypt and Assyria by means of great wonders, and they will dwell in the lands of Gilead and Lebanon, and walk in the name of Jahveh.*

This passage continues the previous prophecy, and predicts the restoration of Israel and Judah after exile.

I. "When [3] Jahveh Sabaoth hath visited
  His flock, the house of Judah,
  He will make them as his war-horse [4] in the battle ;
  From him is the corner-stone, from him the tent-pin,
  From him is the battle-bow,
  From him comes forth every oppressor, together.
  And they will become as heroes trampling under foot
  In the mire of the streets, in the battle ;
  And they will fight when [3] Jahveh is with them,

---

[1] Pss. cx., ii., xlv. See §§ 43, 44, 45, **46.**

[2] Isa. ix. 1–7, xi. 1–9 ; Micah v. 2–5.

[3] It is best to take כִּי in both of these cases as having temporal force rather than causal.

[4] סוּס הוֹדוֹ=his majestic horse in the battle, reminds one of the war-horse of Job xxxix. 20. C. H. H. Wright renders state-horse. The context favours war-horse.

And the riders on horses will be put to shame.
And I will strengthen the house of Judah,
And the house of Joseph will I save.

II. And I will restore [1] them, for I have compassion on **them,**
And will becòme as when I did not cast them off :
For I, Jahveh, am their God ; yea, I will answer them.[2]
And Ephraim will become like a hero,
And their heart will rejoice as with wine ;
And their sons will see and be glad ;
Let [3] their heart exult in Jahveh.
I will hiss for them, and I will gather them ;
When I have redeemed them, they will multiply as **they did**
    multiply ; [4]
And I will scatter them [5] among the peoples,
And in the distant parts they will remember **me,**
And live with their sons, and return.

III. And I will restore them from the land of Egypt,
And from Assyria will I gather them ;
And unto the land of Gilead will they come,
And to Lebanon will I bring them ;
And room will not be found for them.
And he will pass through the sea Trouble,[6]
And smite the sea Billows,
And put to shame all the gulfs of the Nile ;
And the pride of Assyria will be brought low,
And the sceptre will depart from Egypt.

---

[1] הוּשְׁבוֹתִים is a composite form which has arisen from a doubt whether it was הוֹשַׁבְתִּים from יָשַׁב or הֲשִׁיבוֹתִים from שׁוּב. The LXX. read the former, and is followed by the margin of R.V. after Gesenius, Hengstenberg, Chambers, *et al.* The Vulgate and Peshitto read the latter, and are followed by Ewald. This is better, as at the beginning of the next strophe.

[2] The וְ used with וְאֶעֱנֵם should be noted. It is the intensive וְ.

[3] יָגֵל is jussive in form and should have a jussive meaning. So C. H. H. Wright properly renders it.

[4] The multiplication of Israel in the future is based upon their multiplication in former days.

[5] This expression reminds us of Hos. i. 6 seq.

[6] Water is a frequent figure of trouble and distress both for individuals and nations, see Ps. lxix. 2 and Isa. xvii. 12.

> And I will strengthen them in Jahveh ;
> And in his name will they walk about, is the utterance of
> Jahveh."   —Zech. x. 3–12.

This is a prediction of an ultimate victory of the house
of Judah and the house of Joseph combined in a struggle
against their common enemies.   Under the leadership of
Jahveh Sabaoth they become heroic, and like the war-
horse trample under foot all who resist them.   Ephraim
is to go into exile and be scattered as seed in distant
parts, in Egypt and Assyria.   He is to pass through the
sea which is called Trouble and Billows, but he will be
restored from Egypt and Assyria and will walk in the
name of Jahveh.[1]

IV. THE REJECTED SHEPHERD.

57. *The good Shepherd, Jahveh, rejects His flock Israel.
He has been estimated by them at the miserable price of a
slave.   These poor wages are rejected, and the Shepherd's
staves, beauty and concord, are broken as a symbol of the
separation.*

The previous context describes the evil shepherds
destroying the flock for their own advantage, and closes
with the resolution of Jahveh to act as the shepherd of

---

[1] This piece is intermediate in its representations between Hosea
on the one side and Isaiah and Micah on the other.   The reference
to the house of Judah and the house of Joseph is after the manner
of Hos. i. 6, 7.   The scattering and multiplication of Israel is like
Hos. i. 4, 10, ii. 23.   The sea Trouble resembles the Vale of the
Troubler of Hos. ii. 15.   On the other hand, the reference to the
northern frontier, Gilead and Lebanon, corresponds with the reference to the land of Zebulun and Naphtali, Perea and district of the
nations, in Isa. ix. 1.   The restoration from Egypt and Assyria
resembles Hos. xi. 10, 11, but it is much nearer Isa. xi. 15, 16.   The
walking in the name of Jahveh resembles Micah iv. 2–5.   It seems
to us that essentially the same historic situation must be at the
basis of these predictions, and that our passage is intermediate
between Hosea and Isaiah.

this most miserable flock, which is about to be led to the slaughter.

I.   "And I took me two staves,
    One I called Beauty,[1]
    And the other I called Concord ;[2]
    And I served as shepherd of the flock,
    And destroyed the three shepherds in one month ;
    And my soul became weary with them,
    And their soul also loathed me.
    And I said, I will not be your shepherd ;
    The one about to die will die,
    And the one to be destroyed will be destroyed,
    And the rest will devour
    Each the flesh of his companion.

II.   And I took my staff Beauty,
    And cut it asunder,
    To break the covenant
    That I had concluded with all peoples.
    And it was broken in that day :
    And the most miserable sheep knew it was so,
    Those who regard me—
    That it was the word of Jahveh.
    And I said unto them,
    If it seem good to you,
    Give me my hire ;
    And if not, leave it.

III.   And they weighed my hire thirty silverlings,
    And Jahveh said unto me,
    Cast it out for the potter :
    The lordly price
    That I am prized at of them.

---

[1] נֹעַם = beauty, loveliness, the endearing name of the relation of the shepherd to the flock. It is purely ideal of what the relation ought to be.

[2] חֹבְלִים is an abstract intensive plural, meaning, concord (so Ewald renders, "*Eintracht*"). It is usually rendered as bands or bonds.   Orelli renders "confederacy."

And I took the thirty silverlings,
And cast it out
In the house of God for the potter.
And I cut asunder my second staff,
The Concord,
To break the brotherhood
Between Judah and Israel." —Zech. xi. 7–14.

This passage is given by the interpreters generally in the prose form. They are led to do so on the theory that we have here a narrative of what the prophet did in obedience to the command. But the entire piece is a poem of the trimeter movement and of the same strophical organization. In fact, it was impossible for the prophet to illustrate the command of Jahveh in symbolic action. He could take the staves and then break them. He might induce some one to give him the thirty silverlings, and then could cast them away. But these are a very small portion of the shepherd's commission. He is to act as shepherd. He cuts off three other shepherds, probably the kings of the time. He is accepted as a shepherd for a season and then afterwards is rejected, and the money is given him as his hire. The shepherd of Israel is Jahveh the King, and can be no one else.[1] This piece involves the coexistence of the two kingdoms of Judah and Israel. It relates to the final ruin of the kingdom of Israel on account of their rejection of the sovereignty of Jahveh. There is a striking resemblance to Hosea in the silverlings, the price of a slave. Hosea gives this as the price paid by Jahveh for Israel when she was redeemed from her bondage as a slave concubine. It is here the price that Israel pays for the care that Jahveh had exercised over them. The staff Beauty is the symbol of the estimation in which Jahveh held His people. It is parallel with the faithful

[1] See C. H. H. Wright in *l.c.* p. 304.

love of Jahveh as represented by Hosea. The staff
Concord is the symbol of the brotherly union between
Israel and Judah. Hosea represents that this brother-
hood will again be recognized in the final restoration.
The same conception recurs in Ezekiel.[1] The rejection
of the shepherd Jahveh, and of the people of Israel by
Jahveh, is similar to the mutual rejection of husband and
wife in Hosea.[2]

ISAIAH.

Isaiah is beyond question the greatest of the Old
Testament prophets. In a prophetic activity extending
through a long period of varied experiences and historical
changes, he has given us one of the grandest monuments
of inspired thought and utterance. Isaiah was a many-
sided man, indeed we might say all-sided, for his peculiarities consist not in individualities of style or thought,
but in that he combines in his fully rounded character
the excellences of all who had gone before him, adopting
and building into the system of his prophecy the best
thoughts of his contemporaries and predecessors, yet with
such an originality and appropriateness of setting that no
one could regard him as a copyist or a plagiarist. " He is
not the especially lyrical prophet, or the especially
elegiacal prophet, or the especially oratorical and horta-
tory prophet, as we should describe a Joel, a Hosea, a
Micah, with whom there is a greater prevalence of some

---

[1] See § 82.
[2] This passage is applied to the betrayal of Jesus by Judas in
Matt. xxvii. 5. Jesus the Messiah is the divine Shepherd, who
was rejected and sold into bondage for this miserable price. The
correspondence, in fact, is not owing to the precision of the prophetic
prediction, but is owing to the correspondence in situation between
the rejected Jahveh of the times of the decay of the northern kingdom
of Israel and the rejected Messiah of the New Testament. The
prophecy of the rejected shepherd is here not direct prophecy but
simply and alone typical.

particular colour; but, just as the subject requires, he has readily at command every different kind of style and every different change of delineation; and it is precisely this that, in point of language, establishes his greatness, as well as in general forms one of his most towering points of excellence. His only fundamental peculiarity is the lofty majestic calmness of his style, proceeding out of the perfect command which he feels that he possesses over his subject-matter." [1]

The prophecies of Isaiah cover a wide range, both as to subject-matter and as to form. His prophecies relate to Israel, and the nations brought into relations with her. They spring up out of the circumstances of the historical present in order to leap forth into the most distant future. No prophet sees more clearly and describes more vividly the Messiah and His times.

The Book of Isaiah is a collection of several groups of prophecies by Isaiah himself, to which have been attached other anonymous prophecies, which are in his spirit and style, from his own times and also from the period of the exile. It is first necessary to eliminate those that reflect the situation of the exile. These recognise that Babylon is the great enemy, and that deliverance from Babylon is the great Messianic blessing; whereas Isaiah is the great prophet of the Assyrian period. The sections to be removed are (1) xiii.–xiv. 23; (2) xxiv.–xxvii.; (3) xxxiv.–xxxv.; (4) the great prophecy contained in chaps. xl.–lxvi. It seems that these anonymous prophecies were gathered about the name of Isaiah as the sentences of wisdom were grouped about the name of Solomon, the psalms about the name of David, and the laws about the name of Moses. These pieces differ from the writings of Isaiah in style, historic situation, theology

[1] Ewald, *Die Propheten des alten Bundes,* i. p. 280, Göttingen 1867–68.

and conception, although they resemble him in spirit, and appropriate not a few of his ideas.[1]

Limiting ourselves to the genuine prophecies of Isaiah, they may be arranged in three groups. (1) Chaps. i–xii. These relate to divine judgments upon Judah and Israel. There were two successive editings of this group by Isaiah or his disciples. Chaps. ii.–v. were first published, and then the larger collection. Chaps. vi.–xii. were appended, and chap. i. was made the introduction to the whole. (2) Chaps. xiv. 24–xxiii. This is a group of messages against the surrounding nations: Philistia, Moab, Damascus, Israel, Ethiopia, Egypt, Babylon, Edom, Arabia, Tyre and the valley of vision (Jerusalem). (3) Chaps. xxviii.–xxxiii. give a group of woes upon Israel and Judah in view of certain definite transgressions.[2]

In the first group of the prophecies of Isaiah there

---

[1] The unity of Isaiah is still stoutly defended by many scholars, who prefer to adhere to the traditional view with all its difficulties, rather than follow the methods of the higher criticism, and accept its results. The same essential principles are involved in the literary analysis of Isaiah as in the literary analysis of the Pentateuch, the Psalter, and the Book of Proverbs and the Wisdom literature generally. Tradition has ascribed these groups of writings to the four greatest names in Hebrew literary history. But literary and historical criticism in all these cases has disclosed groups of writings of different authors and different times. This literary analysis has disturbed many traditional opinions that seem to have had no other origin than pure conjecture ; but it has enabled us to understand the historic origin of the several writings, has given the key to their correct interpretation, and has shown the wondrous variety of form and content in Hebrew literature. The development of the inspired literature and theology is now beginning to disclose itself with a wealth of meaning which was unknown to those who in an uncritical age imposed their conjectures upon the word of God, and which escapes those who allow themselves to be blinded by these human conjectures and traditions to the real facts and truths of the Scriptures themselves. We have no space here to discuss the question. We shall arrange the writings in their historic order, and let the development of the Messianic idea give its own testimony. See especially Chap. X.

[2] See W. R. Smith, *Prophets of Israel*, p. 210 seq.

is a considerable amount of Messianic material. The first prediction is a quotation from the older prophet that we have already considered [1] with the concluding exhortation—

> "O house of Israel, come ye,
> And let us walk in the light of Jahveh." —Isa. ii. 5.

The Messianic idea of Isaiah is first opened up in Chap. IV.

V. PURIFICATION OF ZION.

§ 58. *Jahveh will come to refine and purify His people, so that the remnant will become holy and blessed. The land will become wonderfully fruitful, and it will be protected by the abiding presence of Jahveh.*

> "In that day the sprout of Jahveh will become splendid and glorious,
> And the fruit of the land will become majestic and illustrious for the rescued of Israel.
> And it will come to pass, that, as for the residue in Zion, and the remainder in Jerusalem,
> They will be called holy,[2] — all who are inscribed unto life in Jerusalem.
> When *Adonay* shall have washed away the filth of the daughters of Zion,
> And the blood of Jerusalem shall put away [3] from her midst by the spirit of judgment, and by the spirit of burning.
> Jahveh will create[4] upon all the established places of Mount Zion, and upon her places of convocation,
> A cloud by day, and smoke and brightness of flame of fire by night :

---

[1] See § 54.

[2] יאמר לך belongs to the style of Hosea, Isaiah, and the great prophet of the exile, instead of the usual יקרא לך. See xix. 18.

[3] דוח for the usual נדח, used only here, Jer. li. 34, Ezek. xl. 38, and 2 Chron. iv. 6.

[4] ברא, a strong word, seldom used in pre-exilic literature.

For upon all the glory a canopy and a pavilion[1] will appear
For a shade by day from heat, and for a refuge and shelter[2] from
    storm and from rain."   —Isa. iv. 2–6.

This prediction is of great importance. It really
opens up two new phases of the Messianic idea. It
lays stress upon the discipline of the people of God
themselves, and also upon a holy remnant to be redeemed
from the fiery trials about to destroy the nation as a
whole. A new line is opened for the doctrine of the
advent of Jahveh. There is a judgment, not upon the
nations as in Joel,[3] but upon perverse Israel after the
manner of Hosea.[4] Israel is disciplined and then
restored. The restoration is through a fiery trial. It is
for the washing away of filth in order to purity, beauty
and holiness. The blessings of the advent are (1)
wonderful fruitfulness of the holy land, usually associated with the divine advent;[5] (2) the purity and
holiness of the people of God, a favourite conception
of Isaiah, which is dwelt upon in subsequent prophecy;
(3) Jahveh dwelling with His people for ever. This
conception is always associated with the advent of
Jahveh. Here, however, the symbolism is taken from
the history of the exodus.[6] The pillar of cloud and

---

[1] סֻכָּה, for the dwelling-place of God, Ps. xviii. 2.

מִסְתּוֹר, a late word, only here for סֵתֶר. We would expect לַיְלָה
over against יוֹם, but it was omitted probably in order to doubling
the epithets.

[3] See § 51.   [4] See § 53.

[5] There has been some dispute as to the meaning of "Sprout of
Jahveh;" some refer it to the Messianic shoot of Isa. xi. 1, Jer.
xxiii. 5, and Zech. iii. 8, vi. 12; but the shoot in these cases is the
shoot of David and from the stump of Jesse. Here the shoot is the
shoot of Jahveh. The parallelism "fruit of the land" favours the
reference of "Sprout of Jahveh" to the sprouting forth of the land
under the reviving influence of Jahveh, as is usual in predictions
of the divine advent. The representation would then be essentially
the same as Joel iii. 18 and Hos. ii. 22.

[6] Ex. xiv. 19 seq.

fire [1] is to be renewed. A divine canopy will protect Israel from all harm.

VI. IMMANUEL.

§ 59. *A wonderful child will be born of a young woman, and be named Immanuel. He is the sign and pledge that Jahveh is with His people, and that He will deliver them. Distress will continue in the land until His maturity.*

The invasion of Judah by the allied Syrians and Israelites, and the great distress resulting therefrom, were the occasion of the prediction of the wonderful child Immanuel. Ahaz the king of Judah is challenged by the prophet Isaiah to ask a sign from Jahveh, with the range of choice from Sheol to heaven. When he declines to ask, a sign is promised by Jahveh Himself.

"Hear now, O house of David ; Is it too little for you to weary men, that you should weary my God also ? Therefore Jahveh [2] Himself will give you a sign ; Lo, young woman, [3] thou art pregnant,

---

[1] See § 51.

[2] הוא is emphatic = himself. Some MSS., followed by Lowth and Cheyne, read יהוה for אדני. The divine name seems unnecessary.

[3] העלמה is a young, marriageable woman, whether virgin or not. בתולה is the usual word for virgin and אשה for wife, but עלמה may be either. The article is taken by some as designed to point out the woman as a distinct and conspicuous one. But then the question arises, What woman ? Some then think of the wife of the prophet on the ground that his children were appointed to be signs to Israel (Isa. viii. 18). Ewald takes the article as generic ; but there seems to be no propriety for such a usage here. It is better to take the article as the sign of the vocative, *O thou young woman.* This is favoured by the קראת, which is pointed as 2 fem. And it is thus rendered by LXX. Aquilla and Symmachus. קראת is taken by Gesen. § 74. 1 ; Ewald, § 194 ; Delitzsch, *et al.*, as a secondary form of the 3 fem. for the usual קראה. But this is improbable. If it were pointed קָרָאתָ, it might refer to Ahaz as subject ; but that is

and about to bear a son, and call his name Immanuel.[1] Curds and honey will he eat at [2] the time of his knowing to refuse [3] evil and choose good. For before the boy knows to refuse evil and choose good, the land, because of whose two kings thou art anxious, will be abandoned."—Isa. vii. 13–17.

Under the solemn circumstances of this prediction one would expect something more than the birth of a child in the family of Ahaz or of Isaiah, or in some unknown household. The significance of the sign is in the child and his name, and not in the mother. The Hebrew word might mean a virgin, but it does not in itself convey the idea of virginity. If the prophet wished to emphasize virginity, he would doubtless have used another and a more definite term. The child bears the significant name *Immanuel, 'El is with us.*

The child is a sign or pledge that God is with His people. It was not so much to convince Ahaz that the predicted events would surely follow in the captivity of Syria and Samaria by the Assyrians, with the desolation of the land of Judah ; but rather that, in the midst of these calamities, God would abide with His people. The child is not represented as the incarnate God, but as the pledge of the divine deliverance. The deliverance was

unlikely. The Syriac and N. T. citation translate as if they read קְרָא. Prof. Toy prefers the participle קֹרֵאת in accordance with יֹלֶדֶת. This is better if the subject is to be the 3 fem. But we should then have three participles in co-ordination.

[1] עִמָּנוּ אֵל is compounded of אֵל, the divine name, and עִמָּנוּ = with us, and thus the child's name is *'El is with us.* It does not affirm the divinity of the child, but that the child bears this name as the sign or pledge of the divine presence. Indeed חִזְקִיָּהוּ = strength of Jahveh, is a similar use of the divine name. If Hezekiah were not too old, he might be regarded as in the mind of the prophet at the time.

[2] לְדַעְתּוֹ. The לְ denotes the point of time, Ewald, § 217*d*, 2 ; Lowth, Delitzsch, Diestel, Cheyne, *et al.* It can hardly express purpose here.

[3] מָאוֹס and בָּחוֹר. These infinitives absolute are used for the classic infins. construct, a usage which begins with Isaiah.

not to be wrought at the birth of the child, for the infancy was to pass in hardship. He would be compelled to live upon curds and honey, the products of a land that had become a wilderness, a place for shepherds and their flocks. The affliction of the land was to continue until the maturity of Immanuel. This pledge was given in a period of impending distress. It remained a predicted pledge until the birth of the Messiah. There is no reason why we should seek a fulfilment of the sign in the time of Ahaz. It is a sign which was expressly assigned to the future. It matters little whether the prophet or his hearers looked for a speedy fulfilment. It was not for them to measure the times and intervals of the divine plan of redemption. If they looked for the birth of such a son in the time of Ahaz or Hezekiah, they were disappointed. There is no historical evidence of any such birth or of any such child. The names assigned to the children of the prophet are plain enough, but there is no connection of this name with any of his children. If, however, any one should prefer to think that a child of the prophet or the royal house bore this name as a sign, the prediction would then become typical and cease to be direct prediction, but the Messianic idea would not be lost. This Immanuel would be a type of the great Immanuel, just as David and Moses and Solomon and others have been such types of the Messiah.

The passage is a Messianic passage, and the prelude to the predictions of the Messianic king which follow in Isaiah and in Micah. Isaiah subsequently gives the child to be born many sacred names ; and Micah points to the mother in Bethlehem.[1] The affliction from the Syrians was followed by an Assyrian period of affliction. The Assyrian was followed by the Babylonian, the Babylonian by the Greek, and the Greek by the Roman.

---

[1] Isa. ix. 6, xi. 1 seq. ; Micah v. 3.

These world - powers rose successively to afflict Israel. Isaiah predicts the approach of the Assyrian affliction, he sees no farther. But he projects into the future the divine pledge in the child Immanuel as a comfort to the faithful remnant in Judah. This pledge remained as the abiding prediction of comfort through all the subsequent periods of affliction until the Messiah was born of the Virgin Mary.[1]

VII. THE PRINCE OF PEACE.

§ 60. *A great light was to shine upon the north-eastern frontier of Israel, exalting the people as highly as they had been previously humiliated, as the first of the Israelites to go into exile. A great deliverance will be wrought, transcending that of Gideon in the day of Midian. A child of the house of David will be born, and bear the names, Wonderful Counsellor, Divine Hero, Distributor of Spoils, and Prince of Peace. He will reign on the throne of David in righteousness for ever. All military equipments will be destroyed in order to universal peace.*

The invasion of Israel and the carrying away into captivity of the inhabitants of Galilee and Perèa by Tiglath Pilezer[2] was the historical basis of the prediction of the Prince of Peace. A thick darkness overshadows the land, and the people are plunged into despair; they are the first of the Israelites to go into captivity, and to suffer its deep humiliation. They are accordingly the first to be exalted, and their exaltation will be as high as their humiliation was deep.

"But she who now has trouble will not have gloom.
As the former time brought into contempt the land of Zebulon and
   the land of Naphtali;

---

[1] Matt. i. 21 25.   [2] 2 Kings xv. 29.

The last time will certainly [1] bring to honour the way of the sea,
    beyond Jordan, the district of the nations.
The people that walk in darkness do see a great light :
Those dwelling in a land of dense darkness, light doth shine upon
    them.
Thou hast increased the nation whose joy thou didst not [2] increase :
They rejoice before thee as the joy in the harvest,
According as men exult when they divide spoil.
For the yoke of his burden, and the staff of his shoulder,
The rod of the one oppressing him, thou hast broken off as in the
    day of Midian.
For as regards every piece of armour [3] of the one arming himself
    with clatter, and garment rolled in blood,

---

[1] There is a contrast between an earlier affliction and a later
blessing, in the first line of the strophe. It is then expanded in
the two following lines. It is then still further expanded in the
remainder of the strophe. The movement of the poetry is hexameter.

[2] The R.V. follows the *Qeri* לוֹ, but the A.V. translates the
Kethibh לֹא. The Babylonian codex agrees with the Western codices
here. The Peshitto, Targum, and Saadia agree with the *Qeri;* but
Symmachus and the Vulgate are with the *Kethibh.* The LXX.
renders, τὸ πλεῖστον τοῦ λαοῦ ὁ κατήγαγες ἐν εὐφροσύνῃ σου. The
documentary evidence favours the *Kethibh,* and the Versions are
divided. Following the LXX., several modern critics change the
text to הגיל, Selwyn and Studer, or חגילה, as Krochmal, Robertson
Smith and Cheyne. The *Qeri* is easy; but the לוֹ would be in an
unnatural position, and apparently superfluous to the sense and the
rhythm. If we render, "Whose joy thou didst not increase," as
Hitzig, Reinke, Hengst. *et al.,* we have a contrast which is in accord
with viii. 23. Orelli follows the *Kethibh,* but takes השמחה as
nominative of the clause. The לֹא is the more difficult reading, and
is to be preferred on that account. The three great principles of
textual criticism count for לֹא.

[3] סאון is only found here in Hebrew. The Versions and authorities greatly differ. The LXX. renders στολή, and thinks of a word
like the Syriac *zayno,* from *zayen,* to arm. This is followed by
Hitzig, Reinke, Knobel, Diestel, *et al.* It has the oldest authority
in its favour, and is in accordance with the context. The Peshitto
read it, however, שאון = tumult ; Saadia, the Vulgate and Targum
render in various ways, showing their doubt as to the form. Joseph
Kimchi suggested the meaning *shoe,* after the Aramaic סֵן. This
has been followed by most recent interpreters. We prefer to
follow the LXX.

It will be for burning, the fuel of fire.
For a child is born to us, a son is given to us; and the rule is upon
    his shoulder.
And his name is called Wonderful Counsellor, Divine Hero, Dis-
    tributor of Spoils,[1] Prince of Peace ;
For the increase of his rule and for peace without end upon the
    throne of David and over his kingdom,
To establish it, and to confirm it in justice and righteousness from
    henceforth even for ever.
The zeal of Jahveh Sabaoth will do this."   —Isa. viii. 23–ix. 6.

The prophet sees a great light shining on the north-
eastern frontier of the land which had been the first to
suffer the humiliation of captivity.   This indicates a
great deliverance, which transcends the victory gained by
Gideon over the Midianites in the plain of Jezreel.   The
nation will reap the harvest of victory, and rejoice in the
division of the spoils.   The victory will be so complete that
all the military equipments will be burned up in order
to the establishment of universal peace.   The victory
has been gained by a prince of the house of David.

---

[1] אֲבִי עַד is usually rendered "Everlasting Father," either thinking of the fatherly rule of the Messiah as an everlasting one
(Delitzsch, Cheyne and Orelli), or as attributing a divine attribute
to the Messiah, as the Everlasting One.   Dathe and Chambers take
אָב as a noun of relation as in Arabic, and render, possessor of the
attribute of eternity.   But the Messianic king is not so closely
identified with Jahveh in the development of the idea.   It is best
to take אָב as a noun of relation, and with Hitzig, Knobel, Diestel,
Kayser, Kuenen, et al., think of עַד in the sense of booty, as in
Isa. xxxiii. 23, Gen. xlix. 27, Zeph. iii. 8 ; so that the meaning is,
owner, possessor, or distributor of booty.   This is most suited to the
context, which lays great stress upon the rejoicing in the spoils of
the victory.   It is best suited to the order of the Messianic titles.   The
climax is the Prince of Peace, as parallel with the destruction of the
weapons of war.   This is preceded naturally by Distributor of Booty,
as parallel with the joy in the division of the spoils above.   The rise
in thought is then clear—(1) the Wonderful Counsellor—the planning
of the campaign and the direction of the battle ; (2) the Divine Hero,
the warrior with divine majesty, valour and irresistible power, in
the conflict itself ; (3) the Distributor of Booty after the conflict ;
and (4) the Prince of Peace, in the everlasting reign of the Messiah.

Names of honour are heaped upon him to indicate his glorious part in the conflict. The names are four—(1) He is a *Wonderful Counsellor*. The victory is due to his wise plans and his marvellous skill in conducting the battle. His wisdom in counsel shines like a great light in the land he has delivered. (2) He is a *Divine Hero*, a heroic *'El*. He has proved himself a hero, a valiant warrior and irresistible conqueror. He has displayed godlike prowess. He has carried on the campaign with godlike majesty and glory. He has surpassed the marvellous victory of Gideon. (3) He is a *Distributor of Spoils*. His victory has been so great, that the spoils are vast. He distributes them to his people, and they greatly rejoice in the rich rewards of the victory. (4) He is above all a *Prince of Peace*. The victory has been a decisive one; so decisive, that all the armour has been consumed with fire. There is no further need of weapons. He is to reign as the Prince of Peace, and secure everlasting peace.

This representation of the Prince of Peace is an enlargement of Zech. ix.[1] The destruction of the weapons of war is after the example of Hos. ii.[2] The everlasting reign on the throne of David is in accordance with the royal Messianic Psalms.[3] This Prince of Peace is no other than Jesus Christ.[4]

VIII. THE FRUITFUL SHOOT.

§ 61. *A twig comes forth from the stump of Jesse, a shoot from his roots bears fruit. The sevenfold gifts of the divine Spirit rest upon him, endowing him to fulfil his*

---

[1] See p. 184.   [2] See p. 171.
[3] Ps. ii., cx., and especially lxxii. See pp. 132–140.
[4] The evangelist Matthew sees this great light shining in the ministry of Jesus in Galilee, Matt. iv. 15, 16.

*work of judging the poor with spiritual discernment, and
the wicked with the rod of his mouth.   Girded with righteousness and faithfulness, He establishes universal peace in
the earth, in which the animal kingdom shares.   The
knowledge of Jahveh becomes universal.   The shoot becomes
the standard about which the nati:ns rally.   The strife of
Ephraim and Judah will come to an end.   A great
deliverance from Egypt and Assyria will take place, and
the people of God return to their land on a highway of
redemption.*

The invasion of Judah by the Assyrians was the
occasion of the prediction of the wonderful shoot.   The
Assyrian was the rod of Jahveh's anger.   He continued
to afflict Judah until the nation became a mere stump in
the ground.   Then Assyria, having served the divine
purpose, will perish.   But the stump will put forth a
shoot that will be fruitful and abide for ever.

I. "And a twig will come forth from the stump of Jesse,
    And a shoot from his roots will be fruitful ;
    And the spirit of Jahveh will rest upon him,
    The spirit of wisdom and understanding,
    The spirit of counsel and might,
    The spirit of knowledge and the fear of Jahveh.[1]
    And not according to the sight of his eyes will he judge,
    And not according to the hearing of his ears will he admonish ;
    But he will judge in righteousness the weak,
    And administer equity to the meek of the land,

---

[1] The Massoretic text gives another line here.   But it is doubtful.
Bickell suggests that it has arisen by repetition from the previous
line,—an easy error of a scribe, as is manifest when the lines are
written one above the other—

רוח דעת ויראת יהוה
והריחו ביראת יהוה

If it be retained, it is the Hiph. infin. of רוח, and is to be rendered,
"his scenting," or "smelling, will be of the fear of Jahveh." This use
of the form is unexampled, and Cheyne is probably correct in following Bickell.   The omission of this line makes the strophe consist of
fourteen lines, a very common strophe for trimeters.

And smite the terrible [1] with the sceptre of his mouth,
And with the breath of his lips will he slay the wicked
And righteousness will be the girdle of his loins,
And faithfulness the girdle of his waist.

II. And the wolf will dwell with the lamb,
And the leopard lie down with the kid,
And the calf and young lion and fatling together,
And a little child be leader over them.
And the cow and bear will graze :
Together will their young lie down,
And a lion like the ox will eat straw ;
And a suckling will play over the hole of the asp,
And over the light hole [2] of the great viper [3]
The weaned child will have stretched out his hand. [4]
And they will not harm or destroy
In all my holy mountain.
For the earth will have been filled with knowing [5] Jahveh,
As the waters are covering the sea.

III. And in that day the root of Jesse will appear,
Which is about to stand as a banner of the peoples,
Unto him will nations resort :
And the place of his resting will become glorious.
And it will come to pass in that day,
Adonay will a second time stretch forth his hand,
To get the remnant of his people,

---

[1] Krochmal, Lagarde and Cheyne rightly regard עָרִיץ as the correct reading instead of אֶרֶץ. There seems to be no proper contrast between the earth and the weak, as there is between the meek and wicked. עָרִיץ would be the most suitable word over against the דַּלִּים.

[2] מְאוּרָה is a noun formed by מ from אוּר. It is the place of light, or light hole.

[3] צִפְעוֹנִי is, according to Tristram, the great viper.

[4] חָדָה is only found here. It is probably equivalent to יָדָה, to put out the hand. The perfect tense is singular in this connection. It is explained by Ewald, Böttcher, et al., as an example of the omission of ו consec. of perfect ; by Driver as a prophetic perfect. But it is better to regard it as a future perfect in order to bring out the fact that the child will remain alive and unharmed after doing this daring thing.

[5] דֵּעָה, fem. of דֵּע ; for the proper infin. דַּעַת, see Hab. ii. 14.

Which remain from Asshur,
And from Egypt, and from Pathros, and from Cush,
And from Elam, and from Shinar, and from Hamath ;[1]
And will lift up a banner to the nations,
And collect the outcasts of Israel,
And the dispersed of Israel will he gather
From the four corners of the earth.

IV. And the jealousy of Ephraim will depart,
And the adversaries of Judah will be cut off ;
Ephraim will not be jealous of Judah,
And Judah will not distress Ephraim,
And they will fly upon the shoulders of the Philistines seaward,
Together they will spoil the sons of the East,
Edom and Moab will become a prize of their hand,[2]
And the sons of Ammon will become their subjects,
And Jahveh will put under a ban the tongue of the Egyptian
    sea,
And wave his hand over the river with his violent blast,[3]
And smite it into seven channels,
And cause them to go over dryshod ;
And a highway will be for the remnant of the people who will
    be left from Assyria,
As it was to Israel in the day of his going up from the land of
    Egypt."

The wonderful shoot springs from the stump of Jesse
and becomes exceedingly fruitful ; for he is endowed with
all the graces of the divine Spirit. These graces are
arranged in three pairs, with a single introductory one :
—(1) Wisdom and understanding, the internal compre-

---

[1] ומאיי הים seems to be a later addition. As Cheyne says : "The
fact that איים and איי הים are specially characteristic of chaps.
xl.–lxvi. renders it a little doubtful whether Isaiah himself wrote
the latter phrase in this verse, which indeed seems complete without it. The earliest absolutely certain occurrences of איים are in
Jer. ii. 10, xxxi. 10. Would Isaiah have used איי הים as a technical
phrase in but one passage of his 'occasional prophecies' ?" (ii. p. 147).

[2] משלח only here and Esth. ix. 19, 22. The מ of the object, that
upon which the hand is put, prize. So משמעת, the audience,
1 Chron. xi. 25, hearers, subjects.

[3] עים only here. It is a mistake for עצם. LXX. has ἐν πνεύματι
βιαίῳ ; so Peshitto and Vulgate.

hensive wisdom and the external practical discernment of things; (2) counsel and might, the counsel to devise the plan and direct it, with the external might to carry it into execution; (3) knowledge and the fear of Jahveh, practical personal acquaintance with Jahveh, and the reverential fear of Him which constitutes true religion. These graces of the divine Spirit enable the Messiah to reign in righteousness and peace. His rule is especially to right the wronged, and to relieve the poor and the afflicted. He judges not according to the eye or the ear, but according to the piety and internal character of his subjects.

The result of such a dominion is the establishment of universal peace. The animal kingdom shares in this peace. The enmity between the wild and the domestic animals disappears. The enmity between man and the beasts of prey departs. The enmity between man and the serpent no longer continues. The little child has dominion over the animals, and the babe sports with the serpent. The curse of Eden is transformed into universal blessing. The knowledge of Jahveh covers the earth as the waters cover the sea, so that there is not only universal peace, but universal personal acquaintance with God.

The second section of the prediction relates to the establishment of peace between the nations. The root of Jesse becomes the standard and rallying point. The strife between the northern and southern kingdoms departs. The nations that are not reconciled are reduced to submission or destroyed. Grand highways of redemption are established, and the exodus from Egypt is transcended by an exodus from all lands of the dispersion. The holy land is restored to its destined glory. This prediction is in all respects an expansion of the ideas of Zech. x.[1]

[1] See § 56.

IX. UNION OF EGYPT AND ASSYRIA WITH ISRAEL.

§ 62. *Egypt and Assyria will be united with Israel as the people of God, speaking the holy language and serving Jahveh with altar and sacrifice. Ethiopia and Tyre will consecrate offerings to Jahveh.*

The second section of Isaiah is a group of prophecies against the nations. These were delivered at different times and under various circumstances. There is one striking Messianic prediction in this collection, and two less important predictions. Ethiopia is to send a present unto Jahveh [1] to Mount Zion. And the merchandise of Tyre will be consecrated unto Jahveh.[2] But the most significant prediction is with regard to the two rival world - powers, Egypt and Assyria, who have been the chief enemies of Israel in her history.

"In that day Egypt will become like women, and tremble, and fear because of the lifting up of the hand of Jahveh Sabaoth, which he is about to lift up against them. And the land of Judah will become a consternation to Egypt : [3] every time when one mentions it unto him, they will fear because of the purpose of Jahveh Sabaoth which he purposeth against them.

In that day there will be five cities in the land of Egypt speaking the tongue of Canaan, and swearing allegiance to Jahveh Sabaoth : one of them will be named the city of protection.[4]

---

[1] Isa. xviii. 7.   [2] Isa. xxiii. 18.

[3] חָגָא or חָגָה is only found here. It is kindred with חָגַג = to dance in a circle, and so in Ps. cvii. 27, to reel from drunkenness. Here it is probably the reeling in terror as synonymous with חָרַד and פַּחַד.

[4] עִיר הַהֶרֶס as pointed by the Massoretes means *city of destruction.* So Peshitto, Aquilla, Theodotion, Cheyne, Orelli. The temples and images of false gods are to be torn down and destroyed. However, the Vulgate, Symmachus, Saadia, Talmud, Rashi, Vitringa, Hitzig, Nägelsbach read חֶרֶם = sun, and render, city of the sun = Heliopolis. The LXX. read צֶרֶק = righteousness, and is followed by Geiger. Gesen., Rosenm., Knobel, Ewald read חֶרֶם = well protected, happy, after the Arabic stem. This best suits the context.

In that day there will be an altar for Jahveh in the midst of the land of Egypt, and a pillar [1] at the side of its boundary for Jahveh ; and it will become a sign and witness for Jahveh Sabaoth in the land of Egypt : when they cry unto Jahveh, because of oppressors, that he will send [2] to them saviours, and strive and deliver them. And Jahveh will be known to the Egyptians, and the Egyptians will know Jahveh.

In that day it will come to pass that they will serve with peace-offering and vegetable-offering, and vow vows unto Jahveh and pay them ; and Jahveh will smite Egypt, continually smiting and healing ; and they will return unto Jahveh, and he will be entreated of them, and will heal them.

In that day there will be a highway from Egypt to Assyria, and Assyria will come into Egypt, and Egypt into Assyria, and Egyptians will serve with Assyrians. [3]

In that day Israel will become a third to Egypt and Assyria, a blessing in the midst of the earth, with which [4] Jahveh Sabaoth will have blessed him, saying, Blessed be my people, Egypt, and the work of my hands, Assyria, and my inheritance Israel."—Isa. xix. 16–25.

Egypt was the ancient enemy of Israel from the times of the exodus. Assyria was the great world-power whose supremacy was at this time most to be dreaded. The little kingdom of Judah was distracted by parties which represented the interests of these two great rivals. Judah was on the verge of ruin. But the kingdom of Judah was the kingdom of God, and Jahveh gives the victory. The prophet predicts the overthrow of Egypt and its subsequent redemption. He rises far above the strife of party and the war of nations, and points to that

[1] The מצבה to Jahveh at the boundary is a memorial pillar or pyramid.

[2] וישלח expresses the purpose of the sign. The R.V. disregards the weak ו, and renders as if it were ו consec. of the perfect.

[3] The easiest rendering of את אשור is as the definite accusative, after the LXX., Targ., Peshitto, and Vulgate. But this is so against the context that interpreters generally regard את as the preposition of association with.

[4] אשר can hardly be, forasmuch as, as Cheyne supposes, or, so that (Orelli). It goes back upon ברכה of the previous line, as Ewald interprets it.

golden age in which all strife and war will cease; when
Egypt and Assyria and Israel will all be one people,
sharing the sacred names that are the peculiar inheritance
of Israel. They will worship Jahveh the God of Israel,
and they will all alike speak the sacred language of
Canaan. "Never had the faith of prophet soared so
high, or approached so near to the conception of a
universal religion, set free from every trammel of national
individuality." [1] Such an era never dawned for Assyria
or for Egypt. But these ancient nations were to the
prophet the enemies of the kingdom of God who were
first to be overthrown and then reconciled. They
represent the nations of the world which were eventually
to be incorporated in the kingdom of God. The prediction can never be realized for these nations, because they
have ceased to exist; but it will yet be realized in that
great peace of the world which is the hope of all the
nations of mankind.

X. THE CORNER-STONE OF ZION.

§ 63. *A corner-stone is laid in Zion that is worthy of
all confidence. It will abide firm in the overwhelming
storm.*

The third section of the prophecies of Isaiah opens and
closes with Messianic features. The Assyrian invasion
brings upon Judah the severest affliction. It is like an
overwhelming flood that sweeps away everything in its
pathway. Those who trust in alliances to save them
will be sorely disappointed. There is only one place of
refuge, and that is in the city of God. Its corner-stone
will be made firm and sure amidst all the troubles. It
will prove the only safe reliance.

[1] W. R. Smith, *Prophets of Israel*, p. 336.

"Therefore hear the word of Jahveh, ye men of scorning,
Ye rulers of this people which is in Jerusalem ;
Since ye say, We have concluded a covenant with death,
And with Sheol have made an agreement,[1]
The overflowing scourge when it passeth along[2] will not come
    to us ;
For we have set lies our refuge, and in falsehood have hidden
    ourselves.
Therefore thus saith Adonay Jahveh,
Lo, I am about to lay[3] a foundation stone in Zion, a test stone ;[4]
A precious corner foundation[5] is about to be laid, he who believeth
    will not be ashamed.[6]
And I will set justice for a line, and righteousness for a plummet ;
And hail will sweep away the refuge of lies,
And the secret place of falsehood[7] waters will wash away,
And your covenant with death will be annulled,[8]
And your agreement with Sheol will not stand.
The overflowing scourge when it passeth along,—ye will be trodden
    down by it."

—Isa. xxviii. 14–18.

The conception of the firm abiding corner-stone of
Zion recurs in the later psalm.

---

[1] חֹזֶה is usually taken as equivalent to חָזוּת of ver. 18, and in the
sense suggested by the parallelism, that is, agreement.

[2] The *Qeri* יַעֲבֹר is correct.

[3] יִסַּד implies a relative clause =*I am he who hath ;* but the LXX.
and Vulgate versions read, *I will found.* Hence it is better, with
Stade, Cheyne, *et al.*, to point יֹסֵד.

[4] בֹּחַן is *test* stone, and not *tested* stone.

[5] פִּנַּת יִקְרַת מוּסָד are combined by the construct states into one idea.
מוּסָד is Hoph. part. parallel with יֹסֵד.

[6] Massoretic text reads יָחוּשׁ, *haste away;* but the LXX., Peshitto
and Targum יֵבוֹשׁ, which is better. Cheyne's suggestion, יָמִישׁ = *give
way*, we cannot follow.

[7] It is necessary on account of the contrast with line 6 to supply
שֶׁקֶר, as Cheyne suggests.

[8] וְכֻפַּר is unique here in the sense usually given to it, and בְּרִית is
fem. It is better, with the Targum, Hupf., Wellh., Cheyne, *et al.*, to
read תֻּפַּר (see Jer. xxxiii. 21).

O

> " The stone the builders refused
> Has become the head of the corner ;
> It is from Jahveh this has happened,
> It is wonderful in our eyes." [1]   —Ps. cxviii. 22, 23.

XI. ZION THE CITY OF THE GREAT KING.

§ 64. *Zion will become the quiet abode of Jahveh the glorious judge, warrior, and king, a place of streams where hostile fleets appear only to be shattered and to become the spoil of the people of God.*

The Assyrian troubles deepen the confidence of the prophet and his disciples in Jahveh the great king of Zion. This confidence reaches its climax in Isa. xxxiii. The prophet sees that the storm has rolled away, the invasion has ceased, Zion is safe, Jahveh reigns supreme over all.

> I. " Hear, ye that are far off, what I have done ;
> And know, ye that are near, my might.
> Sinners in Zion do fear ;
> Trembling doth seize the profane.
> Who of us can abide with devouring fire ?
> Who of us can abide with everlasting burnings ?
> One walking in perfect righteousness,[2] and speaking uprightly,
> Refusing the spoil of oppressors,
> Shaking his palms from holding a bribe,
> Shutting his ears from hearing of bloodshed,
> And closing his eyes from seeing evil;
> He will dwell in the heights ;
> The strong places of rocks will be his high place :
> His bread will be given ; his water will be secured.

> II. A king in his beauty thine eyes will behold :
> Will see a land of remote places.
> Thine heart will muse on terror ;

---

[1] These two passages are frequently cited in the New Testament (Matt. xxi. 42 ; Mark xii. 10 ; Luke xx. 17 ; Acts iv. 11 ; Rom. ix. 33, x. 11 ; 1 Pet. ii. 6, 7), and referred to the Messiah Himself.

[2] צדקות is an emphatic plural.

Where is the scribe, where is the weigher?
Where is the counter of the towers?
The people made strong thou wilt not see,
The people of lip too deep to be heard,
Of stammering tongue which cannot be understood.
Behold Zion, the city of our solemnities:
Thine eyes will see Jerusalem a habitation,
A quiet tent that cannot be packed up,[1]
Whose stakes will not be removed for ever,
And none of its cords will be torn away,
Verily [2] Jahveh is there [3] in majesty.

III. We have a place of rivers.
Channels extended on both sides;
Ships of scourging [4] will not sail therein,
And the majestic ship will not sail over it.
For Jahveh is our judge,
Jahveh is our lawgiver,
Jahveh is our king,
He will save us.
Thy ropes have broken in pieces; they cannot repair them,
The base of the mast [5]—they do not spread the flag.
Then the booty of prey was divided in abundance,
The lame have preyed upon prey.
The inhabitant will not say, I am sick,
The people who dwell therein are forgiven their iniquity."

—Isa. xxxiii. 13–24.

---

[1] צֵעָן is used only here. It means to pack up for a journey.

[2] כִּי אִם is not *but*, as Cheyne, *et al.* It is strong asseveration, as Prov. xxiii. 18. (See Delitzsch on this passage.)

[3] שָׁם of the Massoretic text is suited to the previous context; but שֶׁם of LXX. and Peshitto is more suited to the following context, and is followed by Lowth. We adhere to the Massoretic text, but attach לָנוּ to the following line, which begins the next strophe.

[4] שִׁיט has the same meaning here as in xxviii. 15.

[5] We cannot agree with Delitzsch, Cheyne, *et al.*, that the ship is here Zion, over against the ships of the Assyrian, for the representation is rather of a shipwreck than of a victorious ship. It would not accord with the previous representation of the glory and security of Zion under the dominion of Jahveh. The feminine suffix is entirely appropriate as a lively direct address to Assyria. And then the appropriation of the spoil is entirely suited to the wrecking of the attacking ships.

This passage is an enlargement and development of the prediction of Isa. iv.[1] The passage begins with a description of the true citizen of Zion.[2] Such an one will see the king clothed in his beauty, and will enjoy the happy land of the promise. All unrighteousness of speech and behaviour will be banished from the land. Zion will be a quiet abode, a tent whose cords and stakes will be immoveable; a place of streams and broad channels, like the great cities of the Nile and the Euphrates. But no hostile ships will appear therein. They will be broken up and become the prey of the inhabitants of Zion. Its streams are streams of peace and salvation. Jahveh, the glorious king, warrior, and judge, reigns in Zion, supreme over all.[3] "The record of the prophet's work closes with the triumphant strains of the thirty-third chapter, written perhaps before the catastrophe of Sennacherib, but after the result was already a prophetic certainty, because Judah had at length bent its heart to obedience to Jehovah's word. In this most beautiful of all Isaiah's discourses the long conflict of Israel's sin with Jehovah's righteousness is left behind; peace, forgiveness, and holy joy breathe in every verse, and the dark colours of present and past distress serve only as a foil to the assured felicity that is ready to dawn on Jehovah's land."[4] This splendid ideal seems to the prophet impending after the destruction of the Assyrian invaders; but it is an ideal that still awaits realization in Him who is at once the Son of David and the Son of God, in that glorious time when His reign of peace and righteousness shall have attained its fruition at the end of the age.

---

[1] See p. 193.
[2] This is a variation of Pss. xv. and xxiv. 3–6.
[3] The stream of Zion is another form of the river of God of Joel iii. 18. See p. 158.
[4] W. R. Smith, *Prophets of Israel*, p. 354.

There are two psalms of the Korahite Psalter which describe the glories of Zion as the city of the great king. These descriptions are ideal and not real. Like Isa. xxxiii., they give a picture of what Zion is to be after the destruction of the Assyrian invader. We place them in this period because they reflect its historical situation. They have many features of resemblance with Isaiah.[1]

§ 65. *Zion, the city of the great king Jahveh, is the safe abode of the people of God. Its beauty and glory reflect the majesty of God. Jahveh quiets the commotions of the nations, rebukes the rebellious, and reigns over the earth. The weapons of war are destroyed in order to the establishment of universal peace.*

[1] "In this psalm there occur, moreover, very remarkable coincidences, both of thought and expression, with those prophecies of Isaiah which were uttered in prospect of the Assyrian invasion. The prophet had compared the Assyrian army about to come to a mighty river, the Nile or the Euphrates, overflowing its banks, carrying desolation far and wide, rising till it had submerged all but the most prominent objects. The Psalmist employs a like image when he compares the enemies of his country to an angry sea, its waves roaring, and the mountains trembling at the swelling thereof. Isaiah had described the peace and safety of Jerusalem, weak and defenceless as she seemed to all eyes but the eye of Faith, under the emblem of her own gently-flowing stream of Siloam (viii. 6). The poet also sings the praises of that stream, whose channels make glad the city of God. Thus each has recourse to similar metaphors, and each heightens their effect by contrast. Again, the prophet had assured the house of David that it had a better defence than that of chariots and horses; had laughed to scorn the power of the enemy, saying, 'Associate yourselves, and ye shall be broken in pieces . . . take counsel together, and ye shall come to nought . . . for *God is with us*' (*Immanu'El*); and had symbolized the promised deliverance by the birth of the Child, *Immanuel.* The ever-recurring thought of the psalm is, 'God is our refuge and defence;' 'God is in the midst' of the Holy City; Jehovah (God) of Hosts *is with us* (*Immanu*). The burden alike of prophecy and psalm is *Immanuel, God with us.*"—Perowne, *Book of Psalms*, p. 394 seq., 6th ed. 1886.

I. "God is ours,[1] a refuge and strength,
A help in troubles ready to be found ;
Therefore we shall not fear though the earth change,
And though mountains be moved into the heart of the seas ;
Its waters roar,[2]—be troubled,[3]
Mountains shake with the swelling thereof.
Jahveh Sabaoth is with us ;[4]
The God of Jacob is our refuge.

II. A river [5] (there is) whose streams make glad the city of God,
The holy place of the tabernacles of 'Elyon.
God is in her midst ; she cannot be moved :
God will help her at the turn [6] of the morn.
Nations raged—kingdoms were moved ;
Has he uttered his voice, the earth melteth.
Jahveh Sabaoth is with us ;
The God of Jacob is our refuge.

III. Come, behold the doings [7] of Jahveh,
What wonders [8] he hath done in the earth.
He is causing wars to cease unto the ends of earth ;
The bow he breaketh, and cutteth the spear in sunder.[9]
'Be still, and know that I am God :

---

[1] לָנוּ = ours, belonging to us. It is stronger than our God, or our refuge.

[2] יֶהֱמוּ is concessive, carrying on the construct infinitive.

[3] חמר = boil, ferment, swell, heave, only found here in this sense. It is used of wine in Ps. lxxv. 9 ; and in the Poalal, Lam. i. 20, ii. 11 ; and Job xvi. 16.

[4] The refrain at the close of this strophe has been omitted, and it should be restored, as occasionally elsewhere in Hebrew poetry.

[5] נהר is emphatic in position, in strong contrast to the swelling, raging sea.

[6] לִפְנוֹת = at the turning of the morning, towards morning after the night of trouble. Comp. Pss. xxx. 5, xc. 14.

[7] מִפְעָלוֹת for the older פֹּעַל.

[8] שַׁמּוֹת is taken from Jerome, Calvin, A.V. *et al.* as *desolations* ; by LXX. Peshitto, Hupfeld, Ewald, Perowne, *et al.* as *wonders* or *terrible things.*

[9] The destruction of the instruments of war is, as in Hos. ii. 20 ; Isa. ix. 4. We regard the clause עֲגָלוֹת יִשְׂרֹף בָּאֵשׁ as a later marginal addition that has crept into the text. It is trimeter in the midst of tetrameters, and makes the strophe one line too long.

I shall be exalted among the nations,
I shall be exalted in the earth.'
   Jahveh Sabaoth is with us ;
   The God of Jacob is our refuge." —Ps. xlvi.

Ps. xlviii. describes the glories of Zion as the city of the great King.

I. " Great is Jahveh, and highly to be praised,
 In the city of our God, his holy mount.
 Beautiful in elevation, the joy of the whole earth is Mount Zion,
 On the northern side,[1] the city of the great king.
 God in her palaces is known for a refuge.
 For, lo, the kings assembled,[2] they passed by together ;
 They saw, so they were amazed ; they were dismayed, they hasted away.
 Trembling seized them, writhing as a woman in travail.
 With the east wind thou breakest the ships of Tarshish.[3]
   As we have heard, so have we seen
   In the city of Jahveh Sabaoth, in the city of our God :
   God establisheth her for ever.[4]

II. We have pondered thy mercy, O God, in the midst of thy temple.
 As is thy name, O God, so is thy praise,
 Unto the ends of the earth thy right hand is full of righteousness.
 Let Mount Zion rejoice, the daughters of Judah exult,
 Because of thy judgments, Jahveh.[5]

---

[1] The northern side of Zion was pre-eminently the city or fortress of the king.

[2] The assembled nations before Jerusalem remind us of the Assyrian army as described by Isa. x. 28–34 and Micah v. 1–6.

[3] The reference to the ships of Tarshish is in accordance with Isa. xxxiii. 21.

[4] These three lines seem to us to be a refrain. It is possible that the single line of refrain at the close of the second strophe should be lengthened by the insertion of the first and second lines of this refrain. The second strophe is just two lines short of the first.

[5] The LXX. version reads יהוה here. It is necessary to insert it for the sake of the rhythm.

Go about Zion, and encircle her, count her towers ;
Set thy mind upon her bulwarks, consider her palaces ;
That ye may tell it to the generation following
That God our God is thus : [1]
　　　　For ever and ever he guideth us." [2]　　　　—Ps. xlviii.

MICAH.

Micah and Isaiah were contemporaries. They are
closely related in their range of ideas and the historical
situation that underlies them. The relation is close and
thoroughgoing, extending through the entire book of
Micah and the genuine predictions of Isaiah. They
were either in the relation of master and pupil or of
bosom friendship. The latter is probably the true
relation, although Isaiah represented the higher classes of
the capital and Micah the rural population.[3] They
co-operated in their work of strengthening the faithful in
Judah in the midst of the storms of disaster that came
upon the nation. Jeremiah represents that Micah
delivered his prophecy in the reign of Hezekiah, and that
he produced a profound impression.[4] This seems to
favour the opinion that Micah's prophetic activity began
a little later than Hezekiah's, for his book of prophecy
in its present form is an organic whole.[5] The Messianic

---

[1] זֶה is emphatic, and means thus and so—*this, e.g.* all that the
psalm has described Jahveh to be.

[2] עַל מוּת is a liturgical term, a shortened form of עַל מוּת לַבֵּן of
Ps. ix. 1. It does not belong to the text. It is rendered by the LXX.
as if it were עֲלָמוֹת, and so parallel with עַד עוֹלָם of the last line of
the refrain of the first strophe. But we have already had עוֹלָם
וָעֶד.

[3] See W. R. Smith, *Prophets of Israel*, p. 288 seq.

[4] Jer. xxvi. 18 refers to the passage Micah iii. 12, which is one
of the most striking predictions in the book.

[5] It is possible that the present book was a reissue of earlier
prophecies by the prophet himself ; that he worked them over and
organized them in their present form.

prediction of Micah rises in three stages in chaps. iv.–v. He first cites the production of an older prophet, that the mountain of the house will be established on the top of the mountains.[1] This was in order to relieve his own prediction, that Jerusalem would become a heap of ruins, and the mountain of the house a forest.[2] The second stage of the prophecy resembles the prediction of Amos.[3] The tower of David has lost its ancient dominion, but it will recover it again. The daughter of Zion is to pass through the pangs of childbirth, and to be treated shamefully by the great ones of the earth. But the mind of Jahveh is that the nations are to be gathered as sheaves of the threshing-floor to be threshed out by the bullock Zion, whose horns are of iron and whose hoofs are brass. There is a mingling of symbols, the shepherd's tower, the daughter of Zion, and the bullock. These combine in representing that although Zion may be conquered for a little season, she is ultimately to triumph over all.[4] The highest stage of the prediction is reached in the representation of the Ruler from Bethlehem.

XII. THE RULER FROM BETHLEHEM.

§ 66. *A ruler will be born in little Bethlehem who will bear the name of Peace. He will go forth to fulfil the ancient promises, and become great unto the ends of the earth.*

> " And thou, Bethlehem Ephrathah,[5]
> Little to be among the thousands of Judah,
> Out of thee [6] will come forth for me

---

[1] See p. 181. [2] Micah iii. 21.
[3] See p. 161. [4] Micah iv. 8–13.

[5] אפרתה takes the place of the flock tower of the second section of the prediction, and the mountain of the house of the first section. It is a synonym of Bethlehem.

[6] ממך is emphatic in position. The subject is not expressed. It is indefinite, to be defined by the following משל.

One who is to become ruler in Israel ;
Whose goings forth are from of old, from ancient days.[1]
Therefore he will give them up,
Until the time that one which travaileth [2] has brought forth :
Then the residue of his brethren will return,
Together with [3] the children of Israel.
And he will stand and act as shepherd in the strength of Jahveh,
In the majesty of the name of Jahveh his God ;
And they will abide,[4] for now he will become great
Unto the ends of the earth.
And this one will be Peace." [5]

—Micah v. 1–4.

The prophet sees Zion in great straits. She is besieged and captured. Her ruler is treated shamefully. The line of David returns to the original home of the family at Bethlehem. Thence the royal house had issued from a shepherd life to be the shepherds of Israel. Thither they have returned, and thence they will reissue in Messianic times. The prophet conceives of the restoration of the ruined house of David as in the prediction of Amos,[6] only he uses as a symbol the history of the elevation of David to the throne. The ancient promises will be fulfilled. The ideal king of the Davidic covenant[7]

---

[1] מוצאתיו is parallel with יצא, and therefore מקדם is parallel with ממך. Only the former denote temporal origin, the latter local origin. The reference is not to the eternal generation of the Messiah, as some have hastily supposed, misled by the New Testament doctrine of the Son of God ; but to the ancient promises of the advent as evidences of the ancient purpose of God to raise up the Messiah.

[2] יולדה is the mother of the Messiah, which can hardly be other than personal here. The article is omitted because the mother is emphatically indefinite. We are to think of the same mother as the עלמה of Isa. vii. 14, and the משל is the same as the Prince of Isa. xi.

[3] על־בני = together with, and not unto, as Kleinert, et al.

[4] וישבו. They will dwell, e.g. in safety, as in Micah iv. 4 ; Joel iv. 20 ; Amos ix. 15.

[5] שלום is a name given to the משל. He has the same essential attribute as the king in Zech. ix. 9 and the prince in Isa. ix. 6.

[6] See p. 161.   [7] See p. 126.

cannot fail those who hope for his appearance. He will come forth from little Bethlehem and become a ruler whose dominion will extend to the ends of the earth. The proud invader will be driven back. Under His dominion Israel will become as refreshing dew in the midst of the nations, realizing their everlasting priesthood; and they will ravage their enemies as a lion in the midst of a flock, accomplishing their destiny as the kingdom of God. But the aim of the advent is peace. The ruler from Bethlehem will be Peace. That will be His most characteristic feature and work. And thus our prophet is in accord with Isaiah and the other prophets [1] of the epoch in looking forward through the storms of the time to the realm of peace and the sway of a Prince of Peace.[2]

[1] See pp. 184, 198.

[2] This prediction was cited by the Sanhedrin (Matt. ii. 5 seq.) in response to the inquiry of the Eastern sages where the Messiah was to be born.

CHAPTER VIII.

JEREMIAH AND HIS CONTEMPORARIES.

THE brilliant period of Hezekiah was followed by a sad decline under Manasseh and Amon, which reduced the land so that it could not recover. Josiah, a noble king, attempted a reform, and led the nation in a further advance toward the Mosaic ideal. The Deuteronomic code was brought forth from the neglected temple, sacred psalms again resounded in the house of Jahveh, and holy prophets gathered about the king to encourage him in his work.[1] But this revival separated the pious nucleus from the mass of the people, who declined to follow in the path of progress. The death of the heroic king in a fruitless struggle at the ancient Megiddo brought events to their crisis.[2] The prophets of Jahveh were unable to prevent the reaction which brought in its train the sure ruin of the nation, and severe afflictions to the pious remnant. The great prophet of the age of Josiah was Jeremiah; but he was sustained by lesser prophets, Zephaniah, Habakkuk and others. The earliest of the prophets of this period was Zephaniah, whose prediction was given early in the reign of Josiah.

ZEPHANIAH.

" With the prophet Ssephanya we meet for the first time a considerable diminution of prophetic originality;

---

[1] 2 Kings xxii.; 2 Chron. xxxiv.
[2] 2 Kings xxiii. 29, 30; 2 Chron. xxxv. 20–25.

he repeats a good deal almost verbally from older prophets, and, on the other hand, the style is very ornate
and pointed, ii. 1, 2, iii. 11, 18. What is new is especially
the extended survey of all lands and nations, and the
general review of the spiritual affairs and prospects of
the whole earth, the destruction of Jerusalem being only
incidentally foretold. We see that the small separate
nation, with its ancient national distinctions, must necessarily lose itself more and more in the general life of the
nations of the earth, whilst, nevertheless, the truths which
had lived in it remain the same and gain ever greater
validity in and through all nations." [1]

I. THE GREAT JUDGMENT OF JAHVEH.

§ 67. *Zephaniah predicts that a great and terrible day
of judgment is near upon Judah and Jerusalem and all
nations. But there will be a deliverance of the dispersed
righteous. Israel will again dwell in her land, Jahveh the
Saviour in her midst, rejoicing over her in love. Israel
will be renowned and praised in all the earth, and the
nations, even from the distant parts of Africa, will unite
in the worship of Jahveh.*

It seems that Zephaniah had in mind the Scythian
invaders. Those mysterious hordes from the steppes of
the North filled the inhabitants of Asia with consternation. The prophet sees them as the instruments of the
wrath and judgment of Jahveh for the destruction of the
nations far and near.

"I will utterly consume everything from upon the face of the
    ground ;
The utterance of Jahveh is, I will consume man and beast ;

---

[1] Ewald, *Com. on the Prophets of the O. T.* iii. p. 16, London
1878.

I will consume the birds of heaven and the fish of the sea, and the
stumbling-blocks with the wicked;
And cut off mankind from upon the face of the ground, is the utterance of Jahveh." [1]

This is a strong representation of the utter destruction
of everything. The day of Jahveh is at hand, and
universal ruin is impending. The judgment comes first
upon the idolaters of Jerusalem and Judah. Jahveh
will search Jerusalem with lamps in order to visit them
with punishment.

"Near is the great day of Jahveh, near and greatly hasting.[2]
Hark! the day of Jahveh; the hero is bitterly crying[3] there.
A day of overflowing wrath is that day, a day of distress and
trouble.
A day of waste and wasteness, a day of darkness and gloom,
A day of clouds and thick darkness, a day of the trumpet and alarm,
Against the fenced cities and against the corner towers.
And I will bring distress upon mankind, and they will walk like
the blind,
Because they have sinned against Jahveh;
And their blood will be poured out like dust, and their flesh[4] like
dung.
Neither their silver nor their gold will be able to deliver them, in
the day of the overflowing wrath of Jahveh,
And by the fire of his zeal all the earth will be devoured,
For a completion,[5] yea, a sudden destruction will he make of all the
inhabitants of the earth." —Zeph. i. 14–18.

---

[1] Zeph. i. 2, 3.

[2] מַהֵר is infin. abs. Piel. Knobel takes it as partic. with מ
omitted.

[3] צֹרֵחַ is only found here in Kal, and in Isa. xlii. 13 in the
Hiphil. The cognate languages justify the meaning, cry aloud.

[4] לְחֻמָם is only found here in this sense. It is used in Job xx.
23 and Ps. xi. 6 for *food*.

[5] נבהלה is part. Niph. of בהל, and means, *sudden destruction*.
Comp. נחרצה, Isa. xxviii. 22. כלה is used here in the same sense
as in Isa. xxviii. 22 and Jer. xxx. 11.

In view of this universal judgment, men are called to penitence and seeking Jahveh.

"Gather yourselves together, yea, gather together, O shameless nation,
Before the decree come to the birth, like chaff the day has passed by,
Before the heat of the anger of Jahveh come upon you,
Before the day of the anger of Jahveh come upon you.
Seek ye Jahveh, all the meek of the earth who have wrought his
    judgment ;
Seek righteousness, seek meekness : it may be ye will be hid in the
    day of the anger of Jahveh."   —Zeph. ii. 1–3.

The prophet then describes the destruction of the cities of the Philistines in rapid succession. Moab and Ammon became like Sodom and Gomorrah. The Ethiopians will be slain by the sword. Assyria will be overthrown, and Nineveh become like a desert.

But this judgment has in view a gracious purpose of redemption, and this not only embraces Israel but also the nations.

I. "Therefore wait for me, is the utterance of Jahveh, for the day
    of my rising up for booty : [1]
    For my judgment is to collect nations, that I should gather
        kingdoms ;
    To pour upon them my indignation, all the heat of my anger ;
    For with the fire of my zeal all the earth will be devoured.
    For then I will turn unto [2] the peoples, the lip will be purified,
    That all of them may call on the name of Jahveh, and serve
        him with one shoulder.
    From beyond the rivers of Cush will be my incense ; [3] the
        daughter of Phut will bring a Minchah. [4]

---

[1] Orelli, after the LXX. and Peshitto, reads לְעֵד = to testify. But the Massoretic לְעַד is best sustained.

[2] It is rendered by R.V. "I will turn to the people a pure language," but אל has the force of unto. Jahveh turns unto the people in favour, after the judgment. ברורה is then a participle with verbal force.

[3] עתר, incense, is parallel with מנחה, and cannot be rendered suppliant. Ewald sees the correct meaning and reads פוט = Libya, parallel with Cush, instead of פוץ, which must refer to the dispersed of Israel, and is not in accordance with the context.

[4] For Minchah, see p. 8.

II. In that day thou wilt not[1] be ashamed of all thy deeds wherein
thou hast transgressed against me :

For then I will remove from thy midst thy proudly exulting
ones,

And thou wilt not again be haughty any more in my holy
mountain.

And I will leave over in thy midst a meek and weak people,
and they will seek refuge in the name of Jahveh.

The remnant of Israel will not do iniquity and will not speak
falsehood ;

And there will not be found a deceitful tongue in their mouth;

For they will feed as a flock and lie down, and there will be
none to terrify.

III. Sing, O daughter of Zion, shout for joy, O Israel ;

Rejoice and exult with all thy heart, O daughter of Jerusalem.

Jahveh hath removed thy judgments, hath cleared away thy
enemy :

The King of Israel, Jahveh, is in thy midst ; thou wilt not
fear evil any more.[2]

In that day Jerusalem will be called 'Al-Tira'i ; Zion, 'Al-
yirpu-yadhayikh,[3]

Jahveh thy God is in thy midst, a hero who saveth :

He rejoiceth over thee with joy, renews his love,[4] exults over
thee with singing.

---

[1] The negative לא is difficult, and yet is the best sustained. It
refers to a time when there will be no more shame for sin, because
there will be no more sin. Hitzig would read לֹא, "Mayest thou
be ashamed." This would be more natural. But there is no necessity for forsaking the Massoretic text and the Versions.

[2] The LXX. reads תראי =see, and so many Massoretic MSS., and
these are followed by Henderson, et al. But the Compl. and the
majority of the best Massoretic MSS. read תיראי, and so the
Vulgate. This is best suited to the context.

[3] אל־תראי = Fear not, is a name given to Jerusalem, and
אל־ירפו ידיך =let not thine hands be slack, a name given to Zion, as
Jerusalem is called in Jer. xxxiii. 16, יהוה צדקנו, and in Isa. lxii. 4,
Hephzibah and Beulah.

[4] LXX. and Peshitto read יחדיש, and are followed by Houbigant,
Newcome, Ewald, et al. This is well sustained, and is more suited
to the context than the Massoretic יחריש, be silent, which is followed
by most interpreters.

IV. The afflicted[1] for the place of assembly I have collected. Of
    thee they were, burdened with reproach for her sake.[2]
Lo, I am about to deal with all who afflict thee at that time,
And I will save the halt, and the outcast will I gather,
And make them a praise and a name in all the earth where
    they were shamed.
At that time will I bring you, and at the time will be my
    gathering of you :
For I will make you a name and a praise among all the
    peoples of the earth,
When I restore your prosperity before your eyes, saith
    Jahveh."   —Zeph. iii. 8–20.

This prediction of Zephaniah is remarkable for its
extension of redemption to the nations after the judgment.
It is a further unfolding of Isa. xix. 18–25.[3] As in
Isaiah, Egypt was to speak the language of Canaan, so
here the worship of Jahveh will become universal. All
nations will have their lips purified so as to call upon
the name of Jahveh. The nations that are especially
prominent in this worship, according to the conception
of the prophet, are the distant nations of Africa, the
Ethiopians and the Libyans. These will offer their
incense offerings and their vegetable offerings. This is
similar to the prediction of Isaiah, that there was to be
an altar in the land of Egypt. The universal worship of
Jahveh in Messianic times is represented in the forms of
the ceremonial of the altar and the offerings of the Old
Testament dispensation. This representation is the
clothing of the ideal, and not the ideal itself. For in the

---

[1] נוּגֵי, const. Niph. part. יָנָה=*afflict;* for the usual נוֹגֵי, see Lam.
i. 4 (נּוּגוֹת). Houbigant, Newcome, *et al.* follow the LXX. and read
נוּגַיִךְ=*thy afflicted ones.* מוֹעֵד is taken by LXX., Ewald, Henderson,
et al. as *festival,* as in Lam. i. 4, ii. 6. But it is better to think of
the place of assembling, parallel with Zion.

[2] עָלֶיהָ=*for her sake,* that is, *Zion's* sake. But the Peshitto,
Targum, some Massoretic MSS. read עָלַיִךְ, and these are followed
by Newcome.

[3] See p. 206.

times of the Messiah, universal worship rises above the
local altars and the ceremonial of sacrifice.

The prophet is also remarkable for the tenderness
with which he represents the relation of Israel and
Jahveh.   He advances in the line of Hosea.[1]   The union
is a marriage union.   New names are given in the day of
restoration, and Jahveh rejoices as in a great marriage
festival.   Here we have " one of the boldest, most
wondrous sayings of the Old Testament, which is not
presumptuous only because the seer was vouchsafed a
glimpse into the unfathomable decree of love revealed
in the New Testament." [2]   Israel will no longer be
reproached and afflicted by the nations, but will be
honoured and praised by all the earth.

II. THE ADOPTION OF THE NATIONS IN ZION.

§ 68. *Psalm LXXXVII. describes the adoption of the
nations into the city of God and their enrolment among the
citizens of Zion.*

This in some respects is the most remarkable of the
psalms.   It may be compared with Ps. xlv. and Isa. xix.
18–25 in its attitude to the nations of the world.   But
its outlook is wider even than Zeph. iii. 9, 10.   The
mention of Babylon alongside of Egypt shows that we
have passed from the Assyrian period into the Babylonian.
It is nearer to the representation of Zephaniah, and it is
probable that it belongs to this general period, if not
later.

" His foundation [3] in the holy mountains Jahveh is loving,[4]
  The gates of Zion are better than all the tabernacles of Jacob.

---

[1] See p. 172.   [2] Orelli in *l.c.* p. 321.
[3] יסודתו is only found here for מוסד of Isa. xxviii. 16.
[4] The characteristic tense of this piece is the participle.   It must
be given its classic force, unless we regard the poem as post-exilic,

Glorious things are being spoken in [1] thee, city of God !
I mention Rahab [2] and Babel as belonging to those who know
    me ;
Lo, Philistia and Tyre with Cush : ' This one was born there.'
And as belonging to Zion, it is said,—' This one and that one
    were [3] born in her.'
And 'Elyon, Jahveh—he establisheth her.
He counteth in writing [4] up the peoples,—' this one was born
    there.'
Yea, they are singing as well as dancing all who dwell in thee." [5]

Delitzsch aptly names this psalm " the city of the
regeneration of the nations." [6] Perowne appropriately
says, " Foreign nations are here described, not as captives
or tributaries, not even as doing voluntary homage to the
greatness and glory of Zion, but as actually incorporated
and enrolled, by a new birth, among her sons. Even
the worst enemies of their race, the tyrants and oppressors
of the Jews, Egypt and Babylon, are threatened with no
curse, no shout of joy is raised in the prospect of their
overthrow, but the privileges of citizenship are extended
to them, and they are welcomed as brothers. Nay more,
God Himself receives each one as a child newly born

---

when the participles may represent the other tenses as in Aramaic.
This piece is a pentameter. אהב is correctly attached to the first
line by Hupfeld, Perowne, et al.

   [1] בך may be taken as of thee, with Perowne, R.V. et al. But it
is better, with Hupfeld, to render in thee.

   [2] רחב is a name of Egypt, as in Ps. lxxxix. 11 and Isa. xxx. 7, on
account of her pride, as a sea monster.

   [3] For the thought, compare Isa. xix. 18–25 (see p. 206).

   [4] כתוב is infin. construct as R.V. But Ewald, Hitzig, Delitzsch
follow the LXX. and Targum in regarding כתיב = כתב = book or
writing, for the usual ספר. Jerome renders by participle.

   [5] The LXX. reads κατοικία = מעון. Hupfeld points מעיני.
Böttcher מעיני. The latter is better. Ewald reads מעוני = my arts.
מעיני = fountains, springs, e.g. of life, is retained by Delitzsch, who
puts these words in the mouth of the singers. Perowne regards
them still as words of God. The R.V. also retains this pointing.

   [6] Delitzsch, Psalmen, p. 603.

into His family, acknowledges each as His son, and enrolls him with His own hand in the sacred register of His children."[1]

The representation differs from Ps. xlv., in that there the union with the nations was through the bridal relation established with them by the Messianic king.[2] Here it is a divine adoption into the rank of sonship, and an enrolment in the register of the citizens of Zion. In Isa. xix. 18—25, Egypt and Assyria are united with Israel as the people of God, and share alike the sacred names expressing the covenant relation of Israel to God.[3] Here the still more sacred relation of sonship in the original calling of Israel[4] is extended to them. Israel was then the first-born son of Jahveh, and no other such sons were mentioned. Here Jahveh enrolls many sons in his family, and all distinctions between them have passed away. In Zeph. iii. the nations are purified to worship God with lip and with offerings, and the distant nations of Africa are especially mentioned.[5] Here a family of nations is assembled from all parts, including Babylon and Egypt, Philistia and Ethiopia. In Zeph. iii. Jahveh was represented as reigning over restored Israel. Here the nations who have been assembled in Zion are represented as singing and dancing in celebration of the festival of their adoption and registration and union with one another and with Jahveh.

III. THE RESTORATION OF THE VINE ISRAEL.

§ 69. *The vine Israel has been ravaged by the beasts of the Nile and the Euphrates. Psalm LXXX. is a prayer for restoration, and especially for support to the Messianic son of man, the man of Jahveh's right hand.*

---

[1] Perowne, *Book of Psalms*, ii. p. 133.   [2] See p. 140.
[3] See p. 206.   [4] See p. 100.   [5] See p. 225.

Ps. lxxx. probably belongs to the time of Josiah, when Egypt was the chief enemy of Judah. It has four strophes marked by refrains. The third strophe is a double strophe with a double refrain. The other strophes are of six trimeter lines, with a refrain of two lines.

I. "Shepherd of Israel,[1] O give ear,
   Leader of Joseph like a flock ;
   Enthroned [2] above the cherubim, O shine forth.[3]
   Before Ephraim, and Benjamin, and Manasseh,[4]
   O stir up thy strength,
   And O come for salvation to us.
     Elohim,[5] restore us,
     And let thy face shine that we may be saved.

II. Jahveh, Elohim, Sabaoth.
   How long dost thou smoke [6] during [7] the prayer of thy people ?

---

[1] This is a reminiscence of Gen. xlix. 24. It is a favourite term of the Psalms of Asaph. Comp. Pss. lxxiv. 1, lxxviii. 52, lxxix. 13, and also the group xcv.–c.

[2] ישב is pregnant = *enthroned*, as the cherubim are here conceived as constituting the throne of Jahveh, as in the tabernacle and the temple.

[3] הופיעה. This is a favourite idea of the Psalter of Asaph. See Ps. l. 2 ; Deut. xxxiii. 2 ; Ps. lxxxiv. 11.

[4] The exclusive mention of the tribes in Middle Palestine may be accounted for from that part of the blessing of Jacob upon which the psalm is based. Perowne thinks of their association in the order of the march from Sinai (Num. ii. 17–24). It may also be from the feeling that Judah in her present crisis needs the aid of these tribes. If the psalm was written after the exile of these tribes, there still remained powerful remnants in the time of Josiah. And these might be stirred up to espouse the cause of the national God in the revival of the time of the heroic Josiah.

[5] The refrains of the three strophes differ only in the divine names, which increase from אלהים to אלהים צבאות in the second refrain, and יהוה אלהים צבאות in the fourth. The third refrain uses the same divine names as the second refrain, but heaps up imperatives of supplication.

[6] עשן is the smoking of the nostrils in anger. Comp. Pss. xviii. 8, lxxiv. 1.

[7] בתפלת. The ב can hardly express hostility. It has rather temporal force, *in the time of, during.*

Thou hast given them the bread of tears [1] to eat,
And hast given them to drink out of tears as a measure ; [2]
Thou settest us as a strife to our neighbours,
And our enemies are mocking at us.[3]

    Elohim, Sabaoth restore us,
    And let thy face shine that we may be saved.

III. A vine out of Egypt [4] thou removest,
Thou dravest out nations and so [5] didst plant it ;
Thou didst clear away before it, and cause it to take root,
And the land was filled with its roots.[6]
The mountains were covered with its shadow,
And the cedars of 'El [7] with its boughs.
It put forth its branches unto the sea,
And unto the river its shoots.
Why hast thou broken down its hedges,
So that all the passers-by are plucking it ? [8]

---

[1] לחם דמעה. Comp. Ps. xlii. 3 ; Job iii. 24 ; Lam. iii. 15.

[2] בדמעות. ב is used in a local sense. The tears constitute the cup out of which the Psalmist drinks. The Hebrew says: drink *in* a cup, where we would say : drink *out of* a cup. We might give ב an instrumental force. As we say feed *with* food, the thirst might be satisfied *with tears*. The latter view forces us to regard שליש as adverbial, as LXX. ἐν μέτρῳ. In the other case it is taken as in apposition, a third measure.

[3] למו should be לנו, as LXX. and Vulgate gave it. So Ewald *et al.* A.V. and R.V. have wrongly followed the Massoretic texts.

[4] This allegory of the vine is based upon the blessing of Joseph, even in its phraseology (see p. 97).

[5] ותמעה. The ו consec. expresses result.

[6] We transpose ותמלא with שרשיה on account of the rhythm.

[7] ארזי אל as in הררי אל, Ps. xxxvi. 7. Hupfeld thinks that the idea that the cedars of Lebanon were covered by the boughs of this vine is too enormous a figure, and insists upon the particle of comparison. "Its boughs are *as* those of the cedars of God ;" so A.V. and R.V. But the margin of R.V. gives it correctly after most critics. The parallelism is decidedly for it, and such enormous figures are not unusual in Hebrew poetry. See Micah iv. 1 ; Ezek. xvii. 22. See p. 50.

[8] אָרוּהָ is a rare form, only found here. It is ו consec. perfect, expressing the frequentative imperfect.

The boar out of the forest [1] is ravaging it,[2]
And the beast [3] of the fields is feeding on it.
Elohim, Sabaoth turn now, look from heaven,
See and visit this vine ; [4]
And protect [5] *that which thy right hand planted,*
And be over the branch [6] *thou hast strengthened for thyself.*

IV. It is burnt with fire, it is cut down,[7]
At the rebuke of thy face let them perish.
Let thy hand be over the man of thy right hand,
Upon the son of man thou hast strengthened for thyself :
And we will not depart from thee :—
Quicken us, and on thy name we will call.
Jahveh, Elohim, Sabaoth restore us,
Let thy face shine that we may be saved."

This psalm uses the symbol of the vine to set forth the original planting in the holy land, the present evil condition of affairs and the future restoration. The symbol was taken from the blessing of Jacob, and the

---

[1] יער, with suspended ע, is probably for יאר, as Hupfeld, Grätz, *et al.*, referring to the Nile, and thereby indicating that Egypt is the river swine, the hippopotamus who is ravaging Israel. This would put the psalm in the time of Josiah, as the only period in the history of Israel subsequent to the exodus when Egypt was the chief enemy, except for the brief period in the reign of Rehoboam.

[2] יכרסמנה—a quadriliteral for כסם, only found here. Comp. for the idea, Ps. lxxxix. 40, 41.

[3] זיז = full-breasted beast. See Ps. l. 11, where alone elsewhere it has this sense. These animals from the forest probably refer to the Edomites, Moabites, and other nations on the east of the Jordan.

[4] The Psalmist heaps up the synonymous ראה הבט שוב and פקד.

[5] וכנה. If this pointing be correct, it is an unusual form of the cohort.-imperative כנן for כנה. In this case it would be better to regard the pointing as incorrect. The A.V. and R.V. follow the chief Versions, except LXX., and regard it as a feminine noun, like כן, with the meaning, *stock, stem.* Gratz would read גנה, garden. The context favours the imperative, and Perowne rightly adopts it.

[6] בן is used, after Gen. xlix. 22, as shoot.

[7] כסוחה fem. pass. part. כסח, an Aramaic word, only here and Isa. xxxiii. 12 in Hebrew.

Psalmist makes free use of the original representation.
But there are two Messianic psalms in his mind. The
term "son of man" was derived from the ideal man of
Psalm viii. and the "man of thy right hand" from the
conquering king of Psalm cx.[1] These two Messianic terms
are combined in their reference to the Messianic head of
Israel, who is to be the object of the divine favour in the
times of the restoration. The Messiah is here viewed as
the head of a redeemed people rather than as himself
their Saviour. The divine advent assumes the most important position in the Messianic idea even when the
Messianic head of the nation is brought into view.
Redemption is in the shining forth of the divine glory
from Zion. In this is the hope of Israel.

HABAKKUK.

The prophet Habakkuk belongs to the Babylonian
period. He issued his prophecy somewhat later than
Zephaniah, probably in the reign of Jehoiakin. "Great
as Habaqqûq is in thought, he is no less so in language
and literary skill; he is the last prophet belonging to
the age preceding the destruction of Jerusalem who is
master of a beautiful style, of powerful description, and
an artistic power that enlivens and orders everything with
charming effect. We are still able to admire in him the
genuine type and full beauty of ancient Hebrew prophecy; he is its last pure light, and although he already
reproduces much from older books, he still maintains
complete independence."[2]

Habakkuk complains to Jahveh, and calls upon the
everlasting and holy God to look upon the evil that the
Chaldeans are doing in their invasion, and to visit them

---

[1] See pp. 132 seq., 178 seq.
[2] Ewald, *Prophets*, English edition, iii. p. 32.

with punishment. Jahveh responds to this complaint with a grand representation of the just complaints of the nations against the greedy and unscrupulous kingdom. This response is introduced by a striking contrast between the wicked kingdom and the righteous people of God.

> "Behold a puffed up person, his soul is not upright in him ;
> But a righteous man, by his faithfulness will he live." [1]

This gives the assurance that the faithful, righteous people of Israel will live when the proud oppressor will come to ruin. This piece concludes with an assurance of the powerful presence of Jahveh Himself.

> "Jahveh is in his holy temple :
> Be silent before him, all the earth." [2]

In the midst of the complaint of the nations the prophet quotes a prediction from Isa. xi.

> "Woe to the one building a city with bloodshed,
> And establishing a town with iniquity !
> Behold, is it not from Jahveh Sabaoth
> That the peoples toil for the fire,
> And the nations in vain become weary ?
> For the earth will be filled,
> With knowing the glory of Jahveh,
> As the waters cover over the sea." [3]

The prophet concludes with a sublime representation of the advent of Jahveh for judgment and salvation.

IV. THE ADVENT OF JAHVEH IN GLORY.

§ 70. *Habakkuk describes the advent of Jahveh for the redemption of his people and the destruction of their enemies.*

---

[1] Hab. ii. 4.   [2] Hab. ii. 20.
[3] Hab. ii. 12–14. The last verse is clearly a use of the older Isaiah xi. 9. Hab. uses תמלא for the מלאה of Isaiah, לדעת for דעה, inserts כבוד before יהוה, and uses יכסו על ים for לים מכסים ; but there is no change in the idea.

I. "Jahveh, I have heard the report of thee,
        I fear, Jahveh, thy work.[1]
        In the midst of the years revive him,[2]
        In the midst of the years make known,
        In rage remember compassion.

II Eloah cometh from Teman,
        And the Holy One from Mount Paran,[3]
        His splendour doth cover the heavens,
        And the earth is filled with his renown,
        And brightness appeareth [4] like the light,
        He has rays [5] of light (coming forth) from his hands,
        And he makes [6] a hiding of his splendour.

III. Before him goeth pestilence,
        And fever goeth forth at his feet;[7]
        He doth stand and measure [8] the earth,
        He doth see and shake the nations.
        Then the everlasting mountains are scattered,
        The eternal hills sink down.
        The ancient ways [9] are his.

IV. In trouble I see the tents of Cush,
        The curtains of Midian's land are trembling.
        Is it against rivers it doth burn, Jahveh?
        Or against rivers is thine anger,

---

[1] We arrange the lines in accordance with the parallelism. פעלך is Jahveh's work in theophany, His judgment, especially as in ver. 16, the cause of fear to the Psalmist.

[2] חייהו. The suffix refers to Israel and not the work.

[3] These are the places of theophany in Deut. xxxiii. 2 and Judg. v. 4.

[4] תהיה has here the meaning, become, *appear*.

[5] קרנים = horns or rays of light, as in Ex. xxxiv. 29, 30.

[6] שם = there, is the Massoretic reading followed by Jerome and R.V. The verb שם of the LXX. Aquilla, Sym. and Peshitto is followed by Hitzig, and is the better reading.

[7] לרגליו, at his feet, after him in his steps.

[8] וימדד is taken as Poel of מדד = measure, by Vulgate, Kimchi, Steiner, *et al.* It is derived from מוד = מוט = totter, waver, by LXX., Targ., Delitzsch, Ewald, *et al.*

[9] הליכות = ways, as in Prov. xxxi. 27.

Or against the sea thine overflowing wrath,
That thou ridest upon thy horses,[1]
Thy chariots—for salvation ?[2]

V. Thy bow is made entirely bare ;
Sworn are the rods of thy word.
Thou cleavest streams to the earth.
Have they seen thee, the mountains writhe,
A flood of waters doth overflow,
A great deep doth utter its voice,
On high it doth lift its hands.

VI. Sun and moon stand in their boundary ;
In the light of thine arrows they move,[3]
At the shining of thy lightning-spear.
With indignation thou marchest through the earth,
With anger thou threshest the nations ;
Thou dost go forth for the salvation of thy people,
For the salvation of [4] thine anointed.

VII. Thou dost dash in pieces the chief away from the house of
the wicked,
Laying bare the foundation to the neck.
Thou dost pierce with his rods the chief,[5]
When his rulers [6] are rushing in to scatter me.
Their exaltation is as it were to devour the afflicted in secret.
Thou dost tread on the sea,
With thy horses, the foam of many waters.

---

[1] The horses of Jahveh are to be compared with the cherubic chariot of Ps. xviii. 10.

[2] ישועה is usually taken as the absolute of the previous מרכבתיך. But it is better to regard it as the accusative of purpose or of direction.

[3] יהלכו is taken by some as a relative clause. But it is better to think of the movement of the sun and moon in the light of the arrows of the lightnings, over against the standing still of the sun in the previous context.

[4] It is better to read הושע את. The Massoretic ישע with את is awkward.

[5] The Massoretic accents are incorrect. We follow the parallelism.

[6] פרזו is used here as in Judg. v. 7, 11, dominion for the rulers, chieftains.

VIII. I hear, my belly is agitated,
    At the sound my lips quiver,
    Rottenness comes into my bones,
    And beneath [1] me I am trembling :
    When I am awaiting the day of trouble,
    The coming to a people to crush him.

IX. For the fig-tree was not blooming,
    And there was no produce in the vines,
    The work of the olive failed.
    And the fields did not yield food,
    The flock was cut off from the fold,
    And there were no cattle in the stalls.

X. Verily, I will exult in Jahveh,
    I will rejoice in the God of my salvation ;
    Jahveh Adonay is my army.
    He hath made my feet like hinds,
    To cause me to ride upon the high places."

—Hab. iii.

This sublime piece of poetry is in the trimeter movement. As in the previous prophecy, we have first the
prayer of the prophet for revival and mercy in the midst
of the display of wrath upon the wicked enemies. This
is followed by six strophes describing the advent in
theophany, after the manner of the blessing of Moses,
the song of Deborah and the song of David.[2] The poem
concludes with two strophes describing the terror of the
prophet in the first experience of the glories of the
theophany, and then a final strophe exhibiting his joy in
the experience of redemption. This advent of Jahveh is
the same advent which is ever looked for in the unfolding of the divine side of Messianic prediction. Here the
redemption of his people is the chief object in the view of
the prophet, who advances from a condition of fear to joy
in the contemplation of it.

[1] תחתי = beneath me, or the lower parts.
[2] Deut. xxxiii. ; Judg. v. ; Ps. xviii.

V. THE RIGHTEOUS JUDGE.

§ 71. *Psalm L. represents God as the righteous judge. He comes in theophany for judgment. The righteous and the wicked are alike warned to offer thank-offerings and glorify God, lest they be destroyed by the fire of His wrath.*

Psalm l. describes a theophany from Zion with devouring fire and raging tempest for judgment upon the righteous and the wicked. The ethical tone and high spirituality of the psalm resemble Habakkuk, and the advent is described in somewhat similar terms. It is an advent of light and glory. The historical situation of the psalm is somewhat doubtful, but it is quite well suited to this period, and is best considered in connection with Habakkuk. The righteous and the wicked are alike warned against external sacrifices, and are exhorted to sincere worship with thank-offerings and votive offerings. The psalmist is remarkable for his breadth of view and sublime representation of divine glory and power extending over the entire earth from sunrise to sunset. The psalm is composed of three equal strophes, with a refrain which is essentially the same in thought, and yet varies somewhat in accordance with the strophe to which it is attached. The refrain is missing from the first strophe. And it is not easy to restore it in its original form.

> **I.** "*'El Elohim* [1] Jahveh doth speak,
> And call the earth from the rising of the sun unto the going down thereof.
> Out of Zion, the perfection of beauty, God doth shine forth.
> Let our God come, and let him not keep silent ! [2]

---

[1] אל אלהים יהוה. These three divine names are used side by side as independent names of God.

[2] אל יחרש must be rendered as jussive. The R.V. is in error in rendering it as indicative, "*shall not keep silence*." Ewald renders "*darf nicht;*" Delitzsch "*kann nicht.*"

A fire devoureth before him, and round about him it is very
  tempestuous.
He calleth to the heaven above and to the earth to judge his
  people.
'Gather unto me my favoured ones, who have made a
  covenant with me by a peace-offering,'
The heavens do declare [1] his righteousness, that God is judge
  Himself. [2]

II. 'O hear, my people, and I will speak, Israel,
  And I will testify unto thee, I, God, thy God.
  Not for thy peace-offerings will I reprove thee, or thy whole
    burnt-offerings which are continually before me,
  I will not take from thy house a bullock, from thy folds he-
    goats ;
  For mine are all the wild animals [3] of the forest, beasts upon
    mountains where thousands are. [4]
  I know all the birds of the mountains, and the wild beasts [5]
    of the fields are with me.
  If I were hungry, I would not say it to thee ; for mine is the
    world and its fulness. [6]
  Shall I eat the flesh of bulls, or drink the blood of goats ?
  *Offer unto God a thank-offering, and pay unto 'Elyon thy vows,
  And call upon me in the day of trouble, I will deliver thee, and
    do thou glorify me.'*

III. But unto the wicked God doth say, 'What shall be thine,
  Declaring my statutes, thou hast taken my covenant in thy
    mouth.

---

[1] וַיַּגִּידוּ. The ו consec. imperf. goes back upon the perfect with
which the Psalm begins. This is the strict classic style. It is
wrongly rendered by R.V. " *shall declare.*"

[2] The first strophe has eight lines, but the refrain has been
omitted by the copyist as in Ps. xlvi. at the close of the first
strophe.

[3] חַיְתוֹ יָעַר. The archaic ending for the sake of the rhythm.

[4] הַרְרֵי for the usual הָרֵי tending to Aramaism. The construct
may mean thousands of mountains, or mountains where thousands
are, as in margin of R.V.

[5] זִיז שָׂדַי. Comp. lxxx. 14, where זִיז is used in the same sense
for full-breasted animals. These are the only two passages where
it is so used. Isa. lxvi. 11 uses the word for the breast of women.

[6] תֵּבֵל וּמְלֹאָהּ as in Ps. xxiv. 1.

Seeing that thou hatest instruction, thou hast cast my words behind
thee,
When thou sawest a thief, thou didst run with him, and thy portion
was with adulterers;
Thy mouth thou hast put forth to evil, and thy tongue frameth[1]
deceit;
Thou sittest down, against thy brother speaketh, against thy
mother's son givest a thrust.
These hast thou done, and I have kept silence,[2] thou thoughtest
that I am altogether[3] such an one as thyself;
I will reprove thee, and I will set it in order before thine eyes.
Now consider this.

*Oh, forgetters of God, lest I tear thee in pieces, and there be none to
deliver, offer a thank-offering,*

*Should he glorify me, and prepare his way, I will show him the
salvation of God.'"*[4]

JEREMIAH.

Jeremiah is the second great prophet of the canon.
He was consecrated from the womb to the sad work of
blasting the false hopes of his people, and of tasting
with them the bitterness of their anguish.[5]

Jeremiah is pre-eminently the prophet of sorrow. It
was a mournful task that was imposed upon him, with
iron will and bleeding heart to become the constant
bearer of evil tidings to a perverse generation sinking
ever deeper and deeper into ruin. Jahveh made him
a strong city, an iron pillar and brazen walls against

---

[1] הצמיד only here in Hiphil. It is found in Niph. Num. xxv.
3, 5, Ps. cvi. 28; and in Pual, 2 Sam. xx. 8. It is probably as
Gesenius renders, *bind, fasten* in Kal, and *construct, frame* in Hiph.

[2] והחרשתי. The ו conjunctive co-ordinates in order to the
emphatic contrast of the action of God with the acts of the wicked.

[3] היות אהיה. The infin. construct is used for infin. absolute; an
unusual combination. In Isaiah and later writers the infin. abs.
is used for the construct, but not the reverse. It shows that
the distinction is passing out of use. In Aramaic it is lost altogether.

[4] These lines are wrongly pointed by the Massoretes. We have
here a refrain like the refrain of the second strophe.

[5] Jer. i. 4–10.

the whole land, kings and princes, priests and people;[1] and though they fought against him and persecuted him with cruelty and bitterness, they could not prevail against him, for Jahveh was with him, and he lived to see his evil tidings fulfilled on the land and people, and to accompany the last remnant in their flight from the devastated city and land to Egypt. His own experience is expressed in the words—

> " Oh that my head were waters, and mine eyes a fountain of tears,
> That I might weep day and night for the slain of the daughter of my people !
> Oh that I had in the wilderness a lodging-place of wayfaring men, that I might leave my people,
> That I might go from them, for they are all adulterers, an assembly of treacherous men."   —Jer. ix. 1, 2.

" Yéremyá's literary style has still in these later times much that is peculiar and even original, great wealth of new figures with great delicacy of description, a literary facility that readily adapts itself to the most different subjects, combined with graphic transparency, and with all this an unadorned simplicity which is very unlike the greater artificiality of his contemporary Habaqqûq. Notwithstanding all this, his language already bears the most unmistakeable marks of a declining and depressed age : it no longer possesses such a prompt and firm mastery of itself, the thoughts crumble under the hand of the speaker ; an imposing arrangement and a clearly cut conjunction of the sentences become rare, each thought occurs in a more disconnected and detached manner, is often drawn out to a great length, while it is multiform and not finely articulated like a living whole ; and this greater disjointedness, this longer, slower movement becomes most perceptible when the larger sections, the separate wholes, of his works are

[1] Jer. i. 18, 19.

examined. In certain passages it seems as if the author
were dimly conscious of this defect, the style becoming
suddenly unusually contracted, compressed and terse;
but this artificial terseness is not continued long."[1]

The prophet was associated with Josiah in the reforms
that were conducted on the basis of the Deuteronomic
code. It was natural therefore that he should be greatly
influenced by this code, and that his entire book should
be coloured by its language, style, and doctrines, and
that his spirit and temper should be greatly under its
power.[2]

The prophecies of Jeremiah are divided into three
parts, with an introductory chapter giving the prophet's
call, and a concluding historical chapter. The first part
is a collection of discourses with reference to Judah,
accompanied with historical material (chaps. ii.–xxiv.).
The second part is a collection of prophecies of judgment
and of comfort (chaps. xxv.–xlv.). The third part is a
group of messages to the nations (chaps. xlvi.–li.).[3]

In Part I. we have two Messianic prophecies, the one
relating to the divine advent and the other to the
Messianic king.

---

[1] Ewald, *Prophets*, iii. pp. 65, 66. See also Graf, *Der Prophet
Jeremia*, p. xxxii, Leipzig 1862.

[2] Jeremiah was a priest, and yet he shows no acquaintance with
the priest's code. This seems to imply that he knew it not, whether
it was in existence or not. His code of Mosaic legislation was the
Deuteronomic code, and that was his ideal of reform, and the norm
of Israel's transgression.

[3] In the LXX. parts ii. and iii. are transposed, and the order of
the messages differs. Moreover, there are numerous omissions of
greater or lesser extent, so that the LXX. is only seven-eighths of
the Massoretic text. Graf has shown that these omissions are
largely in the omission of unnecessary matter, belonging to the
diffuse style of the prophet, and are due to his tendency to repeat
himself ; and he pronounces a very unfavourable judgment against
the LXX. version of our prophet (see his *Jeremiah*, p. xli, seq.).
But the judgment of Ewald and other critics is more favourable to
the LXX. version It is clear from the Book of Jeremiah itself

VI. JERUSALEM THE THRONE OF JAHVEH.

§ 72. Jahveh the Saviour marries his exiled people. Selecting one from a city and two from a clan, he restores them to Zion, setting over them shepherds after his own heart. They will come together out of the land of the north unto the inheritance of their fathers. New institutions will be established. Entire Jerusalem will be called the throne of Jahveh, and all nations will gather to it.

"Turn, turncoat children,[1] is the utterance of Jahveh ; for I am lord [2] over you :

And I will take you one [3] from a city, and two from a clan, and bring you to Zion,

And give you shepherds according to mine heart, and they will feed you with knowledge and discretion.

And it will come to pass when ye increase and become fruitful in the land, in those days, is the utterance of Jahveh,

They will not say any more : the ark of the covenant of Jahveh, and it will not again come to mind.

And they will not remember it, and they will not visit it, and it will not be made any more.

At that time they will call Jerusalem the throne of Jahveh.

And all nations will assemble [4] themselves unto it, to the name of Jahveh, at Jerusalem.

---

that several editions of his prophecies were issued from time to time under his direction, and by his pupil Baruch. It seems altogether likely that the differences between the LXX. and the Massoretic text rest upon differences in early Hebrew MSS. The whole subject needs a fresh and thorough investigation. It seems to me that Ewald is correct in his opinion that the LXX. version is correct in its arrangement of parts ii. and iii.—See Ewald, *Prophets*, iii. p. 83.

[1] שובבים = part Polel, with מ omitted, as in Hos. i. 6, means turners, turncoats, apostates ; referring to Israel and Judah.

[2] בעלתי mingles the idea of lord and husband. The ב strengthens the meaning of lordship. The perfect is the perfect of the state. Ewald renders *Schutzherr*.

[3] אחד. The selection is complete, wherever one or two could be found. None will be overlooked. It does not indicate the small number of redeemed, but rather that the number is complete.

[4] נקוו is Niph. perf. of קוה. It is only found here and in Gen. i. 7.

And they will not go any more after the stubbornness[1] of their
    evil heart.
In those days the house of Judah will go with the house of Israel,
And they will come together out of the land of the north[2] unto the
    land that I gave their fathers for an inheritance."

—Jer. iii. 14–18.

    This prophecy dates from the reign of Josiah. It has
the same essential idea that we have found in Hosea[3] of
the marriage relation between Israel and Jahveh. The
people have been dispersed, and are widely scattered in
their exile, but they will not be overlooked. Every one
will be remembered. Every city and tribe will be visited,
and even where there may be but one or two faithful
children, they will be recovered, and all will be brought
back to the inheritance of their fathers. This reminds
us of the prediction of Amos, that in the sifting of Israel
among the nations not a grain would be lost.[4] Israel
and Judah will again be united. But the most significant
feature of this prediction is its transformation of the
institutions of the old covenant. The ark of the covenant
was the most sacred of all the institutions of Israel. It
was the chest that contained the tables of the covenant.
Upon it was the cherubic throne, the place where God was
enthroned in theophanic glory. It was placed in the
throne-room of the temple, the centre and source of every
blessing to Israel. And yet in the new dispensation
that Jeremiah predicts, after the restoration from exile,
the ark of the covenant will cease to exist. The glories
of the ancient ark of the covenant will be forgotten. No
other ark will be made to take its place. For something
higher and better will be given. The entire city of the

---

[1] שְׁרֵרוּת = hardness, stubbornness; a Deuteronomic expression.

[2] Ewald inserts וּמִכָּל הָאֲדָמוֹת after the LXX. This would force
us to break the line into two lines, and make them shorter than the
rhythm seems to require.

[3] Hos. ii. See p. 172.   [4] Amos ix. 9. See p. 161.

new Jerusalem will assume its place. The whole city will be the throne of Jahveh. His theophanic glory will envelope it, and occupy all its streets and houses. The whole city will be as holy as was the most sacred part of the temple, and its inhabitants will enjoy the privileges of its priesthood. The prophet doubtless has the pillar of cloud and fire in mind, and his prediction is an advance in the line of Isaiah.[1]

VII. THE RIGHTEOUS BRANCH.

§ 73. *Jeremiah describes the Messiah as the righteous branch. The name " Jahveh is our righteousness " is given to him and to the New Jerusalem. The exodus from Egypt will no more be remembered because of the greater exodus from all countries of the dispersion and the restoration to the holy land. The Davidic monarchy and the Levitical priesthood will be everlasting.*

The Massoretic text gives two passages, the one from part first of the collection (xxiii. 5–7), and the other from part second (xxxiii. 14–22). These are essentially the same, and yet they differ in certain important particulars, showing that the second passage is an enlargement and an improvement upon the first. The second passage is not found in the LXX. version. It was not in the MSS. used by the Greek translator, but there are no sufficient reasons for doubting its genuineness. We shall place them side by side, that the points of resemblance and difference may be manifest.

" Lo, days are coming, is the utterance of Jahveh, when I will raise up for David a	" Lo, days are coming, is the utterance of Jahveh, when I will accomplish the good word[2] which I have

---

[1] Isa. iv. 5, 6. See p. 194.

[2] הדבר הטוב. This seems to refer to the previous prediction, xxiii. 5, 6, and to show that we have here a new edition of it.

righteous Branch,[1] and he will reign king, and prosper and do justice and righteousness in the earth.

In his days Judah will be saved, and Israel will dwell in confidence: and this is his name which they will call him,[2] *Jahveh is our righteousness.*

Therefore, behold, days are coming, is the utterance of Jahveh, when they will not say any more, as Jahveh liveth who brought up the children of Israel from the land of Egypt; but as Jahveh liveth who led up and who brought the seed of the house of Israel from the land of the

spoken unto the house of Israel and concerning the house of Judah. In those days and at that time, I will cause to sprout for David a righteous Branch;[1] and he will do justice and righteousness in the earth. In those days Judah will be saved, and Jerusalem will dwell in confidence; and this is what they will call her,[2] *Jahveh is our righteousness.*

For thus saith Jahveh, there will not be cut off of David a man sitting upon the throne of the house of Israel; or of the Levitical priests there will not be cut off a man from before me, offering whole burnt-offerings and burning the incense of vegetable offerings and making peace offerings always.

And the word of Jahveh came unto Jeremiah, saying, Thus saith Jahveh, If thou canst break my covenant with the day and my covenant with the night that there be no day or night in their season, then also my covenant with David my servant might be broken that there should be no son for him, reigning on his throne; and with the Levitical

---

[1] צֶמַח צְדָקָה of xxxiii. 15 is but a slight variation of the צֶמַח צַדִּיק of xxiii. 5, the construct relation being employed instead of the adjective. The term is similar to the חֹטֶר and נֵצֶר of Isa. xi. 1.

[2] יִקְרְאוּ of xxiii. 6 has an indefinite subject = they will call him. The nominal suffix is used instead of the proper verbal suffix הוּ—. It is possible that it should be pointed as 3 pl. without suffix יִקְרְאוּ, with the object understood. This would bring the passage into closer relations to יִקְרָא לָהּ of xxxiii. 16, where the suffix certainly refers to Jerusalem. Ewald thinks that the name is given in xxiii. 6 to the people, and would point יִקָּרֵאוּ as Niphal. In Ex. xvii. 15 Moses called the name of an altar he erected to Jahveh יהוה נִסִּי = Jahveh is my banner.

north, and from all lands whither I have dispersed them ; and they will dwell upon their own land."—Jer. xxiii. 5–8.

priests, my ministers. In that the host of heaven cannot be numbered and the sand of the sea cannot be measured, so will I increase the seed of David my servant, and the Levites who minister to me."—Jer. xxxiii. 14–22.

In these passages Jeremiah takes up the prediction of Isaiah with reference to the Messianic king and clothes it with new ideas.[1] The name " *Jahveh is our righteousness* " reminds us of " *'El is with us* " of Isaiah. The Messianic king bears this name as the sacred pledge to Israel that their righteousness was to be found in Jahveh. Accordingly, in the parallel passage, the same name is given to the new Jerusalem, because it is to be the throne of Jahveh. The reign of Jahveh and the king of David's line is to be in the interests of righteousness. The deliverance from the lands of the dispersion will so transcend the exodus from Egypt that the latter will pass out of remembrance of the people. The second passage enlarges the prediction by embracing several ancient covenants, the covenant with Noah as to the perpetuity of the seasons, the covenant with Abraham as to the numbers of his seed, the covenant with Phinehas as to the perpetuity of the priesthood, and the covenant with David as to the everlasting reign of his seed.[2] All these covenants are alike inviolable, and are sure of fulfilment notwithstanding the impending destruction of Jerusalem and dispersion of the nation.

VIII. THE RESTORATION AND THE NEW COVENANT.

§ 74. *Rachel weeping for her children is comforted by the promise that they will return from the land of the enemy.*

[1] Isa. vii. 14, xi. 2 seq. See pp. 195–205.
[2] See pp. 78, 84, 109, 126.

Jahveh loves them with an everlasting love, and after He has chastised them for their sins and brought them to repentance He will restore them. A very great multitude of all classes and conditions will return and will serve Jahveh their God and David their king. Jahveh will plant them in their own land, and it will become wonderfully fruitful, and the people will rejoice with great festivity. A new covenant will be constituted, the divine instruction being written upon the heart so that all will know Jahveh. Jerusalem will be rebuilt, and with all its suburbs it will become holy to Jahveh.

Towards the close of his prophetic activity Jeremiah issued a little book of comfort, which embraces the chief features of the Messianic idea that had been communicated to him by the divine Spirit. This little book is in the spirit of Hos. i.–iii. It is at the basis of the great book of comfort, Isa. xl.–lxvi. It is a poem of the hexameter movement, and is throughout a piece of rare beauty and power.

I. " *Verily, thus said Jahveh :*
 Hark ! we hear a trembling—fear, and there is no peace.
 Ask ye now, and see whether a male is about to bear a child :
 Why do I see every man with his hands on his loins, as a
  woman in travail,
 And all faces are turned into paleness ?
 Woe ! for that day is greater than any like it :
 And it is a time of distress to Jacob ; yet will he be saved
  from it.
 And it will come to pass in that day, is the utterance of Jahveh
  Sabaoth,
 I will break his yoke from off thy neck, and thy bands tear off ;[1]
 And foreigners will no more enslave them ; but they will serve
  Jahveh their God,[2]

---

[1] Comp. Isa. x. 27.
[2] We disregard the accents and follow the rhythm in attaching this clause to this line.

And David their king whom I will raise up for them.

Therefore, O thou my servant Jacob, fear not, is the utterance of Jahveh, and be not terrified, Israel.

For, lo, I am about to save thee from afar, and thy seed from the land of their captivity.

And Jacob will return, and be at rest, and be quiet, and there will be none to make him afraid ;

For I will be with thee, is the utterance of Jahveh, to save thee when I make a full end,[1]

Among all nations whither I shall have dispersed thee, only of thee I will not make a full end,[2]

But I will chastise thee with judgment, and not altogether acquit thee.

II. *Verily, thus saith Jahveh :*

Thy bruise is ill, thy wound is incurable, there is none to espouse thy cause.

For dressing.[3] the wound, medicines, bandage thou hast none, all thy lovers have forgotten thee ;

They seek thee not ; for I have wounded thee with the wound of an enemy ;

With the chastisement of a cruel one on account of the multitude of thine iniquities, because thy sins are strong in number.

[Why criest thou because of thy bruise that thy sorrow is ill ?

Because of the multitude of thine iniquities, because thy sins are strong in number I have done these things to thee.[4]]

Therefore all who devour thee will be devoured, and all thine adversaries, all of them, will go into captivity,

---

[1] כלה as in Zeph. i. 18.

[2] We make both lines close with this word to bring out the antithesis and the parallelism. The rhythm favours it, and we go against the Massoretic points.

[3] למזור = for dressing, binding up the wound. We agree with Graf in attaching this word to the next clause with רפאות, but we cannot agree with him in his rendering, wound.

[4] The LXX. omits this and the previous line. They are a repetition of the previous context in the form of a question. Some think that it belongs to the diffuse style of the prophet, and that it has been omitted by the LXX. on that account. Possibly it was not in the original text at all. The strophe becomes more symmetrical without it.

And thy spoilers will become a spoil, and all who prey on thee
will I give for a prey.

For I will put a bandage upon thee, and from thy wounds will I
heal thee, is the utterance of Jahveh.

For an outcast they call thee, 'it is Zion who has no one seeking her.'

Thus saith Jahveh :

Lo, I am about to restore the prosperity of the tents of Jacob,
and upon his tabernacles I will have compassion ;

And the city will be built upon her hill,[1] and the palace according
to its plan will abide.

And praise will go forth from them, and the sound of merry-
makers :

And I will multiply them, and they will not be few ; and I will
glorify them, and they will not be small in number.

And their children will be as aforetime, and their congregation will
be established before me,

And I will visit upon all their oppressors, and their majestic one
will come forth from themselves,

And their ruler from their midst will go forth, and I will bring
him near, and he will approach unto me.

For who is this who hath pledged his heart to approach unto me ? is
the utterance of Jahveh.

[And ye will become to me a people, and I will become to you a
God.]

Lo, a storm from Jahveh, hot anger is gone forth ;

A storm sweeping all before it, upon the head of the wicked it
whirls,

The heat of the anger of Jahveh will not turn until he has done it,
and until he has accomplished the plans of his heart.

In the last day ye will understand it,[2]

---

[1] תִּלָּה is fem. of תֵּל, hill, like the corresponding word in Arabic.
See Josh. xi. 13 ; Deut. xiii. 17.

[2] Graf looks upon vers. 23, 24 with suspicion, because they are an
exact copy of xxiii. 19, 20 with the exception of the use of מִתְגּוֹרֵר
for מִתְחוֹלֵל, the insertion of חֲרוֹן, and the omission of בִּינָה. It is then
necessary to strike out the last line of ver. 22, for it is impossible
that it should be followed immediately by xxxi. 1, and the line is a
favourite expression constantly recurring in the prophet.   Whatever view we may take of vers. 23, 24, the previous line is suspicious.
It is usual to make the second strophe begin with ver. 23, but I
cannot see the propriety of it. The strophes are indicated by (כִי)כֹה
אָמַר יְהוֹה.

At that time, is the utterance of Jahveh,

I will become God to all the clans of Israel, and they will
become to me a people.

Thus saith Jahveh:

A people, survivors of the sword, found grace in the wilderness.

He went on that he might give Israel rest, from afar Jahveh
appeared unto me.[1]

With an everlasting love I loved thee; therefore I drew
thee in mercy.

Again will I build thee, and thou wilt be built, virgin of
Israel;

Again thou wilt put on thy tabrets, and go forth in the dance
of merry-makers.

Again thou wilt plant vineyards in the mountain of Samaria,
when planters have planted they will praise.[2]

For there is a day when the watchmen in Mount Zion will
proclaim,

'Arise, and let us go up to Zion, unto Jahveh our God.'

III.   *Verily, thus saith Jahveh:*

Sing for Jacob with gladness, and shout for the chief of the
nations:—let it be heard;

Praise and say, 'Jahveh hath saved his people,[3] the remnant
of Israel;'

Lo, I am about to bring them from the land of the north, and
gather them from the sides of the earth,

Among them the blind and the lame, the woman with child
and her that travaileth with child together:

---

[1] Ewald follows the LXX. and reads לוֹ, to him. This is better
suited to the context; but the more difficult reading is to be preferred, with Graf and most others.

[2] The LXX. renders αἰνέσατο and pointed הִלֵּלוּ. This is better
than הִלְּלוּ of the Palestinian and Babylonian codices, which means,
make common or profane. The R.V. "enjoy the fruit thereof" is a
modification of the same idea.

[3] חֹרְשִׁיעַ is pointed by the Massoretic text as an imperative. It
is so taken by the Vulgate, R.V., Ewald, Graf, *et al.* But the LXX.
renders ἔσωσεν as if it were a perfect. This is best suited to the
context.

A great congregation will return hither; with weeping will
   they come and with supplication [1]
I will lead them, I will bring them unto rivers of water, in a
   straight way, wherein they will not stumble.
For I have become a father to Israel, and Ephraim is my
   first-born.
Hear the word of Jahveh, ye nations, and declare it in coasts
   afar off :
Say, 'the scatterer of Israel will gather him, and keep him as a
   shepherd doth his flock.'
For Jahveh has ransomed Jacob, and redeemed him from the
   hand of a stronger than he.
And they will come and sing in the height of Zion, and flow
   unto the goodness of Jahveh,
Unto the corn and unto the new wine, and unto the new oil
   and unto the young of the flock and the herd:
And their soul will become as a watered garden, and they will
   not sorrow any more at all.
Then the virgin will rejoice in the dance, and the young men
   and old men together :
And I will change their mourning into joy, and I will comfort them and cause them to rejoice more than their
   sorrow.
And I will refresh the soul of the priests with fatness, and my
   people will be satisfied with my goodness, is the utterance
   of Jahveh.

IV. *Thus saith Jahveh:*
Hark, in Ramah lamentation is heard, bitter weeping,
Rachel is weeping for her sons ; she doth refuse to be com-
   forted for her children, because they are not.
Thus saith Jahveh:
Refrain thy voice from weeping, and thine eyes from tears ;
For there is hire for thy work, is the utterance of Jahveh ;
   and they will return from the land of the enemy.
And there is hope for thy latter end, is the utterance of
   Jahveh ; and thy sons will return to their boundary.
I distinctly heard Ephraim bemoaning himself,

----

[1] It is better to disregard the accents, with Hitzig and Graf, and
connect בתחנונים with the previous context and make the next line
begin with אובילם.

'Thou hast chastised me, and I was chastised as an untamed
　　calf :

Restore me that I may return ; for thou art Jahveh my God.

For after my turning away, I was sorry ; and after I was
　　taught, I smote upon my thigh ;

I was ashamed, and I was also confounded ; for I bore the
　　reproach of my youth.'

Is Ephraim a precious son unto me, or a child of delights :

That as often as I speak with him I earnestly remember him
　　again ?

Therefore my bowels moan for him ; I will have great com-
　　passion on him, is the utterance of Jahveh.

Set thee up waymarks, set thee up pillars,[1]

Set thy heart to the highway, the way thou hast gone.[2]

Return, O virgin of Israel, return hither [3] unto thy cities.

How long wilt thou go round about,[4] thou turncoat daughter ?

For Jahveh hath created a new thing in the earth, a female will
　　encompass a male.[5]

V. *Thus saith Jahveh Sabaoth, God of Israel :*

Again will they say this thing in the land of Judah and in its
　　cities, when I restore their prosperity :

'May Jahveh bless thee, habitation of righteousness, mountain
　　of holiness,

And let Judah and all its cities dwell together therein—the
　　husbandmen and those who tent about with flocks ;'

When I have refreshed the weary soul and every sorrowful soul
　　I have filled ;

---

[1] תמרורים is only found here.　It is from תמר, like תמרה, pillar ;
see Song iii. 6 ; Joel iii. 3.

[2] הלכתי.　This *Kethibh* is supported by the Vulgate.　But the
LXX. is with the *Qeri* הלכת, and this is rightly followed by R.V.

[3] עד = אלה = אלה = hither.　It can hardly agree with ערים on
account of the failure of the article.

[4] תתהמקין is only found here and in Song v. 6.　חמק, to depart.
The Hithpael is to go round about.

[5] תסובב is commonly understood in the sense that a woman would
get a man with child.　But this has nothing to recommend it in
the context.　The LXX. has quite a different reading, which has
little to commend it.　Ewald renders "turned into a male ;" and
Blayney, cause to turn about, put to flight ; Orelli renders encompass, with the idea of guarding, protecting, as in Deut. xxxii. 10 ;
Ps. xxxii. 10.　This is best.

'On this account I waked and saw, and my sleep was sweet to me.'[1]
Lo, the days are coming, is the utterance of Jahveh,
When I will sow the house of Israel and the house of Judah with
the seed of man and the seed of cattle.
And it will come to pass, according as I watched over them to pluck
up and to break down and to overthrow, and to destroy and to
afflict ;
So will I watch over them to build and to plant, is the utterance
of Jahveh.
In those days they will no more say,
'The fathers have eaten sour grapes, and the children's teeth are set
on edge ; '
But every one will die for his own iniquity.
All men, whosoever eateth the sour grapes, his teeth will be set on
edge.
Lo, days are coming, is the utterance of Jahveh,
When I will conclude with the house of Israel, and with the house
of Judah, a new covenant ;
Not according to the covenant that I concluded with their fathers
In the day of my strengthening their hand to bring them forth
from the land of Egypt;
Which covenant with me they did break, although I was lord over
them, is the utterance of Jahveh.
For this is the covenant that I will conclude with the house of Israel
after those days, is the utterance of Jahveh :
I do put my instruction within them, and upon their heart will I
write it ;

---

[1] This line has great difficulty. It is taken by some as the words
of God who has awaked from a sleep, which is conceived as lasting
during the exile, for the restoration of His people. But God could
hardly represent Himself as sleeping, however appropriate such an
idea might be to an impatient sufferer. It is taken by others as
the words of the prophet, who has given this prediction, as it were
in a sweet dream ; but שֵׁנָה is hardly the state of ecstasy. It is
better to regard it as the words of the people. Ewald thinks of a
quotation from a familiar song. Graf refers to Ps. iii. 6 for a similar
situation. It seems to me that it is best to take the line as the words
to be uttered in the land of Israel at the restoration. There are two
words, the first uttered when "I restore their prosperity," embracing
two lines ; the second uttered "when I have refreshed the weary
soul, and every sorrowful soul have filled," which consists of one
line. This refreshment and comfort was like waking from a sweet
refreshing sleep.

And I will become a God for them, and they will become a people for me ;

And they will not teach any more, each his friend, and each his brother, saying, 'Know Jahveh ;'

For all of them will know me, from the least even to the greatest of them, is the utterance of Jahveh.

For I will pardon their iniquity, and their sins I will not remember any more.

VI. *Thus saith Jahveh:*

Giver of the sun for light by day, the ordinances of the moon and stars for light by night ;

Exciter of the sea, so that its waves moan, Jahveh Sabaoth his name.[1]

If these ordinances can depart from before me, is the utterance of Jahveh ;

Then the seed of Israel may cease from being a nation before me always.

Thus saith Jahveh:

If heaven can be measured above, and if the foundations of the earth can be searched beneath ;[2]

I also may reject all the seed of Israel for all that they have done, is the utterance of Jahveh.

Lo, days are coming,[3] is the utterance of Jahveh,

When the city will be built to Jahveh from the tower of Hananel unto the corner gate,

And a measuring-line will go out over against it,[4] over the hill Gareb, and it will go round about to Goath,

And the whole valley of corpses and ashes and all the pools[5] unto the brook Kedron,

---

[1] Isa. li. 15 and Job xxvi. 12 have essentially the same words. There is a borrowing here. Isaiah and Jeremiah are identical, but Job varies the construction slightly.

[2] The וֹ co-ordinate should be noticed.

[3] The *Kethibh* omits בָּאִים ; but it is rightly given in the *Qeri*, LXX. and Vulgate.

[4] The *Kethibh* reads קָוֶה by repetition of the ה of הַמִּדָּה. The *Qeri* makes the correction. The St. Petersburg codex agrees with the Western codices. קָוֶה may be the correct form here and 1 Kings vii. 23.

[5] The *Kethibh* has הַשְּׁרֵמוֹת, the LXX. ἀσαρήμωθ, so St. Petersburg codex. Ewald follows this and renders pools, on the ground

Unto the corner of the horse gate eastward, *Holy to Jahveh* will
  they become,
It will not be plucked up, and will not be torn down for ever."
—Jer. xxx.–xxxi.

This beautiful and touching hexameter is Messianic
throughout. Its great theme is the restoration of Israel
from exile after severe discipline by Jahveh, and the
establishment of a new covenant and new institutions in
place of the old.

The first strophe describes the great distress about to
come on Jerusalem in the day of Jahveh's visitation.
Israel will go into captivity, but will afterwards be restored. Other nations will be brought to complete ruin,
Israel alone will be chastised on account of sin, but will
not suffer complete ruin. They will return to Jahveh their
God and David their king.

In the second strophe Israel's wound is described as
incurable, his sins are so numerous that he must be
severely punished. But Jahveh will eventually heal him
and restore him to Zion. As he led Israel out of Egypt,
so He has an everlasting love and will have compassion
on him. The city will be rebuilt with its palaces, the
mountains of Samaria will be planted with vineyards,
Zion will again be the resort of pilgrims, and great
festivals will be celebrated with music and dancing. A
king from their own midst will rule over them, and he
will have special access to Jahveh.

The third strophe omits the reference to chastisement,

that שרם is kindred with זרם ; so Reinke. Keil refers to the
cognate Arabic stem with the meaning cut, separate, and renders,
place cut off. Streane renders, quarries or rugged rocks. The *Qeri*
has השרמות, fields. This is followed by R. V. and A.V. ; so
Nägelsbach. The Vulgate reads שדה מות, *regionem mortis.* As
Graf states, השרמות is the more difficult reading, and no one would
be likely to change an easy word into a difficult one. But, on the
other hand, the change of the letter ד into ר is so easy that it is not
surprising, and if once made it would be perpetuated.

except so far as this is involved in the weeping and
supplication of the returning penitents, and deals entirely
with the restoration. There is great rejoicing over Jacob,
who has become chief of the nations. A great multitude
of all classes and conditions return to Zion, under the
leadership of Jahveh their tender Father. The land
regains its ancient fertility, and there is universal joy
and festivity.

The fourth strophe dramatically represents Rachel
weeping for her children, who have gone into exile or
have perished. But she is comforted with the promise
that they will return from their captivity. Ephraim is
then seen confessing his sins and turning to Jahveh with
sincere repentance. Jahveh turns to him with tender
paternal love, and recognises him as His own precious
son in whom He delights. This piece is in the manner
of Hos. xi.[1]

The fifth strophe represents the inhabitants of Judah
congratulating themselves and pronouncing blessings on
the holy city. Jahveh will more than counterbalance
His chastisements by blessings. He will plant them in
the holy land, and discriminate between the righteous
and the wicked. A new covenant will be made in place
of the old. Its instruction will no more be written in
books or on tables of stone, but on the heart; and there
will be no more need of Levitical teachers or prophets,
for all will know Jahveh, both small and great; and all
sins will be forgiven and forgotten. In this prediction
Jeremiah rises above the covenant of Hos. ii.,[2] and
attains a conception of a dispensation so new that the
old is transformed and transfigured.

The prediction reaches its culmination in the last
strophe. The divine covenant is as inviolable as the
ordinances of heaven. The seed of Israel can never be

<hr>

[1] See p. 174.   [2] See p. 171.

entirely rejected. There is to be a separation of the righteous from the wicked. Jerusalem has been destroyed, but it is to be rebuilt in greater glory than ever. Its entire extent is to spring up in palaces. Even the suburbs, the hill Gareb, the abode of lepers; and the valley of Hinnom, the place of refuse, of corpses and of ashes, are to be cleansed, and *Holiness to Jahveh* is to be the title of the whole. The same inscription that was upon the tiara of the high priest of Israel is to be upon entire Jerusalem. This is in accordance with the representation of chap. iii., that the city was to take the place of the ark of the covenant.[1] It is also in accordance with chap. xxxiii., that it was to bear the name, " Jahveh is our righteousness." [2] The new Jerusalem will take the place of the most sacred things of the old covenant. As its inhabitants are to have the divine instruction written on their hearts, to be all alike acquainted with Jahveh, and to be forgiven their sins, and thus to be holy to God; so it is in keeping therewith that the city should be altogether holy as the throne of Jahveh, whose presence and glory will pervade the whole of it.

The Messianic idea of Jeremiah transcends all previous predictions in its representation of the glories of the new covenant. The Messianic king retires into the background of the representation, for it is Jahveh Himself who accomplishes the redemption of His people. This advent is conceived on the basis of the story of the exodus and the covenant of Sinai. But Jahveh will come again in a still more glorious manner, and will deliver His people in a more marvellous way, and will establish a new covenant that will transcend the old in spirituality, in comprehensiveness, and in power.

[1] See p. 242.   [2] See p. 245.

R

IX. THE INVIOLABLE COVENANT WITH DAVID.

§ 75. *Jahveh is faithful to His covenant with David,
notwithstanding the decline of the dynasty. His mercies
are everlasting. He will come and dwell in Zion for ever,
provide abundantly for its inhabitants, and cause prosperity and splendour to sprout forth for David.*

Pss. lxxxix. and cxxxii. are so similar to Jeremiah
xxxiii. in their conception of the inviolability of the
Davidic covenant, that it is most convenient to treat
them here, whatever their date may be. It seems probable, however, that they belong to the last days of the
Jewish monarchy prior to the exile. They differ from
the predictions of Jeremiah in their lyric form, and in
their lamentation and prayer. The Messianic king is in
the background, as in Jeremiah. The only hope is the
advent of Jahveh Himself.

Ps. lxxxix. is composed of four strophes of twelve
tetrameter lines each, enclosing before the last strophe
seven strophes of eight trimeter lines each. The enclosed
piece gives a long paraphrase of the covenant with David,
and a lamentation over its apparent failure. The introductory strophes set forth the faithfulness and the mercy
of God, and the closing strophe is a plea based there-
upon.

> I. "Of the mercies of Jahveh will I sing for ever :
>   I shall make known thy faithfulness with my mouth to all
>   generations.
>   For I said, mercy will be built up for ever ;
>   It is the heavens[1] wherein thou wilt establish thy faithfulness.
>   'I made a covenant with my chosen,
>   I sware unto David my servant ;

---

[1] שמים at the beginning of the line is very emphatic. It is a
local accusative followed by a relative clause defined by בהם.

For ever I will establish thy seed,
And build thy throne to all generations.'
Then let [1] heaven praise thy wonders, Jahveh ;
Yea, in the assembly of the holy ones thy faithfulness.
For who in the skies can be compared to Jahveh ?
Can be like unto Jahveh among the sons of the gods ? [2]

II. '*El* is very terrible in the council of the holy ones,
    Inspiring awe above all round about him is Jahveh.[3]
    O God of hosts, who is like thee ?
    A mighty one, O Jah,[4] and thy faithfulness is round about
       thee.
    Thou art ruler over the pride of the sea :
    When its waves rise thou stillest them,
    Thou hast crushed Rahab as a slain man ;
    With an arm of strength thou hast scattered thine enemies.
    Thine is heaven, yea, thine is earth ;
    The world and its fulness thou hast founded them.
    The north and south thou hast created them.
    Tabor and Hermon rejoice in thy name.

III. Thine is an arm with might :
    Thy hand is strong, thy right hand is lifted up.
    Righteousness and justice are the foundation of thy throne :
    Mercy and faithfulness go to meet thy face.
    Blessed are the people who know the trumpet sound.
    In the light of thy face they walk, Jahveh.
    In thy name they exult all the day,
    And in thy righteousness are they exalted.

---

[1] ויורו. The weak ו shows that the form is jussive. It is an exhortation to praise in view of the covenant promise.

[2] בני אלים, can hardly be "sons of the mighty," as the R.V. The margin is only partly correct in rendering "sons of God." The conception is that the אלים are the heavenly intelligences associated with God, the assembly of angels. בן is a noun of relation, like בני ישראל. The reference then is to the heavenly beings, the race of angels. It is inappropriate to refer אלים here to "the mighty," and in the very next clause translate אל as God.

[3] יהוה is attached to the next verse by the Massoretes. We restore it to its line in accordance with the parallelism and rhythm.

[4] חסין יה should be joined to the following context. The Massoretic points are to be disregarded.

For thou art the glory of their strength
In thy favour thou wilt exalt[1] our horn
For our shield belongeth unto Jahveh ;
And our king to the Holy One of Israel

IV. Then thou didst speak in a vision
To thy favoured ones,[2] and didst say,
'I have laid help upon a hero ;
I have exalted one chosen out of the people.
I have found David my servant ;
With my holy oil I have anointed him,
With whom my hand will be established ;
Yea, mine arm will strengthen him.

V. The enemy will not do him violence ;
And the iniquitous fellow will not afflict him ;
I will beat down his adversaries before him,
And those hating him I will smite.
And my faithfulness and mercy will be with him ;
And in my name will his horn be exalted.
And I will put his hand on the sea,
And his right hand on the streams.

VI. He will call me " My father,
Thou [3] art my *'El* and the rock of my salvation."
Yea, I will make him my first-born,
'*Elyon* [4] to the kings of the earth.
My mercy will I keep for him for ever,
And my covenant will be confirmed for him.
And I will establish his seed for ever,
And his throne as the days of heaven.

---

[1] תרים of the *Kethibh* and Vulgate is to be preferred to the *Qeri* תרום.

[2] The plural is best sustained by MSS. and Versions. But the context is strongly in favour of the singular. The plural is the more difficult reading. The weight of evidence is in its favour.

[3] אתה is attached by the Massoretic accents to אבי. It seems to be better to attach it to אלי.

[4] עליון is a divine name. It is incorrect to render it "highest." It is parallel with "my first-born." The Messianic king is made an עליון to the kings of the earth, as Moses was made an אלהים to Aaron, Ex. iv. 16.

VII. If his sons forsake my instruction,
  And walk not in my judgments ;
  If they profane my statutes,
  And keep not my commandments :
  Then will I visit their transgressions with a rod,
  And their iniquity with blows.
  But my mercy I will not break off,[1]
  And will not be false to my faithfulness.

VIII. I will not profane my covenant,
  And the issue of my lips I will not alter.
  Once I sware in my holiness ;
  I will not lie unto David ;
  His seed will endure for ever,
  And his throne as the sun before me,
  As the moon which is established for ever,
  And a witness made firm in the sky.'

IX. But thou hast cast off and rejected,
  Hast overflowed with anger against thine anointed.
  Thou hast rejected[2] the covenant of thy servant,
  Thou hast profaned his ornament to the ground,
  Thou hast broken down all his hedges ;
  Thou hast made his strongholds a ruin,
  All passing by do spoil him :
  He has become a reproach to his neighbours.

X. Thou hast lifted up the right hand of his adversaries,
  Thou hast made all his enemies to rejoice,
  Yea, thou turnest back the edge[3] of his sword,

---

[1] אפיר is well sustained, but it is difficult in form and in meaning. The proper form of פרר would be אָפֵר. We might, however, think of פור=פרר, the weak stems not infrequently passing over the one into the other. The passage is based on 2 Sam. vii. 15, and the lines are so much alike that we are tempted to read אָסִיר. See p. 127.

[2] נארתה is only found here and Lam. ii. 7. Hupfeld suggests that it is a mistake for נאץ. Delitzsch agrees with Gesenius in comparing the Arabic word of the same form meaning, abhor, and that the stem is kindred with ארר.

[3] צור is ordinarily to be translated rock ; but in Ex. iv. 25 it is a sharp stone or a knife for cutting, and it must have a similar meaning here. Fried. Delitzsch (in his *Prolegomena eines neuen Heb.*

And hast not made him stand in the battle.
Thou hast made his brightness to cease,
To the ground thou hast cast down his throne
Thou hast shortened the days of his youth :
Thou hast covered him with shame.

XI. How long, Jahveh, wilt thou hide thyself for ever ?
Will thy heat burn like fire ?
Remember, Adonay,[1] how fleeting it is :
For what vanity thou hast created all the sons of man,
What man is he that shall live and not see death ?
That can deliver himself[2] from the power of Sheol ?
Where are thy former mercies, Adonay,
Which thou didst swear to David in thy faithfulness ?
Remember, Adonay, the reproach of thy servants ;
My bearing in my bosom all the many peoples ;
Wherewith thine enemies, Jahveh, do reproach,
Wherewith they do reproach the footsteps of thine anointed.'
—Ps. lxxxix.

The three introductory strophes dwell upon the mercy
and faithfulness of God as exhibited in heaven and on
earth.   The throne of Jahveh is founded on righteousness and justice, but mercy and faithfulness are His
attending ministers.   The king of Israel is the anointed
of Jahveh.   He belongs to Him, and the divine faithfulness is pledged to maintain him and exalt him.

The body of the poem enlarges upon the covenant
with David, looking at it from every point of view and
setting it in every light.   It seems as if the author finds

Aram. *Wörterbuchs*, 1886, p. 165) derives the words from צרר, to be
sharp, and thus explains both meanings. It is accordingly unnecessary to render *rock* here.

[1] The זכר־אני of the Massoretic text is extremely difficult.
Delitzsch and Perowne explain the אני as in emphatic position,
אני מה חלד for מה חלד אני, "how short a time I have to live,"
and so R.V. "how short my time is."   But these all paraphrase to
escape the difficulty.   It seems best to adopt the suggestion of
Houbigant, that אני is a mistake for אדני.   See זכר אדני below.

[2] נפשו is the reflexive "himself," as often in Hebrew. It is
incorrectly rendered "his soul" by R.V.

it difficult to leave so attractive a theme. He closes
with a lamentation that the covenant has been rejected,
that the throne of the king has been cast to the ground,
and that the anointed is covered with shame.

The closing strophe is an urgent plea for the speedy
advent of Jahveh to display His former mercies, to fulfil
His ancient covenant with David and to remove the
reproach of His people.

Psalm cxxxii. resembles the previous psalm in its
method of citing the prediction of Nathan in the form of
paraphrase; but it is calmer in tone. It is composed of
four strophes of ten trimeter lines each. The first
strophe gives an account of the anxiety of David to erect
a great tabernacle for Jahveh. The second strophe
describes the removal of the ark of the covenant from
Kirjath Jearim to the holy city. The third strophe
paraphrases the covenant with David. The fourth
strophe gives a prediction that is based on the covenant.

> **I.** "O Jahveh, remember for David
>   All his afflictions;
>   How he sware unto Jahveh,
>   Vowed to the Mighty One of Jacob:
>   'I will not come into the tent of my house,
>   Nor ascend upon the couch of my bed,[1]
>   I will not give sleep to mine eyes,
>   To mine eyelids slumber,
>   Until I find a place for Jahveh,
>   A great tabernacle[2] for the Mighty One of Jacob.'

> **II.** Lo, we heard of it in Ephrathah,
>   We found it in the field of Ja'ar.[3]
>   Let us come to his great tabernacle,[2]

---

[1] The R.V. is inconsistent in rendering "tabernacle of my house,"
and then substituting "bed" for "couch of my bed."

[2] משכנות is an emphatic plural, "great tabernacle." It is improper
to neglect the plural, as the R.V., or to translate "tabernacles," as
in the margin of the R.V.

[3] יער is a proper name, and is not to be rendered "wood" or
"forest." See 1 Chron. xiii. 5.

Let us worship at his footstool.
O arise, Jahveh, to thy resting-place ;
Thou and the ark of thy strength.
Let thy priests be clothed with righteousness,
And thy favoured ones shout for joy.
For the sake of David thy servant,
Turn not away the face of thine anointed.

III. Jahveh sware to David,
In faithfulness [1] from which he will not depart ;
'Of the fruit of thy body
Will I set on a throne for thee.[2]
If thy sons keep my covenant,
And my testimonies that I will teach them,
Also thy children will continue for ever,
They will be enthroned on a throne for thee.'[3]
For Jahveh hath chosen Zion ;
He desired it for a dwelling-place for himself.

IV. 'This is my resting-place for ever.
Here will I sit enthroned ; for I desire it.
Her provision I will abundantly bless ;
Her poor I will satisfy with bread,
And her priests will I clothe with salvation,
And her favoured ones will shout aloud for joy.
There will I cause a horn to sprout for David,
I have prepared a lamp for mine anointed ;
His enemies will I clothe with shame ;
But upon him his crown will be brilliant.' "

—Ps. cxxxii.

This prediction is not only based upon the covenant
with David, but it also involves the predictions of Isaiah
and Jeremiah with regard to the shoot and sprout.[4] The
Messianic king will sprout forth in freshness, vigour,
and glory when Jahveh takes up His abode permanently

---

[1] With Delitzsch and Perowne we detach אֱמֶת from the previous
line and follow the rhythm.
[2] With Delitzsch we find two lines here.
[3] There are two lines here also, as Delitzsch sees.
[4] See p. 201.

in Zion and fills it with blessing.   Zion will become a
centre of salvation as His everlasting throne.   All classes
of the people, and especially the poor, will be abundantly
supplied with provisions for their wants.   This supply is
here attached to the reign of Jahveh, as in Ps. lxxii. it
was the result of the reign of the Messiah.[1]   The priests
will not only be mediators of salvation, but they will be
clothed with it and will personally possess it.   Thus
they will fulfil their ministry of everlasting priesthood
in accordance with Jer. xxxiii.[2]   But the second
David will be the chief recipient of favour.   His horn
will sprout, his dignity will spring up like a tender
plant; his lamp, that is, the light from him, will shine
brightly; his diadem will be brilliant, he will reign in
glory, and all his enemies will be clothed with shame.[3]

---

[1] See p. 138.   [2] See p. 246.
[3] This psalm resounds in the hymn of Zachariah the father of
John the Baptist, Luke i. 68–70.

CHAPTER IX.

EZEKIEL.

EZEKIEL was the first of the prophets of the exile, and as such began a new section in Messianic prophecy. He was carried away captive with Jehoiachin, eleven years before the destruction of Jerusalem, and settled in exile on the banks of the Chebar. In the fifth year of his exile he was called to the prophetic office, and laboured at least twenty-two years. Nothing is known of the prophet outside of his own writings. He was a younger contemporary of Jeremiah, with whom he exchanged prophecies. He was called to be a watchman for Israel, to warn with faithfulness, knowing that their blood would be required of him. Hence he was stern, strict and severe in his prophetic work. He was also a priest by descent, and therefore regarded the temple as of great importance. He depicts its desecration by idolaters, and describes its abandonment by Jahveh in His cherubic chariot. He represents that Jahveh abides as a sanctuary with His people in their temporary exile, and that He will ere long restore them to a new temple in the holy land, where He will dwell with them for ever. His description of the cherubim and of the new temple of the latter days is based upon the temple of Solomon, but it combines in its symbolism the winged creatures and the more massive and stately buildings of the temples of the great cities of the Chaldean empire. The Hebrew ideal of the temple is transformed by the mixture of this foreign material, and it assumes a higher and grander form. Ezekiel was fond of symbols and allegories, and through them he presents graphically and strongly the great truths of the divine discipline and restoration. He is the father of the last form of Old Testament prophecy which may be called Apocalyptic. His language departs from the classic style by the formation of new words and the indulgence of Aramaic terms and expressions. Ezekiel is, as Hengstenberg represents, " a gigantic appearance, well adapted to struggle effectively with the spirit of the times of the Babylonian captivity ; a spiritual Samson who, with powerful hand, grasped the pillars of the temple of idolatry and dashed it to the earth, standing alone, yet worth a hundred prophetic schools, and during his entire appearance, an evidence that the Lord was still among His people although His visible temple was ground to powder." [1]

The prophetic activity of Ezekiel was divided into two parts by the destruction of Jerusalem in the eleventh year of Zedekiah. Previous to this event his office was to scourge the people with the threatenings of the Lord ; but subsequently to comfort them with the promises of restoration.

The introduction describes the manner of his call, chaps. i.–iii. 21. Part I. chaps. iii. 22–xxiv. gives prophecies of judgment against Jerusalem and Judah. Part II. chaps. xxv.–xxxii. gives seven prophecies against the heathen nations, like the corresponding collections in Isaiah and Jeremiah. Part III. chaps. xxxiii.–xlviii. contains prophecies respecting the restoration of Israel, the overthrow of the nations of the world, and the erection of the new temple and the divine kingdom.

There are three Messianic passages in Part I.

[1] Hengstenberg, *Christology,* ii. p. 3, Edinburgh edition.

I. JAHVEH THE SANCTUARY.

§ 76. *Jahveh will be the sanctuary of His people during the short time of their exile, and then restore them to their own land. He will remove all its abominations, and give them one heart of flesh and a new spirit so that they will walk in His ways.*

"Therefore say, Thus saith Adonay Jahveh: Verily I have removed them far off among the nations, and verily I have dispersed them in the lands, and have become for them a sanctuary for a little while in the lands whither they are come.

Therefore say, Thus saith Adonay Jahveh: I will gather you from the peoples, and collect you from the lands in which ye have been dispersed, and give you the land of Israel. And they will come thither and remove all its detestable things and all its abominations from it. And I will give them one heart, and a new spirit will I put within them; and remove the heart of stone from their flesh and give them a heart of flesh, in order that they may walk in mine ordinances and keep my laws and do them, and become a people to me, and I may become a God to them."—Ezek. xi. 16–20.

Jahveh is here represented as the real temple of the exiles for the short period of their dispersion, that is, during the brief interval between the departure of Jahveh from the old temple at Jerusalem until the erection of a new temple by the returned exiles. Jahveh will ere long restore them to their own land after having purged away all their abominations and made them holy. He will give them a new heart and spirit. Their inner man is to be changed. This heart will become a heart of flesh instead of a heart of stone—that is, a truly human heart. It will also be one heart—the people will have true unity, they will be one in the centre of their being. This prediction is in the line of Isa. iv.,[1] which set forth the purification of Israel by divine chastisement. It is also a further unfolding of Jer. xxx.–xxxi. There, the

[1] See p. 193.

divine instruction was to be written on the heart instead of upon tables of stone;[1] here, the heart itself is to be changed. The presence of God will no more be conditioned upon local and geographical relations, or a material temple. God without the temple is better than the temple without God. This the exiles were to learn before God and the temple again could come together. The little while is the interval between the theophanic leaving of the old temple and a divine advent to a new temple. It would be difficult to find such an advent at the restoration under Zerubbabel. We must look to the advent of Jesus the God-man for the renewal of the heart and spirit of the people.

II. THE WONDERFUL CEDAR SPRIG.

§ 77. *The kingdom of God is like a sprig of cedar that will be plucked from a lofty tree and planted upon the mountains of Israel, and grow to be a majestic tree towering above the land.*

"Thus saith Adonay Jahveh : I will take of the foliage[2] of the lofty cedar,[3] from the highest of its shoots will I pluck a tender one, and I will plant it upon a high and exalted mountain ;[4] in the mountain of the height of Israel will I plant it. And it will produce boughs and yield fruit, and become a majestic cedar ; and every wild animal[5] will dwell under it ; and every bird of every wing in the shadow of its hanging boughs[6] will dwell. And all the trees of the field will know that I, Jahveh, have humbled the proud tree, and I have exalted the humble tree, I have dried up the green tree,

---

[1] See p. 256.

[2] עֲמֶרֶת only in Ezekiel. It is rendered by A.V. and R.V.=top.

[3] וְנָתַתִּי is rightly omitted by Cornill, after the Peshitto, as alien to the construction of the verse.

[4] תלול from תלל =sway to and fro, to be exalted.

[5] Cornill inserts כל חיה after the LXX. on the ground that it is required by the context. Birds do not dwell *under* trees, but in them ; animals are therefore needed to justify the preposition תחת.

[6] דלית is bough, from דלה, to hang down.

and I have made fruitful the dry tree : I, Jahveh, have spoken and will do it." [1]—Ezek. xvii. 22–24.

This is a beautiful parable in the manner of Ps. lxxx. and Micah iv.[2] It is a gigantic symbol, and thus all the more suited to represent the wonderful growth of the kingdom of God from a tender shoot to a majestic tree.[3] The sprig represents the faithful and restored remnant of Israel. That faithful remnant will realize in the future all the Messianic predictions of the past. The divine ideal of prophecy is not to be destroyed with the ruin of the nation and the destruction of the majority of the people. It matters little how small the remnant may be. That little remnant inherits all the promises, and will fill the world with its marvellous growth.

III. THE RIGHTFUL KING.

§ 78. *The tiara of the priest and the crown of the king will be removed, and the kingdom remain in ruins until the advent of the one appointed by Jahveh.*

"Thus saith Adonay Jahveh: Remove[4] the mitre, and take off the crown. This is not the one;[5] exalt the lowly one,[6] and abase

---

[1] וְעָשִׂיתִי, a phrase of Ezekiel. ו consec. of perfect after perfect changes the tense from past affirmation to future fulfilment.

[2] See pp. 181 and 229.

[3] The same thought is presented in the parable of the grain of mustard seed, Matt. xiii. 31.

[4] The ancient Versions, LXX., Peshitto, Targ., Vulgate take the infin. construct הרים, הסיר and השכיל as infinitives absolute like הגבה. They rest upon a different pointing. So Cornill at once changes the text to infinitives absolute. So A.V. and R.V. render. Ewald changes the הגבה into הגביה to conform with the three infinitives construct, and renders, "Zu entfernen ist der Kopfbund und wegzunehmen die Krone ! das ist nicht das ! das Niedrige ist zu erhohen und das Hohe zu erniedrigen." If the Massoretic text be more authoritative than the Versions, the one infin. absolute should be assimilated to the three infinitives construct, and not the reverse. But the Versions are more correct, and should be followed here.

[5] זאת לא זאת =this is not this, that is, is not the one to abide, is not the permanent Messianic kingdom.

[6] הַשְּׁפָלָה is pointed as if it were an archaic acc. of שפל, and

the lofty one. An overthrow,[1] an overthrow, an overthrow will I make it—even this.[2] He is not until the coming of the one whose right it is and I give it him."—Ezek. xxi. 31, 32.

The removal of the crown of the king and the tiara of the priest is their deposition from office. The kingdom and the priesthood are to be abolished for a season. The present kingdom is not the Messianic kingdom. The present official priest and king are not those who are to realize the Messianic ideal. They both will remain in ruins until the advent of the one appointed by Jahveh —in other words, until the advent of the Messiah. It is thought by many that this passage is a reminiscence of Gen. xlix.[3] It is vain to find a fulfilment of this prediction in the princedom of Zerubbabel, or the high-priesthood of Jeshua, on the return from the exile. The priesthood and the princedom then were but shadows of the priesthood of Phinehas and the royalty of David. The priesthood lacked the Urim and Thummim as the princedom lacked real authority. The one appointed by Jahveh was and is Jesus Christ.

There are no Messianic prophecies in the second part of Ezekiel, but the third part is chiefly Messianic.

therefore masc. like הגבה. But it is really feminine, and refers to זאת, and should be pointed הִשְׁפָּלָה. Cornill changes הגבה into הגבוהה and makes it feminine.

[1] עוה, thrice repeated, is only found here. It is an intensive noun with the meaning overthrow, ruins. But the LXX., Vulgate and Targum take it as עון, iniquity.

[2] The Massoretic גם זאת לא היה is extremely difficult. If it is to stand, the discrepancy of gender should be noted, and זאת must go with the previous clause and היה with the following clause. The R.V. is incorrect in rendering, "This also shall be no more." Cornill escapes the difficulty by reconstructing the text so as to read : אוי לה כזאת תהיה="Woe to it. Thus it will remain until he come."

[3] See p. 96.

IV. THE FAITHFUL SHEPHERD.

§ 79. *Jahveh, the faithful shepherd of Israel, will recover His scattered sheep, restore them to their own land again, place over them a second David as their shepherd, and make with them a new covenant of peace and blessing.*

"For thus saith Adonay Jahveh : Lo, I will come and seek my sheep and search them out. As a shepherd searcheth out his flock in the day of tempest,[1] so will I search out my sheep and deliver them from all the places whither they have been scattered in the day of cloud and dense darkness : and will bring them out from the peoples, and gather them from the lands, and bring them to their own land, and feed them on the mountains of Israel, by the water-courses, and in all the dwelling-places of the land. In excellent pasture will I feed them, and on the mountain of the height of Israel will be their abode. There will they lie down in excellent abode, and in a fat pasture will they feed on the mountains of Israel. I will feed my flock and I will make them to lie down, is the utterance of Adonay Jahveh. The lost one I will gather, and the outcast will I bring back, and the bruised will I bind up, and the sick will I strengthen, and the strong will I keep.[2] I will feed them with justice. . . . I will save my flock, and they will no more become a prey ; and I will judge between sheep and sheep. And I will place over them one shepherd, and he will feed them, even my servant David ; he will feed them, and he will become a shepherd for them. And I, Jahveh, will become their God, and mv servant David a prince in their midst. I, Jahveh, have spoken it. And I will conclude with them a covenant of peace, and I will cause evil animals to cease from the land. And they will dwell

---

[1] The Massoretic ביום היותו בתוך צאנו נפרשות is certainly very awkward. We sympathize with Cornill in following the Peshitto and reading ביום סופה instead of it. The Versions have found difficulty, and are divided in their testimony. But the simplicity of the Peshitto and its conformity to the context commends it. The Massoretic text has probably arisen from a marginal gloss.

[2] The Massoretic אשמיד involves a contrast with the previous context that is unnatural and unexpected. The LXX. Peshitto and Vulgate read אשמר, which is more appropriate to the context, and is rightly followed by Cornill. It would appear that ואת השמנה was a marginal gloss.

securely in the wilderness, and sleep in the woods. And I will make them and the places round about my hill a blessing,[1] and I will cause the shower to come down in its season : there will be showers of blessing. And the tree of the field will yield its fruit, and the land will yield its produce, and they will be secure upon their own land, and will know that it is I, Jahveh, when I have broken the bars of their yoke, and delivered them from the hand of those who make bondsmen of them. And they will not become any more a spoil to the nations, and the animals of the land will no more devour them ; and they will dwell securely, and there will be none to terrify them. And I will raise up for them a complete plantation.[2] And they will not be taken away by hunger in the land, and they will not bear any more the reproach of the nations. And they will know that I, Jahveh, their God, am with them and that they are my people, the house of Israel, is the utterance of Adonay Jahveh. My sheep, the sheep of my pasture, are ye,[3] and I am your God, is the utterance of Adonay Jahveh."

—Ezek. xxxiv. 11–31.

Jahveh is the shepherd of Israel. The exiles are His flock that have been scattered by storm and tempest. He will not forsake them, but will search them out and gather them together, and restore them to their fold in the land of Israel. The prophet has in mind the same conception that we have found in Ps. lxxx.[4] In Zech. xi. Jahveh the good shepherd rejected his flock after they had treated Him as a miserable slave.[5] Here the good shepherd recovers His sheep. In con-

---

[1] The clause סביבות גבעתי ברכה is exceedingly difficult. The LXX. omits ברכה. The limitation to "round about my hill," that is, Zion, is unnatural. Cornill suggests that the original reading was רביבות = showers, as in Deut. xxxii. 2; Jer. iii.; Ps. lxv. 11, lxxii. 6. This would admirably suit the context. But there is no sufficient reason for departing from the text.

[2] The לשם of the Massoretic text and Vulgate version is not so suited to the context as שלם of the LXX. and Peshitto. There has been a transportation of letters. We agree with Cornill in preferring the שלם.

[3] אדם of the Massoretic text gives a very unsatisfactory sense. It is best with the LXX. to strike it out ; so Cornill rightly judges.

[4] See p. 229.   [5] See p. 187.

nection with the restoration a new covenant is established. This covenant bears the significant name, covenant of peace, because it secures exemption from war and permanent safety in the holy land. The animal kingdom will be at peace with them, and the land will become wonderfully fruitful. The plantation will become so complete in its fruitfulness that there will be no more hunger in the land, but every want will be satisfied. This covenant with nature is in the line of Hosea.[1] The second David appears in the prediction as in Hosea and Jeremiah,[2] but he is in a subordinate position. He is appointed by Jahveh to his shepherd's office, and enters upon his service after the redemption and restoration have been accomplished by Jahveh Himself.

V. THE GREAT PURIFICATION.

§ 80. *Israel will be restored to their own land. They will be sprinkled with clean water and purified. They will receive a new heart and spirit instead of the heart of stone. They will enjoy great prosperity in the land, which will become like the garden of Eden.*

"And I will scatter upon you pure water, and ye will be purified from all your uncleannesses ; and from all your idols will I purify you, and give to you a new heart ; and a new spirit will I give within you, and remove the heart of stone from your flesh, and give to you a heart of flesh ; and my spirit will I give within you, and I will cause that you will walk in my statutes, and that my judgments ye will keep and do them. . . . . And the desolate land will be tilled, whereas it was a desolation in the eyes of every passer-by. And they will say, yonder desolate land is become like the garden of Eden ; and the cities that were waste and desolate and torn down are fenced and inhabited."—Ezek. xxxvi. 25–35.

Ezekiel here represents that the restoration is to be connected with a great purification. The purification in the previous section was accomplished by a great national

[1] See p. 172.   [2] See pp. 174 and 247 seq.

discipline and through suffering. Here it is by the application of pure water. The prophet uses the ceremonial purification of Israel as a great symbol to set forth the great purification that is to transform the nation by transforming its heart and spirit. This is to be accomplished not by any human priests through the use of rites and ceremonies, but by God Himself, who makes a great national baptism. This baptism cleanses the entire nation within and without. It removes all the external uncleanness due to the worship of idols and the indulgence in corrupt practices. But it also removes the deeper impurity of a hard, stubborn and rebellious heart, a reluctant disposition and unruly temper. A new heart takes the place of the old heart, and it is a heart of flesh responsive to the touch of the divine hand. The heart of stone, cold, hard and insensible, is taken away. A new spirit is imparted to Israel, and that is a spirit given directly by God Himself,—a spirit that is in sympathy with the Spirit of God and acts under the divine impulse. Such a purified people are to dwell in a purified land. As there has been a new creation of man after the manner of the creation of Adam by the inbreathing of the breath of God, so there is a renovation of the earth, and it becomes like the garden of Eden, and Paradise is restored. The prophet has in mind the poem of the Temptation and the Fall; and the story of the origin of our race [1] gives him the symbol by which to set forth the new life of Israel in the land of promise, in the new Eden.

VI. THE GREAT RESURRECTION.

§ 81. *Although the nation is dead, and is become a heap of dry bones, the Spirit of Jahveh will bring them to life and animate them with the courage of a great army of God.*

[1] See Gen. ii. 7.

"And I prophesied as I was commanded: and there was a sound when I prophesied, and, lo, an earthquake, and bones approached bone unto its bone. And I saw, and, lo, sinews upon them, and flesh came up, and skin covered them over above: but there was no breath in them. Then he said unto me, Prophesy unto the breath,[1] son of man, and say unto the breath, Thus saith Adonay Jahveh: From the four winds, come thou, O breath, and breathe upon these slain, that they may live. And I prophesied as he commanded me, and the breath came in them, and they lived, and stood up upon their feet a very very great host. And he said unto me, Son of man, these bones are the whole house of Israel: lo, they are saying, Our bones are dried up, and our hope is lost; it is cut off from us. Therefore prophesy, and say unto them, Thus saith Adonay Jahveh: Lo, I am about to open your graves and bring you up from your graves, my people; and bring you to the land of Israel. And ye will know that it is I, Jahveh, when I open your graves, and when I bring you up from your graves, my people, and put my breath in you, and ye live and I place you in your own land; and ye will know that it is I, Jahveh. I have spoken and I will do it, is the utterance of Jahveh."—Ezek. xxxvii. 7–14.

The prophet uses the creation of Adam by the inbreathing of the breath of life from God as a symbol of the restoration of Israel. It is probable that he had in mind also the prediction of a national resurrection that we have found in Hosea.[2] This symbol does not imply the Christian doctrine of the resurrection of all men from the dead. It moves only in the sphere of

[1] There is considerable difference of opinion, in this section, as to the proper rendering of הרוח. The R.V. renders it "wind" twice in this verse; and then once in this verse and once in the following verse "breath." In ver. 14 it renders it "spirit." The margin gives the alternative renderings "breath" for the renderings "wind" and "spirit," and "wind" or "spirit" for the rendering "breath." It seems to us that it is necessary to render uniformly by "breath." The prophet has in mind here, as in the previous section, the creation of Adam in Eden by the inbreathing of the breath of life from the divine nostrils. This breath is still absent from the body. He summons it to come from all quarters and enter with its life the bodies that have come out of their graves. This breath is called the breath of God, because it is conceived here, as in Gen. ii. 7, as having its source in God. The breath and the spirit are not discriminated.

[2] See p. 176.

national death and national resurrection. The nation of
Israel is dead. It has died upon the battlefield. The
field is covered with the slain. The flesh has disappeared
from the bones, and they have become very dry. All
hope seems to have perished. But the divine promises
will be fulfilled. The grace of God is supreme over death.
At the word of divine command, and in obedience to the
prophet's summons, the bones move together to their
proper places, the flesh and the sinews come upon them,
and the body is reconstituted. But it still lacks the
breath of life. At the summons of the prophet, the
breath comes rushing in, and the bodies live and rise to
their feet a very very great army. This resurrection of
Israel is accomplished by the command of God. God
Himself comes in theophany with convulsions of nature
to bring it about. The symbol is a symbol of the resurrection of Israel as a nation, and their restoration to the
holy land. It becomes associated in subsequent prophecy
with the doctrine of a universal resurrection, because the
restoration of Israel, that the prophet had in view, can
be accomplished only in the resurrection of all mankind
in the last great day, and their establishment in the new
Jerusalem upon the new earth. But this wider outlook
was not granted to Ezekiel.

VII. THE GREAT REUNION.

§ 82. *Israel and Judah will be reunited under the
second David. A new and everlasting covenant of peace
will be made with them, and the sanctuary of Jahveh will
abide in their midst for ever.*

"Thus saith Adonay Jahveh: Lo, I am about to take the whole
house of Israel [1] from among the nations, whither they be gone, and

---

[1] Cornill rightly follows the LXX. כל בית ישראל in preference to
the Massoretic בני ישראל, on the ground that the change in the
direction of the Massoretic text was easier than the reverse.

gather them from round about, and bring them unto their land,
and make them one nation in my land [1] on the mountains of Israel;
and one king will they all have for king, and they will not be two
nations any more, and they will not be divided into two kingdoms
any more. And they will not defile themselves any more with
idols or with their detestable things, nor with any of their transgressions; but I will save them from all their apostasies [2] wherein
they have sinned, and will cleanse them; and they will become a
people to me, and I will become a God to them. And my servant
David will be king over them, and they all will have one shepherd,
and in my judgments will they walk, and my statutes will they
keep and do them. And they will dwell upon the land which I
gave to my servant, to Jacob, in which their fathers dwelt; and
they will dwell upon it, they, their children, and their children's
children for ever; and David my servant will be their prince for
ever.

And I will conclude a covenant of peace with them; an everlasting covenant will be with them; [3] and I will give my sanctuary in
their midst for ever. And my dwelling-place will be with them;
and I will become a God to them, and they will become a people to
me. And the nations will know that I, Jahveh, am sanctifying
Israel, when my sanctuary is in their midst for ever."

—Ezek. xxxvii. 21–28.

This prediction is the renewal of several earlier ones
in a new form. The prophet uses a very simple symbol,
the union of two sticks. This sets forth the reunion of
the two sections of Israel, Judah who has just gone
into exile and the northern kingdom that has long been
in exile. They are both to unite under the second David,
as in Hosea.[4] In connection with this reunion a new

---

[1] The LXX. בארצי is preferable to the Massoretic בארץ, as Cornill
states. It is more suited to the style of the prophet, and is warmer.

[2] The Massoretic מושבתיהם = "their dwellings," does not give
good sense in the context. The LXX. translates ἀνομιῶν. It is
better to read משובותיהם = "their apostasies," after Symmachus,
with Ewald and Cornill. So the margin of the R.V. renders "their
backslidings."

[3] The Massoretic ונתתים והרביתי אותם is not in the LXX. The
Peshitto omits ונתתים. The whole is probably a marginal gloss that
has crept into the text. It disturbs the context.

[4] See p. 167.

covenant of peace will be established that will endure
for ever. This is a renewal of Ezekiel xxxiv.[1] The
divine sanctuary will abide in their midst for ever after
they have been consecrated and prepared for it. The
little season when Jahveh was their sanctuary without a
visible sanctuary will be past, and the everlasting union
in the holy land will be accomplished.[2]

VIII. THE JUDGMENT OF GOG.

§ 83. *There will be a great final conflict with Gog at
the head of nations from the ends of the earth. These will
be overthrown by the advent of Jahveh, who will rain fire
and brimstone upon them and utterly destroy them. But
He will pour out His Spirit on His people, and restore
them to their own land.*

"And the word of Jahveh came unto me, saying, Son of man,
set thy face toward Gog, of the land of Magog, the prince of the
chiefs[3] of Meshech and Tubal, and prophesy against him, and say,
This saith Adonay Jahveh: Behold I am against thee, O Gog,
prince of the chiefs of Meshech and Tubal; and I will turn thee
about, and put hooks into thy jaws, and I will bring thee forth,
and all thine army, horses and horsemen, all of them clothed in full
armour, a great company with buckler and shield, all of them
handling swords: Persia, Cush, and Put with them; all of them
with shield and helmet: Gomer, and all his hordes; the house of
Togarmah in the uttermost parts of the north, and all his hordes;

---

[1] See p. 273.   [2] See p. 268.

[3] נְשִׂיא רֹאשׁ is rendered in the R.V. prince of Rosh; so most
interpreters; after the LXX. Sym. Theod. even the latest, Orelli
and Cornill. But the A.V. and the margin of the R.V. render
correctly "chief prince," after the Vulgate, Peshitto, Aquila, and
Targum; so rightly Hengstenberg, Ewald, and Smend. There is
no such country as Rosh known to the Bible, and there is no propriety whatever in referring it to Russia. (See C. H. H. Wright,
Biblical Essays, p. 99 seq., Edin. 1886.) We should also expect a
leader of these hordes, who would bear a more exalted title than
"prince," whereas the prince over chiefs of many tribes and nations
is what the context really requires.

even many peoples with thee. . . . When thou shalt ascend, thou wilt come like a storm, thou wilt be like a cloud to cover the land, thou, and all thy hordes, and many peoples with thee. . . . And it will come to pass in that day when Gog shall come against the land of Israel, is the utterance of Adonay Jahveh, that my fury will come up into my nostrils. Yea, in my zeal and in the fire of my overflowing wrath do I speak, Surely in that day there will be a great earthquake upon the land of Israel ; and the fishes of the sea, and the birds of heaven, and the wild animals of the field, and all creeping things that creep upon the earth, and all the men that are upon the face of the earth, will quake at my presence, and the mountains will be thrown down, and the steep places will fall, and every wall will fall to the ground. And I will call against him every terror,[1] is the utterance of Adonay Jahveh. Every man's sword will be against his brother. And I will plead against him with pestilence and with blood ; and I will rain upon him, and upon his hordes, and upon the many peoples that are with him an overflowing shower, and great hailstones, fire and brimstone. . . . And they that dwell in the cities of Israel will go forth, and make fires[2] of the weapons, both the shields and the bucklers, the bows and the arrows, and the handstaves, and the spears, and they will set fire to them seven years. . . . And it will come to pass in that day, that I will give unto Gog a place for burial in Israel, the valley of Abarim on the east of the sea ; and they will stop up the valley :[3] and there will they bury Gog and all his multitude ; and they will call it the valley of [4] Hamongog. And seven months will the house

---

[1] The Massoretic לְכָל־הָרַי חֶרֶב is not suited to the context. The LXX. πᾶν φόβον μαχαίρας is much better in this respect. It involves the Hebrew כָּל חֲרָדָה, which is rightly adopted by Cornill. We also agree with him in striking out חֶרֶב. This is not suited to חֲרָדָה, and is not found in some of the best MSS. of the LXX. It is a premature specification, which is unnatural in view of the details that follow.

[2] The LXX. and Peshitto omit וּבִעֲרוּ, and it seems to be a marginal gloss explanatory of the unusual הִשִּׂיק. It is therefore properly stricken out by Cornill.

[3] הָעֹבְרִים should be pointed הָעֲבָרִים, the mountains of Moab, outside of the holy land of the restoration ; and the LXX. and Peshitto should be followed, and the Massoretic וַחֲסֹמַת הִיא changed into וְחָסְמוּ אֶת הַגַּיְא after Cornill, and אֶת־הָעֹבְרִים should be elided as a vain repetition from the margin.

[4] הֲמוֹן גּוֹג. The name combines גּוֹג וְכָל הֲמוֹנוֹ above, the multitude of Gog, Gog and all his multitude.

of Israel be burying of them, that they may cleanse the land. . . .
And thou, son of man, thus saith Adonay Jahveh: Say unto the
birds of every wing, and to all the wild animals of the field, Assemble
yourselves, and come; gather yourselves on every side to my sacrifice [1] that I do sacrifice for you, even a great sacrifice upon the
mountains of Israel, and ye will eat flesh and drink blood. Ye
shall eat the flesh of the mighty, and drink the blood of the princes
of the earth, of rams, of lambs, and of goats, of bullocks, all of them
fatlings of Bashan. And ye shall eat flesh [2] till ye be full, and
drink blood till ye be drunken, of my sacrifice which I have sacri-
ficed for you. And ye shall be filled at my table with horses and
chariots, with mighty men, and with all men of war, is the utterance of Adonay Jahveh. . . . Therefore thus saith Adonay Jahveh:
Now will I restore the prosperity of Jacob, and have compassion
upon the whole house of Israel; and I will be zealous for my holy
name. And they will forget [3] their rebellion, and all their trespasses
whereby they have trespassed against me, when they dwell securely
in their land, and there be none to make them afraid; when I have
brought them again from the peoples, and gathered them out of
their enemies' lands, and am sanctified in them in the sight of many
nations. And they will know that it is I, Jahveh their God, in
that I caused them to go into captivity among the nations, and I
gathered them unto their own land; and I will leave none of them
any more there; and I will not hide my face any more from them;
for I have poured out my Spirit upon the house of Israel, is the
utterance of Adonay Jahveh."—Ezek. xxxviii.-xxxix.

The prophet looks forward to the reoccupation of the
holy land by the children of Israel. They will dwell in it
in peaceful security without the need of walled towns

---

[1] Jahveh Himself makes a great זבח, and the flesh of the victims
makes a great feast for the birds and beasts of prey.

[2] בשר is the correct reading, after the Vulgate and Peshitto, in
accord with the context. The חלב of the Massoretic text is not so
good, although supported by the LXX.

[3] ונשׂו is the Massoretic reading, a shortened form of ונשׂאו = " they
will bear." So the Versions and interpreters generally take it.
But it is better, with Hitzig and Cornill, to read נשׁו, and render
"forget." This is more in accordance with the context, and gives
us a thought similar to Zeph. iii. 11. Cornill would change בלמחם
into בל מרתם. This would give a better sense, but it is not
necessary.

and fortresses. Their prosperity and apparently unprotected condition will in the last days provoke the greed
of distant nations. The Scythians, the scourge of the
ancient world, those mysterious hordes of cavalry from
the steppes of Central Asia, whom we have already
met in the predictions of Zephaniah,[1] rise before the
mind of the prophet as the symbol of the last enemies
of the people of God. Gog is the prince of the chiefs of
these savage tribes, who rush upon the holy land like a
horrible tempest. They whirl along with them in their
swift career nations from all parts of the earth. For
Persia, Ethiopia, Libya, Gomer and Togarmah, Meshech
and Tubal, all take part in this great invasion.
Nations from the most distant parts of Europe, Asia, and
Africa simultaneously arise and rush to the centre of the
earth to attack the innocent and unprotected people of
God, and rob them of their peace and wealth.[2] Such
a conflict we have seen already in Joel,[3] but the vision of
that prophet was confined to a narrower range. There
they battle in the vale of Jehoshaphat, here the combat
is upon the mountains of Israel. The hordes of the
enemy cover the whole land like a dense cloud. But
Jahveh has not forsaken His people. He is their only
protector and saviour, but they need no other. Gog and
his host have been gathered together for slaughter.

Jahveh comes with a great earthquake that shakes
all nature and brings every lofty thing to the ground.
He comes with a tempest raining fire, and brimstone, and
hailstones upon the armies of the nations. They are
thrown into a panic and turn their swords against each
other,[4] and pestilence combines with every ill to destroy

---

[1] See p. 221.
[2] See C. H. H. Wright, *Biblical Essays*, p. 108 seq., Edin. 1886.
[3] See p. 157.
[4] The prophet combines several features of theophanies of

them. From all parts the birds and beasts of prey gather to devour their carcases. Their bones are so numerous that for seven months the house of Israel will be busy in burying them, and a great valley will be filled up with their carcases. Their weapons will be so numerous that they will serve the people of the land for seven years with sufficient firewood. The overthrow is to be total, overwhelming, and final. The prophet now concludes with a brief reference to the security of restored Israel. Jahveh has poured out His Spirit upon them, and they recognise God as their deliverer, and His face will no more be hid from them. The advent of the Spirit of Jahveh is not so prominent as in Joel,[1] because the prediction deals chiefly with the great deliverance wrought in the last conflict, and the prophet has in mind another great prophecy of the restoration.

This prediction has no historical reference. It is in its nature apocalyptic. It points to a conflict to follow the restoration. It is taken up again by the author of the New Testament Apocalypse as the appropriate symbol of the final conflict of the world.[2]

IX. THE HOLY LAND OF THE RESTORATION.

§ 84. *Ezekiel gives a detailed description of the holy land of the restoration, its division among the tribes, the sacred portions of the priests, Levites, and prince; the holy city named Jahveh Shammah; the temple, its stately structure and sanctity; the priesthood limited to the faithful and holy line of Zadok; and the ritual, which differs from*

ancient times. The earthquake is frequent in theophanies, Ex. xix. 18; Num. xxvi. 10; Ps. xviii. 7; fire, hailstones, and tempests are mentioned, Gen. xix. 24; Josh. x. 11; Judg. v. 20; and the panic, Judg. vii. 22; 1 Sam. xiv. 20; 2 Chron. xx. 23.

[1] See p. 155.   [2] Rev. xx. 7–10.

*that of the priest code by its relative simplicity and the stress
laid upon the sin-offerings at the beginning of the year.
From the temple a stream of life issues, increasing as it
goes in depth and power. Its waters give life to the barren
portions of the land, and even the Dead Sea and its shores,
with the exception of a few salt tracts. The banks of the
river are lined with trees of life, yielding healing leaves
and monthly fruits. The garden of Eden and the new
Jerusalem are combined.*

Ezekiel closes his book of prophecy with the greatest
symbol that he or any other prophet ever conceived. He
combines in his representation the story of Paradise, the
holy land of the conquest, the temple of Solomon, and
the structures of the great cities of the Babylonian empire,
—all that was greatest and best in the history and experience of his own nation and other nations, in order to
set forth the wondrous excellence of the holy land of
the restoration. Most modern interpreters hesitate to
accept the entire section, chaps. xl.–xlix., as Messianic.
Even Hengstenberg limits the Messianic element to chap.
xlvii. 1–12.[1] Wellhausen and his associates regard the
whole as the programme for the returning exiles that
was afterwards expanded into the priestly legislation.
But it seems to us that the whole section is one great
symbol.

"It is Ezekiel's peculiarity not to picture the days to
come in general outline, but thoroughly to enter into
and appropriate such anticipations of the future, both in
inward and outward respects. Hence he does not simply
foretell the re-erection of the temple and holy nation in
whose midst God will take up His abode for ever; but
this perfect restoration of God's house, in which nothing
that ever belonged to it will be lost, is carried out before

---

[1] Hengstenberg, *The Prophecies of the Prophet Ezekiel*, p. 348,
Edin. 1874.

his eyes to the least minutiæ. In this process, indeed, the O. T. limitation asserts itself more strongly than in the prophets elsewhere, while often transcended in spirit it cannot be permanently overcome by the existing power of conception. In great measure the picture is only a prophecy of the true consummation of God's kingdom, in so far as the Mosaic cultus is so also. Here, where prophecy sketches the concrete shape of the future Church, it falls back into the typical. It is a description of God's perfect residence in the imperfect figurative language of the Old Covenant." [1]

It is necessary for us to remember that the symbolism is elaborate and intricate, but this is in order to set forth clearly and strongly the ideal that it is our privilege to determine.

The temple of Ezekiel is situated on an exceeding high mountain, as in Micah and Isaiah. [2] It is a stately structure like a city. It is enclosed in a wall, a reed high, and is five hundred cubits square, and has an outer border of fifty cubits. This area is in the midst of a sacred portion of Jahveh, assigned to the priests of the line of Zadok, $25,000 \times 10,000$. North of this portion is the portion of the Levites of the same dimensions. On the south is the portion of the city of equal length, but only half the width. The portion of the prince extends along the east and west sides of these three portions. The holy land is a narrow strip along the Mediterranean Sea, from Hamath to the river of Egypt, all of it on the west of the Jordan. The tribes receive their portion beginning at the north. Seven are on the north of the four reserved portions, in the order, Dan, Asser, Naphtali, Manasseh, Ephraim, Reuben, Judah. Five are on the south, in the order, Benjamin, Simeon, Issachar, Zebulon, and Gad: This

[1] Orelli, in *l.c.* pp. 373, 374.
[2] See p. 181.

arrangement differs so greatly from the original division of the land that it must be regarded as a new arrangement.

It is not difficult to discern the ideal element here. The land of the restoration is to be distributed among the tribes of Israel in accordance with the new conditions and circumstances that may arise. The temple of Ezekiel is separated from the holy city, each of these having its own sacred enclosure. The temple is in the midst of the portion of the faithful and holy priests of the line of Zadok. It is to be regarded as vastly more sacred than the ancient temple. It is much more magnificent, and is more carefully guarded. The walls of the temple enclosure are like the walls of a city, and they have three gates of elaborate construction and stately buildings in which are the guard-rooms of the Levitical priests. Access to the sacred places is guarded with extreme care.

At the distance of 100 cubits from the outer gates are three inner gates leading to the inner court. These are of the same stately character as the outer gates, only the apartments of the north and south gates are places of purification for the washing and slaughter of the victims, and they have associated with them in the outer court additional buildings containing dressing-rooms for the priests. The east gate is the gate through which Jahveh enters to take possession of the temple. After the divine entry in theophany, the outer gate must remain closed for ever. The east gate of the inner court is to be opened on the sabbaths and new moons, and the prince is to enter therein and worship at the threshold while the priests offer his offerings. It is also to be opened for the prince to make a free-will offering.

The inner court is 100 cubits square. None but the priests of the line of Zadok can enter it. The Levitical

priests are degraded from the priesthood for unfaithfulness, and are assigned the duty of guarding the outer
court of the temple. But the line of Zadok are exalted
to higher privileges of sanctity owing to their faithfulness.[1]
This is an unfolding of the Messianic idea of the
covenant with Phinehas, the faithful priesthood that was
to be substituted for the house of Eli, and the eternal
priesthood of the prediction of Jeremiah.[2] The priests of
the line of Zadok are clothed in pure white linen in
their ministry. These garments are to be worn in the
ministry in the inner court, and are to be deposited in
the halls for the priests. The priests are to keep themselves from every form of impurity. They are the
ministers of the inner court of the temple, and as such are
exalted in holiness beyond anything that had been previously prescribed. The priests of the new dispensation
are to be faithful and holy. None but such priests will
be able to minister before Jahveh when He comes in His
glory. The priests have the additional office of instructing
the people and judging causes according to the law of
Jahveh. This function is an unfolding of the provisions
of the Deuteronomic code.[3] The divine instruction flows
forth from them to the people of God. The temple is
situated in the inner court. It is of the same size and
general character as the temple of Solomon. But it is
distinguished by the absence of the ark of the covenant
from the most holy place. Here Ezekiel is in entire
accord with Jeremiah.[4] The glory of Jahveh, which has
entered through the east gates, has filled the house and
dwells there for ever. Furthermore, the temple has no
lamp-stand, and it combines the altar of incense and the
table of shew-bread of the old temple in the one wooden

---

[1] Ezek. xl. 46, xliii. 19, xliv. 15 seq.
[2] See pp. 110, 122, 246.   [3] Deut. xvii.
[4] Jer. iii. 14–18. See p. 242.

altar table before Jahveh.   The inner court has no lavers
and no brazen sea, for the places for purification are in
the chambers of the inner gates and the halls of the
priests.   The only thing in the court is the great altar
upon which the offerings to Jahveh are made.   And
thus there is greater simplicity in the furniture of the
new temple, as greater stress is laid upon the glory of
Jahveh that occupies it and the sanctity of His priesthood.

The offerings embrace the same kinds as the priest
code, and yet the ritual is simpler and differently
arranged.   The offerings are all to be made by the
priests of the line of Zadok who receive them from the
prince whose duty it is to provide them.   The prince
receives them from the people.   This gradation of
responsibility in providing and making the offerings is a
better security than the looser provisions of the priest-
code.   The ritual service embraces the morning sacrifice,
the sabbaths, the new moons, passover, and tabernacles.
No mention is made of the evening sacrifice, Pentecost,
the feast of trumpets, or the day of atonement.   On the
other hand, there is a special emphasis upon the first and
the seventh days of the first month, in the offering of the
sin-offerings of expiation, that seems to exclude the day
of atonement of the priest-code.   These sin-offerings
differ from the sin-offerings of the day of atonement in
that they consist of a bullock, and that the blood is
applied to the door-posts of the temple, the corners of
the base of the altar, and the gate-posts of the inner
court, to purify the sanctuary and cleanse it in its most
essential parts from the uncleanness of the people in
which it was situated.   As the inner court is the place
of sacrifice into which only the Zadokite priests may
enter, and from which even the other Levitical priests
are excluded, so it appears that even the Zadokite priests

are not permitted to enter the temple itself, for the blood of the most sacred sin-offering, which in the prescription of the priest code is taken into the holiest of all and applied to the base of the throne of Jahveh, the *Kapporeth* above the ark of the covenant, is here applied only to the doors of the temple. It appears that the whole temple has assumed the sanctity of the holy of holies of the Solomonic temple, and there is no high priest in Ezekiel's representation to enter even the outer room of the temple. This is in keeping with the absence of the ark of the covenant, the lamp-stand, the shew-bread and the incense, and the limitation of the temple furniture to a simple altar table before Jahveh.

The ideal of Ezekiel thus emphasizes so greatly the sanctity of the new temple and its priesthood that it increases the difficulty of access to God. This at first seems to be a decline in the development of prophecy rather than an advance, and to be far from what we should expect in a Messianic prediction. But we observe that the prophet has in view just this thing, to exalt the majesty and sanctity of the new temple and its ritual ; and if the difficulty of access is enhanced here, it is relieved in part by the provision of faithful and holy priests of the line of Zadok who are all alike faithful and holy, and who need no high priest of superior rank and sanctity to mediate for them with God. It is also still further relieved by the prophecy that we have already considered where a new spirit and a heart of flesh were promised to God's people.[1] If the prophet dwells on the external here, and presses it even to extremities, he certainly is no less extreme in his unfolding of the internal there. The holy land of the restoration will solve all these paradoxes. Each prediction is a separate glance into a future that is transcendently glorious.

[1] See p. 274.

T

The time had not yet come for faithfulness and sanctity, the characteristic features of the line of Zadok, to be extended to the entire people as a kingdom of priests. And the great high priest who was to embody these traits of character in perfection had not yet risen from the line of Zadok as its culmination. The prediction is absorbed in the glories of the divine advent, and the second David appears merely as the princely head of the nation, providing the national sacrifices to be offered by the priests of the line of Zadok, and leading the nation in its devotions.

The prophecy concludes with a description of the river of life issuing from the temple. This stream we have already found in Joel, Isaiah, and the Psalter.[1] But our prophet is much more elaborate. He describes it as it trickles down from the side of the gate, then increasing as it goes with wonderful rapidity so that its waters rise about the soles of the feet, to the knees, to the loins, and finally become a flood that cannot be passed. These waters are waters of life. They impart life to the waste and desolate regions, so that even the waters and banks of the Dead Sea are healed and filled with life, with the exception of a few salt tracks reserved for desolation. On the banks of the stream are trees of life, with healing leaves and monthly fruits.[2] The prophet thus uses the imagery of the garden of Eden to show that in his conception Paradise is to be restored and attached to the new Jerusalem.[3] The prophecy concludes with the name of the city, "*Jahveh is there*," which reminds us of the name of the same city in Jeremiah,[4] "*Jahveh is our righteousness.*"

---

[1] See pp. 158 seq., 211, and 214.
[2] Ezek. xlvii. 1–12.
[3] This conception of Ezekiel is resumed in Rev. xxii.
[4] See p. 246.

CHAPTER X.

THE destruction of Jerusalem by Nebuchadnezzar, king of Babylon, and the removal of its inhabitants into exile, seemed to be the death of the Jewish nation. But the destruction of the temple and its furniture by fire, and the desecration of its sacred places by the tramp of the heathen, seemed to the pious Jew still more dreadful. It looked as if God had abandoned His people, and that the national religion had died also. But the religion of Jahveh was indestructible. It was not to perish with the exile of the nation as so many other religions had perished. In the greatest calamities it displayed its power. It rose fresh and vigorous from the ruins of its holy places. These were but the external forms of the religion of Jahveh, and not the religion itself. It at once assumed newer and higher forms suited to the condition of the exile, and it pointed forward to forms of external manifestation that infinitely transcend the ancient forms. The destruction of the holy city and temple was indeed the work of Jahveh Himself. The Chaldean was His servant, to accomplish His purpose of chastisement upon His people. This chastisement was a striking to death, a turning the world upside down; but the Chaldean, like the Assyrian before him, is to perish in the divine judgment that will come upon him for his sins. Israel will rise from the dead and a new world will take the place of the old.

In these times of exile Jahveh raised up His greatest prophet, one who mastered the situation, grasped the problem of the exile, and saw its solution in a great act of divine judgment and of redemption. The name of this prophet has not been handed down to posterity. He issued his prophecies anonymously. They were circulated among his countrymen in the different regions of the dispersion. It was not likely that he could safely attach his name to his predictions, or that they could be circulated in public during the period of the Babylonian supremacy. His prophecies were issued from time to time, and subsequently gathered into that masterly poem that is contained in chaps. xl.–lxvi. of Isaiah. It seems to us that chaps. xiii.–xiv. and chaps. xxxiv.–xxxv. of Isaiah are from the same great author. They are so complete in themselves, and of such length, that he did not deem it best to include them in his final collection. Indeed, they are the preludes to his great composition.

The great unknown did not stand alone. There were others associated with him who have left us their prophecies. Some of these are also contained in the Book of Isaiah, and others are preserved in the Psalter. The literary difference between these writings and those that were issued previous to the exile is well stated by Ewald: "All the writings which arose in this transition time are alike in this, that they bear the common impress of being purely literary productions, and exhibit no traces whatever of a previous public prophetic work and speech. In the case of the earlier prophets, every book, indeed almost every piece, is a glass through which we can clearly discern by a hundred signs the public work of the prophet which lies behind it; and even in the Book of Hézeqiél a large portion of his public life and work is interwoven, at least of the time before the destruction of Jerusalem. Now, however, after the people had for

many decades entirely lost their freedom, and conse-
quently the captivity had long silenced the public
ministry of all the prophets of Israel, a longer or shorter
book, though bearing the outward form used by the old
prophets, nevertheless could no longer be the ripe fruit of
public labours, and could nowhere show real traces of
them.   The word had no choice but to adopt literature
as its vehicle; the prophet was compelled to become a
writer.   These writings came forth indeed from the
heart of this excited and agitated time, for the most part
without much elaboration as genuine pamphlets of the
day, reflecting with the freshest life and warmth the
feelings of the passing day, and speaking straight from
the heart; yet throughout, as proceeding simply from
the inspiration of an individual, not as from the public
national life of Israel.   And really this is a chief mark
which distinguishes all these pieces from those of the
older prophets; they may indeed be recognized by a
hundred other signs, and the more closely we compare
them with older pieces, the more evidence we find that
they could not have been written earlier than in this
extraordinary time.   But this one mark is of the greatest
significance; any one who is really acquainted with the
older prophets, will feel that writings which exhibit in every
respect the characteristics of literary effort and diction
must belong to quite another sphere of prophetic labour."[1]

Whatever opinion of their authorship may be held,
these writings take their place in the exile, so far as the
development of the Messianic idea is concerned.   They
exhibit a marked advance beyond Jeremiah and Zephaniah; and the great unknown is certainly at a higher
stage of religious development than Ezekiel.[2]

[1] Ewald, *Prophets*, English edition, iv. pp. 228, 229.

These pieces all exhibit features of the period of the exile.
Those who still maintain that Isaiah was their author admit this,

The sufferings of the Jews as they went forth into exile were greatly enhanced by the cruelty of the neighbouring tribes of Moab and Edom, who were united by ancient ties of kinship. These joined with the oppressor in the bitterest hours of Judah, and without cause outdid the Babylonian in deeds of violence and crime. It was natural, therefore, that Israel's hope of restoration should be mingled with anticipations of judgment upon these nations as well as upon the great world-

and hold that these pieces are apocalypses, in which the situation of the prophet is ideal as well as the predictions themselves. But there is no reason for such a violent hypothesis. It is a law of prophecy that the historical situation of the prophet should be the basis of his prediction. See p. 56; also A. B. Davidson, *The Expositor*, August 1885, p. 86; and Orelli in *l.c.* p. 415. This alone makes the prediction useful to his contemporaries. There is no reason for an anticipation of the situation of the exile in the age of Hezekiah to make it the basis of a prediction of the Messianic time. God does not raise up prophets before their time. He does not give predictions until they are needed. Isaiah lived in the Assyrian period, and his prophecies dealt with that period and its issues. The prophecies we are now to consider all deal with the Babylonian period and its relation to the Messianic age. The theology of these pieces is in decided advance beyond that of Isaiah —all along the line of doctrine, religion, and morals. It is also in advance of Jeremiah and of Ezekiel. There are sufficient evidences that these authors were familiar with Isaiah, but there are also evidences no less great of their use of Jeremiah, Zephaniah and other prophets. It is indeed characteristic of the great unknown that he grasps the theology of the past, and reconstructs it for the future in higher and grander forms.

The language of these pieces is also different from that of the age of Hezekiah or of Josiah. There are large numbers of words of late formation. But the most striking feature is the difference in syntax. The syntax of this prophet is at a considerable stage of decay beyond that of Jeremiah, and is nearer to Ezekiel in its neglect of the *vav* consecutive and use of the simple *vav*. This is all the more striking in a prophet of such elegance of style as the great unknown shows himself to be throughout his poem. It is sufficient for us to state that the four great principles of internal evidence, upon which the science of the higher criticism depends, are decidedly in favour of exilic writers for these compositions, namely—(1) Their historical situation; (2) their style; (3) their theology; (4) their depending upon Zephaniah and Jeremiah and

power, Babylon. There are several predictions of this
kind belonging to the early days of the exile, from prophets
who had themselves witnessed the destruction of the city.
The most important of these is the apocalypse contained
in Isa. xxiv.–xxvii.[1] This is one of the finest pieces of
poetry in the Old Testament. It is composed of twelve
strophes in the hexameter movement, and is remarkable
for its alliteration, rhyme and play upon words;[2] in all

other prophets. The external evidences in favour of their composition by Isaiah are purely traditional. They rest upon nothing
more substantial than the fact that the sections were appended to
Isaiah at an early period. It is noteworthy that there is an historical section xxxvi.–xxxix., which includes a prediction of Isaiah and
a song of Hezekiah. This clearly was designed to be the close of
the book by the editor who made it. It is extremely improbable
that any editor or author would have inserted such an historical
section before the great prophecy. It is probable that these anonymous writings were appended to Isaiah in order to make the book
of similar size with the other three great prophetic books, Jeremiah,
Ezekiel and the Twelve. It is also noteworthy that Isaiah is placed
third in order, in the most ancient Jewish tradition, between Ezekiel
and the Twelve, as if its composite character was recognized. And
the Talmud represents that the work was edited by the college of
Hezekiah and not by the prophet himself. See my *Biblical Study*,
p. 176.

[1] This piece has so many peculiarities of style and doctrine, that
it must be ascribed to an anonymous author, who has left this piece
as his only literary monument. See Knobel, *Jesaia*, p. 205 seq.,
4 Aufl. There is some difference of opinion as to the exact location
of the prophecy in the period of the exile. It is not easy to determine this question. It seems to me to belong to the earlier years
of the exile, when the destruction of Jerusalem and the evil conduct
of Moab were fresh to the experience of the people.

[2] The word-play of these lines should be noted—

xxiv. 3. הבוק תבוק הארץ והבוז תבוז

xxiv. 4. אבלה נבלה הארץ אמללה נבלה תבל

xxiv. 16. ואמר רזי לי רזי לי אוי לי

xxiv. 16. בנדים בגדו ובגד בגדים בגדו

xxiv. 17. פחד ופחת ופח עליה יושב הארץ

xxiv. 19. רע התרעעה ארץ פור התפוררה ארץ מוט התמוטטה ארץ

xxv. 6. משתה שמנים משתה שמרים

xxv. 6. שמנים ממחים שמרים מזקקים

xxvii. 7. הכמכת מכהו הכה אם כהרג הרגיו הרג

these respects transcending every other piece of Hebrew
poetry.

I. THE DESTRUCTION OF THE GREAT METROPOLIS AND THE ANNIHILATION OF DEATH AND SORROW.

§ 85. *This apocalypse depicts the judgment of the nations,
among whom Moab and the great world-powers, the
leviathan Babylon and the dragon Egypt, are especially
mentioned. The earth staggers like a drunkard and
swings like a hammock. It is utterly laid waste, and all
classes and conditions of its population are scattered. The
kings of the earth and the evil powers of the heaven are shut
up in the dungeon and are punished. The wicked oppressors
will die for ever. But Israel's corpse belongs to Jahveh. The
light of life will quicken their dead bodies, and their shades
will come forth from Sheol. Death and sorrow will be
abolished for ever. The people will be gathered one by one
from all lands of their exile, and restored to Mount Zion,
where they will unite with all nations in the banquet provided for them by Jahveh.*

    I. "Behold, Jahveh is about to make the earth empty, and make
        it waste,
        And turn it upside down, and scatter abroad the inhabitants
            thereof.
        And it will be as with the people, so with the priest; as
            with the servant, so with his master;
        As with the maid, so with her mistress; as with the buyer,
            so with the seller;
        As with the lender, so with the borrower; as with the taker
            of usury, so with the giver of usury to him.
        The earth will be utterly emptied, and it will be utterly
            spoiled:
        Verily, Jahveh hath spoken this word.
        The earth doth mourn, doth fade away, the world doth
            languish, doth fade away.

The highnesses[1] of the earth do languish, the earth also is
    polluted under the inhabitants thereof :
Because they have transgressed the instructions, changed the
    ordinance, broken the everlasting covenant.

II. Therefore the curse doth devour the earth, and they that
    dwell therein are found guilty :
Therefore the inhabitants of the earth are burned, and few
    men left.
The new wine doth mourn, the vine doth languish, all the
    merry-hearted do sigh.
The mirth of tabrets doth cease, the noise of them that
    rejoice doth end, the joy of the harp doth cease.
They cannot drink wine with a song ; strong drink is bitter
    to them that drink it.
The city of chaos[2] is broken down : every house is shut up,
    that no man may come in.
There is a crying in the streets because of the wine ; all joy
    is darkened, the mirth of the land is gone into captivity.
In the city is left desolation ; and the gate is smitten with
    destruction.
For thus will it be in the midst of the earth among the
    peoples,
As the beating of an olive tree, as the grape gleanings when
    the vintage is done.

III. Those lift up their voice, they shout ;
Because of the majesty of Jahveh, they do cry aloud from
    the sea.
Therefore the glory[3] of Jahveh is in the coasts,[4]
The name of Jahveh, the God of Israel, in the coasts of the sea.

---

[1] מָרוֹם must have the same meaning here as in ver. 21, where it
is clearly a collective ; so Knobel and the margin of the R.V.
Cheyne renders quite appropriately " highnesses." This line is
completed in the first half of the next verse.

[2] קִרְיַת תֹהוּ. The city or town is doomed to תֹהוּ, that is, the
original chaotic condition of the earth before the creation of light
(Gen. i. 2).

[3] The pointing of the Massoretic text כְּבֻדוּ is against the context.
The LXX. read כָבוֹד, which is better suited to the parallel שֵׁם, and
to the context, which is not an exhortation, but a statement of a fact.
There has been a transposition of וֹ. See also ver. 23.

[4] בָּאֻרִים is difficult. It is omitted by the LXX. The Vulgate
renders *in doctrinis*, thinking of the *Urim and Thummim.* Gesenius

From the°skirt of the earth have we heard songs, 'glory to
  the righteous.'

I said, I pine away, I pine away, woe is me !

The treacherous dealers have dealt treacherously ; yea, the
  treacherous dealers have dealt very treacherously.

Fear, and the pit, and the snare are upon thee, O inhabitant
  of the earth.

And it will come to pass, that he who fleeth from the noise
  of the fear will fall into the pit ;

And he that cometh up out of the midst of the pit will be
  taken in the snare.

IV. For the windows on high are opened, and the foundations of
  the earth do shake.

The earth is utterly broken,[1] the earth is clean dissolved, the
  earth is entirely moved.

The earth staggereth like a drunken man, and moveth to and
  fro like a hammock ;[2]

And the transgression thereof rests heavy upon it, and it
  falls, and will not rise again.

And it will come to pass in that day, Jahveh will visit,

Upon the host of the high ones[3] on high, and upon the kings
  of the earth upon the earth.

---

renders, region of light, and is followed by the R.V. It is better,
with Lowth, Hitzig, Knobel, and Cheyne, to read באיים. This is
favoured by the style of the author. He first mentions the praise
as coming from the sea, מים ; then in the coasts באיים, and finally
combines them in באיי הים. The omission of the LXX. is due
probably to the feeling that איים was merely a repetition, and
without force.

[1] The Massoretic text should be corrected by striking out the ה
of רעה, which is an anomalous form, and against the analogy of
פור and מוט. It has arisen by repeating the initial ה of the next
word. הארץ should be deprived of the ה, which is against the
analogy of the other clauses, and has arisen by repeating the closing
ה of the previous word. Moreover, the rhythm requires the striking
out of these two unnecessary syllables in a line sufficiently long
without them. The line is composed of three parts of two accents
each.

[2] מלונה is rendered by the R.V. hut ; but it is better, after Knobel,
Gesenius, Ewald, and Cheyne, to render hammock.

[3] The host of the high in the height are the heavenly host,
including possibly the angel princes of the nations in hostility to
Israel, who are contrasted with the kings of the earth's surface.

And they will be gathered together, as prisoners are gathered
in a dungeon,[1] and shut up in the prison.
And after many days will they be visited, and the moon will
be confounded, and the sun ashamed ;
For Jahveh Sabaoth doth reign[2] in Mount Zion and in
Jerusalem,
And before his elders will be glory.[3]

V. Jahveh, thou art my God : I will exalt thee, I will praise
thy name ;
For thou hast done wonderful things, counsels of old, perfect
faithfulness,
For thou hast made of a city an heap ; of a defenced city a ruin :
A palace of strangers to be no city ; one that will never be
built,
Therefore will a strong people glorify thee, the city of the
terrible nations will fear thee.
For thou art a stronghold to the poor, a stronghold to the
needy in his distress,
A refuge from the storm, a shadow from the heat,
For the blast against the terrible ones[4] is as a storm against
a wall.

This is a conception that belongs to the exile, and the times that
follow. Cheyne compares Ps. lxxxii., where, after Bleek, he explains
the אלהים as the patron spirits of the nations. See also Dan. x. 13.
Cheyne also refers to the LXX. of Deut. xxxii. 8, "He set the
bounds of the nations according to the number of the angels of
God." Ewald and Delitzsch also think of the evil powers of heaven.

[1] The pit is from the context a place of imprisonment, so that
it is better to render dungeon. The reference may be to the prison
house of Sheol, where the evil spirits and wicked kings are reserved
for punishment. See 2 Pet. ii. 4 ; Jude 6.

[2] מלך is not the perfect of the sure future, as R.V., but either
"hath become king," as Cheyne, or "doth reign," as an emphatic
present.

[3] The last line is a shortened line, as is common in Hebrew
strophes. It is apart from the previous line, and does not qualify
it, but has its own copula. The elders are either the elders of the
people over against the evil angels and kings, or the heavenly elders,
as in Rev. iv. 4, over against the evil host of the high on high.

[4] כורם קיר loses its difficulty if we regard it as parallel with
בחרב בציון, and make the line begin with כי רוח ערצים. רוח is then
the construct of the object, wind or blast beating against the terrible
ones as a storm against a wall. It is similar to אש צריך of xxvi. 11.

As the heat in a dry place wilt thou bring down the noise
of strangers,
As the heat by the shadow of a cloud, the song of the terrible
ones will be brought low.

VI. And Jahveh Sabaoth will make for all peoples in this
mountain
A banquet [1] of fat things, a banquet of wine on the lees,
Of fat things full of marrow, of wines on the lees well refined,
And he will swallow up in this mountain the face of the
covering that is cast over all peoples,
And the veil that is spread over all nations,
He doth swallow up death for ever;
And 'Adonay Jahveh will wipe away tears from off all faces;
And the reproach of his people will he take away from off
all the earth: verily, Jahveh hath spoken it.
And it will be said in that day, Lo, this is our God; we have
waited for him to save us:
This is Jahveh: we have waited for him to be glad and
rejoice in his salvation.

VII. When [2] the hand of Jahveh shall rest on this mountain,
Moab will be trodden down in his place, even as straw is
trodden down in the water of the dunghill.
And when he spreads forth his hands in the midst thereof,
as he that swimmeth spreadeth forth his hands to swim;
He will lay low his pride together with the craft of his hands,
and the fortress of the high fort of thy walls:
He doth bring it down, lay it low, and bring it to the ground,
even to the dust.
In that day will this song be sung in the land of Judah:
A city of strength have we: salvation is put for walls and
ramparts.

---

[1] משתה is a banquet. It is not a feast in the Biblical sense,
which is always associated with sacrificial meals of the peace-offering.
Even Cheyne has been misled to think of a great peace-offering in
which Jahveh is the host. But there is nothing in the context to
suggest such a thing. The peoples are rather invited to a rich
banquet, as a symbol of the joy of the great deliverance when all
sorrow and death will disappear.
[2] The particle כי introduces a new strophe and a temporal clause.
Moab is brought into view, in order to contrast his ruin with the
redemption of Jerusalem.

Open the gates, that a righteous nation keeping faithfulness
may enter.

One in purpose firm thou keepest in peace ; in peace, for in
thee he trusteth :

Trust in Jahveh for ever : yea, in Jah Jahveh [1] a rock everlasting.

VIII. Verily he hath brought down them that dwell on high, a city
inaccessible ;

He layeth it low, he layeth it low even to the earth ; he
bringeth it even to the dust.

The foot trampleth it ; the feet of the afflicted, the steps of
the weak.

The righteous hath a way : smooth, level, thou rollest the
path of the righteous :

Yea, on the way of thy judgments, Jahveh, have we waited
for thee : to thy name and to thy memorial is the desire
of our soul.

With my soul have I desired thee in the night : yea, with
my spirit within me I seek thee early :

For according as thy judgments are in the earth, the inhabitants of the world do learn righteousness.

Should favour be showed to the wicked, he doth not learn
righteousness, in the land of uprightness he deals
wrongfully ;

And he beholds not the majesty of Jahveh.   Jahveh, should
thy hand be lifted up, they see it not : [2]

Let them see and let them be ashamed ; zeal for the people,
yea, fire for thine adversaries, let it devour them. [3]

---

[1] יָהּ יְהוָֹה.   This combination of divine names is only found here
and in xii. 2.   יָהּ is a shortened form of יְהוָֹה.   It is not infrequent
in Hebrew poetry by itself.   It is thought by some that יְהוָֹה here is
a later marginal gloss.   There can be no doubt that the rhythm of
the line would be better without it, and the omission is favoured by
the LXX.

[2] This clause is parallel with the first clause of the previous line,
giving us an example of introverted parallelism, which has escaped
the notice of the Massoretes, who connect it with the wrong verse.

[3] אֵשׁ צָרֶיךָ is the construct of the object, fire against thine adversaries in antithesis with zeal for thy people.   The R.V. follows
Knobel, Delitzsch and most interpreters in taking the suffix in
תֹּאכְלֵם as pleonastic.   The advent of Jahveh is in a blaze of glory,
which on the one side is zeal for His people, and on the other fire to
devour their adversaries.

IX. Jahveh, thou wilt ordain peace for us : for thou hast also
wrought all our works for us.

Jahveh our God, other lords beside thee have had dominion
over us ;

But by thee only will we make mention of thy name.[1]

They are dead, they shall not live ; they are deceased, they
shall not rise :

Therefore hast thou visited and destroyed them, and made
all their memory to perish.

Thou hast increased the nation, Jahveh, thou hast increased
the nation, thou hast glorified thyself : thou hast enlarged
all the borders of the land.

Jahveh, in trouble they visited thee, they poured out a
prayer [2] when thy chastening was upon them.

Like as a woman with child, that draweth near the time of
her delivery, is in pain and crieth out in her pangs ;

So have we been before thee, Jahveh. We have been with
child, we have been in pain,

We have as it were brought forth wind ; we have not wrought
any deliverance in the earth ; neither have the inhabitants of the world fallen.

X. Thy dead shall live ; my dead body,[3] they will arise.
Awake and sing, ye that dwell in the dust :

---

[1] If we could follow the LXX. ἐκτός σου ἄλλον οὐκ οἴδαμεν, and
insert לֹא יְדַעֲנוּ before לְבַד בְּךָ, we would have a better line than the
present Hebrew text.

[2] לַחַשׁ is the whisper of incantation, magic. There is no other
example of its use in a good sense. And yet the context so strongly
urges it that most interpreters, Knobel, Nägelsbach, Delitzsch,
Cheyne and R.V. render " prayer." But Ewald and Böttcher look
for a solution of the difficulty in a different interpretation of צָקוּן.
The LXX. ἐν θλίψει μικρᾷ and the Vulgate in tribulatione murmuris,
suggested to Böttcher the rendering, " trouble was the ban of thy
chastisements." Ewald from an Æthiopic word gets the meaning
ring, circle, and renders צָקוּן לַחַשׁ, " magic circle." The rhythm
forces us to combine these two words by a Maqqeph. This favours
taking צָקוּן as a noun. The LXX. probably read the text קְטַן לַחַץ.

[3] נְבֵלָתִי is incorrectly rendered by R.V. " my dead bodies." It
is singular, " my corpse." Israel is here conceived in its unity as a
nation. It lies dead in the dust of the grave, but it belongs to
Jahveh and will rise again. Ewald and others render the imperfects as jussives ; but it is better, with Cheyne and others, to regard
them as predictive.

For thy dew is as the dew of the light of life,[1] and the earth
will cast forth the dead.

Come, my people, enter thou into thy chambers, and shut thy
doors about thee :

Hide thyself for a little moment, until the indignation be
overpast.

For, behold, Jahveh cometh forth out of his place to punish
the inhabitants of the earth for their iniquity :

The earth also will disclose her blood, and will no more cover
her slain.

In that day Jahveh will visit with his sore and great and
strong sword

Upon leviathan the swift serpent and leviathan the crooked
serpent ;

And he will slay the dragon that is in the sea.[2]

XI. In that day, a pleasant[3] vineyard, sing ye of it.

I, Jahveh, do keep it ; I water it every moment,

---

[1] אורות is taken by Gesenius, Fürst, Böttcher, Hitzig, R.V. and
others as plural of אוֹר, herbs. But this seems inappropriate. It
is best, with Ewald, Delitzsch, Cheyne and margin of R.V., to take
it as plural of אוֹר, light. The plural is then the emphatic plural,
the light of life (Ewald, Delitzsch), or everlasting light : the light
from God which quickens the dead bodies, as the dew quickens the
plants of the earth. The רפאים are the shades, departed spirits.
The R.V. renders "the dead," and misses the sense.

[2] These three lines have been wrongly separated from their
strophe by the Massoretes, and attached to the following chapter.
There is the same contrast between Israel and his oppressors as
we have found in the previous strophes. There is considerable
difference of opinion as to the reference of these terms. Most
interpreters think of three empires, of which Egypt is the last,
according to li. 9 and Ezek. xxiv. 3, the other two being Media
and Babylon (Hitzig), Scythia and Babylon (Böttcher), Media and
Persia (Ewald), Assyria and Chaldea (Delitzsch). Vitringa, Knobel
and Reinke think that but one empire is referred to. Cheyne
thinks that there is a mythical reference to the storm dragon. It
seems best to think of two empires. The latter, Egypt, is sufficiently
designated by התנין אשר בים ; the former, Babylon, by the term
לויתן,—the two epithets נחש בריח and נחש עקלתן are simply an
emphatic description of the same monster.

[3] חמר, fermented wine, is only found here and in Deut. xxxii.
14. Some MSS., the LXX. and Targum read חמד. These are
rightly followed by Lowth, Hitzig, Ewald, Delitzsch, Knobel and
Cheyne.

Lest any visit upon it, I keep it night and day.

Fury I have none : would that I had briers, thorns;

I would march upon them in battle, I would burn them together.

Or else let him take hold of my strength, that he may make peace with me : make peace with me.

In days [1] to come let Jacob take root ;

And Israel will bloom and be fruitful, and the face of the world will be full of fruit.

Hath he smitten him as he smote those that smote him ? or is he slain according to the slaughter of them that were slain by him ?

In exact measure,[2] when thou sent her away, thou didst contend with her.

XII. He hath expelled [3] with his rough blast in the day of the east wind.

Therefore by this will the iniquity of Jacob be covered over,

And this is all the fruit of taking away his sin ;

When he maketh all the stones of the altar as chalkstones ;

Beaten [4] in sunder, the Asherim and the sun-images will rise no more.

Verily the defenced city is solitary, an habitation deserted and forsaken, like the wilderness :

There the calf feeds, and there he lies down, and consumes the branches thereof.

When the boughs thereof are withered, they are broken off ; the women come and set them on fire ;

For it is a people of no understanding :

---

[1] הבאים. We should supply ימים, as in Jer. xxxi. 38. The early omission of this word made the line obscure, and the Versions differ greatly in their rendering of it.

[2] סאסאה is only found here. It is usually taken as סאה סאה, the repetition being in the style of our poet, that is, in measure by measure, thus by careful measurement so as not to exceed the bounds ; see Jer. xxx. 11 : So R.V. after most interpreters. Hitzig, Ewald, Knobel take it as Pilpal of סוא = זוע = disquiet, drive away. But this is more suited to the following context than to the previous line.

[3] הגה is only found here and Prov. xxv. 4. It is similar to ינה, and after Syriac and Arabic analogies means expel, reject.

[4] מנפצות refers to אבני מזבח, but belongs to the following line, and is in emphatic position.

Therefore he that made them has no compassion upon them,
and he that formed them shows them no favour.

And it will come to pass in that day, that Jahveh will beat
off his fruit, from the flood of the River unto the brook
of Egypt,
And ye will be gathered one by one, O ye children of Israel.
And it will come to pass in that day, that a great trumpet
will be blown,
And they will come which were ready to perish in the land
of Assyria, and they that were outcasts in the land of
Egypt;
And they will worship Jahveh in the holy mountain at
Jerusalem."

This apocalypse is Messianic throughout. It presents
vividly and strongly the divine judgment upon the world
and the redemption of God's people. These two contrasted results of the divine advent are not kept apart,
but are mingled and repeated again and again as the
poet advances in strophe after strophe.

The first strophe predicts that the earth will become
a waste, and that all classes of its inhabitants will be
scattered and will perish because of their transgressions.
In the second strophe the great city of the world is
brought into view and called the city of chaos, to indicate
that it is doomed to return to the condition of the earth
before God created the light upon it. The third strophe
begins with a glance at the glory of God sounding forth
from the redeemed upon the distant coasts of the sea;
and then vividly describes the vain efforts of the fugitives
to escape the divine judgment.[1] The fourth strophe
enlarges the judgment scene until it embraces heaven and
earth. The windows of heaven are opened for a great
storm; the sun and the moon hide their light in shame
and confusion;[2] there is a great earthquake, the earth
staggers like a drunkard and swings like a hammock,

[1] See Amos ix. 2 seq.　　　　　[2] See Joel iv. 15, p. 158.

U

and then is entirely broken up and removed.[1] All this is but an intensification of previous predictions. But in one respect this judgment scene transcends all others, for it not only includes the kings of the earth, but also alongside of them and distinguished from them, the host of the high on high, which can only be understood of the evil spirits of the air, the evil angels and angel princes of the hostile nations. These are imprisoned in the dungeon of Sheol and visited with punishment. Here then is the original of those representations of the judgment of the evil angels which recur in later prophecy.[2]

In striking contrast with these imprisoned evil spirits and kings are the elders on Mount Zion, before whom the glory of Jahveh, the King of Israel, is manifested. These might be referred to the elders of Israel were it not for the late origin of this prediction, the contrast with the host of the high on high, and the fact that they are the elders of Jahveh, belonging to Him in a peculiar sense. We are therefore to find here the origin of the conception of the twenty-four elders of the Apocalypse of the New Testament who have immediate access to the throne of God, and before whom His glory is peculiarly manifest.[3]

The fifth strophe is a song of praise to Jahveh for His acts of judgment and mercy. The sixth strophe describes a great banquet provided by Jahveh for the redeemed from all nations on Mount Zion. In connection with this banquet it is proclaimed that death, the great shroud that envelopes all peoples, is abolished for ever; and Jahveh wipes away tears from all faces, and removes

---

[1] See Ezek. xxxviii. 19 seq., p. 280 seq. See also Rev. xvi. 19–21, which is based on this passage.

[2] The apocalypse of Enoch lays great stress upon the judgment of the evil angels; but we find it sufficiently represented in 2 Pet. ii. 4; Jude 6; Rev. ix. 1 seq., xii. 7, xx. 1.

[3] See Rev. iv. 4 seq.

sorrow and shame for ever. The apocalypse reaches its height in this Messianic triumph over death and sorrow, and it gives us a unique feature of the divine advent which becomes the basis of the predictions of the New Testament.[1] The original curse of man pronounced in the garden of Eden upon our race is overcome. The divine blessing has transformed the curse; the divine judgment has transformed the world; the wicked have been destroyed, the righteous have been redeemed, death has been swallowed up in victory.

The seventh strophe contrasts the ruin of Moab, and his strong city, with the city of Israel, the city of God whose walls and rampart are salvation, and whose trust is in an everlasting rock. The eighth strophe triumphs over the world's metropolis, that has been brought so low that the feet of the afflicted people of God trample it under foot. The judgment of God is greatly desired by the righteous, but the wicked refuse to see until the blaze of the divine glory destroys them. The ninth strophe begins with a feeling of gratification. The proud oppressors who had lorded it over Israel have been destroyed, they are dead and will never revive, but Israel has been marvellously increased and his borders have been extended. The strophe concludes with the humiliating thought that all the sufferings of Israel were fruitless in themselves until Jahveh wrought deliverance in answer to his prayer. The tenth strophe is an anti-strophe to the previous one. The wicked oppressors will have no resurrection, but Israel will rise again. Israel is the corpse of Jahveh. It belongs to Him, and He will watch over it, and at the proper time raise it from the dead. Though it may have become dust in the ground and its shades may wander in Sheol, the divine light, the light of life will quicken it as the dew quickens the herbs of the field, and the shades

[1] See 1 Cor. xv. 54; Rev. vi. 12–17, xxi. 4.

will come forth from Sheol, the dust will rise in the body, and Israel will live again. This is the same idea of a national resurrection that we have found in Hosea and Ezekiel.[1] In view of this hope Israel is to seek refuge in God during the brief period of trial, and wait until the divine judgment has been executed upon the swift and crooked leviathan, Babylon; and upon the dragon of the sea, Egypt.

The eleventh strophe is a beautiful song of Jahveh's vineyard. It touchingly describes His care over it, the zeal with which He defends it from its enemies, and the certainty of its marvellous increase. The face of the world will be filled with its fruit.[2] The present and past discipline has been carefully measured. Its end was redemption from sin. Israel has not been smitten to death as Babylon, has not been slain as Egypt—the smiting has been of a different sort, and, although it has resulted in the death of the nation, Israel will revive, but Babylon and Egypt will not revive. The twelfth strophe describes the exile and punishment of Israel as in order to their redemption. The heathen altars, with their pillars in honour of Ashera and Baal, will be utterly destroyed, and all the iniquity of Jacob will be covered over in this punishment.

This apocalypse has a supplement of five lines. This may have been taken from an older prophet, possibly Isaiah. But it gives a very suitable conclusion to the apocalypse, although not in such a high poetic strain as the body of the piece. There is to be a great harvest in the entire region from the Euphrates to Egypt, and the exiles are to be gathered one by one.[3] A great trumpet

[1] See pp. 176 and 275.
[2] This song of the vineyard is based partly upon Isa. v. and partly resembles Ps. lxxx. See p. 229.
[3] See Jer. iii. 14, p. 242.

will be blown as a signal for all the exiles to return to the holy mountain at Jerusalem.[1]

At a considerably later date the great unknown issued a prediction of the destruction of Babylon by the Medes and the judgment of the world. It is contained in Isaiah, chaps. xiii.–xiv. 23. It is the prelude to the judgment upon Babylon by Cyrus of chaps. xl.–xlviii., and is possibly one of the earlier predictions referred to therein.[2] There is nothing that we have not found already in older prophecies so far as the Messianic idea is concerned. The predictions of Joel, Zephaniah, and Ezekiel with reference to the day of Jahveh are repeated. The same great conflict reappears with the convulsions of nature that accompany it.[3]

> "Set ye up an ensign upon the bare mountain, lift up the voice unto them,[4]
> Wave the hand, that they may go into the gates of the nobles. I have commanded my consecrated ones,[5]
> Yea, I have called my mighty men for mine anger, my proudly exulting ones.[6]
> Hark ! a multitude in the mountains, like as of a great people !
> Hark ! a tumult of the kingdoms of the nations gathered together !
> Jahveh Sabaoth mustereth the host for the battle.
> They come from a far country, from the uttermost part of heaven,
> Jahveh, and the weapons of his indignation, to destroy the whole earth.
> Howl ye ; for the day of Jahveh is at hand ; as destruction from Shadday it cometh.[7]
> Therefore all hands will be feeble, and every heart of man will melt :

---

[1] There can be no doubt that this little section resembles very much Isa. xi. 15, 16.

[2] See A. B. Davidson, *Expositor*, April 1884, p. 257.

[3] See pp. 150 seq., 221 seq., and 279 seq.

[4] This line resembles Isa. xl. 9.

[5] מקדשי. The warriors of Jahveh were consecrated for the holy war. See Joel iv. 9 ; Jer. xxii. 7, li. 27, 28 ; Zeph. i. 7.

[6] עליזי גאותי. This same phrase is found in Zeph. iii. 11.

[7] This line is identical with Joel i. 15.

And they will be dismayed ; pangs and sorrows will take hold of
them ; they will be in pain as a woman in travail ;

They will be amazed one at another ; their faces will be faces of
flame.

Behold, the day of Jahveh cometh, cruel, with wrath and heat of
anger ; [1]

To make the land a desolation, and to destroy the sinners thereof
out of it.

Verily the stars of heaven and the constellations thereof will not
give their light ;

The sun will be darkened in his going forth, and the moon will
not let her light shine. [2]

And I will visit upon the world for their evil, and upon the
wicked for their iniquity ;

And I will cause the arrogance of the proud to cease, and will lay
low the arrogancy of the terrible.

I will make a man more rare than fine gold, even a man than the
pure gold of Ophir.

Therefore I will make the heavens to tremble, and the earth will
be shaken out of her place, [3]

In the overflowing wrath of Jahveh Sabaoth, and in the day of
the heat of his anger."   —Isa. xiii. 1–13.

Another anonymous apocalypse has been preserved in
Isa. xxxiv.–xxxv. It differs from the previous apocalypse
in poetical structure, and in its entire style and representation. It resembles very much the great prophecy
contained in Isa. xl.–lxvi. It seems to be an earlier
piece by the same author, the prelude and outline of
that great composition. In the previous apocalypse
Babylon was the great enemy, but Egypt, and especially
Moab, were associated with him. In this apocalypse
Edom takes the place of Moab, and becomes the central
figure of the judgment scene. This apocalypse differs
from the previous one in the unfolding of its theme.
There, the judgment and the redemption were presented
in a series of contrasted pictures running through the

---

[1] Comp. Zeph. i. 14–16.   [2] Comp. Joel iv. 15.
[3] Comp. Ezek. xxxviii. 20.

several strophes of the poem. Here, the prophet first presents the judgment scene and then the redemption in the second half of his piece. This enables us to consider the two scenes apart, and to attach to them corresponding representations from other writings.

II. THE BLOOD-BATH OF JAHVEH.

§ 86. *This apocalypse gives a picture of the judgment of the earth. The judgment is a great slaughter. Edom becomes the blood-bath of Jahveh. Heaven and earth are contaminated with the blood and carcases of the slain. The heavens are rolled up as a scroll, and their host fade as the foliage of a tree.*

" Draw near, ye nations, to hear ;
  And ye peoples, hearken ;
  Let the earth hear, and the fulness thereof ;
  The world, and all things that spring forth out of it.
  For Jahveh hath indignation against all nations,
  And wrath against all their host :
  He hath put them under the ban, he hath given them to the slaughter,
  And their slain will be cast out,
  And the stink of their carcases will come up,
  And the mountains will be melted with their blood,
  And all the host of heaven will consume away.[1]
  And the heavens will be rolled together as a scroll :

---

[1] נמקו is the Niphal of מקק. It is used in Ps. xxxviii. 6 of running ulcers ; in Zech. xiv. 12, of the wasting away of eyes and tongue as by the plague of leprosy ; in Lev. xxvi. 39, Ezek. xxiv. 23, xxxiii. 10, of the pining or wasting away in iniquity. These passages all force us to see here the figure of a foul disease, a running sore. Gesenius, after Vitringa, thinks of the melting of the lights of heaven like wax candles ; but the Oriental lights were lamps, not candles. The rendering of the R.V., " dissolved," has no justification. The host of heaven are contaminated with the rotting carcases upon the surface of the earth, and break out in foul ulcers, so that they waste away as by disease. This is a dreadful figure, but it suits the context and Zech. xiv. 12.

> And all their host will fade away,
> As the leaf fadeth from off the vine,
> And as a fading leaf from the fig-tree.
> For my sword hath drunk its fill in heaven :
> Behold, it will come down upon Edom,
> And upon the people of my ban, to judgment;
> The sword of Jahveh is filled with blood,
> It is made fat with fatness,
> With the blood of lambs and goats,
> With the fat of the kidneys of rams :
> For Jahveh hath a sacrifice in Bozrah,
> And a great slaughter in the land of Edom,
> And the wild oxen will come down with them,
> And the bullocks with the bulls ;
> And their land will be drunken with blood,
> And their dust made fat with fatness,
> For it is the day of Jahveh's vengeance ;
> The year of recompense in the controversy of Zion.[1]
> And the streams thereof will be turned into pitch,
> And the dust thereof into brimstone,
> And the land thereof will become burning pitch.
> It will not be quenched night nor day ;
> The smoke thereof will go up for ever ;
> From generation to generation, it will lie waste ;
> None will pass through it for ever and ever."

. . . . . .

The symbols of the divine judgment are quite new to the Messianic idea. The great slaughter of the final conflict has appeared in many previous predictions.[2] But here it is described in dreadful details. The mountains flow with the blood, the bodies of the slain defile the earth, and the foul odours of the rotting carcases rise to the heavens and contaminate them with running sores, so that they waste away as if afflicted with leprosy.[3]

---

[1] This same idea is found in Isa. lxi. 2 and lxiii. 4.
[2] See Joel iv. 18–21, p. 158. Ezek. xxxviii., xxxix. ; see p. 279.
[3] This representation recurs in Isa. lxvi. 24, and especially in Rev. xiv. 20.

There are two other significant figures.   The heavens are
rolled up as the leaves of a scroll, and the heavenly
bodies fade and fall like leaves from a tree.[1]   This indicates that in the view of our prophet heaven and earth
are to pass away, and that the primeval chaos is to
return again.   The special doom of Edom is that of
Sodom and Gomorrah.[2]

The counterpart to the reduction of the earth to
chaos is the renovation of nature described in chap. xxxv.
But before we enter upon this delightful theme, we shall
bring into consideration two other pieces of prophecy that
deal with the judgment of Edom.   The first of these is
that wonderful dramatic poem that the great unknown
has taken up into his marvellous composition in Isa.
lxiii. 1–6.   It has no organic connection with its context,
and it is best to treat it here.

(*Prophet*)   "Who there[3] is coming[4] from Edom,
   Stained red[5] in his garments from Bozrah ;
   Who there made glorious in his apparel,
   Stretching himself[6] in the greatness of his strength?

---

[1] These figures reappear in Matt. xxiv. 29 and Rev. vi. **13.**

[2] Gen. xix. 24–28.

[3] מִי זֶה is here as usual, "Who there," or "Who then."   זֶה has
the same force in the third line as Knobel rightly gives it.   The
demonstrative emphasizes the interrogative.

[4] בָא should have its force as a participle.   It is followed by three
other participles in the parallel lines.   These should all have their
full force.

[5] חָמוּץ is rendered by Gesenius, "splendid;" by Ewald, "crimson;"
by Cheyne, "bright red," all thinking of the colour.   The R.V.
renders "dyed," and leaves the colour to be understood.   It is best
to render in accordance with the context, "stained red," thinking
of the blood-bath.

[6] צֹעֶה is rendered by the R.V., after the Vulgate, Lowth, Cheyne
and others, "marching."   But this is not justified by the usage of
the word or the context.   Gesenius ánd Nägelsbach render "tossing
the head ; " Delitzsch, "bending to and fro ; " Ewald and Knobel,
"stretching himself."   The victor is exulting, and expresses it in the
stretching of the body as he moves along.

(*Jahveh*) I that speak in righteousness,
          That am mighty to save.

(*Prophet*) Wherefore art thou red in thine apparel,
          And thy garments like him that treadeth in the winefat?

(*Jahveh*) I have trodden the wine-press alone;
          And of the peoples there was no man with me:
          Yea, I have been treading [1] them in mine anger,
          And trampling them in my fury,
          So that their juice [2] is sprinkled upon my garments,
          And all my raiment I have stained. [3]
          For the day of vengeance was in my heart;
          And the year of my redeemed is come.
          Yea, I was looking and there was none to help;
          And I was wondering and there was none to uphold;
          And so mine own arm brought salvation for me,
          And my fury it upheld me.

---

[1] ודרכם. The interpretation of the piece depends upon the pointing of the vavs in this verb and those that follow. The Massoretic pointing seems to involve the interpretation that they are futures, and so the A.V. renders them. But the classic syntax would require that the imperfects that follow דרכתי should be vavs consecutive, all the more that we have a distinct jussive form in יד (ver. **3**), and that it is followed by a perfect at the close of the verse. If the pointing be thus changed, as urged by Cheyne and others, the rendering of the R.V. is correct. The Massoretic pointing involves, in accordance with classic Hebrew syntax, that all these imperfects with weak vavs should be final clauses, for a change of tense from the perfect to the imperfect is made by a vav consec. of the perfect. But this piece agrees with the syntax of the great unknown in disregarding strict classic rules, and therefore we should follow the usage of our prophet in his preference for weak vavs with the imperfect for the ordinary uses of the imperfect. Driver and Diestel are certainly correct, however, in pointing the jussive of ver. 3 וַיֶן, and we should notice the Massoretic וַתְּשֵׁע. It seems to us that we should follow the Massoretic pointing in other respects and give the imperfects the force of continued action in the past. This will remove all the difficulties of the syntax. Then we have to notice that וַיֶן and וַתְּשֵׁע both change the tense in order to express the result of the previous actions.

[2] נצח is the juice of the grape—and here the life-blood of the enemies.

[3] אנאלתי is an Aramaism for הגאלתי. It may have arisen from a copyist mistake.

Verily, I have been stamping the peoples in mine anger,
And I have been breaking them to pieces [1] in my wrath,
And I have been pouring down their juice on the earth."
—Isa. lxiii. 1–6.

Edom is here, as in the previous prophecy, a symbol of
the enemies of God. He has been visiting them in
judgment. He has trodden them in the wine-press of
His wrath, and so great has been the slaughter that it
has become a blood bath to the conqueror himself. This
is described by the victor himself in response to the inquiry
of the prophet, who sees him approaching, coming up from
Edom with blood-stained garments, and with triumph
displayed in his entire attitude and in every step. There
can be no doubt that this conqueror of Edom is Jahveh
Himself.[2]

There is still another prediction of triumph over Edom
that belongs to the early times of the exile, namely, the
prophecy of Obadiah.[3] We should not be surprised at

---

[1] אשברם is followed by the LXX. Vulg. Vitringa, Gesenius,
Delitzsch and R.V. But Houbigant, Lowth, Hitzig, Knobel, Ewald
and Cheyne follow some Hebrew MSS., after the Peshitto and Targum, read ואשברם, and render " break in pieces," which seems to be
required by the parallelism.

[2] There can be no doubt that Rev. xix. 13 seq., in its representation of the triumph of the Messianic Word of God, has our passage
in view. This has induced many of the older interpreters to refer
this prediction to the servant of God. But the Messiah is the antitype of the conqueror of Edom, in that He is not only the servant
of Jahveh, but is also Jahveh Himself.

[3] There is great difference of opinion among interpreters as to
the date of Obadiah. Many, even Orelli, regard him as the earliest
of the prophets, whose little prophecy has been used by Joel and
Jeremiah. But he properly belongs to this period, as Ewald and
J. J. S. Perowne show. He uses Joel freely. The relation between
Jeremiah and this prophet is not so easily determined. Obad. 1–4
and Jer. xlix. 14 seq. are very much alike, and yet there are striking
differences. Each omits something contained in the other, and each
gives new matter that is not contained in the other. Obadiah's piece
is a little fuller, and this might favour the opinion that he was later ;
but, on the other hand, Obadiah is briefer than Joel in the matter
common to them. We cannot agree with Perowne in the opinion

the number of predictions that use Edom as the symbol
of the enemies, for the cruelty and treachery of Edom
were deeply impressed upon the minds of the exiles.[1]

" For the day of Jahveh is near [2] upon all nations :
As thou hast done, it will be done unto thee; thy recompense will
    return upon thine own head.[3]
For as ye have drunk upon my holy mountain, all nations will drink
    continually,
And they will drink, and swallow down, and become as though they
    had not been :
But in Mount Zion will he rescue,[4] and there will be a holy place; [5]
And the house of Jacob will possess their possessions,
And the house of Jacob will be a fire, and the house of Joseph a
    flame,
And the house of Esau will become stubble, and they will burn
    among them, and devour them :
And there will not be any survivor [6] to the house of Esau; for
    Jahveh hath spoken it.

---

that Jeremiah borrowed from Obadiah. We incline to the opinion
of Ewald, that both of them used an older prophet. It is the custom
of all these later prophets to use earlier ones, some of them known
to us and others unknown.

[1] "Deepest of all was the indignation roused by the sight of the
nearest of kin, the race of Esau, often allied to Judah, often independent, now bound by the closest union with the power that was
truly the common enemy of both. There was an intoxication of
delight in the wild Edomite chiefs, as at each successive stroke
against the venerable walls they shouted, ' Down with it ! down
with it ! even to the ground.' They stood in the passes to intercept
the escape of those who would have fled down to the Jordan valley ;
they betrayed the fugitives ; they indulged their barbarous revels
on the temple hill. Long and loud has been the wail of execration
which has gone up from the Jewish nation against Edom. It is the
one imprecation which breaks forth from the Lamentations of
Jeremiah ; it is the culmination of the fierce threats of Ezekiel ;
it is the sole purpose of the short sharp cry of Obadiah ; it is the
bitterest drop in the sad recollections of the Israelite captives by
the waters of Babylon ; and the one warlike strain of the evangelical prophet is inspired by the hope that the divine conqueror
should come knee-deep in Idumæan blood. Lam. iv. 21, 22 ; Ezek.
xxv. 8, 12–14; Obad. 1–21 ; Jer. xlix. 7–22 ; Isa. lxiii. 1–4."—
Stanley, *Jewish Church*, ii. p. 556.

[2] See Joel i. 15 and Zeph. i. 14.   [3] See Joel iv. 3.
[4] See Joel iii. 5.   [5] See Joel iv. 17.   [6] See Joel iii. 5.

And they of the south will possess the Mount of Esau ; and they of the lowland, the Philistines ;

And Ephraim [1] will possess the field of Samaria ; and Benjamin, Gilead.

And the captivity of this host [2] of the children of Israel will possess that which belongeth to the Canaanites, even into Zarephath ;

And the captivity of Jerusalem, which is in Sepharad, will possess the cities of the south.

And saviours will come up on Mount Zion, to judge the Mount of Esau ;

And the kingdom will be Jahveh's."   —Obad. 15–21.

The only additional feature in this prophecy is the reoccupation of the holy land in sections. There is a specification of several of the more prominent tribes, and of the two great divisions of Israel, which reminds us in part of Ps. lxxx., and in part of Ezek. xlix.[3]

III. THE TRANSFORMATION OF NATURE.

The second section of the apocalypse, Isa. xxxiv.–xxxv., is the counterpart to the first section. There, we saw a picture of the corrupting of the earth and its return to primeval chaos. Here, we see a picture of the transformation of the wilderness into a garden.

[1] את שדה before אפרים has arisen by repetition of the same words before שמרון. They make the line too long for the rhythm. They are against the parallelism, which, in the other cases, makes a section of Israel the subject of ירשו. They involve the exclusion of Ephraim from the land of the restoration, against the context, which represents the house of Joseph as united in the war against Edom. It would make Judah the inheritor of the country of Ephraim in violation of the covenant and contrary to all precedents.

[2] הַחֵל הַזֶּה of the Massoretic text is "this host or army." But it is difficult to understand what is meant. The LXX. renders ἡ ἀρχὴ αὕτη, reading הָחֵל, infin. abs. Hiph. of חלל, to begin. This would then refer to the northern kingdom as the first to go into exile. These are to return and occupy the region of the Canaanites on the north, as in the next clause the Jerusalemites are to occupy the cities of the south.

[3] See pp. 228, 285.

§ 88. *A highway of redemption is provided for the redeemed to return to their land. It is transformed from a desert into a garden. All evils, physical and moral, are removed. Sorrow flees away, and everlasting joy comes in its stead.*

I. " Let the wilderness and the solitary place be glad ;[1]
    And let the desert rejoice,[2] and let it blossom as the rose,
    Let it blossom abundantly, and let it rejoice
    Even with joy[3] and singing ;
    The glory of Lebanon has been given unto it,
    The excellency of Carmel and Sharon ;
    They see the glory of Jahveh,
    The excellency of our God.
    Strengthen ye the weak hands,
    And confirm the feeble knees.
    Say to the fearful of heart, be strong ;
    Fear not : behold your God.
    He cometh with vengeance, with a divine recompense
    He cometh to save you.

II. Then the eyes of the blind will be opened,
    And the ears of the deaf will be unstopped,
    Then will the lame man leap as an hart,
    And the tongue of the dumb will sing :
    For in the wilderness waters will break out,
    And streams in the desert,
    And the mirage[4] will become a pool,
    And the thirsty ground springs of water ;

---

[1] יְשֻׂשׂוּם is difficult. The ם cannot be the suffix, for the verb is intransitive, and there is nothing in the context to which it can refer. Luther, Lowth, Eichhorn and Hitzig take it as a repetition by mistake of the initial letter of the following word. Most critics think that the archaic plural ן has been assimilated to the following letter, so after Aben Ezra, Ewald, Delitzsch, Fürst, Cheyne, Diestel.

[2] וְתָגֵל seems to be jussive, unless we suppose that at this stage of the language the distinction in form between the jussive and indicative has well-nigh disappeared.

[3] גִּילַת is an example of the construct before the conjunction vav. Other examples are found in Isa. xxxiii. 6 and Ezek. xxvi. 10 ; so Ewald, Gesenius, Böttcher and Green.

[4] שָׁרָב is the mirage, like the corresponding Arabic word.

In the habitation of jackals, where they lay,
There will be grass with reeds and rushes.

III. And an highway will be there,
And it will be called the way of holiness ;
The unclean will not pass over it,
Nor will it be theirs ;[1]
Wayfaring men and fools will not wander there,[2]
No lion will be there,
Nor will any ravenous beast go up thereon,
They will not be found there ;
But the redeemed will walk there ;
And the ransomed of Jahveh will return,
And come with singing unto Zion ;
And everlasting joy will be upon their heads ;
Gladness and joy will overtake them,
And sorrow and sighing will flee away."

This is a beautiful picture of the land of the redeemed.
It reminds us of the representations of Ezekiel with
regard to the wonderful fertility of the holy land, his
comparison of it with the garden of Eden, and the vision
of the river of life and its wonderful trees.[3] But our
prophecy transcends these and all previous prophecies in
its elaborate representations, and becomes the basis of
the description of Isa. xl.–lxvi. The advent of Jahveh is
the source of all these blessings. Nature is transformed
at His presence. The earth had been transformed by His

---

[1] והוא למו is difficult. It is taken as a circumstantial clause by
Knobel, Ewald and others, and rendered, "inasmuch as it is theirs,"
namely, it belongs to the people of God. It is probable that vav
carries over the force of the negative, and we should render "nor
shall it be theirs."

[2] This clause is commonly taken as indicating those who have a
right to the way ; but this disturbs the movement of the thought
and spoils the climax by a premature announcement. The prophet
first indicates those who have no right to the way in six lines, and
then in the closing six lines those who have possession of it.
Accordingly we take תעה in a good sense, "wander it," and give
אויל the bad sense that it invariably has. The highway of redemption was no place for wayfarers or fools.

[3] See Ezek. xxxiv. 25–27, xxxvi. 35, xlvii. 12, pp. 272, 274, and 290.

wrath into a wilderness, and had returned to its original chaos. It now responds to His blessing in a greater transformation, and becomes like the garden of Jahveh. The most fertile portion of Palestine, Lebanon, Carmel and Sharon are selected as representatives of what the entire land is to be.

But the blessings extend beyond physical nature. Man is to be redeemed. His bodily ills disappear. The blind, the lame and the dumb are healed, and unite in this universal joy of nature. All sin is banished. A holy highway is established leading into the holy land. No unclean person will enter it, no beast of prey will be found there; even the fools and wayfarers will have no place there. For it is a highway of redemption—a royal road to the garden of God. All sorrow and sighing are banished, they flee away like evil demons from the holy way of redemption, and joy and gladness fly thither like angels of blessing to crown the heads of the holy people with everlasting happiness.[1]

IV. THE GREAT SUFFERER.

The exile was a bitter experience for the pious Israelite. It transcended the woes of the Egyptian bondage. For then the holy land was a bright prospect that had not yet been attained; but now the holy land had been lost through the sin and folly of the people of God. The pious keenly felt that they were deprived of blessings which they ought to have inherited. They needed redemption from sin even more than deliverance from oppressors. The pious were indeed the greatest sufferers, for they shared in the persecution to which Jeremiah and others like-minded had been sub-

---

[1] This reminds us of the banquet of joy and the wiping away of tears of Isa. xxv. 6-8. See p. 300.

jected by the wicked princes and their followers among
the people. Piety was now synonymous with affliction
and sorrow. The ideal of the suffering Messiah had its
genesis in these circumstances, and yet it was not without connection with earlier Messianic prophecies. The
ideal man of the poem of the creation [1] and of the codes
of the Pentateuch [2] had not been realized in the experience of Israel or mankind. The curses were earned and
the blessings were forfeited. The problem of redemption was no longer simply the education of the race for
its attainment of the divine ideal, or the training of
Israel in the sacred institutions of redemption ; but first
of all they must be delivered from the curse of sin and
the penalties of broken covenants and vows. The
problem of redemption became complicated owing to the
fact that not only did the sinner suffer for his evil deeds,
but the righteous man who strove to serve God, to attain
the divine ideal, and to gain the promised blessings,
increased his sufferings and sorrows thereby. He separated himself from his evil surroundings only to incur
enmity and persecution. He suffered no longer for sin,
but for righteousness' sake. Ideal manhood is to be
gained only through the real manhood of fortitude, per-
severance, and the patient endurance of persecutions
even unto death. This conception is found in germ in
the Protevangelium.[3] The conflict with Satan and the
forces of evil was accompanied with peril, and the victory
was to be gained only through suffering. It is also
contained in the covenants with Abraham [4] and David.[5]
What Egypt was to the seed of Abraham, that the exile
became to the seed of David and the children of Israel.
The wilderness was the way to the holy land of redemption, and the entrance was through the vale of tribula-

[1] See p. 68.   [2] See p. 115.   [3] See p. 71.
[4] See p. 87.   [5] See p. 126.

X

tion.[1]   But the circumstances of the exile, and especially
the experience of the persecuted Jeremiah and his
associates, taught the people of God lessons they had
never learned before.   The sufferings of the nation in
exile were to discharge the penalties of its transgressions,
but were not to result in ultimate ruin.   The nation
had indeed died, but it was to rise again in a great
resurrection.[2]   The faithful prophets, the teachers of the
nation, are not to suffer persecution and death in vain;
they are to earn and receive the rewards of their faithfulness.   There are several psalms of the exile that
present to our view a great sufferer who can hardly be
any other than the Messiah.   It seems probable that
Jeremiah was the type of the great sufferer, for he was
the hero of the exiles, the great historical sufferer for God.
But even this prince of sufferers does not attain the
heights of the ideal of these psalms.   He is the basis of
the representation, but the divine Spirit guided the
psalmists to discern and describe a sufferer whose experience was vastly more bitter than that of Jeremiah,
and whose sufferings were rewarded with a redemption
which Jeremiah did not gain.

There is a vividness of intense realization of suffering
on the part of these psalmists.   They must have been
great sufferers themselves.   They describe sufferings in such
minute details and with such an intensity of feeling, that
these must be real though extravagant.   The ideal seems
to be real, so keenly is it apprehended and so vividly is
it described.   The psalmists sink deep in the apprehension of their own sorrows, but these lead to depths of
woe which are apprehended in the imagination and fancy
through foreboding and presentiment.   Deep in the
depths of their own sorrows, from the lowermost pit into
which they have fallen they are conscious of deeper woes

[1] See p. 172.   [2] See pp. 176, 275, 302.

that surge up about them, filling them with trembling
and horror.

§ 88. *Ps. XXII. describes a sufferer with stretched body,
feverish frame, and pierced hands and feet.   He is surrounded by cruel enemies, who mock him for his trust in
God, and divide his garments as their spoil.   He is abandoned by God for a season, until he is brought to the dust
of death.   He is then delivered, and praises his deliverer
with sacrifices, in which the great congregation of Israel
join.   The ends of the earth are called upon to turn unto
Jehovah.*

I. "My 'El, my 'El, why dost thou forsake me?
   Far from my salvation are the words of my roaring.[1]
   My God, I cry in the daytime, but thou answerest not;
   And in the night; and there is no silence to me.
   But O thou holy one,
   Enthroned upon the praises of Israel:
   In thee our fathers trusted:
   They trusted, and thou didst deliver them:
   Unto thee they cried, and they were rescued:
   In thee they trusted, and were not ashamed.

II. But I, a worm and no man;
    A reproach of mankind, and despised of the people:
    All seeing me laugh me to scorn;
    They shoot out the lip, they shake the head,
    (Saying) 'Roll on Jahveh; let him deliver him;
    Let him rescue him, if he delight in him.'
    But O thou who took me from the belly;
    Who made me trust, upon the breast of my mother;
    Upon thee was I cast from the womb,
    From the belly of my mother thou art my 'El.

---

[1] דברי.   The construction is disputed.   The A.V., R.V., so
Perowne, render as if the force of the preposition מן with ישועתי
were carried over to this word.   But it is better, with Jerome,
Delitzsch, and the margin of the R.V., to make the clause complete
in itself.   There is a chasm between the words of the cry and the
redemption.   This is the inexplicable feature of the sufferings.

III. Be not far from me, for there is trouble;
 Be near, for there is no helper.[1]
 Many bulls have encompassed me:
 Mighty ones of Bashan have enclosed me;
 They gape upon me with their mouth—
 A lion ravening and roaring.
 As water I am poured out,—
 Yea, all my bones have parted themselves:
 My heart is become like wax;
 It is melted in the midst of my bowels.

IV. My strength is dried up like a potsherd,
 And my tongue is made to cleave to my jaws;
 And in the dust of death thou layest me;[2]
 For dogs have encompassed me:
 The assembly of evil ones have enclosed me;
 They are piercing my hands and my feet.[3]
 I count all my bones;
 They look, they stare upon me;
 They divide my garments among them,
 And over my clothing they cast a lot.

V. O thou, Jahveh, be not far off:
 My strength, O haste to my help;
 O deliver my life from the sword,

---

[1] קרובה is wrongly attached to the previous line by the Massoretes and most interpreters.

[2] The R.V. renders תשפתני as a perfect, "Thou hast brought me." Perowne renders as future, "Thou wilt lay me." It is better, with Delitzsch, to render as present, "Thou layest me."

[3] כָּאֲרִי, as pointed in the Massoretic text, is difficult of explanation. It seems to require the rendering "like the lion." But the figure of the lion has been left above where the form אַרְיֵה was used; אֲרִי is not used for lion in the Psalter. The ancient Versions all render by a verb, though they differ somewhat in the meaning given to the form. The LXX., Peshitto, Arabic and Vulgate render "they pierced" or "bored through," taking כאר as equivalent to כרה = כור. But Aquila, Symmachus and Jerome follow the corresponding Arabic word, and render "bound." The consensus of the Versions can be explained only by a different pointing. In this case it is easier to point as a construct participle כָּאֲרִי, as Perowne, than to change the form into a perfect כארו, as Delitzsch after several Hebrew MSS.

From the power of the dog my darling,
Save me from the mouth of the lion.
Yea, from the horns of the yore ox thou hast answered me.
I will declare thy name to my brethren,
In the midst of the congregation I will praise thee.
Ye that fear Jahveh, praise him ;
All the seed of Jacob, glorify him.

VI. Yea, stand in awe of him, all the seed of Israel,
For he hath not despised,
And he hath not abhorred the affliction of an afflicted one ;
And he hath not hid his face from him ;
But when he cried unto him he heard.
From thee comes my praise in the great congregation :
My vows I shall pay in the presence of those who fear him.
The meek will eat and they will be satisfied :
Those who seek him will praise Jahveh,
(Saying) ' Let your heart live for ever.'

VII. Let all the ends of the earth remember, and let them turn
unto Jahveh,
And let all the kindreds of the nations worship before thee ;
For Jahveh's is the kingdom, and he is ruling over the
nations.
Have all the fat ones of the earth eaten and worshipped,
All who go down to the pit and he who did not keep his soul
alive will bow down ;
A seed will serve him. It will be told of 'Adonay to the
generation,
They will come, and they will declare his righteousness to a
nation to be born, that he hath done it."

This psalm is composed of six strophes, of ten trimeter lines each, with a supplementary strophe of seven
pentameter lines.[1]   The first strophe presents the sufferer
in his extremity.   He is abandoned by God, and unable

[1] This psalm bears the name of David in the title. But it is
well known that the titles of the psalms do not come from their
authors, but from very late editors. It is disputed whether לדוד
denotes authorship by David, or indicates that the psalm originally
belonged to another Psalter that bore the name of David without
meaning to imply that David was the author of the psalms contained

to explain an experience so different from that of the fathers. Those who seek refuge in Jahveh have ever been delivered, but he seems to be an exception. The second strophe describes the cruel mockery of his enemies. They make sport of his trust in God, and exult over his abandonment. The next two strophes describe the terrible situation of the sufferer. He is surrounded by his enemies, who combine the evil dispositions of dogs, wild bulls, lions and wicked men. They gloat over his sufferings and greedily wait for his death, that they may appropriate his garments and divide them as a spoil. He suffers as a man whose body is racked with pain, so that every bone stands forth in its own individuality with its special ache. He is consumed with fever, and burns with intense thirst. His hands and feet are pierced or bored through, and he is alone in his agony, with no helper. These sufferings transcend those of any historical sufferer, with the single exception of Jesus Christ. They find their exact counterpart in the sufferings of the cross. They are more vivid in their realization of that dreadful scene than the story of the Gospels. The most striking features of these sufferings are seen there, in the piercing of the hands and feet, the body stretched upon the cross, the intense thirst, and the division of the garments.[1] The next two strophes set forth the divine answer to the prayers and vows of the sufferer. He is delivered from the dust of death, and praises his deliverer in the congregation of Israel; and there is great joy at the sacrificial feast in commemoration of the event. The supplementary strophe

therein. Critics are agreed that the date of a psalm is to be determined chiefly from internal evidence. Dean Perowne is in accord with most recent critics in assigning this psalm to the period of the exile (see *Book of Psalms*, 6th ed. 1886, i. p. 244).

[1] Matt. xxvii. 39–46; Mark xv. 29–34; Luke xxiii. 35–38; John xix. 23–30.

sets forth the world-wide importance of this deliverance. All the ends of the earth are exhorted to turn unto Jahveh and worship before Him, who is the universal king and ruler of all nations.   His praise will resound in generations yet unborn.

The sufferings of this psalm are ideal sufferings, based upon the experience of Israel in exile, and especially of the pious prophets; but they look forward to severer sufferings than any that have yet been endured.   This ideal is a Messianic ideal, that finds its only historical realization in Jesus Christ.

The great sufferer of Ps. xxii. also appears in Pss. xl., lxix., lxx.   These have the same pentameter movement, and seem to have been originally one poem,[1] comprising seven strophes, of ten lines each.

§ 89. *Pss. XL., LXIX., and LXX. describe a sufferer who is entirely consecrated to the divine service.   He suffers*

[1] Ps. lxx. is only another version of Ps. xl. 14–18. Pss. lxix. and xl. have the same historical situation, and their correspondence in style and phrases is so evident, that it is generally agreed that they have the same author.   Although Delitzsch adheres to the traditional view of the authorship of Ps. xxii., he agrees with Hitzig that Pss. xl. and lxix. have a common origin, and that Ps. lxix. is best explained from the life of Jeremiah.   There are many features of resemblance with that prophet, and also with the Book of Lamentations.   The difference between the first and second half of Ps. xl. is recognized by Delitzsch, who agrees with other critics that the two parts were once separate, and that they were combined for use in worship.   But notwithstanding the break between vers. 12 and 13, there is yet, as Perowne remarks, a play in the second half of the psalm on words already occurring in the first half, which shows an original connection between them.   The break occurs at ver. 13, and this is not included in Ps. lxx.   A study of the strophical organization of the three psalms has convinced me that all the facts of the case are best harmonized by regarding Pss. xl. and lxix. as originally one.   Ps. xl. 13 is in striking accord with the beginning of Ps. lxix., and is not included in Ps. lxx.   It seems to me therefore that the whole of Ps. lxix. ought to be inserted here.   This explains the omission of ver. 13 from Ps. lxx., and also its omission from Ps. lxix., where it was deemed best in making the separation that the psalm should begin with prayer.

*reproaches for the people of God. He is consumed with
zeal for the house of God. He fasts and prays, and yet is
abandoned by God to his enemies. They persecute him
bitterly with mocking words and cruel deeds. He is plunged
in a miry and watery pit, and is in peril of life. He
suffers intense thirst, and is dying of a broken heart. He
finds no compassion. Even his own kindred have forsaken
him, and he is the scorn of the wicked. They give him
vinegar and gall for his nourishment. But his patient
waiting is at last rewarded. His enemies incur a terrible
doom, while he proclaims his deliverance in the great
congregation to the joy of all the meek.*

I. "I waited patiently on Jahveh ; and he inclined unto me,
    And heard my cry, and brought me up from the pit of deso-
        lation, from the clay of the mire,[1]
    And set my feet upon a rock, established my steps,
    And gave a new song [2] in my mouth—praise to our God.
    Many see [3] and they fear, and they trust in Jahveh.
    Blessed is the man who has made Jahveh his trust,
    And hath not turned unto the proud [4] and lying apostates.
    Many things thou hast done, Jahveh my God,
    Thy wonders and thy thoughts respecting us—there is no
        estimating unto thee.
    Should I tell and should I speak them, they are stronger [5] in
        number than can be counted.

II. Peace-offering with vegetable-offering thou hast no delight in ;
    ears [6] hast thou bored me :

---

[1] The same situation is described in similar terms in Ps. lxix.
3, 14 (see strophes iii. lines 4–6, v. lines 1–3), also in Lam. iii.
53–58, and in Jer. xxxviii. 6.

[2] שיר חדש. See Isa. xlii. 10 ; Pss. xcvi. 1, xcviii. 1.

[3] Compare Isa. xlix. 7, lii. 15.

[4] רהבים is only found here. The singular רהב is used of Egypt
as the boastful and insolent power, the sea-monster, Ps. lxxxix. 11 ;
Isa. li. 9.

[5] עצם is used in this sense in Ps. lxix. 5 and Jer. xxx. 14, 15.

[6] The LXX. and Heb. x. 5 use σῶμα, which is certainly no translation of אזן. Some regard this as a mistake of a Greek copyist,

Whole burnt-offering with sin [1] thou hast not asked : then
said I,

Lo, I am come with the book roll, written concerning me ;

To do thy pleasure, my God, I delight, and thy instruction is
in the midst of my bowels.

I have preached righteousness in the great congregation,[2]
behold my lips.

I cannot refrain, Jahveh, thou knowest.

Thy righteousness I have not covered in the midst of my heart ;
thy faithfulness and thy salvation.

I said, I have not concealed thy mercy and thy faithfulness
from the great congregation.

Thou, Jahveh, wilt not refrain thy compassion from me ;

Thy mercy and thy faithfulness will continually preserve me.

III. For evils have encompassed me until there is no number,
Mine iniquities have overtaken me, and I am unable to see ;
They are stronger in number than the hairs of my head, my
heart doth forsake me.

Save me, O God, for waters are come unto my life.[3]

I am plunged into the mire of the abyss, and there is no
standing ;

I am come into the depths of water, and a flood doth overwhelm me :

---

who repeated the last letter of the previous word, and wrote σῶμα
instead of ὠτία, on the ground that some Greek MSS. have ὠτία,
and the Vulgate renders, aures. But it is more likely a correction
after the Hebrew. It is possible that the LXX. found עצם in the
Hebrew MSS. used by them. See Lam. iv. 7.

[1] חטאה is usually translated "sin-offering" here. But the technical
term for sin-offering is חטאת, an intensive noun, which corresponds
with the Piel of the verb. These intensive forms are alone suited
to the idea of expiation, as we see likewise in the corresponding
verbs קדש ,כפר ,טהר. Other technical terms are used in this passage,
עולה, זבח and מנחה. There is no reason for an exception in the case
of the sin-offering. חטאה is seldom used in the Old Testament.
In the other passages, Gen. xx. 9, Ps. xxxii. 1, it can only mean
sin. Why should it mean anything else here ? The context does
not require it. For the זבח and מנחה are closely associated offerings,
but there is no manner of connection between the עולה and the
חטאת. See my article, *The Argument e silentio*, in the *Journal of
the Soc. of Bib. Lit. and Exegesis*, 1883, p. 14 seq.

[2] Compare Ps. xxii. 23, 26.

[3] With this line Ps. lxix. begins.

I am weary with my calling, my throat is become hot, mine
eyes do fail.

While waiting for my God, those hating me without cause
have become more than the hairs of my head ;

Mine enemies in a lie have become stronger in number than
my locks.[1] What I did not spoil I then returned.[2]

O God, thou dost know of my folly ; and my faults from thee
are not hid.

IV. Let not those who wait on thee be ashamed through me,
'Adonay Jahveh Sabaoth :

Let not those who seek thee be upbraided through me, God
of Israel :

Because for thy sake I have borne reproach ; upbraiding hath
covered my face ;

I am become a stranger to my brothers, a foreigner to the
sons of my mother.

For zeal for thine house consumed me, and the reproaches of
them that reproached thee have fallen on me.

When I myself wept with fasting, it became a reproach to me ;

When I made my garments sackcloth, I became a proverb to
them ;

Those sitting in the gate compose against me, even the songs
of wine-bibbers.

But as for me, my prayer is to thee, Jahveh, at the time of
acceptance.

O God, in the abundance of thy mercy answer me, in the
faithfulness of thy salvation.

V. Deliver me from the mire, and let me not be overwhelmed.
Let me be delivered from those that hate me.

Let not the flood of waters overwhelm me, and let me not be
swallowed up in the abyss.[3]

---

[1] מַצְמִיתַי is followed by the R.V. and most interpreters, but the
thought is inappropriate. It should be pointed מִצָּמְתִי, with Ewald.
Hupfeld would follow the Peshitto, and read מֵעַצְמוּתַי = than my bones.

[2] אָז אָשִׁיב is difficult. Delitzsch and Perowne regard אָז as
equivalent to זֹאת. But with their rendering, which is followed by
the margin of the R.V., we should expect the jussive form. It is
better to take אָז as the particle of time, and give it its usual force
as a vav consec.

[3] וּמִמַּעֲמַקֵּי מַיִם has crept into the text by repetition from ver. 3.

Let not the well keep guard over me with its mouth.

Answer me, Jahveh, according [1] to the excellence of thy mercy, according to the abundance of thy compassion turn unto me.

And hide not thy face from thy servant. I am straitened. Haste, answer me.

Draw near unto my life. Ransom it : on account of mine enemies redeem me.

Thou knowest my reproach, and my shame and my upbraiding. Before thee are all my adversaries. Reproach hath broken my heart.

When [2] I was sore sick, and hoped for some to pity and for compassionate ones, and found them not :

They gave in my eating gall,[3] and in my thirst they give [4] me vinegar to drink.

VI. Let their table before them become a snare, and for their recompense [5] a trap.

Let their eyes be darkened from seeing, and their loins be continually tottering.

Pour out upon them thine indignation, and let the heat of thy wrath overtake them.

Let their habitation be desolate, in their tents let there be no inhabitant.

For O thou who hast smitten,[6] they have pursued, and they recount the pain of thy pierced ones.

---

[1] The כי טוב should be changed to כטוב, in accordance with the parallel כרב. A similar copyist mistake we have found in Num. xxiii. 7. See p. 105.

[2] The vav consecutive of the imperfect introduces a temporal clause.

[3] See Lam. iii. 15. בְּרוּת is only found here.

[4] יַשְׁקוּנִי. The change of tense is difficult. We might suppose with some that this is a case where the vav consec. is used with a qualifying word between it and its verb. But it is better to regard it as changing the colour of the action.

[5] The Massoretic שְׁלוֹמִים = peaceful, secure, is not so well suited to the context as the reading שִׁלֻּמִים, = recompense, of the LXX. The R.V. renders, after the Massoretic text, "when they are in peace."

[6] כִּי אַתָּה אֲשֶׁר, etc., is rendered by the R.V. "for they persecute him whom Thou hast smitten." But the אַתָּה is emphatic in position, and the relative seems to refer more naturally to it. The Psalmist

Add iniquity unto their iniquity, and let them not come into
thy righteousness.

Let them be blotted out of the book of life, and let them not
be written with the righteous.

Since I am an afflicted one, and a sufferer of pain, O God, let
thy salvation lift me on high.

I will praise the name of God with a song, and I will magnify
him with a thank-offering.

Yea, it will please Jahveh better than an ox or bullock with
horns—with hoofs.

VII. Have the afflicted seen, the seekers of God will rejoice (saying),
'Let your heart live,'[1]

For Jahveh is a hearer of the poor, and the prisoner he hath
not despised.[2]

O God [3] to deliver me, Jahveh to my help, O haste.[4]

Let them be ashamed and let them be confounded, the seekers
of my life to destroy it.[5]

Let them be turned backward and dishonoured who delight
in my evil.

Let them be desolate [6] for a reward of their shame, who say [7]
to me, Aha! Aha!

Let them exult, and let them rejoice in thee, all who seek thee.

---

means to emphasize the fact that Jahveh had smitten him, and that
then his enemies had pursued him in addition. The same thought
is found in Job xix. 6–22.

[1] Compare Ps. xxii. 27.

[2] The remaining lines of Ps. lxix. constitute a trimeter, and are
a later liturgical addition, and do not properly belong to the psalm.

[3] The 70th Psalm begins here. We shall give a translation of the
text that comes from a critical comparison of Ps. lxx. with Ps. xl.
14–18.

[4] Ps. lxx. reads אלהים להצילני, Ps. xl. רצה יהוה להצילני. The former
is more difficult. The latter repeats יהוה, and makes the line too
long. It would be more natural to add the imperative than to
leave it off.

[5] Ps. lxx. omits יחד and לספותה of Ps. xl. This makes the line
too short. ספה is an unusual word that a copyist would not be
likely to add to an original text, but יחד is probably an addition.
It makes the line too long.

[6] Ps. lxx. reads ישובו, Ps. xl. ישמו. The latter is more difficult,
and more likely to be original.

[7] Ps. xl. gives לו after האמרים. This is more likely to be
original.

Let them say continually, Jahveh be magnified, the lovers of
thy salvation.[1]

Seeing that I am afflicted and poor, let 'Adonay think upon me.[2]

O thou my help and my deliverer, my God, do not tarry." [3]

This psalm evidently has Jeremiah's experience in
view as the basis of its representation.   The first strophe
gives a brief reference to the miserable situation of the
sufferer, and then praises God for the deliverance He has
wrought.   The order of topic is the reverse of that of
Ps. xxii., for the description of sufferings follows the
statement of the deliverance.   But it is probably chiefly
a past experience that the Psalmist is describing.   The
second strophe sets forth the entire consecration of the
sufferer to the divine service.   Instead of offering the
sacrifices of the ritual, the whole burnt-offerings, peace-
offerings, and vegetable-offerings, connected as they might
be and often were with sin in the offerer, he offers himself a sacrifice to God, and is assured that God accepts
him.   The sufferer has his delight in doing the pleasure
of Jahveh.   The roll of divine instruction is in his hands,
but the divine instruction itself is in his heart; and he
proclaims the faithfulness, mercy and compassion of God
to the great congregation of Israel.   This reminds us of
the new covenant of Jeremiah, of the roll of the law discovered in the temple and used as a basis of the reform
of Josiah, and of the language of Deuteronomy itself.[4]

---

[1] Ps. lxx. has יגדל אלהים, where Ps. xl. has יגדל יהוה and ישועתך
for תשועתך.   The readings of the latter are better.

[2] Ps. lxx. has אלהים חושה לי, and Ps. xl. אדני יחשב לי.   The
latter is more likely to be correct.

[3] Ps. lxx. has עזרי for עזרתי of Ps. xl., and אלהים for אלהי.   The
latter is better.

[4] Jer. xxxi. 33.   See p. 256; 2 Kings xxii. 8 seq. ; Deut. xxx.
11–14.   The Epistle to the Hebrews (x. 8 seq.) applies this passage to
Jesus Christ.   It follows the LXX. in its deviation from the original
text, and yet does not miss the meaning of the passage.   The sufferer of
the psalm offers himself instead of the offerings of the ritual, and this
offering of his own person is accepted by God.   None but Jesus Christ
could in fact make such a substitution and find entire acceptance.

The third strophe begins the description of the sufferings of the Psalmist. His iniquities have indeed overtaken him and overwhelmed him. He does not exclude
himself from the company of sinners notwithstanding he
has become a sacrifice acceptable to God. The Psalmist's
ideal is mingled with the historical reality. He is unable
to remove his ideal entirely from the connection of sin
and suffering in actual experience. We have no direct
prophecy, but typical prophecy.[1]

This sufferer's woes are very great. He is plunged,
like Jeremiah, in a pit whose filth defiles him, and whose
waters rise up about him and threaten his life. His
throat is parched with thirst and with agony in his
calling upon God. His enemies have prevailed over him,
and they are innumerable, so that they cannot be resisted.
They have spoiled him, and forced him to give up that
which he had not taken from them. God knows his
faults, but they are not against his enemies. These are
treating him with injustice and wrong.

---

[1] "The history of prophets and holy men of old is a typical history.
They were, it may be said, representative men, suffering and hoping,
not for themselves only, but for the nation whom they represented.
In their sufferings, they were feeble and transient images of the
Great Sufferer, who by His sufferings accomplished man's redemp-
tions : their hopes could never be fully realized but in the issue of His
work, nor their aspirations be truly uttered save by His mouth.
But confessions of sinfulness and imprecations of vengeance, mingling with these better hopes and aspirations, are a beacon to guide
us in our interpretation. They teach us that the psalm is not a prediction ; that the Psalmist does not put himself in the place of the
Messiah to come. They show us that here, as indeed in all Scripture, two streams, the human and the divine, flow on in the same
channel. They seem designed to remind us that if prophets and
minstrels of old were types of the Great Teacher of the Church, yet
that they were so only in some respects and not altogether. They
bear witness to the imperfection of those by whom God spake in
time past unto the fathers, in many portions and in many ways,
even whilst they point to Him who is the Living Word, the perfect
revelation of the Father."—Perowne, *Book of Psalms*, i. p. 562, 6th
ed. 1886.

The fourth strophe gives the reason of the sufferings. He is persecuted for righteousness' sake, on account of his devotion to God and his consecration to the divine service. His prayers, fastings and tears have excited their contempt, and the sufferer fears lest all the pious will be discouraged and put to shame because of his abandonment by God. He has borne reproaches for the sake of God. He has been consumed with zeal for the temple now in ruins. His own brothers have turned against him, and wine-bibbers have made him their sport and song of derision. But he still perseveres in prayer, and looks forward to the time of acceptance when the faithfulness and mercy of God will be disclosed.

The fifth strophe describes more vividly the sufferings themselves. The pit of mire and water is like a covered well, it shuts him in so that he cannot escape. His enemies with their reproaches have broken his heart. He is sore sick, and his condition is such that it should excite sympathy and compassion; but his enemies multiply his sorrows so that his nourishment consists in bitter, sour and poisonous[1] food and drink.

The sixth strophe is a terrible imprecation upon the wicked and cruel enemies of the sufferer. His deliverance by his faithful God is sure, but his persecutors will incur a dreadful doom. He will praise God with thank-offerings of songs of praise that will be more acceptable than animal sacrifice, but they will be blotted out of the book of life, and have no portion with the righteous.[2]

---

[1] This is a figure that is frequent in the Old Testament. See Job iii. 24 ; Pss. xlii. 4, lxxx. 6; but especially Lam. iii. 15. The evangelist found a realization of this situation in the thirst of our Saviour upon the cross, when the Roman soldiers offered Him gall and vinegar (Matt. xxvii. 34 ; John xix. 28, 29).

[2] The Apostle Peter sees this fearful imprecation realized in the death of Judas Iscariot, and the exclusion of the traitor from the band of the apostles (Acts i. 19, 20).

The last strophe agrees with the last strophe of Ps. xxii. in representing that the deliverance of this sufferer has universal relations. All the afflicted and the seekers after God will rejoice with him, and be comforted with the additional evidence that God is a rewarder of the pious, and that the wicked will surely be confounded and destroyed.

These psalms of the great sufferer prepare the way for the suffering servant of Isa. liii.

CHAPTER XI.

ISAIAH xl.–lxvi. is a book of comfort, cheering the exiles of Israel with the promise of the advent of Jahveh to redeem them from bondage and restore them to their holy land. It is a further unfolding of Jeremiah's book of comfort.[1] The apocalypse of Isaiah xxxiv.–xxxv. is its prelude, but it differs from that apocalypse in that the order of judgment and redemption is inverted. The judgment of the nations is separated from the judgment of Babylon, and is associated with the new Jerusalem in a final conflict there after the model of Ezekiel.[2] This is given in the appendix to the prophecy, and does not enter into the unfolding of its great theme. The prophecy itself is rather a presentation of the glories of redemption. The author stands on the loftiest peak of prophecy. He masses more Messianic predictions in his book than any of the prophets that preceded him. He carries the Messianic idea to a much higher stage of development, so that he becomes the evangelical prophet, who seems to be the nearest to the Messiah and the theology of the New Covenant. The circumstances of the exile were favourable to this. It is doubtful whether it was possible for a prophet living in the land of Israel in the use of the ceremonial of the temple of Solomon, or the temple of Zerubbabel, to attain those profound spiritual conceptions of God and divine things that per-

[1] See p. 247.   [2] See p. 279.

vade the whole of this sublime poem. Even Ezekiel was too near the old temple to escape altogether from the influence of its institutions. But the prophecy of the great unknown reflects the experience of a prophet who had lived long in exile. To him the worship of Jahveh consists in prayer and fasting, in observance of the Sabbath, and keeping pure from the abominations of the heathen.[1] By these more spiritual religious exercises the faithful people of God could testify their attachment to the religion of their fathers, without any sacred places or sacred institutions. They were thereby brought into closer communion with their God, when priestly mediation and ceremonial access were out of the question.

This marvellous prophecy is certainly in its present form a single composition, and yet it is difficult to show any close connection between its parts. Many of them can be removed without disturbing the flow of its thought and emotion. There is indeed a lack of connection in several places that has attracted the attention of critics, and has led to the conjecture that the prophet uses several more ancient prophecies. This should not surprise us, for it is characteristic of the writers of the period to use older prophets. There are not a few citations from earlier writings that are evident.[2] These examples suggest that there are others that are not so evident, but that may be detected by the methods of literary criticism.

The prophecy is divided into three sections of nine chapters each by the refrains,[3] xlviii. 22, lvii. 20, 21, lxvi. 24.

But these refrains are more suited to the last chapter than to the body of the prophecy. We should expect

---

[1] See especially Isa. lii. 11, lvi. 1–8, lviii., lxvi. 17.
[2] See Isa. li. 11, lxv. 25.
[3] See Delitzsch *Isaiah*, ii. p. 129.

that the refrains of the prophecy would emphasize rather
its great theme. A closer examination of the piece discloses just such refrains as we should expect in xlii.
14–17, xlviii. 20–22, lii. 11–12, lvii. 14–21, lxii.
10–12. These all involve the divine advent and the
deliverance from Babylon.

The last of these refrains corresponds so closely with
the introduction to the prophecy xl. 1–12 that we may
regard it as the original conclusion. This is in accord
with other peculiarities of the closing section. We have
already considered the little piece, lxiii. 1–6, elsewhere.[1]
It has no sort of connection with its present context.
And the section lxiii. 7–lxvi. betrays a later period of composition, and a different train of thought from that which
pervades the body of the prophecy. The division of the
prophecy into three parts seems to have come from the
final arrangement when the appendix was added.

A careful examination of the body of the prophecy
discloses other features that show earlier and later
sections. There are differences in rhythm,—trimeters,
pentameters, and hexameters.[2] These differences might
have been designed to give variety of movement to a
poem of such great length. But there are certain facts
that seem to imply that the trimeters were originally
a prophecy by itself. The introduction, the conclusion, and the intervening refrains have the longer
movement. If there be a difference in date, the trimeters
must be earlier than the framework of the prophecy

---

[1] See p. 313.
[2] It is not always easy to distinguish hexameters from trimeters,
for the cæsura of the hexameter usually falls in the middle of the
line dividing it into two trimeters. But they may be distinguished
in part by the occurrence of the cæsura sometimes after the second
accent and sometimes after the fourth accent; and in part by the
fact that the second half of the hexameter line is complementary to
the first. See my *Biblical Study*, p. 283.

that encloses them. There are also several long pieces of the pentameter movement, and lyrics in the hexameter movement. But there are several other important differences, among which we may mention—(1) That the great theme of the trimeters is the divine advent for the deliverance of the servant of Jahveh, and that in the pentameters and hexameters the wife and mother, Zion, takes the place of the servant in a parallel representation; (2) that the great conqueror who is to be the divine instrument in the deliverance of Israel is referred to in the trimeters in general terms; but in the other part of the poem is named by his name, Cyrus;[1] (3) that the pentameters use quite frequently the divine name 'Adonay Jahveh. It seems to me therefore that there was an earlier prophecy with the trimeter movement, whose great theme was the divine deliverance of the servant of Jahveh; and that this was taken up into a larger prophecy in a second edition and associated with a parallel theme, the divine deliverance of Zion, the wife of Jahveh.

But whatever view we may take of these differences, it is certainly more convenient to recognise them and to discuss the Messianic idea of the prophecy in accordance with the lines thus marked out.

The trimeter poem that constitutes the original basis of the prophecy of the great unknown seems to have had its own divisions. We may distinguish five parts— (1) xl.–xli. 10, xli. 13–xlii. 13; (2) xlii. 18–xliv. 23; (3) xlviii. 1–11, xiix. 1–13; (4) lii. 13–liii., lv.; (5) lviii.–lix., lxi. These parts close with little hymns or pieces of similar character. The theme of these trimeters is the deliverance of the servant of Jahveh. There is considerable difference of opinion as to the meaning of this term. It is new to the Messianic idea. It is the contribution of this great prophet toward the unfolding of the doctrine

---

[1] Isa. xliv. 28, xlv. 1; comp. xlvi. 11.

of redemption. Moses and David most frequently bear the title, servant of Jahveh,[1] but it is also used with reference to other holy men, such as Joshua, Job, Daniel, and Zerubbabel.[2] The prophets Jeremiah and Ezekiel use the term for Israel as a whole.[3] There can be no doubt that we have the same usage in the great unknown. Israel as a body is the chosen servant of Jahveh, whom He has called and taken to Himself. This is clear in the first passage where it occurs in our prophet.

> " But thou, Israel, my servant,
> Jacob, whom I have chosen,
> Seed of Abraham, that loved me,[4]
> Thou whom I took hold of from the ends of the earth,
> And called from the corners thereof,
> And to whom I said, Thou art my servant;
> I have chosen thee and not cast thee away.
> Fear not, for I am with thee;
> Be not dismayed, for I am thy God;
> I do strengthen thee, yea, I do help thee,
> Yea, I do uphold thee by the right hand of my righteousness."
> —xli. 8–10.

Israel is here contrasted with the idolaters, as the servant of Jahveh. They have reason to fear the judgment that is impending in the approach of the great conqueror from the east, but Israel has nothing to fear; for Jahveh is all-powerful, and He has raised up this conqueror to do His service. Israel is now called the servant of Jahveh as he was once called the son of God, and a kingdom of priests.[5] The term servant is generic,

---

[1] See especially Deut. xxxiv. 5 ; Jer. xxxiii. 21 seq. See p. 245.
[2] Josh. xxiv. 29 ; Job i. 8 ; Dan. vi. 21 ; Hag. ii. 23.
[3] Jer. xxx. 10, xlvi. 27, 28 ; Ezek. xxxvii. 25.
[4] אֹהֲבִי. The participle with the suffix is commonly objective. So Knobel and Cheyne rightly take it. But the R.V. adheres to the A.V., and follows most interpreters in taking the suffix as referring to the subject, " whom I love," or " my friend."
[5] See pp. 100, 101.

as the term son and kingdom in those earlier conceptions. If all the passages that we have to consider remained at this level they would still be Messianic, and find their only sufficient fulfilment in Jesus Christ. We shall consider them in their order.

I. THE SERVANT IN WHOM JAHVEH IS WELL PLEASED.

§ 90. Jahveh is the redeemer of His servant Israel. He transforms the wilderness into a paradise before him, and provides for all his wants. He raises up a servant in whom He is well pleased, and upon whom He bestows His Spirit. This servant is gentle in his dealings with the weak, and meek in all his relations to the world. But he will deliver the captives, will become a covenant for Israel and a light to the Gentiles.

> "Behold, I do make thee a threshing instrument,
>   A sharp new one having teeth :
>   Thou wilt thresh the mountains, and wilt beat them small,
>   And wilt make the hills as chaff.
>   Do thou fan them,[1] that the wind may carry them away,
>   And the whirlwind may scatter them ;
>   And thou wilt rejoice in Jahveh,
>   Thou wilt glory in the Holy One of Israel.
> The poor and needy—
>   Seeking water when there is none,
>   Whose tongue doth fail for thirst,—
>   I, Jahveh, will answer them,
>   I, the God of Israel, will not forsake them.
> I will open rivers on the bare heights,
>   And fountains in the midst of the valleys ;
>   I will make the wilderness a pool of water,
>   And the dry land springs of water.

---

[1] The R.V. renders the jussive תְּרֵם, "thou shalt fan them," ignoring the form. This might be correct if we supposed that at this period of the exile the distinction between the jussive and indicative was passing away ; but we prefer to follow the classic usage.

I will plant in the wilderness the cedar, the acacia tree,
And the myrtle, and the oleaster ;
I will set in the desert the fir-tree,
The pine and the box-tree together ;
That they may see, that they may know,
That they may consider, that they may understand together,
That the hand of Jahveh hath done this,
And the Holy One of Israel hath created it."

—Isa. xli. 15–20.

This passage retains the generic reference to Israel as
a whole.   The redemption is wrought by Jahveh.   He
makes Israel like a threshing instrument, and all nature
is transformed under His blows.   This reminds us of the
symbol of Micah, where the daughter of Zion is compared
with a bullock with iron horns and brass hoofs to thresh
the nations.[1]   But the representation soon changes, and
Jahveh Himself is the actor in the redemption.   The
poor and needy exiles are provided by Him with supplies
for all their wants.   Though their way to the holy land
be through the desert, they will not thirst.   Springs will
come forth for them, and pools of water, and all the
delightful shade trees will be in their path.   This is the
same transformation of nature that we have found in
Isa. xxxv.[2]

The conception of the servant rises in the next passage
to a higher stage.

I. " Behold my servant, whom I uphold ;
     My chosen, in whom my soul delighteth ;
     I have put my Spirit upon him ;
     He will bring forth judgment to the nations.
     He will not cry, nor lift up,
     Nor cause his voice to be heard in the street.
     A broken reed will he not break off,
     And the faint wick will he not quench :
     He will bring forth judgment in truth.

---

[1] Micah iv. 13.   [2] See p. 318.

He will not faint nor be broken,[1]
Till he set judgment in the earth ;
And the coasts wait for his instruction.

II. Thus saith 'El Jahveh,
He that created the heavens, and stretched them forth ;
He that spread abroad the earth and that which cometh out
of it ;
He that giveth breath unto the people upon it,
And spirit to them that walk therein ;
I, Jahveh, have called thee in righteousness,
In order to hold[2] thine hand and to keep thee,
And to give thee for a covenant of the people, for a light of the
nations ;
To open the blind eyes,
To bring out the prisoners from the dungeon,
And them that sit in darkness out of the prison-house.
I am Jahveh ; that is my name ;
And my glory will I not give to another,
Neither my praise unto graven images.
Behold, the former things are come to pass,
And new things am I declaring :
Before they spring forth I tell you of them.

Sing unto Jahveh a new song,
And his praise from the end of the earth ;
Ye that go down to the sea, and all that is therein,
The coasts, and the inhabitants thereof.
Let the wilderness and the cities thereof lift up their voice,
The villages that Kedar doth inhabit ;
Let the inhabitants of Sela sing,
Let them shout from the top of the mountains.

---

[1] It should be noticed that there is a contrast in the condition of
the Messianic servant and the people to whom he ministers. They
are like a broken reed, רָצוּץ ; but he will not be broken, יָרוּץ. They
are like the faint, dim, and expiring wick of a lamp, כֵּהָה ; but he
will not faint, יִכְהֶה.

[2] וְאֶחְזָק. The jussive form of the first person is unusual. Are
we to give it its jussive force or regard it as an evidence that the
distinction between the indicative and jussive is passing out of use
in the time of our prophet ? Reasons may be given on both sides
of this question. We prefer to adhere to the classic usage, and
regard the ן as a weak Vav expressing purpose.

Let them give glory unto Jahveh,
And declare his praise in the coasts.
Jahveh will go forth as a mighty man ;
He will stir up zeal like a man of war ;
He will cry, yea, he will shout aloud ;
He will do mightily against his enemies." —Isa. xlii. 1–13.

Here we have a distinction between Israel and the
servant of Jahveh, for the servant has a work to do
for Israel as well as the nations.   To Israel he is the
embodiment of the covenant, namely, the prophetic
covenant, the new covenant that we have seen in
Jeremiah and Ezekiel.[1]   He is a light to the nations
to enlighten them, to instruct and to guide them as well
as Israel.   This reminds us of the calling of Israel to
be a kingdom of priests.[2]   The servant is not a king,
but a prophet, and yet he is a deliverer, for he rescues
the captives from their prisons.   He is above all the
teacher of the nations.   For this office he has been
anointed with the divine Spirit, as the Messianic king
was anointed in the prediction of Isaiah.[3]   He is a
servant who is entirely acceptable to Jahveh, and thus
is distinguished from the sinful and backsliding people.
He is gentle and meek in his ministry.   He has to deal
with the weak and perishing.   These are compared to
broken reeds and spent wicks.   Though they be broken,
he will not break them off.   He will rather bind them
up.   Though they shine but dimly, their wicks being
destitute of oil, he will not put out the lamps that give
no light.   He will pour in the oil, and cause them to
shine again.   It should be noted here as a hint of the
work of the servant that is described in subsequent
passages, that the same terms are used of the servant as
of the people whom he is to redeem, only there is a contrast
between them.   They are broken and faint.   But he will

[1] See pp. 247 and 272.   [2] See p. 101.   [3] See p. 202.

not be faint, and will not be broken. He will have success in his ministry. There is no conception thus far of a suffering servant. His work is a quiet and unostentatious work of ministry to the weak and suffering. The section concludes with a refrain of praise.

Who then is this servant? Most recent critics think that the prophet presents by personification the ideal Israel, the pious nucleus of the nation, as the Messianic servant. Dr. A. B. Davidson calls attention to the parallel between the prophet's use of the term servant and Zion.[1] He rightly states, " The personification of the community as a mother, is as old as Hosea; and if personified Zion be distinguished from their own members, there is nothing strange in Israel personified being distinguished

---

[1] "The other essential point in the conception of the servant, his activity, is suggested by the word 'servant' itself. And here the prophet's personification of Israel differs from another of his personifications, Zion or Jerusalem (for there is no difference between these two, just as there is none between Israel and Jacob). The conception of the servant Israel is that of a 'people' in opposition to the other peoples of the world; the idea of Zion is rather that of a community inhabiting the holy hill and chosen land of the Lord. The one is, so to speak, masculine, active, and entrusted with a mission to the peoples; the Lord is the husband of the other, who is passive and recipient, and instead of executing any service among the nations is served by them—they bring back her sons in their bosom, and carry home her daughters upon their shoulders. The personification Israel, though said to be 'loved' by Jehovah (chap. xliii. 4), was a less suitable subject for pouring out all the floods of Jehovah's affection upon than Jerusalem, the daughter of Zion—a woman forsaken and grieved in spirit, even a wife of youth when she is cast off (chap. liv. 6). But the two personifications are really identical, for as kings bow down before Zion with their faces to the earth, and lick the dust of her feet (chap. xlix. 23), so before the servant kings shall stand up, and princes shall worship (ver. 7, chap. lii. 15); and the promise made to the servant, that he should be the light of the Gentiles, is fulfilled in the restored Zion, to whose light the Gentiles come (chap. lx.). And, what is not unworthy of attention, especially by those who find difficulty in conceiving how the servant Israel could be called 'a covenant of the people,' Zion personified, i.e. the community, inhabitress of Zion, is distinguished from the individual members of the community, her sons and daughters."—A. B. Davidson, Expositor, Nov. 1884, pp. 356-57.

from Israelites, from the fragments of Israel scattered in every land—the tribes of Jacob and the preserved of Israel."[1] There can be no doubt that these conceptions are parallel, as indeed they represent two stages in the composition of the prophecy; and there is much in favour of this interpretation. And it makes very little difference, so far as the reference of these passages to Jesus Christ is concerned, whether he be the realization of this ideal Israel, as he is of the ideal man of Ps. viii.,[2] or whether he be predicted in the form of an individual prophet. Delitzsch uses the figure of the pyramid to describe the use of the term servant in this prophecy. "The conception of the servant of Jehovah is, as it were, a pyramid, of which the base is the people of Israel as a whole, the central part Israel 'according to the spirit,' and the summit the person of the mediator of salvation who arises out of Israel."[3]   To this Oehler[4] and Cheyne[5] agree. It is true there is a difficulty in rising from the base to the apex, and then descending again to the base, or in rising or descending half way; but there is a difficulty in any case, for we have the distinction, whether we define that distinction as a personification or a person, and there is a rising and falling from the one to the other. The difference is simply whether the ascent be in two grades or in three.

We are now at a late period in the development of the Messianic idea. We have seen the term seed in its development from the whole human race, through the seed of Abraham, to the seed of David and a personal Messiah.[6] We have seen the term son first applied to

[1] A. B. Davidson, *Expositor*, Nov. 1884, p. 358.
[2] See p. 147.
[3] Delitzsch, *Isaiah*, ii. p. 174.
[4] G. F. Oehler, *Old Testament Theology*, ii. pp. 399–400.
[5] Cheyne, *Prophecies of Israel*, ii. p. 264, 3rd ed. 1884.
[6] See pp. 71, 83, 126, 202, 244.

Israel as a nation, then to the dynasty of David, and then at last to the Messianic king.[1] The great unknown uses the term servant for Israel as a whole. He was only following the analogy of the terms seed and son, if he unfolded the term servant in the same way until he reached the conception of a great prophet who would for the first realize the ideal of the faithful servant. With Moses and David and Jeremiah in his mind, all of whom bore the title servant of Jahveh, he could not find it difficult to conceive of a Messianic servant greater than they. It is difficult to distinguish a personification from a person. Zion as the mother is an easy personification, and the usage of prophecy is so plain that there can be no mistake. But we have no such usage to guide us with reference to the term servant. Usage is all the other way. The application of the term servant to Moses and David and other prophets, would lead the prophet and his readers to understand by servant a prophet like them.

II. JAHVEH DELIVERS HIS SERVANT ISRAEL.

§ 91. *Jahveh will gather His servant Israel from all lands of their exile. He will blot out all his sins, will cause him to pass through fire and water unharmed, will make for him a highway in the wilderness, and transform it into a garden. He will pour out His Spirit upon their seed, and they will become fruitful. The name of Jacob will be assumed as a title of honour.*

In the previous section of the original prophecy the servant was at first Israel as a whole, and then in the conclusion a ministering servant was distinguished from Israel. In this the second section of the prophecy the

[1] See pp. 100, 126, 135, 198.

prediction deals with Israel as a nation.   There are several pieces in which the redemption of the servant is presented in varied forms.

> "And now thus saith Jahveh,
> Thy creator, O Jacob, and thy former, O Israel :
> Fear not, for I do redeem thee ;
> I have called thee by thy name, thou art mine.
> When thou passest through waters I will be with thee ;
> And in the rivers, they will not overflow thee :
> When thou goest in the fire thou wilt not be burned,
> And the flame will not consume thee.
> For I, Jahveh, am thy God,
> The Holy One of Israel is thy Saviour ;
> I have given Egypt as thy ransom,
> Cush and Seba in thy stead.
> Since thou art precious in mine eyes ;
> Thou art honoured, and I love thee ;
> And I will give mankind in thy stead,
> And peoples instead of thy life.
> Fear not, for I am with thee :
> From the sun-rising I will bring thy seed,
> And from the sun-setting I will gather thee :
> I will say to the North, give up ;
> And to the South, withhold not :
> Bring my sons from afar,
> And my daughters from the ends of earth ;
> All who are called by my name,
> Whom I have created for my glory,
> Whom I have formed, yea, have made."   —Isa. xliii. 1–7.

This piece predicts the redemption of Israel from all lands of their dispersion, in accordance with many previous prophecies.   But it gives two new features.   The one indicates a miraculous preservation in the midst of all perils, whether these were of fire or water.   The people might be called to pass through waters, but these would not overwhelm them.   They might be constrained to pass through the midst of the fire, but they would not be burned.   The faithful care of Jahveh will deliver them from all evil, and bring them safely to their own land. The rivers are here not dried up as in the prediction of Isa. xi.,[1] but they are passed over in safety. This reminds us of the Sea Trouble of the earlier Zechariah.[2] The passing through the fire is not viewed as a divine chastisement as in Isa. iv.;[3] but the fire indicates perils on the journey to the holy land. It is parallel with the rivers and the wilderness.[4] The other important feature is seen in the use of the other nations as the ransom price of Israel. Israel is to be redeemed from bondage. The other nations will be given to the conqueror of Babylon to satisfy him, and induce him to restore Israel to his land.

The second Messianic prediction in this section is similar to the first.

> "Thus saith Jahveh—
> He who giveth a way in the sea,
> And in the strong waters a path;
> He who leadeth forth chariot and horse, army and force,
> Together they lie down, they will not rise up.
> They are extinguished, as a wick they are quenched;
> The former things remember not,
> And things of old do not consider.
> Behold, I am about to do a new thing.
> Now it will sprout forth, will ye not know it?
> Yea, I will make a way in the wilderness,
> In the desert rivers.
> The wild animals of the field will glorify me,
> The jackals and the ostriches;
> For I do give waters in the wilderness,
> Rivers in the desert,
> To give drink to my people, my chosen:
> The people which I formed for myself,
> That they might declare my praise."   —Isa. xliii. 16–21.

The returning exiles are to pass through the sea and strong waters in safety. Their enemies will be destroyed,

[1] See p. 204.
[2] See p. 185.
[3] See p. 193.
[4] Comp. Isaiah xli. 18.

as were the chariots and forces of Pharaoh at the crossing of the Red Sea. They will pass through the wilderness, and rivers will burst forth to give them refreshment.[1]

The third prediction is more important.

> " And now hear, Jacob, my servant ;
> And Israel whom I have chosen :
> Thus saith Jahveh, thy maker,
> And thy framer from the womb, who will help thee.
> Fear not, my servant Jacob ;
> And Jeshurun whom I have chosen.
> For I will pour water upon the thirsty land
> And streams upon the dry ground :
> I will pour my Spirit upon thy seed,
> And my blessing upon thine offspring :
> And they will sprout forth between the waters as grass,[2]
> As poplars by the water-courses.
> This one will say I am Jahveh's ;
> And this will name with the name of Jacob ;
> And this will subscribe with his hand unto Jahveh,
> And use the name of Israel as a title."   —Isa. xliv. 1–5.

This passage renews the familiar promise of the transformation of the desert into a garden, but associates with it the outpouring of the divine Spirit upon the seed of Israel. In the previous section the Messianic servant, who ministered to Israel and the nations, received the gift of the divine Spirit ;[3] but here the divine Spirit comes upon Israel as a whole. This is then in accordance with the predictions of Joel and Ezekiel.[4] The result of this gift of the Spirit is great fruitfulness and great honour. The

---

[1] This is in accordance with the representations of Isa. xxxv. and xli. 14–20. See pp. 318 and 342.

[2] בבן of the Massoretic text is a compound preposition defectively written for בבין, and is rendered by the R.V. "among the grass," after most interpreters. But the LXX. inserts מים, and this is rightly followed by Lowth, Ewald, and Cheyne as more suited to the parallelism.

[3] See p. 343.   [4] See pp. 154 and 283.

other nations will come and attach themselves to **Jacob**
and claim a share in his honourable titles.   This is in
accordance with the prediction of Isa. xix., that Egypt
and Assyria would assume the titles of Israel,[1] and recalls
the adoption of the nations in Zion of Ps. lxxxvii.[2]   It is
evident that our prophet here conceives that Israel is the
ministering servant of Jahveh to the nations, as in the
previous section he conceived of a Messianic servant
who had a ministry to do for Israel as well as the
nations.

This section closes with a brief prediction of redemption from sin and the hymn of refrain.

> "Remember these things, O Jacob
> And Israel, for thou art my servant:
> I formed thee, thou art a servant to me;
> O Israel, thou wilt not be forgotten of me!
> I have blotted out as a thick cloud thy transgressions,
> And as clouds thy sins;
> Oh, turn unto me, for I do redeem thee.
>
> *Sing, oh heavens,*
> *For Jahveh hath done it.*
> *Shout, ye lower parts of the earth;*
> *Break forth into singing, ye mountains,*
> *Oh forest, and everything therein;*
> *For Jahveh hath redeemed Jacob,*
> *And in Israel will He beautify Himself."*

III. THE HIGH CALLING OF THE SERVANT.

§ 92. *The servant of Jahveh is called from the womb to*
raise up the tribes of Jacob.   At first he will be concealed
in a condition of humiliation, but at last he will be
honoured by kings and princes.   He will restore Israel to
his inheritance, and become the light and salvation of the
nations.   The exiles will come up from the most distant

---

[1] See p. 206.   [2] See p. 226.

parts.   Jahveh Himself will conduct them.   They will no more suffer from hunger, or thirst, or heat, for nature will be transformed for them into a highway of redemption.

I. "Listen, oh coasts, unto me ;
   And hearken, ye peoples, from far :
   Jahveh hath called me from the womb ;
   From the bowels of my mother hath he made mention of my name :
   And he hath made my mouth like a sharp sword,
   In the shadow of his hand hath he hid me ;
   And he hath made me a sharp arrow,
   In his quiver hath he concealed me.
   And he said unto me, 'Thou art my servant
   Israel, in whom I will beautify myself.'

II. But I said, I have laboured in vain,
    I have spent my strength for waste and vanity :
    Yet surely my judgment is with Jahveh,
    And my recompense with my God.
    And now saith Jahveh,
    That formed me from the womb to be his servant,
    To bring Jacob again to him,
    In that Israel is not assembled ;
    That I may be glorified in the eyes of Jahveh
    In that my God is my strength.[1]
    And he said, 'It is too light a thing that thou shouldest be my servant
    To raise up the tribes of Jacob,
    And to restore the preserved of Israel :
    I will therefore give thee for a light to the nations,
    To become my salvation unto the end of the earth.'

---

[1] The Kethibh לֹא is the more difficult reading.   It is given also in the Vulgate and by Symmachus, and is followed by Henderson, Hitzig, Hengstenberg, and others.   The Qeri is more suited to the previous line, and is the rendering of Aquila, the Targum, R.V. and most interpreters.   But this line is part of a hexastich, in which the third and fifth lines are parallel in construction.   The structure of the fourth and sixth lines is also parallel.   In both of them the subject precedes its verb.   This indicates that they are circumstantial clauses.   From this point of view the Kethibh is more suited to the context, and being the more difficult reading, and having the best external authority, is to be preferred.

z

III. Thus saith Jahveh,
    The redeemer of Israel and his Holy One.
    To one despised of person,[1] to the abhorred of the nation, to
        the servant of rulers :
    ' Kings will see and arise,
    And princes, verily they will do homage,
    Because of Jahveh that is faithful,
    The Holy One of Israel, and he hath chosen thee.'
    Thus saith Jahveh,
    ' In an acceptable time have I answered thee,
    And in a day of salvation have I helped thee :
    And I will preserve thee, and give thee for a covenant of the
        people
    To raise up the land,
    To make them inherit the desolate heritages ;
    Saying to them that are bound, " Go forth ; "
    To them that are in darkness, " Show yourselves." '

IV. They will feed in the ways,
    And on all bare heights will be their pasture.
    They will not hunger nor thirst ;
    Neither will the mirage [2] nor sun smite them :
    For he that hath mercy on them will lead them,
    Even unto springs of water will he guide them.
    And I will make all my mountains a way,
    And my highways will be exalted.
    Lo, these will come from far :
    And, lo, these from the north and from the west ;
    And these from the land of Sinim.[3]

    Sing, oh heavens ; and be joyful, oh earth ;
    And break forth into singing, ye mountains ;
    For Jahveh hath comforted his people,
    And will have compassion upon his afflicted."

---

[1] בזה נפש is variously explained. נפש is taken by the A.V. and
R.V., Gesenius, Hengstenberg, and others as a collective, " persons,"
" whom man despiseth." Ewald, Knobel, Cheyne take the נפש as
the seat of the feeling, " despised in soul "—" heartily despised." It
is better to follow the LXX. and Vulgate, Hitzig and Delitzsch, and
think of the נפש as the object of the feeling, " of contemptible soul,"
or despised in person. See Ps. xxii. 7, בזוי עם. See p. 323.

[2] שרב, see Isa. xxxv. 7, p. 318.

[3] ארץ סינים. This land must from the context be a distant one.
China is the most probable reference, but this is not altogether certain.

This section is an advance upon the conception of the servant of the previous section.   There, he was endowed with the divine Spirit;[1] here, he is called from the womb, and assigned his ministry prior to birth.   There, he was made a sharp threshing instrument; here, his mouth is made like a sharp sword[2] hidden in the hand of Jahveh, and a sharp arrow concealed in His quiver.   This reminds us of the representation of the fruitful shoot of David's line, whose mouth was a sceptre, and the breath of whose lips would slay the wicked.[3]   He has the same ministry here as there both to Israel and the nations,[4] but the ministry to the nations is emphasized.   It was too light a thing for this servant to restore Israel—he has a much greater work assigned him, to become the light and salvation of the nations even to the ends of the earth.

A new feature of this servant appears in this section. He is represented in a state of humiliation.   He is despised in person, he is abhorred of the nation, he is a servant of rulers.   He is in bondage to the heathen rulers.   He is an abhorrence to the nation.   He is in his own person one to be despised.   This corresponds with the representation that he was concealed in the hand and quiver of Jahveh.   His condition of humiliation veiled the glorious destiny that was in him.   And yet this servant of rulers is to display his glory.   The sword will flash, and the arrow will reach its mark.   Kings will see the flashing of that sword; they will rise in honour of him who had been abhorred by the people.   Princes will prostrate themselves, and do homage to him whose person had once been despised.   He will be the light and salvation of all nations.   He will restore Israel, and they will come from the most distant parts and take part in

[1] Isa. xlii. 1.   See p. 343.
[3] Isa. xi. 4.   See p. 203.
[2] Isa. xli. 15.   See p. 342.
[4] Isa. xlii. 6.   See p. 344.

this day of redemption. Nature will transform itself before them, and they will no more suffer hunger or thirst or the scorching of the sun.[1]

The servant is here distinguished from Israel, and the same question arises here as in the previous section, whether we are to think of a prophet or of ideal Israel. It seems to us that it is most natural to think of a Messianic prophet who was called from the womb like Jeremiah to be the teacher and saviour.[2] This prophet is the second Jacob, as the Messiah is elsewhere the second Adam, the second Moses, and the second David. Each of these persons becomes in turn the type of the Messiah.[3]

IV. THE SIN-BEARING SERVANT.

§ 93. *The servant of Jahveh is a sufferer, unattractive in form, despised and rejected, a man of sorrows, and an outcast. He is innocent as a lamb, and yet is pierced, scourged, and crushed for his people. Jahveh lays upon him as a trespass-offering the iniquities of all. He suffers as a substitute, and then is highly exalted and rewarded with spoils of victory, a prosperous ministry, and great honour.*

[1] Isa. iv. 6, xxxv. 7. See p. 193.   [2] Jer. i. 5.
[3] Another picture of a sufferer is given in Isa. l. 4–11. This is a piece that stands by itself. It is composed of two strophes of ten pentameter lines each. It resembles Ps. xl. even more than the passages relating to the servant in the great unknown. There is nothing in this piece that indicates that it is Messianic. The sufferings are not extraordinary. The work of this prophet is no more than any prophet of the time might be expected to do. No one would have thought it Messianic were it not for its position between chaps. xlix. and liii. I agree with Knobel and others in the opinion that the prophet is here giving his own experience. It belongs to the second edition of the prophecy, as it is pentameter in rhythm.

I. " Behold, my servant will prosper,[1]
He will be lifted up and be exalted and be very high.
According as many were astonished at thee—
So disfigured more than man was his appearance,
And his form than the sons of men ;
So will he startle [2] many nations ;
Because of him kings will stop their mouths;
For what had not been told them they will see,[3]
And what they had not heard they will attentively consider.

II. Who believed our report,
And the arm of Jahveh, unto whom was it revealed ?
When [4] he grew up as a suckling plant before him,
And as a root out of a dry ground ;
He had no form and no majesty that we should see him,
And no appearance that we should take pleasure in him ;
Despised, and forsaken of men,[5]
A man of sorrows, and acquainted with grief,[6]

---

[1] ישׂכּיל may mean either "deal wisely," as the R.V., Cheyne,
Delitzsch, Orelli, or " prosper," as the margin of the R.V. after the
Targum, Lowth, Gesenius, Hitzig, Ewald, Knobel and Rodwell.

[2] יַזֶּה is the Hiph. imperf. of נזה = leap for joy, exult.   The
Hiphil means either to cause to leap for joy, to rejoice, or sprinkle
with water, blood, or oil. The LXX. renders θαυμάσονται. The
Peshitto and Vulgate render "sprinkle," and are followed by
Luther, A.V., R.V., Hengstenberg and most interpreters.   But
this rendering does not suit the context. It is not in accordance
with the parallelism, and is alien to the thought of the entire piece,
which does not touch upon the work of the priest or of purification,
but deals with the sufferer as a victim and an offering for the redemption of his people. Furthermore, usage requires the preposition
עַל or אֶל, with the meaning to sprinkle. Hence it is better to fall
back, with Ewald, Delitzsch, Nägelsbach, Hitzig, Knobel, Rodwell,
Orelli, upon the original meaning, to spring or leap, and render
"cause to leap in wonder" or "startle." This is nearer the LXX.,
and is in accordance with the other gestures of wonder in the
context. Cheyne does not decide, and Lowth retained sprinkled,
but doubted its correctness.

[3] See Isa. xlix. 7.

[4] וַיַּעַל is the protasis of a temporal clause. It is improper to
render ו consec. as causal with the R.V. We might, with Ewald,
Delitzsch, Knobel, and others, render it as an independent clause.

[5] See Isa. xlix. 7 and Ps. xxii. 7.   See pp. 323 and 354.

[6] Compare Ps. lxix. 21   See p. 330.

And as one before whom there is a hiding of the face,[1]
Despised, and we regarded him not !

III. Verily our griefs he bore,
    And our sorrows he carried them.
    But we regarded him as stricken,
    Smitten of God, and humbled.
    But he was one pierced because of our transgressions,
    Crushed because of our iniquities;
    The chastisement for our peace was upon him;
    And by his stripes there is healing for us.
    We all like sheep strayed away;
    Each one turned to his own way,
    While Jahveh caused to light on him the iniquity of us all.[2]

IV. He was harassed while he was humbling himself,
    And he opens not his mouth;
    Like a sheep that is being led to the slaughter,
    And as an ewe that before her shearers is dumb,
    And he opens not his mouth.[3]
    From oppression and from judgment he was taken away,
    And among his contemporaries [4] who was considering,
    That he was cut off from the land of the living,
    Because of the transgression of my people he had the blow ?[5]

---

[1] מַסְתֵּר is taken by Lowth, Hengstenberg and others, after the
LXX. and Vulgate, as an unusual form of the part. Hiph. of סתר,
and rendered "as one covering his face from us" in shame. The
Messiah is here conceived as a leper, an outcast from the congregation. The pointing might be changed to get this meaning. But it
is better, with Ewald, Knobel, Delitzsch, Cheyne, R.V., to take it as
a noun formed by מ and render "a covering of the face before
him," as one so disfigured that one could not look upon him.

[2] כלנו both at the beginning and close of the verse is exceedingly
emphatic. It indicates that all, including the author, are strayed
sheep, and that this sufferer is the representative and substitute
for all.

[3] ולא יפתח פיו is repeated for emphasis.

[4] את דורו is an adverbial accusative. The object of the verb
ישוחח is found in the clause with כי, as Ewald, Delitzsch, Cheyne
and R.V. The older view, that את דורו is the object of the verb,
maintained by Hengstenberg and given in the A.V., has little to
support it.

[5] נגע למו. The rendering depends upon the interpretation of the

With the wicked his grave was assigned,
And with the rich [1] in his martyr death ; [2]
Although he had done no violence,
And there was no deceit in his mouth.

V. But Jahveh was pleased to crush him with grief ! [3]
When he himself offers a trespass-offering, [4]
He will see a seed, he will prolong days ;
And the pleasure of Jahveh will prosper in his hands ;
On account of his own [5] travail he will see ;
He will be satisfied with his knowledge ; [6]

---

suffix. It may be either singular or plural. It is taken as plural
by the Targum, Gesenius, Ewald and others. It may then be
rendered either, the blow came upon them, or the blow due to them,
or the blow for them. But it is better, with R.V., Delitzsch, Knobel,
Cheyne, Rodwell and Orelli, to take it as singular.

[1] עָשִׁיר is a collective, rich men. This is taken by Knobel, Orelli,
et al., in a bad sense, parallel with רְשָׁעִים. Ewald would read עָשִׂיק,
and is followed by Rodwell. Cheyne does not decide between these
two views.

[2] בְּמֹתָיו. The plural is the emphatic plural, violent death or
martyr death. See Ezek. xxviii. 10. There is no sufficient reason
for reading it as a singular, with Cheyne. Lowth, Gesenius, Böttcher,
Ewald, Orelli, Rodwell derive it from בָּמָה, high place, and think of
the tomb or mound on the high place. This is a possible rendering,
and is strongly supported, but is not sufficiently plausible to induce
us to leave the easiest meaning which is appropriate to the context.
The plural of sepulchral mound is urged by Knobel as an evidence
that the servant is collective.

[3] הֶחֱלִי is taken by Gesen., Knobel and others as a Syriac form
for הֶחֱלָה, and rendered as a verb ; so R.V., "he hath put him to
grief." But it is better, with Hitzig, Ewald, Böttcher and others,
to take it as a noun with the article and change the pointing. It
is an accusative of closer definition.

[4] אִם תָּשִׂים is a conditional or temporal clause. It is not the
2nd pers. referring to Jahveh, as R.V., for a sacrifice was not made
by God, but by the offerer, and it was accepted by God. It is the
third fem. with נַפְשׁוֹ as the subject (so the margin of R.V.), only
נֶפֶשׁ here is reflexive, the person himself. The אָשָׁם is the trespass-
offering or guilt-offering of the priest code, which is distinguished
from the other offerings by the stress that it puts upon satisfaction
and compensation. The R.V. follows the A.V. in rendering sin-
offering. But this is חַטָּאת, and has a different signification that is
not suited to the context.

[5] נַפְשׁוֹ is reflexive, "himself," and not "his soul," as R.V.

[6] בְּדַעְתּוֹ is attached by the Massoretes to the following clause,

> My righteous servant will justify many,
> And their iniquities he will carry.
> Therefore will I give to him a portion among the great;
> And with the strong will he divide spoil,
> Because he exposed himself to death,
> And he was numbered with transgressors,
> And he did bear the sin of many;
> And for transgressors interposes." [1]

This piece begins the fourth section of the original prophecy, and the conception of the Messianic servant rises to a greater height. In the first section the gentleness and meekness of the servant was emphasized, and it was predicted that he would not faint or be broken until he had accomplished his work. In the second section the prediction did not rise above Israel as a whole. In the third section the servant was represented as concealed for a season in a state of humiliation, and then subsequently brought forth by Jahveh to accomplish His work of redemption. Here these two conditions are more strongly contrasted, and the stress is laid upon the sufferings of the servant as the means of redemption. There is here an advance upon the conception of the suffering Messiah of the Psalter, whose

and regarded as in emphatic position; so most interpreters. But this makes both lines too long for the rhythmical movement of the piece. It is then difficult to explain the knowledge as the instrument of justification; some think that the suffix is objective, "knowing of him;" others, as R.V., take it as subjective, "his knowledge." It is better to connect it with ישבע.

[1] יפגיע. This verb has already been used in ver. 5. It must have a similar meaning here. There "Jahveh caused to light upon him the iniquity of us all." Here the context suggests the same thought. He is numbered with "transgressors," He bears the sin of many. It is best therefore to render interpose, or mediate, or act as a substitute—for the sin-bearing, and the suffering from divine infliction, are the essential features of his work. The rendering of the R.V., "made intercession," changes the tense, and suggests the doctrine of the priestly intercession of Christ, which is contrary to the theme of the entire piece, which sets forth the victim and not the priest.

sufferings were indeed of world-wide significance, but were not represented as the means of redemption. Here the servant is a sin-bearing servant, and the Saviour of his people from their sins.

The prediction begins with a distich setting forth the success of the servant and his great exaltation. This corresponds with the previous representation.[1] The remainder of the first strophe presents the servant in two contrasted conditions. In the former his face and form are so disfigured that he excites the astonishment of men. His sufferings are extraordinary. In the latter his exaltation is so great, transcending all experience, that the nations are startled and their kings are dumb in wonder.[2]

The second strophe describes the sufferer more fully. He grows up before God as a sapling, as a root out of a dry ground. His origin is in an humble sphere, and in an unpromising condition. This reminds us, on the one hand, of the fruitful shoot that comes forth from the stump and roots of Jesse,[3] and, on the other hand, of the concealment of the servant by Jahveh.[4] When he attains manhood, he has no majesty of form and no attractiveness of appearance that men should be drawn to him and recognise him as their prophet and leader. Outward appearances are all against him. He is not only unattractive, but he is also repulsive. Men of rank and condition turn away from him. His face and form are so dreadful in their expression of sorrow and woe, that men forsake him. They treat him as if he were a leper, and had been smitten by God with a foul disease. They

---

[1] The order of topic is the same as we have seen in Ps. xl. See p. 329.

[2] This is a fuller statement of the contrast of Isa. xlix. 7. See p. 354.

[3] Isa. xi. 1. See p. 201.   [4] Isa. xlix. 2. See p. 351.

cover their faces that they may not see him.　The third
strophe gives the reason of these intense sufferings.　He
is not suffering for his own sins, but for the sins of his
people.　His face is bathed in sorrow, and his form is in
an agony of suffering because of their transgressions.　He
bears their sins and their sorrows as their representative
and substitute.　The sorrows of the nation and the sins
of the race are concentrated in his features and embodied
in his form.　He is pierced, scourged, and crushed, and
suffers cruel persecution.　But this is not the cause of
his agony.　He suffers for sin, and that not his own.
He is an innocent sufferer, whose grief is enhanced by
injustice and wrong, and is intensified by the keen apprehension of the ill-desert of those for whom he suffers.
All else have strayed from the fold of God, he only is
faithful, and Jahveh imposes upon him the sum of the
iniquity of his people.　As the only faithful and innocent
one, he comes to the front, stands in the breach and takes
upon himself the curse of the nation.　We cannot see
in this sin-bearing servant any other than an individual
prophet, for the author of the prophecy includes himself
with all others among the straying sheep, whose sins the
servant bears, and for whose redemption he suffers.

The prophet now advances to the climax of these
sufferings.　They culminate in death.　This is described
as the sacrifice of a sheep, and as the death of a martyr.
His contemporaries all misunderstand him.　He is innocent, and yet is esteemed guilty.　He does no violence,
and yet suffers extreme violence.　He has no deceit in
his mouth, and yet he is treated deceitfully.　He dies
as their redeemer, and is cut off because of their transgressions, and yet they assign him a grave with the
wicked.　It is difficult to see in this martyr death anything but the death of a prophet.　It is true that
national death and national resurrection are now familiar

Messianic ideas;[1] but in all these representations the death of Israel is ever a judicial death in punishment for their own sins. Here, however, the prophet describes a martyr, one who suffers for the sins of his people, and not for his own sins. His innocence is contrasted with the guilt of all others, including the author of the prophecy.

The prophet finally represents that this suffering has been in order to accomplish a divine plan of redemption. He suffers in obedience to the divine appointment. He offers a trespass-offering for the sins of the people, in order to purchase their redemption thereby. The trespass-offering has as its idea the payment of a fine in compensation for neglected duties and breaches of the divine law. His death is such a substitution and compensation for sin. When this has been accomplished, the condition of humiliation has come to an end, and the exaltation of the servant begins. There is no explicit mention of a resurrection, but this is implicitly involved, for he who has died a martyr's death must rise from the dead in order to receive the rewards of his service. The rewards are success in his ministry, the enjoyment of the spoils of his victory, and exaltation to great honour as the redeemer. This prophecy of the servant who dies and rises from the grave, finds its only fulfilment in the death of Jesus Christ, and in his resurrection and exaltation to his heavenly throne.

V. THE GREAT INVITATION.

§ 94. *A great invitation is extended to all to partake freely of the blessings of the New Covenant. These are the realization of the mercies of God, assured to David and his seed. The word of Jahveh is as sure as the ordinances of heaven. It will accomplish His purpose, and all nature will rejoice in the redemption of His people.*

[1] See pp. 176, 275, and 302.

I. " Ho, every one that thirsteth, come ye to the waters,
   And he that hath no money ;
   Come ye, buy, and eat ;
   Yea, come, buy without money,
   And without price wine and milk.
   Wherefore will ye spend money for that which is not bread ;
   And your labour for that which satisfieth not?
   Hearken constantly unto me, and eat ye that which is
      good,
   And let your soul delight itself in fatness.
   Incline your ear, and come unto me ;
   Hear, and your soul shall live :
   And I will make an everlasting covenant with you,
   Even the sure mercies of David.
   Behold, I gave him for a witness to the peoples,
   A prince and commander to the peoples.
   Behold, a nation that thou knowest not thou wilt call,
   And a nation that know not thee will run unto thee,
   Because of Jahveh thy God,
   And for the Holy One of Israel ; for he hath beautified thee.

II. Seek ye Jahveh while he may be found,
   Call ye upon him while he is near :
   Let the wicked forsake his way,
   And the iniquitous his thoughts :
   And let him return unto Jahveh, and he will have compassion
      upon him ;
   And to our God, for he will abundantly pardon.
   For my thoughts are not your thoughts,
   And your ways are not my ways, is the utterance of Jahveh.
   For the heavens are higher than the earth :
   So are my ways higher than your ways,
   And my thoughts than your thoughts.
   For as the rain cometh down,
   And the snow is from heaven, and returns not thither
   Except it hath watered the earth,
   And made it bring forth, and made it sprout,
   And given seed to the sower and bread to the eater ;
   So will my word be that goeth forth out of my mouth :
   It will not return unto me empty,
   Except it hath accomplished that which I please,
   And it hath prospered in the thing whereto I sent it.

> *For ye will go forth with joy,*
> *And be led forth with peace to the mountains,*[1]
> *And the hills will break forth before you into singing,*
> *And all the trees of the field will clap their hand.*
> *Instead of the thorn will come up the fir tree,*
> *And instead of the brier will come up the myrtle tree:*
> *And it will be to Jahveh for a name,*
> *For an everlasting sign that will not be cut off."*

This section of the prophecy sets forth the fulness and freeness of the new covenant of redemption. This covenant is the realization of the sure mercies of David, that is, the everlasting mercy of Jahveh promised to David and his seed in the prophecy of Nathan.[2] These mercies will be extended to the people, to all who accept the invitation to partake of the blessings of the covenant. They are offered freely to all who repent of their sins, and turn unto Jahveh with sincere obedience. The word of God is sure of success. It will be fruitful and accomplish the divine purpose of redemption.[3] All nature will rejoice in the restoration of Israel. Thorns and briars, the fruit of the original curse, will give place to trees of beauty to reward the righteousness of the redeemed people.[4]

VI. THE REWARD OF RIGHTEOUSNESS.

§ 95. *Israel is called to repentance, true fasting, deeds of righteousness and mercy, and sabbath keeping, with the promise of the advent of Jahveh as their light and glory.*

---

[1] ההרים is attached by the Massoretes to the next clause, but this spoils the rhythm of both lines. The mountains are the mountains of Israel.

[2] See p. 126 seq.

[3] This reminds us of the reference to the Davidic covenant in Jer. xxxiii. See p. 244 seq.

[4] This description corresponds with Isa. xxxv. See p. 318. So the new covenant is connected with fertility of the land in Ezek. xxxiv. See p. 272 seq.

He will come as a warrior, to interpose on their behalf and deliver them from their enemies. He will bestow upon them a new covenant, and the Spirit of Jahveh will abide with them for ever.

The fifth section of the original prophecy begins with a trumpet call to repentance. It then gives a careful discrimination between formal fasting and the true fasting that is accompanied with deeds of righteousness and mercy. To the latter the promise of redemption is made.

"Then will thy light break forth as the dawn,
And thy health will spring forth speedily :
And thy righteousness will go before thee ;
The glory of Jahveh will bring up the rear.
Then wilt thou call, and Jahveh will answer ;
Thou wilt cry, and he will say, Here am I.

If thou take away from the midst of thee the yoke,
The putting forth of the finger, and speaking vanity ;
And shouldest thou [1] draw out thy soul to the hungry,
And satisfy the afflicted soul.
Then will thy light rise in darkness,
And thy thick darkness be as the noon day :
And Jahveh will guide thee continually,
And satisfy thy desire in drought,
And make strong thy bones :
And thou shalt become like a watered garden, and like a spring
    of water,
Whose waters fail not.
And they that shall be of thee will build the old waste places :
Thou wilt raise up the foundations of many generations ;
And thou wilt be called, The repairer of the breach,
The restorer of paths to dwell in.

---

[1] The form וְתָפֵק is difficult. The weak vav with the jussive seems to be out of place. Strictly it should have its jussive force, and yet most interpreters render it as if it were vav consec. of the perfect carrying on the protasis of the condition. Ewald, Knobel and Delitzsch take it as a new protasis with modal force. This is best, although the indicative form is used in the next clause, and the vav consec. of perfect in the apodosis.

If thou turn away thy foot from the sabbath,
From doing thy pleasure on my holy day ;
And call the sabbath a delight,
And the holy thing of Jahveh honourable ;
And honour it, so as not to do thine own ways,
Nor find thine own pleasure, nor speak words :
Then shalt thou delight thyself in Jahveh ;
And I will make thee to ride upon the high places of the earth ;
And I will feed thee with the inheritance of Jacob thy father.
Verily the mouth of Jahveh hath spoken it." —Isa. lviii. 8-14.

The sins of Israel have brought them into trouble and
darkness.   Jahveh is their light and salvation.   The
people are called to repentance, to put aside their formal
fasting and engage in the real fastings, that alone give
pleasure to Jahveh, namely, deeds of righteousness and
mercy.   They are also exhorted to be faithful to the
Sabbath, the holy day of Jahveh.   All other holy things
have been destroyed.   All the more is their fidelity to
be shown by the sanctification of the holy day.   In
response to such repentance Jahveh will come.   His
glory will be revealed, and His light will shine, and
dispel their darkness and gloom.   He will guide them
continually, and satisfy all their needs, so that they will
become like a well-watered garden ; and the wastes of
Zion, which have now been long desolate, will be rebuilt.

Chap. lix. is a severe indictment of Israel for their
sins and the evil condition into which they have brought
themselves.   But the more desperate the condition, the
greater the necessity for the divine interposition.

" When Jahveh saw,
    And it was evil in his eyes that there was no one,
    And saw that there was no man,
    And wondered that there was no one to interpose : [1]

---

[1] מַפְגִּיעַ is used here of Jahveh as the verb יַפְגִּיעַ is used of the
servant in liii. 12.   Both Jahveh and His servant must interpose for
the redemption of his people.

His own arm brought salvation unto him;
And his righteousness, it upheld him.
And he put on righteousness as a breastplate,
And an helmet of salvation upon his head;
And he put on garments of vengeance,
And was clad with zeal as a cloke.
According to their deeds, accordingly will he repay
Fury to his adversaries, recompense to his enemies;
To the coasts he will repay recompense.
Verily they will fear the name of Jahveh from the sun-setting,
And his glory from the rising of the sun:
For he will come as a rushing stream,
Which the wind of Jahveh [1] driveth.
And a redeemer will come to Zion,
And unto them that turn from transgression in Jacob, is the
        utterance of Jahveh.
And as for me, this is my covenant with them, saith Jahveh:
My Spirit that is upon thee,
And my words which I have put in thy mouth,
Will not depart out of thy mouth, nor out of the mouth of thy
        seed,
Nor out of the mouth of thy seed's seed, saith Jahveh,
From henceforth and for ever."   —Isa. lix. 16–21.

This section of the prophecy represents Jahveh Himself interposing for the redemption of His people, as He
had constituted His servant the mediator and the sin-
bearing victim.   There must be a mediation on the
divine side as well as on the human side of the Messianic idea.   Jahveh's interposition is not in suffering;
that was the work of the servant.   He interposes as an
almighty conqueror to reward all the enemies of His
people according to their ill deserts.   For this end He is

---

[1] רוח יהוה is rendered spirit of Jahveh by the A.V., after the
Targum and the older interpreters.   But Lowth, Delitzsch and
others, after the Vulgate, render, wind or tempest from God, in
accordance with the context.   The R.V., after Knobel, Ewald,
Cheyne and Rodwell, renders breath of God, which has essentially
the same meaning.   The wind is called the wind of Jahveh, after
the analogy of cedars of God, mountains of God, and other the like
expressions.

seen arming Himself from head to foot for the conflict, whose result is final victory for His people, and inevitable ruin for their adversaries. The result of this interposition is that the glory of Jahveh extends over the world from sunrise to sunset. The new covenant is established with the people of God. This covenant is internal, so that the divine words are in the mouths of the seed of Israel unto all generations. This is similar to the representations of Jeremiah and Ezekiel. In Jeremiah the words are written upon the heart;[1] in Ezekiel, a new heart and a new spirit are given with which to walk in the divine commands;[2] here the words are in the mouth. All these are varied representations of the same great thought, that the external, formal, and legalistic observance will give place to internal, real and spiritual obedience. The divine Spirit also abides with the seed of Israel for ever. This is a reiteration of the promises of Joel, Ezekiel, and also of the great unknown himself.[3]

This fifth part of the original edition of the prophecy gives a final representation of the servant. Some have thought it strange that the prophet should add anything more after he had reached the height of the sin-bearing servant, but really there was something still lacking to complete the picture, and this is now given us in chap. lxi.

VII. THE GREAT PREACHER.

§ 96. *The servant of Jahveh is anointed with the divine Spirit, and becomes the gentle preacher of redemption to the poor and afflicted. He proclaims the year of grace, as well as the day of judgment. He transforms sorrow into joy. The people of Jahveh become the priests, and the nations their servants. The cities of Judah are rebuilt,*

[1] See p. 253.　　[2] See p. 274.　　[3] See pp. 154, 283, and 343.

2 A

*and the returning exiles enjoy the blessings of the new
covenant, and are recognised as the seed who enjoy the
divine blessing.   In view of this accomplishment of his
work the servant rejoices in a song of praise.*

I. "The Spirit of Jahveh [1] is upon me ;
    Because Jahveh hath anointed me.
    To preach good tidings unto the meek he hath sent me,
    To bind up the broken-hearted,
    To proclaim liberty to the captives,
    And deliverance to them that are bound ;
    To proclaim the acceptable year of Jahveh,[2]
    And the day of vengeance of our God ;
    To comfort all that mourn ;
    To provide for the mourners of Zıon,
    To give unto them a headdress instead of ashes,[3]
    The oil of joy for mourning,
    The garment of praise for the spirit of faintness ; [4]
    And they will be called terebinths of righteousness,
    The planting of Jahveh to beautify himself.

II. And they will build the old wastes,[5]
    They will raise up the former desolations,
    And they will repair the waste cities,
    The desolations of many generations.
    And strangers will stand and feed your flocks,
    And the sons of the alien will be your plowmen **and your**
        vinedressers.
    But ye will be named the priests of Jahveh :
    Ye will be called the ministers of our God :
    Ye will eat the riches of the nations,

---

[1] רוח אדני יהוה.   The LXX., N. T. citation (Luke iv. 18), and
Vulgate omit the אדני, and this is doubtless correct.   יהוה אדני is
characteristic of the pentameter sections of the book, and is not
found in the trimeters.   Cheyne follows Lowth in omitting it.   It
should also be omitted, for the same reasons, in the last line but one
of the piece.

[2] Compare Isa. xlix. 8 ; Ps. lxix. 14.

[3] There is a word-play here.   The mourner receives פאר instead
of אפר.

[4] כהה.   See Isa. xlii. 3.   [5] See Isa. lviii. 12.

And in their glory will ye pride yourselves.[1]
For your shame ye will have double ;
And for confusion they will rejoice in their portion :
Therefore in their land they will possess the double :
Everlasting joy will be theirs.

III. For I, Jahveh, love judgment,
I hate robbery with iniquity ;[2]
And I will give them recompense in faithfulness,
And I will make an everlasting covenant with them,
And their seed will be known among the nations,
And their offspring among the peoples :
All that see them will acknowledge them,
That they are the seed which Jahveh hath blessed.

I will greatly rejoice in Jahveh,
Let my soul be joyful in my God ;
For he hath clothed me with the garments of salvation,
He hath covered me with the robe of righteousness,
As a bridegroom putteth on a priest's turban,
And as a bride adorneth herself with her jewels.
For as the earth bringeth forth her increase,
And as a garden causeth that which is planted in it to spring forth,
So will Jahveh cause righteousness to spring forth,
And praise before all nations."

In this passage the idea of the servant of Jahveh
reaches its climax. It was not without reason that the
Messiah recognised himself most distinctly in this picture,
and employed it in his discourse in the synagogue of
Nazareth to explain his mission to his unbelieving
kindred and townsmen,[3] for here we see the Messiah

---

[1] תחימרו is taken by Knobel, Gesenius, Ewald, Nägelsbach,
Reinke, as Hithp. of ימר, change, and rendered exchange themselves. But Delitzsch, Böttcher, and Cheyne follow the LXX.,
Peshitto and Jerome in taking ימר as equivalent to אמר, stand
forth, and render exalt oneself. This is favoured by Ps. xciv. 4.

[2] בעולה as pointed in the Massoretic text is whole burnt-offering.
So Jerome, Talmud, Luther, etc. But Ewald, Knobel, Delitzsch,
Reinke, Nägelsbach, Cheyne follow the LXX., Targum, Peshitto,
and Saadia in reading עַוְלָה.

[3] Luke iv. 17-22.

preaching the gospel of redemption that he has already
achieved, enjoying the fruits of his ministry, and rejoicing
in the accomplishment of his work.   He is anointed
with the divine Spirit, as in the first passage, and becomes
a gentle preacher.[1]   There he was unostentatious and
meek in his entire work, not breaking off the broken
reed or putting out the faint wick, but yet releasing the
captives.   Here he has the same work, but as he describes
his own mission and work he enlarges upon this feature
of it, and we see him binding up the broken-hearted,
comforting mourners, giving them festal robes, instead
of the ashes and sackcloth of humiliation and mourning.
There he was the light of the nations, as well as the
covenant of Israel.   This feature was enlarged in the
second representation.   He raises up the tribes of Jacob,
restores them to their own land, and becomes salvation
to the ends of the earth.[2]   Here this is still further
enlarged.   The redeemed become like terebinths of
righteousness, they build the wastes of Judah and
Jerusalem, they become the priests of the nations, and
the nations become their servants.   Thus they realize
their original ideal as set forth in the covenant of
Horeb.[3]   They are recognised by the nations as the seed
that enjoy the blessing of Jahveh, and thus attain the
Abrahamic covenant.[4]   They enjoy the new covenant
with its everlasting joy and prosperity, which is now
familiar to us from the representations of Jeremiah,
Ezekiel, and the great unknown himself.   This prophecy
thus sums up in itself, and enlarges upon all the previous
descriptions of the servant, with the exception of those
relating to the suffering substitute.   That picture
presented fully the servant's condition of humiliation.
It mentioned the servant's exaltation only at the begin-

[1] xlii. 1–7.   See p. 343.   [2] xlix. 1–7.   See p. 353.
[3] Ex. xix. 3–6.   See p. 101.   [4] Gen. xii. 1–3.   See p. 83 seq.

ning and at the conclusion.   That which was left undeveloped there is here the substance of the picture. The servant is here not engaged in the work of substitution and interposition, but he is employed in proclaiming the results of it, and in applying the fruits of it, in the preaching of the gospel of redemption to the poor and miserable.   The sin-bearing servant needs as his counterpart the joyful preacher of the glad tidings of a redemption that has been accomplished.   The servant no longer bears the name of servant, he is preparing the poor and sorrowful for the festival of redemption of the year of grace.   It is most fitting, therefore, that the prophecy should conclude with a song of joy in the mouth of the great preacher.   He has accomplished his mission, and is entitled to its rewards, and the saddest of all sorrows has been transformed into the purest and loftiest joy.

CHAPTER XII.

THE PROPHECY OF THE RESTORATION OF ZION.

THE second edition of the prophecy is a book of comfort to Zion, who is personified and represented as the wife of Jahveh and the mother of its inhabitants. The introduction, the conclusion, and the four intermediate refrains, together with the several pieces with which they are connected, all set forth the same theme. The advent of Jahveh is at hand. He comes to comfort Zion and restore her wastes. His people are to go forth from Babylon and pass through the wilderness to the holy land. The scenes of the exodus from Egypt are to be transcended in marvellous transformations of nature and by the wonders of the divine guidance. Zion is the central figure of this second edition of the prophecy, as the servant of Jahveh is the chief feature of the first edition. The theme is developed in several sections.

I. JAHVEH'S HIGHWAY TO ZION.

§ 97. *The time of Zion's suffering for sin is completed. The ancient promises will now be fulfilled. The advent of Jahveh is heralded by messengers, prepared by a transformation of nature and proclaimed by Zion as glad tidings. Jahveh comes with the strong arm of a ruler and with the tenderness of a shepherd on the highway of redemption.*

I. "Comfort ye, comfort ye, my people, saith your God ;
    Speak unto the heart of Jerusalem, and proclaim unto her,
    That her warfare is accomplished, that her iniquity is discharged,
    That she hath received from the hand of Jahveh double for all
        her sins.
    Hark ! one proclaiming, 'in the wilderness clear the way of
        Jahveh,
    Level in the desert a highway for our God.
    Let every valley be lifted up, and every mountain and hill be
        depressed,
    And the crooked place become straight, and the rugged place a
        plain,
    And the glory of Jahveh will be revealed, and all flesh will see it
        together,
    For the mouth of Jahveh hath spoken it.'

II. Hark ! one saying proclaim.   And one is saying, what shall I
        proclaim ?
    All flesh is grass, and all its glory [1] as the flower of the field.
    The grass withereth, the flower fadeth, when the spirit of Jahveh
        hath blown thereon.
    Surely the people are grass.   The grass withereth, the flower
        fadeth,
    But the word of God standeth for ever.
    Go up on the high mountain, Zion that bringest good tidings,
    Lift up thy voice with strength, Jerusalem that bringest good
        tidings,
    Lift it up, fear not, say to the cities of Judah, behold your God !
    Behold, 'Adonay Jahveh cometh as a strong one,[2] his arm ruling
        for him,

---

[1] חסדו of the Massoretic text has the meaning of mercy elsewhere.
But Knobel, Delitzsch, Cheyne and others suppose that it means
here, grace, elegance or beauty, as its synonym חן.   But there is no
evidence for it unless it be found in this passage.   The LXX. and
1 Pet. i. 24 render δόξα as if they read כבוד.   This harmonizes
with the context, and accordingly is adopted by Ewald.   Lowth
would read הדרו.

[2] בחזק.   Ewald regards this as a simple and beautiful variation of
יד חזקה of Ex. xiii. 9.   It is taken by the LXX., Peshitto, Targum
and Gesenius as an abstract, " with strength."   But the R.V. and
most recent interpreters take it as a concrete with the ב essentiæ.

Behold, his wage is with him and his recompense before him ;
Like a shepherd he feedeth his flock, with his arm gathereth the
  lambs,
And in his bosom lifteth them,—those that give suck he leadeth.'
                                                    —Isa. xl. 1–11.

This introduction is dramatic in form. The message
of comfort is first given by the prophet in four lines.
The warfare of Zion is now about to come to an end.
Her iniquity has been discharged. She has suffered for
her sins in double measure. She is now about to receive
her reward in the advent of her God. The herald of the
advent first appears calling upon nature to prepare a
highway. The mountains and hills are to fall down, the
valleys are to rise, the crooked places are to become
straight, and the rough places smooth, in order that the
way of Jahveh may be entirely level, straight, and without
impediment. Such a transformation of nature is ever the
accompaniment of the divine advent; but here nature is
to prepare the way for Jahveh's advance in the redemption
of His people; for He comes in glory as the saviour of Zion.

In the second strophe two voices are heard, the one
receiving from the other the message contrasting the
perpetuity and infallibility of the word of divine promise
with the frailness and perishableness of man. Finally,
Zion and Jerusalem are seen ascending the mountains
and announcing to the cities of Judah the glad tidings of
the advent. God comes as a strong one, distributing His
awards according to the desert of men; but He is the
gentle Shepherd of His people, providing especially for the
lambs of the flock and the mothers who are caring for
their young. In these closing words the shepherd of
Israel reaches the height of its representation. In the
earlier Zechariah the shepherd rejects his flock on account
of their low estimation of his services.[1] In Ps. lxxx.

[1] See p. 187.

the shepherd of Israel is still angry with his people, who earnestly beseech him to come for their salvation.[1]   In Ezekiel the faithful shepherd is seen recovering his scattered flock and restoring them to their own land.[2] Here the shepherd is seen leading his flock on the highway of redemption.   He is tender and gentle, and provides especially for the little suckling lambs and their mothers.   These might be weary on their journey.   But he takes the lambs in his bosom, and with patient, gentle step conducts the mothers from the land of exile to Zion. Every one, even the feeblest, will share in the great salvation.

The first refrain of the prophecy is in a little piece of ten lines inserted at the close of the first part of the original trimeter prophecy.   It presents the same theme with additional features.

" I have been long time silent. Shall I be still ?   Shall I restrain myself ? "[3]

As a woman in labour will I groan, I will gasp and I will pant together.

I will lay waste mountains and hills, and all their herbs dry up ;

And make rivers into coasts, and pools I will dry up ;

And lead the blind in a way they know not,

In paths they know not will I make them go ;

I will make darkness into light before them, and rugged places into a plain,[4]

These things I do with them, and I do not forsake them.[5]

They are thrust back and are ashamed with shame, those who trust in graven images.

Those who say to the molten images, ' Ye are our gods.' "

—Isa. xlii. 14–17.

---

[1] See p. 228.   [2] See p. 272.

[3] אחריש and אתאפק are rendered by the R.V. and many interpreters as if they were the same tense as החשיתי. The difference in tense should be noted. It is best, with Ewald, to regard the imperfects as interrogatives.

[4] Compare Isa. xl. 4.

[5] These are prophetic perfects. It is better to render them by emphatic presents than by futures.

As in the introduction the time of warfare had to be accomplished, so here Jahveh has been long silent. But the time has come for the advent. He is eager for it as a mother to give birth to her child. He is even in the pangs of child-birth, and in His labour there will be a transformation of nature. The mountains and hills will be laid waste, as in the previous representation they were depressed. The rivers and pools that might be in the way are dried up. Even the blind are to be led in a way unknown to them, and their darkness will give place to light. Jahveh will not forsake them, but will accomplish all these things for them. Only the idolatrous will be brought to shame. As in the previous piece Jahveh was gentle to the suckling children and their mothers, so here He is especially kind to the blind.[1]

II. JAHVEH THE ONLY GOD AND SAVIOUR.

The second section of the prophecy deals especially with the overthrow of Babylon by Cyrus. The prophet gives a very striking representation of the work of Cyrus in the deliverance of Israel and the execution of the divine judgment upon Babylon and the nations. Cyrus now has the same work of judgment to accomplish that the Assyrians and Babylonians had done before him. But this judgment was not a chastisement of Israel as the Assyrian and Babylonian oppressions had been. Cyrus is the conqueror of the enemies of Zion, and her deliverer and restorer. Jahveh raised him up for this purpose, and assigned him his career of conquest. The prophet is thus guided to take a more friendly view of the relation of Israel to the nations, and to discern that Jahveh is the only God and Saviour of the world.

[1] This reminds us of Isa. xxxv. 5.   See p. 318.

§ 98. *Israel will go forth from Babylon with songs of joy. Jahveh will guide them through the wilderness and quench their thirst by water from the rocks. All the ends of the earth will turn unto Jahveh, and every tongue will swear allegiance to Him.*

" Declare ye, and bring it forth ; yea, let them take counsel
        together ;
Who hath showed this from ancient time, hath declared it of old?
Have not I, Jahveh? and there is no God else beside me ;
A just 'El and a Saviour ; there is none beside me.
Look unto me, and be ye saved, all the ends of the earth : for I
        am 'El, and there is none else.
By myself have I sworn, the word is gone forth from my mouth
        in righteousness, and will not return,
That unto me every knee shall bow, every tongue shall swear.
Only in Jahveh, one said to me,[1] are perfect righteousness[2] and
        strength :
Even to him will come,[3] and will be ashamed all they that were
        incensed against him.
In Jahveh will all the seed of Israel be justified, and boast them-
        selves."   —Isa. xlv. 21–25.

Jahveh is the only God and Saviour.   There is no other God.   It follows, therefore, that He and He alone must be the Saviour of the world, if salvation is to extend beyond the Jewish race.   Our prophet attains this conception, and looks forward to the time when the people will turn unto Jahveh from all parts of the earth,

----

[1] לִי אָמַר. This is a voice to the prophet, such as we have seen in
וְאָמַר of xl. 3, and will see again in lvii. 14.

[2] צְדָקוֹת is probably the emphatic plural.

[3] יָבוֹא. The singular is rendered as a plural by the Peshitto, Vulgate, some MSS. of the Hebrew and LXX. There has probably been a transposition of the ו, and we should read יָבֹאוּ. The construction of the pentameter line favours this. There are often two verbs at the beginning of a line such as we should have in יָבֹאוּ וְיֵבֹשׁוּ. It is difficult to find a good reason for the singular form without introducing an awkward contrast into the line. We have the proper contrast between this line and the next. Lowth, Knobel, Ewald, Cheyne and most critics rightly read the plural.

and when every knee will bow in His worship, and every tongue swear allegiance to Him. This universal salvation is the result of that line of prophecy that has been extending the boundaries of redemption beyond the borders of the chosen people. We have seen it extended in the earlier Isaiah to Egypt and Assyria, Ethiopia and Tyre,[1] and in Zephaniah to the Ethiopians and Libyans.[2] Ps. lxxxvii. describes the adoption of the nations: Egypt, Babylon, Philistia, Tyre, and Ethiopia, one after another in the city of God.[3] Jeremiah sees all nations assembling to the new Jerusalem.[4] But the great unknown first grasps the problem of the world-wide extent of redemption, and sees all mankind united in the worship of the one only true God and Saviour.

The second refrain becomes more specific with reference to the departure from Babylon, as we should expect from its relation to the prophecy respecting Cyrus and the overthrow of Babylon.

" Thus saith Jahveh, thy Redeemer, the Holy One of Israel :
I, Jahveh, thy God, which teacheth thee to profit,
Which leadeth thee in the way thou shouldest go.
Oh that thou hadst hearkened to my commandments !
Then had thy peace been as a river, and thy righteousness as the waves of the sea ;
Thy seed also had been as the sand, and the offspring of thy bowels like the grains thereof ;
His name will not be cut off nor destroyed from before me.
Go ye forth from Babylon, flee ye from the Chaldeans with a voice of singing,
Declare ye, tell this, utter it even to the end of the earth :
Say ye, Jahveh hath redeemed his servant Jacob.
And they thirsted not, he led them through the deserts ;
He caused the waters to flow out of the rock for them ; he clave the rock also, and the waters gushed out.
There is no peace, saith Jahveh, to the wicked."

—Isa. xlviii. 17-22.

---

[1] See p. 206. [2] See p. 225.
[3] See p. 226. [4] See p. 242.

In this piece we have the reason of the exile. As in the introduction it had been the discharge of a debt of iniquity, so here it had been because of neglect of Jahveh's commands. If Zion had followed the teaching of Jahveh, the ancient promises would have been fulfilled. The seed promised to Abraham would have been as the sands of the sea,[1] and their peace would have been like an ever-flowing river, and their righteousness as the waves of the sea. The exile has been only a temporary failure. The promises will yet be fulfilled. The exile is to be followed by restoration, and the exiles are summoned to go forth from Babylon. As in the exodus from Egypt, so will it be in this greater exodus. Waters will burst from the rock to quench the thirst of those whose path leads through the desert to the promised land.

III. JAHVEH IS FAITHFUL TO ZION.

§ 99. *Jahveh is more faithful than a mother. He will never forget Zion, but will restore her and multiply her children. He will make bare His holy arm, and redeem Jerusalem. They will march forth from Babylon, a holy people, bearing the sacred vessels, Jahveh being at once their vanguard and rearguard. Kings and queens will be their foster-fathers and mothers. The watchmen of Zion tell the glad tidings of the advent, and the wastes of Jerusalem break forth in responsive songs.*

The third section of the prophecy gives the complaint of Zion and the response of the faithful Jahveh, immediately after the parallel representation of the servant of Jahveh. The piece is a hexameter of twenty lines.

"And Zion said, Jahveh hath forsaken me, and 'Adonay hath forgotten me.

Can a woman forget her suckling child, that she should not have compassion on the son of her womb?

---

[1] See p. 84.

Yea, these may forget, yet will not I forget thee.

Behold, I have graven thee upon the palms of my hands; thy walls are continually before me.

Thy builders [1] do make haste; thy destroyers and they that made thee waste shall go forth of thee.

Lift up thine eyes round about, and behold: all these do gather themselves together, they do come to thee.[2]

As I live, is the utterance of Jahveh, thou shalt clothe thee with them all as with an ornament,

And like a bride thou wilt gird thyself with thy waste, and thy desolate places and thy land that hath been destroyed.

Surely now shalt thou be too strait for the inhabitants, and they that swallowed thee up will be far away.

The children of thy bereavement will yet say in thine ears,

The place is too strait for me; give place to me that I may dwell.

Then wilt thou say in thine heart, Who hath borne [3] me these,

Seeing I have been bereaved of my children, and am barren, an exile, and wandering to and fro, and who hath brought up these?

Behold, I was left alone; these where were they?

Thus saith 'Adonay Jahveh,

Behold, I will lift up mine hand to the nations, and set up my banner to the peoples:

And they will bring thy sons in their bosom, and thy daughters will be carried upon their shoulders.

---

[1] בָּנַיִךְ of the Massoretic text is followed by the R.V. and most interpreters in the rendering "thy sons." But the LXX., Vulgate, Targum, Saadia are rightly followed by Lowth, Eichhorn and others in reading בֹּנַיִךְ. So the margin of the R.V. Ewald would insert בֹּנַיִךְ after בָּנַיִךְ, and thus combine the two readings.

[2] The same line in Isa. lx. 4 shows where the line must be divided. This compels us to connect חַי אָנִכִי, etc., with the next line, and this forces us to begin the next line with וְתִקְשְׁרִים, and connect it with ver. 19. The כִּי is then out of place. It has crept into the text by a very natural assimilation to כִּי כֻלָּם and כִּי עַתָּה.

[3] מִי יָלַד. The R.V. follows Lowth, Gesenius, Ewald and others in rendering, "Who hath begotten me these." But it is better, with the margin of the R.V., Knobel, Hitzig, Delitzsch and Cheyne, to render, "Who hath borne." The context shows that the mother is surprised at the number of her children. She does not inquire for the father, but for the mother.

And kings will be thy foster-fathers, and their queens thy nursing
    mothers ;
They will bow down to thee with their faces to the earth, and lick
    the dust of thy feet ;
And thou wilt know that it is I, Jahveh, and they that wait for me
    will not be ashamed."   —Isa. xlix. 14–23.

This piece magnifies the faithfulness of Jahveh. He
is the gentle Father here, as He is the gentle shepherd
in the introduction. He is more faithful than the
mother to the babe at her breast. He will never forget
Zion. Her walls are graven on His palms as a perpetual
memorial. The old Zion is in ruins, and her children
are scattered in exile. But the real Zion is the ideal
that Jahveh Himself has planned, and the destruction
of the old Zion was in order to the erection of the new
Jerusalem. The builders make haste to their work.
The desolaters will soon be expelled from its ruins.
Her children are now scattered, and few in number.
But they will be gathered, and marvellously increased.
They will become so numerous that it will be difficult
to find place for them, and Zion herself will be unable
to understand that she can be the mother of such a
multitude.

The relation of Zion to the nations is also unfolded.
They will obey the call of Jahveh, and take part in her
restoration. They will become the servants of Zion, and
bring her children in their bosoms and on their shoulders.
Yes, even the kings and queens of the nations will delight
in doing honour to the children of Zion. They will
become foster-fathers and foster-mothers. They will
bow down to the earth in obeisance, and lick the dust
of Zion's feet. Zion will be exalted high above all.
This exaltation of Zion after a season of humiliation
is entirely parallel to the exaltation of the servant of
Jahveh after a season of obscurity and servitude, as set
forth in that part of the trimeter section of the prophecy

that immediately precedes.[1]   The exaltation of Zion over
the nations is not conceived as a triumph; but rather
as an enthronement to such a height of excellence that
the nations will render willing homage and service.   As
in the previous section every knee bows to Jahveh, and
every tongue swears allegiance to Him, so here those
who worship Jahveh will honour Zion likewise.

This section has as its chief piece a beautiful lyric in
three great strophes, enclosed by an introduction, and
a conclusion that constitutes the refrain.

The introduction is an appeal to Zion to remember
the ancient promises, and a renewal of the assurance that
Jahveh is the comforter of Zion.

"Hearken to me, ye that pursue righteousness, that seek Jahveh:
Look unto the rock whence ye were hewn, and to the hole of the
        pit whence ye were digged.
Look unto Abraham your father, and unto Sarah that bare you:
For when he was but one I called him, that I might bless him [2] and
        multiply him:
For Jahveh doth comfort Zion: he doth comfort all her waste
        places,
And make her wilderness like Eden, and her desert like the garden
        of Jahveh:
Joy and gladness will be found therein, thanksgiving and the sound
        of melody.
Attend unto me, my people; and give ear unto me, my nation:
For instruction will go forth from me, and I will make my judgment
        to rest for a light of the peoples.
My righteousness is near, my salvation is gone forth, and mine arms
        will judge the peoples;
The coasts will wait for me, and on mine arm will they trust.

---

[1] xlix. 2, 7.   See p. 353.

[2] וַאֲבָרְכֵהוּ as pointed by the Massoretes is a change of tense.
We may follow classic usage and render this and the following
verb as in final causes.   These are rendered by the R.V. and
interpreters generally as if the vavs were vavs consecutive.   But
it is better to think of the blessing of Abram, and the multiplication of his seed as the purpose of God when He called him alone.
See Gen. xii. 1, 2.   See p. 84.

Lift up your eyes to the heavens, and look upon the earth beneath:
For the heavens will vanish away like smoke, and the earth will
    wax old like a garment,
And they that dwell therein will die like gnats,[1]
But my salvation will be for ever, and my righteousness will not be
    abolished.
Hearken unto me, ye that know righteousness, the people in whose
    heart is my instruction ; [2]
Fear ye not the reproach of men, neither be ye dismayed at their
    revilings.
For the moth will eat them up like a garment, and the worm will
    eat them like wool :
But my righteousness will be for ever, and my salvation unto all
    generations."   —Isa. li. 1–8.

Zion is comforted by a reference to the covenant with
Abraham. God called him alone, and yet it was with
the design of blessing him with a numerous posterity.
Zion has nothing to fear on account of the diminished
number of her children and the sufferings of the exile.
The Abrahamic covenant will be fulfilled. Zion's waste
places will be restored. Her wilderness will become like
the garden of Jahveh in Eden, and joy and gladness will
be found therein. This piece reminds us of Jeremiah's
book of comfort,[3] and of Ezekiel's promise that the land
would become like the garden of Eden.[4] Both of these
earlier prophecies are presupposed. The promise of
Jahveh is sure. The earth will become old like a
garment, and the heavens vanish as smoke, and all the
inhabitants of the world will die like gnats, and all their
persecutors will pass away as garments consumed by

---

[1] כמו־כן. כֵּן is rendered by the Versions and most interpreters,
"so, thus, in like manner." But Lowth, Ewald, Gesenius, Hitzig,
Knobel and others render gnat. It is only found here in the
singular, and in the Talmud it assumes the feminine form. Hence
Cheyne follows Weir in reading כנים.

[2] Compare Jer. xxxi. 33.
[3] Jer. xxx.–xxxi. See p. 246.
[4] Ezek. xxxvi. 25–35. See p. 274.

moths. There is indeed to be a new world in place of the old. But the righteousness and the salvation of Jahveh will abide for ever to all generations of His people, who have His instruction written in their hearts.

This introduction is followed by the three great strophes of the poem, the first calling upon the strong arm of Jahveh to awake for the redemption of His people; the second calling upon Jerusalem to wake up, for Jahveh will take from her the cup of His wrath and give it to her oppressors ; the third calling upon Zion to awake and put on her garments of strength and beauty. The poem closes with the heralds proclaiming the advent.

"How beautiful upon the mountains are the feet of him that
    bringeth good tidings, that publisheth peace,
That bringeth good tidings of good, that publisheth salvation ; that
    saith unto Zion, thy God is king.
Hark ! thy watchmen do lift up the voice ; together they sing:
For they see eye to eye, when Jahveh returneth to Zion.
Break forth into joy, sing together, ye waste places of Jerusalem :
For Jahveh doth comfort his people, redeem Jerusalem.
Jahveh doth make bare his holy arm in the eyes of all the nations ;
And all the ends of the earth see the salvation of our God.
Depart ye ! depart ye ! go ye out from thence, touch no unclean
    thing ;
Go ye out of the midst of her ; purify yourselves, ye that bear the
    vessels of Jahveh.
For ye will not go out with haste, nor go by flight :
For Jahveh is the one going before you ; and the God of Israel the
    one bringing up your rear."   —Isa. lii. 7–12.

This piece is dramatic in style, and in this respect also resembles the introduction. There, we saw Zion and Jerusalem proclaiming from the mountains the divine advent. Here, the preachers are on the mountains, and are admired by those who hear their message of peace. They are heard singing with joy, and the waste places of Jerusalem break forth into a glad, responsive song. For the holy arm of Jahveh has been displayed before all nations. The holy arm of this passage takes the place of the ruling arm of the introduction.[1] The people are then called upon to depart from Babylon, as in the previous refrain.[2] The piece concludes with a new thought. The departure from Babylon will not be a flight, as at the exodus from Egypt, but like a band of peaceful worshippers, in holy garments, bearing the sacred vessels of their God. As at the exodus from Egypt in the pillar of cloud and fire, Jahveh is at once their vanguard and their rearguard, protecting them on all sides.

The fourth section of the prophecy gives a companion piece to the picture of the exaltation of the suffering servant of Ps. lii. 13–liii. in the exaltation of Zion after a brief period of suffering under the divine wrath, in a condition of widowhood and barrenness. This is a beautiful hexameter poem of two strophes of fifteen lines each.

IV. JAHVEH THE COMFORTER OF ZION.

§ 100. *Zion has been forsaken for a short time, and suffered affliction. But Jahveh is her husband and saviour. He is faithful to her, and will bestow upon her His covenant of peace. He will restore her to her land, and her children will become so numerous that they will break forth on every side and take possession of the nations. Jerusalem will be rebuilt of precious stones. All her children will be disciples of Jahveh, and enjoy everlasting peace.*

I. "Sing, O barren, thou that didst not bear; break forth into singing, and cry aloud, thou that didst not travail with child:

For more are the children of the desolate than the children of the married, saith Jahveh.

---

[1] See p. 375.   [2] See p. 380.

Enlarge the place of thy tent, and let them stretch out the
curtains of thine habitations :
Spare not, lengthen thy cords and strengthen thy stakes.
For thou wilt break forth on the right hand and on the left ;
And thy seed will inherit the nations, and make the desolate
cities to be inhabited.
Fear not ; for thou shalt not be ashamed : neither be thou
confounded ; for thou shalt not be put to shame :
For thou shalt forget the shame of thy youth, and shalt not
remember the reproach of thy widowhood any more,
For thy Maker is thine husband : Jahveh Sabaoth his name ;
And thy Redeemer is the Holy One of Israel ; the God of the
whole earth is He called.
For as a woman forsaken and grievẹd in spirit, Jahveh called thee,
And a wife of youth when she is rejected, saith thy God ;
For a small moment have I forsaken thee : but with great
compassions will I gather thee.
In a gush [1] of wrath I hid my face from thee for a moment :
But with everlasting mercy I have compassion on thee, saith
Jahveh thy Redeemer.

II. For this is as the days of Noah [2] unto me ; when I swore that
the waters of Noah should not flow over the earth ;
So have I sworn that I will not be wroth with thee, nor rebuke
thee.
For the mountains will depart, and the hills be removed ;
But my mercies will not depart from thee, neither will the
covenant of my peace be removed,
Saith Jahveh, that hath compassion on thee, O thou afflicted,
tost with tempest, and not comforted. [3]

---

[1] שֶׁצֶף is only found here. It is a variation of שֶׁטֶף of Prov.
xxvii. 4, as Gesenius, Ewald, Delitzsch, Cheyne and others, meaning
overflow, gush. The LXX., Vulgate, Targum, A.V., Lowth and
others render "little," which suits the context, but has no justification in etymology.

[2] The common Massoretic כִימֵי is followed by the R.V. and most
interpreters. But the Babylonian codex and some Palestinian
codices agree with the Peshitto, Vulgate, Targum, and Saadia in
reading כִי יְמֵי. The LXX. מִמֵי can best be explained as a corruption of כִימֵי. Matt. xxiv. 37 also favours this reading. The external
evidence for יְמֵי is unusually strong, and the context favours it. We
do not hesitate to follow it, with Lowth and Delitzsch.

[3] The rhythm requires that we should disregard the Massoretic
accents, and construct the line as we have given it.

Behold, I am about to lay thy stones with kohl,[1] and thy foundations with sapphires,

And make thy pinnacles rubies, and thy gates of carbuncles, and all thy borders of pleasant stones,

And all thy children will be disciples of Jahveh; and great will be the peace of thy children, in righteousness wilt thou be established;

Thou wilt be far from oppression; for thou wilt not fear: and from terror; for it will not come near thee.

Behold, they may gather close together, but not by me; whosoever shall gather together against thee shall fall for thy sake.

Behold, I have created the smith that bloweth the coals in the fire,

And that bringeth forth an instrument for his work; and I have created the waster to destroy.

Any weapon that is formed against thee shall not prosper:

And any tongue that is raised against thee in judgment thou shalt condemn.

This is the inheritance of the servants of Jahveh, and their righteousness is of me, is the utterance of Jahveh."

—Isa. liv. 1–17.

This beautiful poem carries on the thought of xlix. 14–23, and combines therewith the representations of several previous prophets, Hosea, Zephaniah, Jeremiah, and Ezekiel. The two contrasted conditions of Zion are set forth in stronger terms than in the previous section of our prophet. She is a wife of youth, who has been rejected by Jahveh on account of sin. In an outburst of wrath He gave her up, and she has suffered the reproach of widowhood. She has been grieved in spirit, has been afflicted, has been tossed about as by a tempest, and has had no comfort. This rejected wife of Jahveh reminds us of the same idea in Hosea and Jeremiah.[2] But the humiliation of Zion is to continue only for a brief season.

---

[1] פוּךְ is the kohl or stibium with which Oriental ladies paint their eyebrows and eyelids. It is here the cement of the precious stones.

[2] See pp. 168, 246.

Jahveh is still her husband, His love is unquenchable, His compassions fail not, his covenant is inviolable. The time has come for her restoration. This is the chief theme of the poem. The restoration is compared with the days of Noah. Then the wrath of God destroyed the inhabitants of the earth by a deluge, and only Noah and his family were left; but he received the promise that there should never be another deluge. So when Zion is restored, Jahveh will assure her with an oath of covenant that He will never be angry with her any more, and will never rebuke her again. This reference to the Noachic covenant reminds us of Jeremiah.[1]

The restoration is also accompanied with a multiplication of the children of Zion in accordance with the ancient promises. This is presented in the striking contrast between the married and the desolate. The time of her marriage was a time of fruitfulness and large increase in the holy land; but in her exile her children have been slain and scattered, and she has become desolate. We are here reminded of Rachel weeping for her children.[2] But the desolate wife will again enjoy the love of her husband, and her children will be much greater than ever before, so great that there will not be room enough for them in the holy land, and they will break out in all directions and take possession of the nations.[3] The restoration will result in the rebuilding of Jerusalem in greater beauty and magnificence than ever. The new Jerusalem has already been described in Jeremiah and in Ezekiel as greatly enlarged and adorned with holiness and the divine presence;[4] but this passage sets forth its wondrous beauty. Its walls and gates are constructed

[1] Jer. xxxiii. 14–22.   See p. 245.
[2] Jer. xxxi. 15, 16.   See p. 251.
[3] Compare Isa. xlix. 19–21.   See p. 382.
[4] See pp. 254 and 286.

of sapphires, rubies, carbuncles and all kinds of precious
stones; and they are cemented by the costly stibium
with which the Oriental ladies beautify their eyelids and
eyelashes. "The stones of its walls would look like the
eyes of a woman shining forth from the black framework of their painted lids, *i.e.* they would stand out in
splendour from their dark ground." [1]

The restoration has its new covenant of peace. This
reminds us of Ezekiel.[2] This covenant involves security
from oppression and fear. No enemy will be able to
harm her with weapon or with tongue. She will be
delivered from fear, and will possess her inheritance in
righteousness, and her children will be the disciples of
Jahveh, will be under His divine instruction and guidance,
and will enjoy great peace.[3] But above all, the tender
compassion and everlasting mercy and comfort of her
husband and saviour will abide with her for ever.[4]

V. JAHVEH'S HOUSE OF PRAYER FOR ALL NATIONS.

§ 101. *Not only the faithful in Israel, but all foreigners
who keep the covenant and the Sabbath, will inherit the
holy mountain, for Jahveh dwells with the humble and
contrite, and His house will become a house of prayer for
all nations. The righteous will enjoy the covenant of peace,
but there is no peace for the wicked. The word of command is issued to prepare the highway and remove the
stumbling-blocks out of the way of the returning exiles.*

The fourth section of the prophecy gives a little piece
of prediction with regard to the share of foreigners in the

---

[1] See Delitzsch, *Isaiah*, ii. p. 349. This is the basis of the description of the new Jerusalem in Rev. xxi.
[2] Ezek. xxxiv. 25, xxxvii. 26. See pp. 272, 278.
[3] Compare Zeph. iii. 16, 17. See p. 224.
[4] Compare Jer. xxxi. 33, 34; Ezek. xxxvi. 25–35. See pp. 253, 274.

blessings of the Messianic times. The eunuchs, who were not admitted to a share in the institutions of the old covenant, and the foreigners will alike be welcomed to the new Jerusalem and enjoy its privileges.

> " And the foreigners who join themselves unto Jahveh to minister to him,
> And to love the name of Jahveh, to become servants unto him,
> Every one keeping the Sabbath from polluting it, and those who are firm in my covenant,
> I will bring them unto my holy mountain, and I will make them rejoice in my house of prayer;
> Their burnt-offerings and their peace-offerings will be for acceptance upon mine altar,
> For my house will be proclaimed a house of prayer for all peoples."
> —Isa. lvi. 6, 7.

This passage is the most advanced of all those that we have met, relating to the share of the nations in the redemption of Israel. Isaiah predicts that Egypt will serve Jahveh with peace-offerings, vegetable-offerings and votive-offerings;[1] and in Zephaniah the Cushites bring incense-offerings, and the Libyans vegetable-offerings.[2] So here foreigners in general will bring burnt-offerings and peace-offerings to the divine altar and find acceptance. The temple is no longer a merely Jewish temple, it has become a universal temple. As such it is more than a place of sacrifice, it is a place of prayer. The prophet rises above the conception of Ezekiel to the idea of a universal religion. The sacrifices are still here, for the Old Testament point of view cannot yet be abandoned; but the sacrifices are in the background. As the qualifications for participation in the blessings of redemption are no longer national, but covenant-keeping and Sabbath observance, conditions that all nations might fulfil; so the most significant feature of the new worship is prayer,

[1] Isa. xix. 21. See p. 207. [2] Zeph. iii. 10. See p. 223.

and the world-wide name of the temple of Jahveh will be—*house of prayer for all peoples.*

This section of the prophecy closes with a little piece, and a refrain which is in accord with its sublime ideas.

"Have I not been silent,[1] even a long time, and thou fearest me not?.

I will declare thy righteousness and thy works,

They will not profit thee. When thou criest, let them which thou hast gathered deliver thee;

But the wind will take them, a breath will carry them all away;

But he that putteth his trust in me shall possess the land, and shall inherit my holy mountain.

And one saith,[2] Cast ye up, cast ye up, prepare the way,

Take up the stumbling-block out of the way of my people.

For thus saith the high and lofty One, that inhabiteth eternity, whose name is holy;

I dwell in the high and holy place, with him also that is of a contrite and humble spirit,

To revive the spirit of the humble, and to revive the heart of the contrite ones.

For I will not contend for ever, neither will I be always wroth;

For the spirit should fail before me, and the persons which I have made.

For the iniquity of his covetousness was I wroth and smote him, I hid my face and was wroth;

When he went on turning away in the way of his heart, I saw his ways.

Verily I will heal him; I will lead him also, and restore comforts to him and to his mourners.

Creator of the fruit of the lips: 'Peace,

Peace, to him that is far off and to him that is near,' saith Jahveh, and I will heal him.

But the wicked are like the sea that is tost up,

For it cannot rest, and its waters toss up mire and dirt.

There is no peace, saith my God, to the wicked."—Isa. lvii. 11-21.

As in a previous section, Jahveh has long been silent,

---

[1] This begins with the same thought and the same verb, חשה, as xlii. 14.

[2] Compare xl. 3. The ואמר reminds us of ואמר of xl. 6.

and it is now time to speak and act. There will be a distinction between the righteous and the wicked. The idolaters will be destroyed, there is no peace for the wicked. But they that trust in Jahveh will inherit the holy mountain. They that are humble and contrite in heart and spirit will enjoy the divine presence. Those far and near will enjoy the peace of the restoration. The time of suffering for sin is over. God will hide His face no more, He will have compassion and will comfort the mourners of Zion, and will heal them. A voice is heard, commanding to prepare the way, to remove the stumbling-blocks, for Jahveh is about to lead His people to His holy mountain.

VI. ZION THE LIGHT OF THE WORLD.

The idea of the servant of Jahveh reaches its culmination in Isa. lxi. This passage is enclosed by two hexameter pieces, in which the idea of the restoration of Zion reaches its height. The former of these is a hymn of wondrous beauty, the latter, the real conclusion of the second edition of the prophecy.

§ 102. *The advent of Jahveh to Zion is like the rising of the sun that illuminates her and makes her a light to all the world. Thither the nations assemble with their treasures to do homage to Zion and her God. The city will be built of precious metals. Peace and righteousness will be its rulers. The people will be all righteous, and the city will be altogether glorious.*

I. " Arise, shine, for thy light is come, and the glory of Jahveh is risen upon thee ;
For lo, darkness covereth the earth, and dense darkness the peoples.
But upon thee Jahveh riseth and his glory upon thee appeareth,

And nations walk in thy light, and kings in the brightness of thy rising.

Lift up round about thine eyes and see : they all do gather themselves together, they do come to thee ; [1]

Thy sons from afar come, and thy daughters at the side are carried. [2]

Then wilt thou see and be bright, [3] and thy mind will be reverent and be enlarged ;

For the abundance of the sea will be turned unto thee ; the wealth of nations will come to thee ;

The multitude of camels will cover thee, the young camels of Midian and Ephah, all of them. [4]

From Sheba will they come, gold and frankincense will they bring, and the praises of Jahveh they will tell in glad tidings ;

All the flocks of Kedar will gather themselves to thee, the rams of Nebaioth will minister to thee,

They will ascend for acceptance on mine altar, and the house of my beauty I will beautify.

II. Who are these that fly like a cloud and like doves unto their lattices ?

Surely to me the coasts will assemble, [5] and the ships of Tarshish first,

To bring thy sons from afar, their silver and their gold with them,

To the name of Jahveh thy God and to the Holy One of Israel ; for he doth beautify thee.

And foreigners will build thy walls, and their kings will minister to thee.

---

[1] Comp. Isa. xlix. 18, where the line is identical with this one.

[2] See Isa. xlix. 22.

[3] נהר=נור, to shine, be bright, is only found here and in Ps. xxxiv. 6.

[4] כלם is separated by the accents from the previous line. But attaching it there the verse is easily divided into two hexameters, otherwise we have a third short line.

[5] יְקַוּ is usually rendered, hope for, expect, wait ; but it is better to follow Gen. i. 9 and Jer. iii. 17, where the Niphal is used for the assemblage of waters and nations. Thus the context seems to require יִקָּווּ, with Geiger and Luzzato.

For in my wrath I smote thee, but in my favour I have compassion on thee,

And thy gates will be open continually, day and night they will not be shut,

For bringing unto thee the wealth of nations and their kings will be conducted.[1]

For the nation and the kingdom that will not serve thee will perish,

Yea, the nations will be utterly wasted.[2]

The glory of Lebanon will come unto thee, the cypress, plane, and sherbin tree together,

To beautify the place of my holiness, and the place of my feet I will glorify.

III. And the sons of thy oppressors will go unto thee to submit themselves,

And all who despised thee will prostrate themselves at the soles of thy feet,

And they will call thee the city of Jahveh, Zion of the Holy One of Israel.

Instead of being forsaken, and hated, and without a traveller,

I will make thee an everlasting excellency, a joy of generation and generation;

And thou wilt suck the milk of nations, and the breast of kings wilt suck;

And wilt know that I, Jahveh, am thy Saviour, and thy Redeemer, the Mighty One of Jacob.

Instead of brass I will bring gold, and instead of iron I will bring silver,

And instead of wood brass, and instead of stones iron,

And I will make peace thy magistracy,[3] and righteousness thine exactors;

---

[1] נהוגים has nominal force according to Knobel, with the meaning guides—that is, the kings lead the nations to Jerusalem. Most interpreters think of the kings as led captive, but this does not suit the context or the usual meaning of the word. Lowth and Gesenius think of the kings as conducted by a large train of attendants.

[2] This seems to be a broken line.

[3] פקדתך is abstract, meaning oversight, government. It is taken by the R.V., after many interpreters, as for the concrete, overseers, as in 2 Chron. xxiv. 11. But Ewald, Delitzsch, Cheyne and others retain the abstract, government, magistracy. Delitzsch, Nägelsbach and Cheyne rightly think that peace and righteousness are personified and constituted the rulers of the new Jerusalem.

Violence will no more be heard in thy land, oppression and
destruction in thy boundaries,
But thy walls will be called 'salvation,' and thy gates
'praise.'

IV. The sun will no more become a light by day, or for brightness
the moon shine for thee,
But Jahveh will become thine everlasting light, and thy God
thy beauty ;
Thy sun will no more go down, and thy moon will not withdraw itself,
For Jahveh will become for thee an everlasting light, and the
days of thy mourning will be ended.
And thy people will be all of them righteous, for ever they
will inherit the land,
The branch of my planting, the work of my hands to beautify
myself.
The least will become a thousand, and the smallest a strong
nation :
I, Jahveh, will hasten it in its time."　　　　　　　—Isa. lx.

This song is the gem of the book. Here the glory of
Zion attains its height. It is based upon the previous
passages, especially xlix. 14–23. In the first strophe
Zion is called upon to rise and let her light shine upon
the dark places of the earth, that the nations and their
kings may walk in her light. Jahveh has arisen in her
as the sun to shine forth from her upon all the world.
This is a further unfolding of the conception of Jeremiah
that the entire city will become the throne of Jahveh
and be as sacred as the holy of holies and the ark of
the covenant ;[1] and of the names of the city, " Jahveh is
there," of Ezekiel; and " Jahveh is our righteousness,"
of Jeremiah.[2] Zion is then called upon to look about
and see her children brought back to her by the nations
that have become her servants.[3] Her heart is cheered

---

[1] Jer. iii. 14–18, xxxi. 40.　See pp. 242, 254.
[2] Jer. xxxiii. 16 ; Ezek. xlviii. 35.　See pp. 244 and 290.
[3] Comp. Isa. xlix. 18, 22.　See p. 382.

and brightened as she beholds the wondrous spectacle. They not only bring her children to her, they bring their wealth with them, wealth of flocks and herds and camels, gold and frankincense, all the riches of the sea and the land, to enrich Zion; and above all, they tell the glad tidings of the praise of Jahveh which has spread over the world as the light of the sun.

The second strophe again calls attention to the approaching multitudes by a question. They come like a cloud of doves flying home to their cotes. The distant coasts appear, with the ships of Tarshish leading the way on the sea with their snow-white sails. These ships bring her children to Zion laden with gold and silver. The foreigners now take part in the building of the new Jerusalem, and the kings of the nations serve her. Her gates remain open day and night that the crowding multitudes may enter the city with their treasures. The nations and kingdoms that refuse their service will be destroyed. The precious timber of Lebanon will be brought in to beautify the holy places, as it had been used in the erection of the ancient temple.

The third strophe briefly contrasts the state of humiliation with the state of exaltation. Her days of oppression and despisement are over. She now sees the sons of her oppressors, and all who despised her, lying prostrate at the soles of her feet,[1] recognising her as the city of Jahveh, the Zion of the Holy One of Israel. Zion has been forsaken, hated, and with no one to visit her ruins even as a traveller, but now she has become the joy of the generations, an everlasting excellency, and will be nourished by the best of the nations. As in the previous section kings and queens were to be her foster-fathers and mothers, so here she is to suckle at the breast of the nations and their monarchs, and be sustained by

[1] Comp. Isa. xlix. 22. See p. 383.

their riches.[1]   The days of her poverty, when iron, and
brass, and stones were her portion, have past.   She is
now to have gold and silver as well.   In the former
times she has suffered from oppression and destruction,
but now these will no more be heard of in her boundaries.
Peace and righteousness are appointed as her magistrates.
This is a further unfolding of the covenant of peace of
the previous section, where peace was to be the portion
of her children and she was to be shielded from every
evil.[2]   And so the walls of Zion are no more to be of
stones; even the precious stones of the previous section[3]
are no more thought of; the walls are called " salvation,"
and the gates " praise." [4]

The last strophe of this wonderful poem goes back
upon the thought with which it began.   Jahveh is the
sun and the moon, the everlasting light and beauty of
Zion.   She no longer needs the light of sun or moon.
Her people will be all righteous, the planting of Jahveh ;
and the least of them will be as strong as a thousand,
and the smallest of them as a strong nation.   This is an
unfolding of the blessings of the Mosaic codes which are
now to be realized to the full.[5]   This marvellous picture
of the glory of Zion is taken up into the representation
of the new Jerusalem in the great Apocalypse of the
New Testament.[6]

The climax of the glory of Zion has been reached in
the piece just considered.   This is followed in the second
edition of the poem by the trimeter poem in which the
idea of the servant of Jahveh attains its climax.   The

---

[1] Isa. xlix. 23.   See p. 383.   [2] Isa. liv. 13–17.   See p. 389.
[3] Isa. liv. 11, 12.   See p. 389.
[4] This reminds us of the salvation that was made the walls and
bulwarks of Zion in the great apocalypse, Isa. xxiv.–xxvii.   See
Isa. xxvi. 1, p. 300.
[5] Comp. Deut. xxxii. 30 ; Lev. xxvi. 8.   See pp. 116, 117.
[6] See Rev. xxi. 22–27, xxii. 5.

whole is then concluded with a hexameter piece of thirty
lines which is the counterpart of the introduction to the
whole prophecy, and resumes the principal thread of
thought in the intermediate representations of the restoration of Zion.

§ 103. *Zion has been named " Forsaken " and " Desolate,"
but she is to receive the new names, " Married " and " My
delight is in thee." Jahveh will rejoice over her as His
bride, and will make her His crown of glory. Jahveh will
not be silent any longer. The watchmen on the walls
cannot be silent. The advent is at hand. The heralds are
crying, " Prepare the way." The proclamation has gone
forth to the ends of the earth, " Salvation cometh."*

I. "For Zion's sake will I not be silent, and for Jerusalem's sake
    I will not be quiet,
  Until the righteousness thereof go forth as brightness, and
    the salvation thereof as a torch that burneth.
  And the nations will see thy righteousness, and all kings thy
    glory :
  And thou shalt be called by a new name, which the mouth of
    Jahveh will name.
  And thou shalt be a crown of glory in the hand of Jahveh,
  And a royal diadem in the hand of thy God.
  Thou shalt no more be termed ' *Forsaken;*'
  Neither will thy land any more be termed ' *Desolate:*'
  But thou shalt be called ' *My delight is in thee,*' and thy land
    ' *Married,*'
  For Jahveh doth delight in thee, and thy land will be married.
  For as a young man marrieth a virgin, so will thy great
    builder [1] marry thee ;
  And as the bridegroom rejoiceth over the bride, so will thy God
    rejoice over thee.

---

[1] בָּנָיִךְ of the Massoretic text, although followed by the Versions
and interpreters generally, does not give an intelligible sense. It is
best, with Lowth, to point בֹּנַיִךְ as in xlix. 17, and render, "thy great
builder." This is demanded by the context. It is God alone who
marrieth Zion. There is no sense in her sons marrying her.

II. Upon thy walls, Jerusalem, I have appointed watchmen,
    All day and all night continually they are not silent.
    Ye that remind Jahveh, let there be no rest to you,
    And give no rest to him until he establish,
    And until he make Jerusalem a praise in the earth.
    Jahveh hath sworn by his right hand and by the arm of his
        strength,
    ' I will not give thy corn any more as food for thine enemies,
    And the foreigners will not drink thy new wine with which
        thou hast toiled ; '
    For those that have garnered it will eat it, and praise Jahveh,
    And those that have gathered it will drink it in my holy court.

III. Go through, go through the gates ; prepare [1] ye the way of the
      people ;
    Cast up, cast up the highway ; gather out the stones ; [2]
    Lift up an ensign over the peoples.
    Behold, Jahveh hath proclaimed unto the end of the earth,
    Say ye to the daughter of Zion, Behold, thy salvation cometh ; [3]
    Behold, his wage is with him, and his recompense before him.
    And they will call them, 'The holy people, the redeemed of
        Jahveh ; '
    And thou shalt be called 'Sought out,' 'A city not forsaken.'"
                               —Isa. lxii.

This piece opens with the same expression of impatience
on the part of Jahveh that we have seen in two previous
pieces.[4] The advent is at hand. The salvation of Zion
will go forth as a flaming torch. All nations will see
her righteousness and glory. The old names suited to
her state of humiliation, " Forsaken " and " Desolate," are
to be put away. These were the names that Zion
thought appropriate to her when Jahveh began to comfort
her.[5] But those times are past. She is to be a diadem
and a glorious crown in the hand of Jahveh, and new
names are to be given suited to her state of glory. She
is to be called " My delight is in thee " and " Married."

[1] Comp. Isa. xl. 3.   [2] Comp. Isa. lvii. 14.   [3] Comp. Isa. xl. 10.
[4] Isa. xlii. 14, lvii. 11. See pp. 377 and 393.
[5] Isa. xlix. 14. See p. 381.

2 c

The forsaken wife is to be taken back and remarried, and Jahveh her great builder will rejoice over her as his bride. Thus the prophet sums up all those previous predictions of the remarriage of Zion that we have seen in Hosea,[1] and especially in Zephaniah,[2] and the previous section of this prophecy.[3]

The second strophe brings into view the watchmen on the walls of Jerusalem impatiently pleading with Jahveh night and day to accomplish His promises. This is similar in style to the watchmen of Isa. lii. 8,[4] singing the advent song. The last strophe renews the call of the refrains to pass through the gates of Babylon and enter upon the highway to Zion. The same voice issues the command to prepare the way for the people by removing the stones. We then have a concluding proclamation which is a renewal of the introduction and a summary of the theme of the book. Salvation cometh. Jahveh is at hand with His recompense and wage suited to Zion and her enemies. Zion will be universally recognised as " the holy people," " the redeemed of Jahveh." The city that has been forsaken will be recognised as the one that is not forsaken, but has been sought out by Jahveh and restored.

VII. THE NEW JERUSALEM, THE NEW HEAVENS AND NEW EARTH.

The prophecy of the great unknown was finally issued with an appendix embracing chaps. lxiii.–lxvi. This is composed of one little piece of trimeter poetry of an early date, already considered in an appropriate place,[5] and two larger pieces of longer rhythm. The earlier

---

[1] Hos. ii. 19, 20. See p. 171.
[2] Zeph. iii. 17. See p. 224.
[3] Isa. liv. 5. See p. 388.
[4] See p. 386.
[5] Isa. lxiii. 1–6. See p. 313.

of these, chaps. lxiii. 7–lxiv., is a lamentation and supplication that contains no Messianic prediction.   The latter,
chaps. lxv.–lxvi., is apocalyptic in character, resembling
those apocalypses that we have considered at the opening
of this chapter.   The judgment is here a discrimination
between the righteous and the wicked without regard to
nationality.

§ 104. *The divine advent will result in the creation of
new heavens, a new earth, and a new Jerusalem.   There
will be no more weeping or premature death, but the people
will rejoice with great joy.   Jahveh will extend peace to
Zion like a river.   The nations will take part in the
restoration, and will furnish their share in the new priesthood and offerings.   There will be a universal assemblage
before Jahveh on every new moon and sabbath.   But the
wicked will not share in these blessings.   They will be
visited with fire and sword.   Outside the holy city their
carcases will rot and burn in the place of refuse.*

" For, behold, I am about to create new heavens and a new earth ;
    And the former things will not be remembered, nor come to
        mind.
    But rejoice ye and exult for ever in that which I am about to
        create ;
    For, behold, I am about to create Jerusalem an exultation, and
        her people a joy.
    And I will exult in Jerusalem, and rejoice in my people ;
    And the sound of weeping will be no more heard in her, nor the
        sound of crying,
    There will be no more thence an infant of days,
    Nor an old man that will not fill up his days ;
    For the child will die an hundred years old,
    But the sinner an hundred years old will be accursed.

    And they will build houses, and inhabit them ;
    And plant vineyards, and eat their fruit ;
    They will not build, and another inhabit ;

They will not plant and another eat;[1]
For as the days of a tree will be the days of my people,
And my chosen will consume the work of their hands.
They will not labour in vain,
And they will not bring forth for sudden destruction,
For they are the seed of the blessed of Jahveh, and their offspring
    with them.
And it will come to pass that, before they call, I will answer;
And while they are yet speaking, I will hear.
The wolf and the lamb will feed together,
And the lion will eat straw like the ox;[2]
But dust will be the serpent's food.
They will not hurt, and they will not destroy,[3]
In all my holy mountain, saith Jahveh."[4]

.   .   .   .   .   .

" Be glad with Jerusalem, and exult for her, all that love her;
Rejoice for joy with her, all that mourn over her;
That ye may suck and be satisfied with the breasts of her consola-
    tions;
That ye may milk out, and be delighted with the breast[5] of her
    glory.
For thus saith Jahveh,
Behold, I am about to extend peace to her like a river, and the
    glory of the nations like an overflowing stream,
And ye shall suck thereof; ye shall be borne upon the side, and
    shall be dandled upon the knees.[6]
As one whom his mother comforteth, so will I comfort you; and
    ye shall be comforted in Jerusalem.

---

[1] Compare Amos ix. 14.

[2] This line is identical with Isa. xi. 7c.

[3] This and the previous line are identical with Isa. xi. 9a, b.

[4] This passage may be constructed as a hexameter strophe, with seven hexameter lines, two pentameter lines, and one shortened trimeter line. But there is but one line that must be a hexameter, and this is followed by the two pentameters. The most natural arrangement of the other lines is to arrange them as trimeters after the example of Isa. xi. and Amos ix., upon which they are based. In this case the prophet is using extracts from older prophecies throughout. This section could be removed from the prophecy without marring it in any way. See Knobel, *Jesaia*, p. 509.

[5] זיז. Compare Pss. l. 11, lxxx. 14. See pp. 231 and 238.

[6] Compare Isa. xlix. 22, lx. 4.

And ye shall see it, and your heart will rejoice, and your bones
　will flourish like the tender grass ;
And the hand of Jahveh will be known toward his servants, and
　he will have indignation against his enemies.

For, behold, Jahveh will come with fire, and his chariots will be
　like the whirlwind ;
To render his anger with fury, and his rebuke with flames of fire,
For by fire will Jahveh plead, and by his sword, with all flesh ;
　and the slain of Jahveh will be many.
They that sanctify themselves and purify themselves for the
　gardens, entering one after another [1] the innermost place ;
The eaters of swine's flesh and the abomination and the mouse,
　will come to an end together, is the utterance of Jahveh.
Verily, I,[2] their works and their thoughts am going to gather
　with all nations and tongues ;
And they will come and see my glory, and I will set a sign
　among them,
And I will send such as escape of them unto the nations, Tarshish,
　Pul, and Lud,
Those that draw the bow, Tubal and Javan, the coasts afar off
　that have not heard my fame :
Those who have seen my glory will declare my glory among the
　nations.

And they will bring with all your brethren, out of all the nations,
　a minchah unto Jahveh,

---

[1] The Massoretic text reads in the Kethibh אַחַר אַחַד, and in the
Qeri אַחַר אַחַת, either after one (masc.) or one (fem.), thinking of a
god or goddess. The LXX. omits these words. The Peshitto,
Targum, Symmachus and Theodotion read אַחַר אַחַר one after
another. Interpreters are in doubt. Cheyne regards the text as
hopelessly corrupt. Ewald would read אַחַר אַחַר, "behind, behind,"
"in the innermost house," in imitation of the language of those who
desire to celebrate the mysteries. Knobel and Delitzsch adhere to
the Kethibh, and regard the אַחַר as the hierophant who leads the
people in the mysteries. Lowth takes אַחַד as the name of a deity.

[2] וְאָנֹכִי of the Massoretic text stands without a verb. Some
supply יֹדֵעַ after the Peshitto, Targum, Saadia. Delitzsch and
Cheyne supply אֶפְקֹד, I will punish. בָּאָה also stands alone. This
is usually supposed to represent בָּאָה הָעֵת. Compare Isa. xxvii. 6
and Jer. li. 33. But it is easier to follow the LXX., Vulgate, and
Peshitto, and read בָּא instead of בָּאָה. This will then supply
אָנֹכִי with its verb. The objects would then be in emphatic
position between the pronoun and its verb.

Upon horses, and in chariots, and in litters, and upon mules,
    and upon swift beasts,
To my holy mountain Jerusalem, saith Jahveh ;
As the children of Israel bring their minchah in a clean vessel
    into the house of Jahveh.
And of them also will I take for priests, for Levites, saith Jahveh.
For as the new heavens and the new earth, which I am about
    to make,
Are about to remain before me, is the utterance of Jahveh, so
    will your seed and your name remain.
And it will come to pass that, from one new moon to another,
    and from one sabbath to another,
Will all flesh come to worship before me, saith Jahveh,
And they will go forth and look upon the carcases of the men
    that have transgressed against me ;
For their worm will not die, neither will their fire be quenched ;
And they will be an abhorring unto all flesh."

—Isa. lxv. 17–lxvi.

This apocalypse is in some respects more remarkable than any of its predecessors. The prophet sees new heavens, a new earth, and a new Jerusalem taking the place of the old; and these are created by the divine advent, as the present world was created out of primeval chaos. On this new earth and in this new Jerusalem there is universal joy. Weeping and crying no more appear, and the years of life are greatly lengthened. This reminds us of the great apocalypse with which the chapter begins. There we see the earth staggering like a drunkard, swinging like a hammock, and then broken up and removed, and its great city reduced to chaos; but no mention of new heavens and a new earth. Here the destruction of the old is presupposed by the creation of the new. There we noted the wiping away of tears and the abolition of death. This seems to be stronger than the representation of this passage, that the years of life would be lengthened.[1] The author now inserts a number

[1] See especially Isa. xxiv. 10, 19, 20, xxv. 7, 8. See pp. 296 seq.

of passages from older prophets to enlarge the picture of felicity. These are in the style of Amos and Isaiah, representing the fruitfulness and security of the land, the prolonged life of the people, the success of all their labours, their enjoyment of the blessing of Jahveh, His ready response to their desires, and the share of the animals in this universal peace.[1]

The prophecy calls upon all who love Jerusalem to rejoice with her. She is the nursling child of Jahveh, and He nourishes her with comfort and glory. Her peace is like an everflowing river, and her glory like an overflowing stream. The theme of the second edition of the book, that Jahveh is the comforter of Zion, is here resumed. The prophecy then turns to the side of the judgment. Jahveh comes with fire and sword to destroy the idolaters, and reveals His glory to the nations. From all parts of the earth they recognise Him and take part in the restoration of the children of Zion. They bring them in horses, in chariots, in litters, and upon mules and swift animals to the holy mountain. They conduct them as if they were princes of the earth. This is a further unfolding of the representation of Isa. xlix. and lx., that they would be carried in the arms as children by maid - servants and man - servants, and brought in ships from the most distant coasts.[2] The nations will also bring their offerings, as the Israelites bring them, in clean vessels, and Jahveh will select priests from among them to represent them, to share with the Levites in the holy priesthood. This is another phase of the prediction that the new temple will become a house of prayer for all nations.[3] This participation of the nations in the priesthood and worship of Jahveh involves a transformation of the times and mode of worship. As Israel used

---

[1] See pp. 161 seq., 201 seq.   [2] See pp. 382 and 395.
[3] Isa. lvi. 6, 7. See p. 392.

to meet in great congregations in the courts of the
tabernacle and the temple on the holy days, so in these
Messianic times all flesh are to assemble in great congregations every sabbath and every new moon to worship
Jahveh.

The prophecy concludes with a dreadful contrast.
Within the city, the righteous are assembled from all
mankind and engaged in the worship of God.   Without
the city, in the place of refuse, the wicked are a mass of
rotting, burning carcases, an abhorrence to all mankind.
On the one side is the new world of the redeemed, on
the other the Gehenna of the lost, the final abodes of the
righteous and the wicked after the advent of Jahveh to
judgment.   Here the Messianic idea opens up new paths
for the doctrine of the future life.   This apocalypse gives
the later Jewish theology its doctrine of Gehenna, and
the New Testament its doctrine of hell.   It also
furnishes to the apostles their doctrine of the new world.
The sublime representations of the New Testament Apocalypse are drawn chiefly from this source.[1]

This wondrous prophecy, as it has expanded in three
successive editions, finds its only appropriate historical
situation in the exile.   Looking forward from thence it
builds on all the previous prophets, and transcends them
all in the bulk and grandeur of its representations.   It
is related to the Book of Ezekiel as the inner to the
outer; as the essential spirit and substance to its formal
envelope.   It seems to us that Ezekiel could never have
written his apocalypse if he had seen or heard of the
doctrines of Isa. xl.–lxvi.   It is indeed not at all strange
that some Jewish Rabbins and some modern scholars
have doubted the inspiration of Ezekiel, who differs so
greatly from the Mosaic codes on the one side and from
Isa. xl.–lxvi. on the other.   The difficulty is resolved

[1] See 2 Pet. iii. and Rev. xxi.

only when we see that Ezekiel stands on a lower stage in the development of the Messianic idea than the great unknown, who had Ezekiel and Jeremiah, the exile and the body of ancient prophecy behind him; and thus could grasp the whole doctrine of his predecessors, and rise from it to greater heights of prediction.

CHAPTER XIII.

DANIEL.

DANIEL is generally ranked as the fourth of the greater Hebrew prophets; but this is not the ancient Jewish view of the book, for Daniel does not appear among the books of the prophets in the Jewish Canon, but among the miscellaneous writings. And this is manifestly correct. Daniel was not a prophet by office, but a sage. His predictions are in visions or the interpretation of dreams, like those of Joseph in Egypt; and they have been preserved in a book which is essentially a collection of marvels of prediction and of event.

Little is known of Daniel outside of this book. He is therein represented as a captive of noble birth in the third year of Jehoiakim,[1] and as a famous sage during the period extending from Nebuchadnezzar to Cyrus.

The Book of Daniel is marked by a singular feature in which it resembles the Book of Ezra. It is written in two different languages, Hebrew and Aramaic. The Aramaic section extends through chaps. ii. 5—vii. The book is ordinarily divided at chap. vii., where the Aramaic section closes. But this is an unnatural division. For chaps. i.–ii. 5 are also in Hebrew, and the topical division of the book is at chap. vi., making two equal parts, twelve chapters in all. Chaps. i.–vi. give the marvellous events in the experience of Daniel and his three associates, including his interpretation of the dreams

[1] Dan. i. 1–6.

of Nebuchadnezzar and of the handwriting on the wall that heralded the downfall of Babylon.

These six chapters are in strict chronological order, beginning with events in the time of Nebuchadnezzar (i.–iv.), then giving the story of Belshazzar's feast (v.), and the delivery from the lion's den in the reign of Darius (vi.), and closing with the statement, "so this Daniel prospered in the reign of Darius and in the reign of Cyrus the Persian."[1] It would seem that we have here a complete work, a compilation of stories by a late hand, in which Daniel and his associates are the heroes of the exile.

The second part is another collection in chronological order, beginning with a dream in the first year of Belshazzar (vii.), then giving a vision in the third year of Belshazzar (viii.); a vision in the first year of Darius (ix.), and concluding with a vision in the third year of Cyrus (x.–xii.). The first of these visions is in Aramaic, the others in late Hebrew. The second part is therefore a collection of the visions and dreams of Daniel. Sometimes Daniel is represented as speaking in the first person, and then he is spoken of in the third person, as in the first part. The book makes no claim to be the production of Daniel himself. It is a compilation of stories relating to Daniel and visions of Daniel, and was edited by a later writer probably in the Maccabean age. We are not surprised, therefore, that the collection was enlarged by apocryphal insertions and additions in the Septuagint version.

If we deny the traditional theory that Daniel was the author of the book which bears his name as the hero of its pages, it is not necessary to deny the historicity of its miracles and predictions. We have simply to inquire whether the book is sufficiently credible to assure us of

[1] Dan. vi. 28.

their truth. The internal character of the book is such as to prove its divine inspiration. There is nothing in the book save the supernatural element that makes it objectable to any one. Its spirit and tone are high, and indeed sublime. We should not be disturbed if its stories were fiction, composed with the design to point the lesson of fidelity to God, or if the predictions were pseudepigraphic, because we can see no valid objection to these literary styles in the Bible, and indeed we have an example of such fiction in Esther, and of such a pseudepigraph in Ecclesiastes.[1] But we are not convinced that Daniel has the features of these types of Hebrew literature. There are strong reasons in favour of these views, but there are also strong reasons against them. And it seems to us that the latter are prevalent. There are historical difficulties in connection with the stories which are not easy to explain. But subsequent discoveries may give us better information. There is but one difficulty in connection with the predictions, and that is a difficulty which can be removed in accordance with the principles of predictive prophecy, as we shall see. We hold therefore that the predictions were delivered by the Daniel of the exile, but that they were written down in their present form by a Maccabean editor, and we should not be surprised to find traces of his editorial work in the historical setting and in the colouring of the predictions.[2]

I. THE KINGDOM OF THE SON OF MAN.

§ 105. *Daniel represents the kingdoms of the world in conflict with the kingdom of God. These are symbolized by one great and terrible image with four parts diminishing*

---

[1] See my *Biblical Study*, pp. 224, 232.
[2] See Orelli in *l.c.* p. 454 seq.

*successively in glory and becoming more heterogeneous in
their elements; and also by four beasts rising successively
from the sea, increasing in the extent of their dominion
through the symbolical numbers 3, 4 and 10. Out of the
last beast a little horn arises, an anti-Messiah. The
kingdom of God is symbolized by a little stone which is cut
out of the mountain without hands. It breaks in pieces
the image, and grows to a great mountain filling the earth.
The Son of man comes enthroned on the clouds to destroy
the anti-Messiah and the beasts, and to assume universal
dominion. The Ancient of days also comes to judgment
on a throne of flames, from which issues a river of fire.*

The Book of Daniel gives two symbolical representations of the destruction of the kingdoms of this world by
the kingdom of the Messiah. The one of these is in a
dream of Nebuchadnezzar in chap. ii., the other in a
vision of Daniel in chap. vii.

"Thou, O king, sawest, and behold one[1] great image. This image,
which was mighty, and whose brightness was excellent, stood before
thee; and the aspect thereof was terrible. As for this image, his
head was of fine gold, his breast and his arms of silver, his belly
and his thighs of brass, his legs of iron, his feet part of iron and
part of clay. Thou sawest till that a stone was cut out without
hands, which smote the image upon his feet that were of iron and
clay, and brake them in pieces. Then was the iron, the clay, the
brass, the silver and the gold broken in pieces together, and became
like the chaff of the summer threshing-floors; and the wind carried
them away, that no place was found for them: and the stone that
smote the image became a great mountain, and filled the whole
earth. This is the dream; and we will tell the interpretation
thereof before the king. Thou, O king, art king of kings, unto
whom the God of heaven hath given the kingdom, the power, and

---

[1] חַד is used for the indefinite article, according to Winer, Gesenius,
R.V. and most interpreters; but it is better to give it its proper
force as a numeral, with Kliefoth and Keil. The image was *one*.
This needed to be emphasized at the beginning, on account of the
subsequent description of its parts.

the strength, and the glory; and wheresoever the children of men dwell, the beasts of the field and the fowls of the heaven hath he given into thine hand, and hath made thee to rule over them all : thou art the head of gold. And after thee will arise another kingdom inferior to thee ; and another third kingdom of brass which will bear rule over all the earth. And the fourth kingdom will be strong as iron : forasmuch as iron breaketh in pieces and subdueth all things, and as iron that crusheth all these will it break in pieces and crush. And whereas thou sawest the feet and toes, part of potter's clay and part of iron, it will be a divided kingdom ; although there may be in it of the strength of the iron, forasmuch as thou sawest the iron mixed with miry clay. And as the toes of the feet were part of iron and part of clay, so the kingdom will be partly strong and partly broken. And whereas thou sawest the iron mixed with miry clay, they will mingle themselves with the seed of men ; but they will not cleave one to another, even as iron doth not mingle with clay. And in the days of those kings the God of heaven will set up a kingdom, which will never be destroyed, nor will the sovereignty thereof be left to another people ; but it will break in pieces and consume all these kingdoms, and it will stand for ever. Forasmuch as thou sawest that a stone was cut out of the mountain without hands, and that it brake in pieces the iron, the brass, the clay, the silver and the gold ; the great God hath made known to the king what will come to pass hereafter ; and the dream is certain, and the interpretation thereof sure."

—Dan. ii. 31–45.

The symbolism of the dream of Nebuchadnezzar is entirely original in Daniel. There is nothing to correspond with it in the previous predictions, not even in Ezekiel, the master of symbolic prophecy. The artificial image, rich, costly and elaborate, but nevertheless composed of heterogeneous materials, is a very suitable symbol of the kingdoms of the nations. The living stone rolling down from the mountain, growing as it descends in strength and in power, is a simple but appropriate symbol of the kingdom of God. But this symbol does not stand alone. It has its mate in a vision of Daniel in chap. vii. The kingdoms are there represented by four wild beasts coming up from the sea one after another.

Over against them the dream presents the Son of man and the Ancient of Days. These two great symbols are best considered side by side, because they are parallel representations of the same Messianic ideal.

"Daniel spake, and said, I saw in my vision by night, and, behold, the four winds of the heaven brake forth upon the great sea. And four great beasts came up from the sea, diverse one from another. The first was like a lion, and had eagle's wings: I beheld till the wings thereof were plucked, and it was lifted up from the earth, and made to stand upon two feet as a man, and a man's heart was given to it. And behold another beast, a second, like to a bear, and it was raised up on one side, and three ribs were in his mouth between his teeth: and they said thus unto it, arise, devour much flesh. After this I beheld, and lo another, like a leopard, which had upon the back of it four wings of a bird; the beast had also four heads; and dominion was given to it. After this I saw in the night visions, and behold a fourth beast, terrible and powerful, and strong exceedingly; and it had great iron teeth; it devoured and brake in pieces, and stamped the residue with his feet: and it was diverse from all the beasts that were before it; and it had ten horns. I considered the horns, and, behold, there came up among them another horn, a little one, before which three of the first horns were plucked up by the roots: and, behold, in this horn were eyes like the eyes of a man, and a mouth speaking great things. I beheld till thrones were placed, and one that was ancient of days did sit; his raiment was white as snow, and the hair of his head like pure wool; his throne was fiery flames, and the wheels thereof burning fire. A fiery stream issued and came forth from before him: thousand thousands ministered unto him, and ten thousand times ten thousand stood before him; the judgment was set, and the books were opened. I beheld at that time because of the voice of the great words which the horn spake; I beheld even till the beast was slain, and his body destroyed, and he was given to be burned with fire. And as for the rest of the beasts, their dominion was taken away: yet their lives were prolonged for a season and a time. I saw in the night visions, and, behold, there came with the clouds of heaven, one like unto a Son of man, and he came even to the Ancient of Days, and they brought him near before him. And there was given him dominion, and glory, and a kingdom, that all the peoples, nations, and languages should serve him: his dominion is an everlasting dominion, which will not pass away, and his kingdom that which will not be destroyed. As for me, Daniel, my spirit was grieved in the midst of my body, and the visions of my head troubled me. I came near unto one of them that stood by, and asked him the truth concerning all this. So he told me, and made me know the interpretation of the things. These great beasts, which are four, are four kings, which will arise out of the earth. But the saints of the Most High shall receive the kingdom, and possess the kingdom for ever, even for ever and ever. Then I desired to know the truth concerning the fourth beast, which was diverse from all of them, exceeding terrible, whose teeth were of iron and his nails of brass; which devoured, brake in pieces, and stamped the residue with his feet; and concerning the ten horns that were on his head, and the other horn which came up, and before which three fell; even that horn that had eyes, and a mouth that spake great things, whose look was more stout than his fellows. I beheld, and the same horn made war with the saints, and prevailed against them, until the Ancient of Days came, and judgment was given to the saints of the Most High; and the time came that the saints possessed the kingdom. Thus he said, the fourth beast will be a fourth kingdom upon earth, which will be diverse from all the kingdoms and will devour the whole earth, and will tread it down, and break it in pieces. And as for the ten horns, out of this kingdom will ten kings arise: and another will arise after them; and he will be diverse from the former, and he will put down three kings. And he will speak words against the Most High, and will wear out the saints of the Most High; and he will think to change the times and the law; and they will be given into his hand until a time and times and half a time. But the judgment will sit, and they will take away his dominion, to consume and to destroy it unto the end. And the kingdom and the dominion, and the greatness of the kingdoms under the whole heaven, will be given to the people of the saints of the Most High: His kingdom is an everlasting kingdom, and all dominions will serve and obey Him."   —Dan. vii. 2–27.

The visions of Daniel agree in representing the kingdoms of this world over against the kingdom of the Messiah. These kingdoms are four in number, united in chap. ii. in one great and terrible image, in chap. vii. separated in four successive wild beasts. These four kingdoms are variously interpreted as to their reference and fulfilment. Some seek to limit the range of the prophetic symbols by the Greek Empire, and explain either the Median and Persian kingdoms as separate,[1] and so go against their constant association in the Scriptures, or else distinguish between the Greek Empire of Alexander and that of his successors, which is no less unnatural.[2] The common view is that Rome is the fourth kingdom, as the one most naturally fulfilling all the conditions of the symbolism. The chief difficulties in this theory are, (1) the Roman Empire had not yet arisen even in the most distant horizon of the prophecy, and it is against the analogy of prophecy to transcend its horizon;[3] and (2) that the little horn of chap. viii. is supposed to be identical with the little horn of chap. vii. It seems to us that interpreters have generally erred in overlooking the essential symbolical character of the prophecy. If the image and the beasts are symbols, so also are the numbers.[4] The number four is usually symbolical of the wide extent of a thing. It indicates here the wide extent or compass of the kingdoms rising up against the holy people, and subjecting them as it were from the four quarters of the earth. That this is the true conception we see from the analysis of the successive kingdoms into other symbolical members.

The head of gold and the lion correspond. These represent the Chaldean Empire, in accordance with the interpretation of the prophet. The breast and arms of silver, and the bear, with three ribs in his mouth, represent the next kingdom that would arise, which historically was the Medo-Persian. The three ribs are generally referred to Egypt, Babylon and Lydia as the conquered

[1] So Ephraim Syrus, Bleek, Kayser, De Wette, Hitzig, Delitzsch, Kranichfeld.
[2] Grotius and Rosenmüller.
[3] See p. 56.　　　　　　　　　　[4] See pp. 53 and 57.

2 D

kingdoms; but the number is rather symbolical, and as the simplest number of completeness represents a complete number of kingdoms that would be absorbed by that empire, the full number allotted it. The belly and thighs of brass, and the leopard with four heads and four wings, represent another great empire which suits very well historically the Greek dominion of Alexander and his successors. The four heads and four wings are generally referred to the four kingdoms of the successors of Alexander; but they rather indicate the wide extent of that kingdom, its comprehensiveness and world-wide supremacy. The legs of iron, and feet of clay and iron mixed, and the terrible beast with ten horns, represent the final empire, which historically suits the Roman. The ten horns are referred to successive forms of it, or the monarchs ruling over it, or the ten kingdoms into which it resolves itself; but really the number ten, as the number of the highest completeness, represents the dominion as world-wide and thus embracing a complete number of petty kings or kingdoms of diverse nationalities, in accordance with the mixture of materials in that part of the image representing it. Thus, whilst the successive kingdoms increase in comprehensiveness, as represented by the numbers three, four and ten, they diminish in unity and intrinsic worth and glory. Out of the fourth and last kingdom springs up the little horn, having the eyes of a man, speaking great things, and making war with the saints, until the appearance of the Ancient of Days. This little horn seems to be a small rebellious power that overcomes a definite number of other horns, or to be a section of the empire complete in itself. It becomes proud, defiant and oppressive of the saints. This horn is by the description individualized, so that it presents the appearance of a definite person. It is a concentration of power and oppression in an individual, in the climax or culmination of the period of oppression previous to the deliverance. It is an anti-Messiah, or an anti-christ.

The little horn of chap. vii. is usually interpreted as the same as the little horn of chap. viii. But it seems to us that the two are different in conception. The one is associated with the third kingdom, the other with the fourth kingdom, so that the one is a forerunner of the other. This little horn is the chief difficulty in the interpretation. It suits so closely Antiochus Epiphanes, that one is tempted to find in him the type of the anti-Messiah of the prediction. And yet every other feature of the prediction has its basis in the history of the exile. The difficulties have not been entirely removed. The great majority of recent critics urge this as a strong reason for the origin of the prediction in the Maccabean age, and insist that it is a pseudepigraph. It seems to us, however, that interpreters have not sufficiently estimated the analogy of other predictive terms. We have seen that the terms seed, son and servant have unfolded in the hands of the prophets from generic terms to personal designations of the Messiah. It is not unnatural, therefore, it is rather in accordance with the analogy of prophecy, that the hostile kingdoms should not only increase in comprehension or extension, but also increase in intensity or in intension, and we might reasonably expect that a great hostile monarch—an anti-Messiah—would precede the advent of the Messiah Himself.

The sufferings of the people of God reach their climax under the oppression of the anti-Messiah. He persecutes them in the most sacred institutions of their religion. But his time is very limited. It is measured by the prophetic three times and a half, which is half a week of prophetic time, a very short interval, for God will cut it short.   He will come in an advent of judgment to destroy the oppressor and to save His people.

The stone cut out of the mountain without hands, that grows to be a mountain filling the whole earth, and that breaks in pieces all the kingdoms, is the kingdom of the Messiah.   The symbol is enormous, but it is similar to the exaltation of the temple mount in Isaiah and Micah,[1] the marvellous growth of the vine in Ps. lxxx.,[2] and the cedar twig in Ezekiel.[3]   This stone has as its parallel the Son of man, who would accordingly seem to represent likewise the kingdom of the Messiah over against the wild beasts; but in this passage the Son of man is brought into contrast, not so much with the wild beasts as with the little horn, and if that be an individual this must also be an individual, and therefore the Messiah Himself.   This Son of man comes enthroned on the clouds of heaven to the Ancient of Days, and receives the everlasting dominion.   The advent of the Ancient of Days is the advent of God, enthroned on a throne of flames of fire, with streams of fire flowing forth from it. These are flames of wrath and judgment.   They are the reverse of the river of grace in other representations of prophecy.[4]   The books of judgment are opened, and judgment is pronounced.   The advent is therefore both on the part of God and of the Messiah an advent to judgment, and therefore a second advent from the point of view of the New Testament.

This judgment differs from all previous representations in the appearance of the divine records or book of judgment, upon the basis of which the judgment is pro-

---

[1] Isa. ii. 2 ; Micah iv. 1.   See p. 181.
[2] Ps. lxxx. 10–12.   See p. 228.
[3] Ezek. xvii. 22–24.   See p. 269.
[4] Joel iv. 18 ; Ps. xlvi. 5 ; Isa. xxxiii. 21 ; Ezek. xlvii. 6–12 ; pp. 158, 212 214, and 290.

nounced, and also of the river of fire into which the enemies of the kingdom are cast. This is another form of the flames of Gehenna that we have seen in Isa. lxvi.,[1] and is the basis of the judgment-scene of the Apocalypse of the New Testament.[2]

II. THE LAST TIMES.

§ 106. *Daniel predicts that seventy sacred year-weeks will elapse from the decree to rebuild Jerusalem until the end. The last week is resolved into days. In the middle of this last year-week there will be intense affliction. The Messiah will be cut off, the worship brought to an end, and the holy city destroyed. The affliction will extend a short time beyond the middle of the week, and then after a still further brief delay the blessing will come. There will be a resurrection of the dead and a day of judgment, when the righteous will receive their inheritance, and shine for ever as the stars.*

There are two Messianic passages in the second part of Daniel that are best considered together. Daniel in the first year of Darius, in answer to supplication, receives in a vision a prediction of the interval to the advent of the Messiah and of the last times.

"Seventy weeks are decreed upon thy people, and upon thy holy city, to finish [3] transgression, and to make an end [4] of sins, and to

---

[1] Isa. lxvi. 24. See p. 406.   [2] Rev. xx. 9–11.

[3] לבלא is taken by LXX., Vulgate, Gesen., Ewald, Hitzig, R.V. and most interpreters as for כלה, to complete, finish; but the margin of R.V. agrees with Keil and Kranichfeld in reading כלא, to restrain, hold back.

[4] התם of the Qeri is followed by R.V. after most interpreters; but the Kethibh חתם, to seal, is given in the margin; so Keil, Kliefoth, Kranichfeld and Orelli.

cover over [1] iniquity, and to bring in everlasting righteousness, and to seal up vision and prophet,[2] and to anoint the holy of holies.[3] Know therefore and discern, that from the going forth of the word to restore and to build Jerusalem, until an anointed one, a prince,[4] will be seven weeks and sixty-two weeks; [5] it will be built again with street and moat even in troublous times. And after the sixty-two weeks an anointed one will be cut off, and will have nothing: [6] and the people of the prince that will come will destroy the city and the sanctuary; and his end will be with a flood, and even unto the end will be war; desolations are determined. And he will confirm a covenant [7] with many for one week; and in the middle of the week he will cause peace-offering and vegetable-offering to cease; and upon the wing of abominations will be a desolator; [8] and even

---

[1] כפר is the technical term for covering over sin, used in the priest code and throughout the Old Testament.

[2] נביא is prophet, as the margin of R.V., so Orelli, and not the abstract prophecy, as R.V. itself after most interpreters.

[3] קדש קדשים is the holy of holies, the most sacred place of the temple. There is no propriety in referring it to the Messianic person.

[4] משיח נגיד. These terms are indefinite, unless we suppose that משיח has already become a proper name. It is just as strong a reference to the Messiah as if it were definite. We cannot agree with those who find any other historical reference than the fulfilment in Jesus Christ.

[5] The Massoretic accents break up the times into three periods of 7+62+1 weeks. But the Versions generally favour two periods, 69 weeks and 1 week. The R.V. agrees with most modern interpreters in following the Massoretic text. But the American Company of Revisers rightly consult the context, and agree with the rendering of the margin of the R.V. The Massoretic text is also followed by Keil and Kliefoth, who make seven sacred times until the advent of the Messiah, and then sixty-two weeks of the building of the sacred city, with a final week of affliction in the last days. But this is introducing into the Old Testament the New Testament doctrine of an interval between the first advent of the Messiah and the end of the world.

[6] ואין לו=and he will have nothing—that is, all will be lost with his death. So it will seem at the time. The A.V., "but not for himself," has nothing to recommend it in the context. It introduces the innocence of the sufferer from Isa. liii.

[7] הגביר has as its subject the hostile prince according to most interpreters, and not the Messiah, as Hävernick, Hengstenberg, and others suppose.

[8] על כנף. The desolator is compared to a gigantic vulture or bird of prey. He comes down with his foul and abominable wings to defile and destroy the sacred places.

unto the consummation, and that determined, will it be poured out upon the desolator."—Dan. ix. 24–27.

The second Messianic passage gives another view of these last times. It is assigned to the third year of Cyrus.

"And at that time will Michael stand up, the great prince who standeth over the children of thy people ; and there will be a time of trouble, such as never was since there was a nation even to that same time ; and at that time thy people will be delivered, every one that will be found written in the book. And many of them that sleep in the dust of the earth will awake, some to everlasting life, and some to reproach and everlasting abhorrence. And they that be wise will shine as the brightness of the firmament ; and they that turn many to righteousness as the stars for ever and ever. . . . And I heard the man clothed in linen, that was over the waters of the river, when he held up his right hand unto heaven, and sware by him that liveth for ever, that it will be for a time, times and a half ; and when they have made an end of breaking in pieces the power of the holy people, all these things will be finished. . . . Many will purify themselves, and make themselves white, and be refined ; but the wicked will do wickedly, and none of the wicked will understand ; but they that be wise will understand. And from the time that the continual burnt-offering shall be taken away, and the abomination that maketh desolate set up, there will be a thousand two hundred and ninety days. Blessed be he that waiteth, and cometh to the thousand three hundred and five and thirty days. But go thou thy way till the end be ; for thou wilt rest, and wilt stand in thy lot at the end of the days."—Dan. xii. 1–3, 10–13.

The interpretation of these passages depends upon the explanation of the seventy weeks. There are three views. (1) The ancient theory was that they refer to the appearance of Christ in the flesh, his death and the destruction of Jerusalem by the Romans. (2) Most recent interpreters refer the whole passage to the time of Antiochus Epiphanes. (3) Some of the Fathers and many recent interpreters regard the prophecy as referring to the development of the kingdom of God from the end of the exile to the fulfilment of the kingdom at the second advent. The primary question is whether to attach the sixty-two weeks to the previous seven and make two periods, or to separate them and regard the prophecy as distinguishing three periods of seven weeks, sixty-two weeks, and one week. The difficulty with the last method of interpretation is that it cannot satisfactorily explain the cutting off of the Messiah. Furthermore, the representation of a long interval of sixty-two weeks between the advent of the Messiah and the end, is against the Old Testament point of view, which does not distinguish the two advents of the New Testament. It seems to us that the prophecy predicts that sixty-nine weeks will elapse from the decree of Cyrus to the advent of the Messianic prince, and that the final week is the time of his advent, in the middle of which he is cut off and the Old Testament worship is brought to an end, the holy city destroyed, and the new covenant established. In connection with this event the prophet sees the end of the world. The cutting off of the Messiah is not strange to us in Daniel, for we have already seen the martyr death of the servant of Jahveh in Isaiah and the psalms of the exile.[1] The suffering Messiah is the great Messianic idea of the period of the exile. Daniel has no more idea of a Messianic king in this passage, than has the great unknown in his representation of the suffering servant. The enthroned son of man of the previous section does not appear until the great judgment. The Messiah here is a sufferer who dies in the last times of suffering, prior to the judgment and prior to the establishment of the kingdom of God. Daniel does not see the combination of these two representations in one person. This could not be disclosed until the first advent of Jesus Christ in a state of humiliation showed that he himself, and not another, would come again in his kingdom of glory at the end of the world.

[1] Ps. xxii. 16; Isa. liii. 9. See pp. 323 and 358.

We cannot accept the theory, which prevails with the majority of modern critics, that the prophecy relates to the afflictions in the time of Antiochus Epiphanes. It is true that the term "anointed one" might refer to a high priest slain at that time, and there is no reasonable objection to referring the term "an anointed one," "a prince," to any heathen monarch who might be used to advance the interests of God's people; but, on the other hand, the terms are more commonly applied to the Messiah as a prince of Israel and an anointed one of Jahveh. The terms do not decide. It may also be admitted that the Maccabean editor of this prediction of Daniel may have had in mind the Antiochan persecution, which might very well be regarded as a prelude to the Messianic end; but this does not decide the goal of the prediction of Daniel. If we suppose that Daniel was the original author of the prediction, there would be less likelihood of his thinking of the Antiochan affliction, and more intrinsic probability of his thinking of the ultimate affliction in accordance with the usage of Old Testament prophecy. From this point of view the Antiochan times may be regarded as an historical anticipation of the Messianic affliction, but not as the fulfilment of the prediction of Daniel,[1] who agrees with all the prophets in looking forward to the times of the Messiah and disregarding intervening events, and is in especial accord with the great unknown in his conception of a suffering Messiah.

The last prediction gives an expansion of the final week. As the seventy years of the duration of the captivity, according to Jeremiah,[2] unfolded apparently in the last year, in Dan. ix. into seventy weeks from the decree to rebuild Jerusalem till the Messianic end, so the last week of the seventy is analysed into days.

[1] See p. 65.   [2] Jer. xxix. 10.

The entire year-week is 2520 days; of these 1290 days are mentioned, or 30 days beyond the first half of the year-week, and 1335 days, or 45 more beyond. Similar numbers occur in chap. viii., viz.—2300 days of evening and morning—equivalent to $6\frac{7}{18}$ year-days, or the greater portion of the year-week. The earlier affliction of the little horn of the third kingdom was to last the greater part of a year-week, but the later and greater affliction was to last only for half the year-week and a very little beyond.

These numbers are entirely symbolical, and are to be interpreted in their relations, but cannot be reduced to measures of historic time. They show that the times of the world-power have been strictly limited by God, and that the last times of affliction will be very brief, and that these will be speedily followed by a divine advent, when all the promises of blessing will be realized to the full.

The final blessedness is not only for those living at the time, but also for the faithful Daniel and those who have acted wisely, and brought others to righteousness. There is indeed to be a resurrection of the dead. There have been already three predictions of the resurrection of the dead,[1] but these have all looked forward to a national resurrection of Israel, and have not presented the doctrine of the resurrection of individuals in Israel. Here for the first time the doctrine of the resurrection of individuals comes into the Messianic idea, and there is a distinction in the character of these. Some are to rise to receive their everlasting reward, and some to shame and everlasting abhorrence : these two classes are in strong antithesis. The righteous dead are to share in the felicity of the holy land. Daniel is to

---

[1] Hos. xiii. 14; Ezek. xxxvii. 7–14; Isa. xxvi. 19. See pp. 176, 275, and 307.

stand in his lot, that is, receive his share of the inheritance in the land of redemption. This involves the conception of Ezekiel, of a redistribution of the holy land, after the method of the original distribution in the times of the conquest by Joshua.[1] But the wicked are also to receive their ill-deserts, they are to rise from the dead for this purpose. In the closing apocalypse of the great unknown, we saw the wicked a mass of rotting, burning carcases outside the holy city, in the vale of Gehenna,[2] an abhorrence to all mankind. These were the wicked enemies living in the time of the great judgment. But here Daniel adds to that mass the wicked dead who rise from their graves in order likewise to become the everlasting abhorrence of the righteous. Daniel does not yet conceive of a universal resurrection, but only a resurrection of some, the righteous and a portion of the wicked. He is probably thinking of the wicked children of Israel, the apostates. He has not learned that the heathen will rise from the dead also. That is a doctrine of the New Testament, which has not yet arisen in the Messianic idea.

[1] Ezek xlviii. See p. 285.   [2] Isa. lxvi. 24. See p. 285

CHAPTER XIV.

THE MESSIANIC IDEA IN THE TIMES OF THE RESTORATION.

THE destruction of the Chaldean empire and the erection of the Persian empire in its stead was a wonderful divine interposition on behalf of the chosen people. The friendliness of Cyrus and his decree permitting them to return to Jerusalem, and restore the temple and institutions of their religion, was a fulfilment of the predictions of their prophets that aroused their admiration and exerted their hopes to the highest pitch. They remembered the wonders of the deliverance from Egypt and the march through the wilderness to Canaan, and, encouraged by the predictions of Isaiah, Jeremiah, Ezekiel, and the great unknown, they looked forward to a divine advent and a march to Zion through the wilderness, that would transcend all the ancient theophanies. Psalm lxviii. was composed at this time,[1] and gives expression to these hopes in language borrowed largely from ancient poems, and especially from the great unknown.

---

[1] There is no psalm which has troubled critics so much as this psalm. The history of its interpretation is a marvel of errors and contradictions. There is still considerable difference of opinion as to its date. But its dependence upon other pieces of poetry, and especially upon Isa. xl.–lxvi., seems to me to fix its date at the close of the exile or in the time of preparation for the return from Babylon.

I. THE MARCH OF JAHVEH.

§ 107. *Psalm LXVIII. describes the march of Jahveh to Zion. He triumphs over all enemies, leads the captives, whom He has rescued, in triumphant procession, laden with spoils, and enters with them the sanctuary of Zion. Egypt, Ethiopia, and all nations unite in His worship and in songs of praise.*

I. " When God arises,[1] his enemies will be scattered ;
　　Yea, those that hate him will flee from his presence.
　　As smoke is driven away, thou wilt drive them ;[2]
　　As wax melteth from the presence of fire,
　　The wicked will perish from the presence of God ;
　　But the righteous will rejoice, will exult before God,
　　And they will shout for joy.
　　Sing unto God, play his name,
　　Cast up a way for his chariot in the wastes.
　　Jah is his name, therefore exult before him.
　　A father of orphans and a judge of widows
　　Is God in the habitation of his holiness ;
　　God is one who makes the solitary to dwell in a house,
　　Who bringeth out prisoners into prosperity,
　　Only the stubborn do inhabit a parched land.

II. O God, when thou wentest forth before thy people, {
　　When thou didst march in the wastes, the earth trembled,[3]
　　Yea, the heavens dropped at the presence of God,

---

[1] יקום is not jussive, as A.V., R.V., Perowne, and Delitzsch, but indicative and hypothetical, as Ewald and Hitzig, or, better still, the protasis of a temporal clause.

[2] The הִנְדֹּף and תנדף of the Massoretic text are difficult. The LXX., Peshitto, Targum, and Vulgate read יִנָּדֵף. Perowne would read תִּנָּדֵף . . . כְּהִנָּדֵף, taking both forms as Niphal. Ewald makes תנדף, 3 fem. intransitive. Delitzsch explains הִנְדֹּף as an infinitive absolute for infin. construct by assimilation to תנדף.

[3] The rhythm requires that we should disregard the accents of the Massoretes, and attach ארץ רעשה to this line. Reuss makes it an independent line.

Yon Sinai at the presence of God, the God of Israel.[1]
With a copious rain thou used to sprinkle it,[2] O God ;
Thine inheritance, if it were weary, thou didst establish it.
Thy living[3] creatures dwelt in it.
Thou used to prepare in thy goodness for the afflicted, O God.[4]
'Adonay giveth the word,
The women that bring the glad tidings are a great host,
(*Saying*), 'Kings of hosts flee, they flee,
And she that tarrieth at home, shall she divide spoil?
Will ye abide among the cotes ?[5]
The winged dove is covered with silver,
And her pinions with yellow gold.'[6]

III. When[7] Shadday would scatter kings,
      It will snow therein in dense darkness.

---

[1] These four lines are a free use of the song of Deborah, Judg.
v. 4, 5.

[2] The Massoretes divide the verse here according to the rhythm.
And yet Hupfeld, Delitzsch, and Perowne follow the versions, and
attach נחלתך to the first half of the line. That makes it a pentameter.

[3] חיתך is taken by A.V. and R.V. as congregation, and in the
margin as troops, after Gesenius. But it is better, with Hupfeld,
Delitzsch, and Perowne, to think of living creatures.

[4] These imperfects are frequentatives, referring to the continued
care of Jahveh over His people in the holy land.

[5] שפתים is evidently essentially the same as משפתים of Judg. v. 16.
But the context shows that we are to think of dove-cotes rather than
sheep-folds.

[6] This is very difficult, and is variously understood. The interpretation depends upon our idea of the connection of this distich
with the distich that follows. Ewald, Perowne, and others think
there is a contrast here. We think that the strophe closes here, and
that these are all the words of the women who are heralding the
great victory. They are calling upon their sisters to go forth and
take possession of the rich spoil of gold and silver that lies upon the
ground. It is not in accordance with the song of Deborah to
suppose that the one who stays at home will share the spoil. It is
better, therefore, to regard the clause as interrogative with the
answer *No*, she shall not. The doves in the dove-cotes do not show
their bright plumage. It is only when they are on the wing in the
sunshine that the gold and silver colours appear. So let the
damsels of Israel take flight to the battle-field, and they will be
rewarded with the rich spoil of the victory. The heralds are women,
and they are exhorting the women of Israel. The men are supposed
to be already on the battle-field.

[7] This third strophe begins, like the others, with the protasis of a

O mountain of God,[1] mount Bashan ;
O mountain of summits, mount Bashan ;
Why look ye askance, ye mountain of summits,
At the mountain God has desired to dwell in ?
Surely Jahveh will inhabit it for ever.
The chariots of God are two myriads, thousands repeated :
'Adonay among them came from Sinai [2] into his holy place.
Thou hast gone up on high, thou hast led captives, captive ; [3]
Thou hast taken gifts of men,
And even the rebellious are to dwell with Jah Elohim.[4]

---

temporal clause. This clause has בְּפָרֵשׂ in the protasis, and תַּשְׁלֵג in the apodosis. It reminds us of Deut. xxxii. 8. Both clauses have modal force. צַלְמוֹן is not the name of a mountain, but is a noun similar to צַלְמוּת, with the meaning dense darkness, as the Targum, many Rabbins, and Reuss. I can see no good sense in snowing on Zalmon. Some think that it is the place where the battle took place, and the shields, spears, and weapons of the slain were scattered upon the ground as snow in a snow-storm. The easiest interpretation is to think of a theophany, as in Judg. v. 20, 22, where there was a severe storm. Comp. Josh. x. 11 and Job xxxviii. 22–23. Snow-storms and hail-storms are conceived as the special means used by God when He interposes in battle for His people. The Psalmist looks for such a great snow-storm in a time of dense darkness, in which the enemies of God will be defeated and slain.

[1] הַר אֱלֹהִים is mountain of God, as a very great mountain, comp. Ps. xxxvi. 7. It does not imply that it was a sacred place.

[2] סִינַי is difficult to construct and understand. It is mentioned here, because the Psalmist has in mind the blessing of Moses (Deut. xxxiii. 2, 3). בָּם is taken by Hupfeld and Stade as a corruption of בָּא מִסִּינַי. This is indeed suggested by Deut. xxxiii. 2, מִסִּינַי בָּא. But Perowne and Reuss insert בָּא מ after בָּם. It seems to us that the historical reference is more in accord with the style of this psalm than the insertion of בְּ before סִינַי, and rendering " as in Sinai in the sanctuary," or with Delitzsch and the margin of the R.V., render " Sinai is in the sanctuary," or with Ewald, " Sinai in holiness." Zion had to the Jew a much greater sanctity than even Sinai. Zion was a holier name, as the abode of the theophanic God for hundreds of years. Why should it be called a Sinai as if the theophany at Sinai for a brief period made that more holy than Zion ?

[3] Comp. Judg. v. 12.

[4] אַף סוֹרְרִים is the subject of the infinitive, and יה is the accusative, as Ewald and Hupfeld. Most interpreters connect it with the previous line, and make the infinitive the purpose of the whole previous clause. Perowne makes the infinitive take the place of the imperf. and renders, " Yea, with the rebellious shall Jah God abide."

Blessed be 'Adonay, who day by day beareth our burdens,
'El is our salvation, 'El is unto us an 'El for saving acts,
To Jahveh 'Adonay belong the issues for death.

IV. Yea, God will crush the chief of his enemies,[1]
The hairy scalp of one walking on in faults;
'Adonay said, ' From Bashan I will recompense,
I will recompense from the depths of the sea,
That thy foot may be bathed in blood,[2]
And the tongue of thy dogs have its portion [3] of the enemies.'
They have seen thy goings, O God,
The goings of my 'El, my king, into the holy place:
The singers went before, behind the minstrels,
In the midst damsels playing on timbrels, (*saying*,)
' In the congregations bless ye God,
'Adonay, ye from the fountain of Israel.'[4]
There is little Benjamin, their ruler,
Princes of Judah with their company,
Princes of Zebulun, princes of Naphtali.

V. O God, command Thy strength,[5]
O strengthen, God, what thou hast done for us from thy
temple.[6]
Unto Jerusalem, to thee will kings bring presents.

---

[1] Comp. Deut. xxxii. 42.

[2] The Massoretic תִּמְחַץ does not give good sense. It is best to
follow the LXX., Peshitto, Vulgate, Hupfeld, Reuss, Perowne, and
most critics, and read תִּרְחַץ.

[3] The Massoretic מִנֵּהוּ is variously explained. The A.V. follows
the LXX., Calvin, and others, in taking it as the preposition מִן with
the suffix "of the same," that is, of the blood. Delitzsch and Perowne
take it as the noun מִן = מְנָה, portion, and refer the suffix to the
tongue. It is still better, with Olshausen and Hupfeld, to read מְנָתוּ,
and thus gain the noun מְנָה, which has the authority of usage in its
favour.

[4] Comp. Isa. xlviii. 1, li. 1.

[5] The Massoretic צִוָּה is not so suited to the context as עֻזָּה of the
LXX. and Symmachus, which latter is followed by Ewald, Hupfeld,
Perowne, and others.

[6] מֵהֵיכָלֶךָ is to be attached to the second line, with Hupfeld and
Perowne. The lines in the last strophe are longer than usual. They
are generally tetrameters. There is considerable variation from
trimeter to tetrameter in this hymn, as in the song of Deborah, after
which it is modelled.

Rebuke the wild beast of the reeds, the assembly of bulls,
With the calves of the peoples trampling under foot for pieces
of silver ;
Disperse [1] the people which delight in wars.
Rich ones will come out of Egypt,
Cush will haste to spread forth his hands unto God. [2]
Ye kingdoms of the earth, sing unto God,
Play to 'Adonay, to him who rides upon the ancient heavens.
Lo, he uttereth with his voice, a strong voice.
Ascribe strength to God,
Over Israel is his majesty and his strength in the skies.
God is to be feared in thy holy places,
'El of Israel also giveth strength and great power to the
people.
Blessed be God."   —Ps. lxviii.

This psalm is composed of five strophes of fifteen
lines each. It is constructed after the model of the
song of Deborah, and is full of reminiscences of other
pieces of Hebrew poetry ; but it is especially animated
by the spirit and guided by the conceptions of the great
unknown.

The first strophe begins with the general statement
that when God comes in theophany, the wicked will flee
like smoke and melt like wax,[3] but the righteous will
shout for joy. The second part of the strophe is a call
to cast up a highway for Jahveh, whose chariot is to
march through the wastes,[4] and describes Him as a
father of orphans, a judge of widows, the deliverer of
prisoners, and the bestower of fruitfulness.[5]

The second strophe begins with a reference to the

---

[1] בַּזֵּר of the Massoretic text is not so good as בַּזֵּר of the LXX.,
which is adopted by Ewald.

[2] Comp. Isa. xliii. 3, xlv. 14, lx. 5, 6.

[3] The author evidently had in mind the song of Moses, when the
ark of the covenant set forward. See Num. x. 35.

[4] This reminds us of the refrains of the great unknown, Isa. xl. 3,
lvii. 14, lxii. 10.

[5] This is in the style of Isa. xl. 11, xlii. 16, xlix. 15 16.

2 E

divine march from Sinai through the wilderness to
Palestine,[1] and of His provisions for His people in the
holy land.[2]   In the second half of the strophe, God Himself gives the word of victory, and the damsels push on
to proclaim it as glad tidings to the women of Israel.[3]
The announcement is made that the victory has been gained,
the spoil is ready, and a warning is given lest any should
neglect to secure her share in it.[4]   The kings of the nations
are in full flight, and the battle-field is covered with
spoils.   She who tarries at home will not share in them.
Let the dove leave her cote and spread her wings of gold
and silver, and fly forth to take her share in the victory
of God.

The third strophe begins with a brief reference to
God's interposition by snow-storm for the discomfiting of
the hostile kings.   It then points to Zion as the place
that God had chosen above all others as His everlasting
habitation.   It again describes the march of God with
His innumerable chariots of angels from Sinai[5] into His
holy place, and concludes with the glad statement that
Jahveh has delivered the captive Israelites from the
exile, and is on His march with the train of rescued ones
to His holy place.[6]   He is a God of salvation, He is
a God of saving acts and of deliverance even from death.
He will restore the redeemed, even those that have been
rebellious, and they will dwell with Him as their God
and Saviour in Zion.[7]

[1] This is a free use of the song of Deborah, Judg. v. 4, 5.

[2] This is in the manner of the song of Moses, Ex. xv. 13, 17.

[3] This damsels' song reminds us of the singing women of Ex. xv.
21.   The heralds themselves are like the heralds of the great unknown, Isa. xl. 9, xlviii. 20, lii. 7, 8, lxii. 6, 11.

[4] The rebuke to the slothful and easy-going is in the manner of
Judg. v. 16.

[5] The myriads of chariots that accompany Jahveh on His march,
are after the manner of the blessing of Moses, Deut. xxxiii. 2.

[6] The train of rescued captives is in the style of Judg. v. 12.

[7] The Epistle to the Ephesians, iv. 8, applies this ascent to the

The fourth strophe first describes the crushing of the enemies. They will not be able to escape, they will be caught between the heights of Bashan and the depths of the sea, and Israel will bathe his feet in their blood. The strophe concludes with a dramatic description of the entrance into the sanctuary. In front march the singers, then comes Jahveh the great king, with damsels playing on timbrels to the right and left of Him. Behind Him march the players on stringed instruments, and then the tribes of Israel. Those especially mentioned are Benjamin and Judah in the south, and Zebulun and Naphtali in the north, the former because they constituted the body of the exiles who returned, the latter because they were the warlike tribes of Deborah's song.[1]

The last strophe is a petition based upon the triumphant march, a prayer that Zion may be strengthened and her enemies destroyed. These enemies are described as the wild beast of the reeds, Egypt; the assembly of bulls and their calves, the princes and people of the nations in general, all the warlike powers. The psalmist yearns for the destruction of all the violent, and the establishment of peace. Then he sees that Egypt and Ethiopia will turn unto God with tribute and worship. All the kingdoms will sing His praise. His chariot is in the highest heavens, His strength is in the skies; and yet His holy places are in Zion, there is His majesty, and there He is to be revered. He giveth strength and great power unto His people. The universal relations of this triumphant march of Jahveh to Zion are no less prominent than in the corresponding prophecies of the great unknown.

height of Zion, with a train of rescued captives, to the ascension of Jesus Christ from the abode of the dead to heaven. The victorious march of Jahveh finds its appropriate fulfilment in that greatest of all victories, and that greatest of all triumphal processions.

[1] See Judg. v. 18.

The decree of Cyrus permitting the Jews to return to their own land, and to rebuild the temple at Jerusalem, was followed by the joyful compliance of considerable numbers, under the governor Zerubbabel of the house of David, and Joshua the chief priest. They began the erection of the temple by setting up the altar in its ancient place, and undertook the rebuilding of the city. Great difficulties were encountered, owing to the jealousies of the inhabitants of Samaria and Edom, and continued misrepresentations at the court of Persia. Two prophets arose in the reign of Darius to cheer them in their work, Haggai and Zechariah.

Little is known of Haggai apart from his predictions, and the brief mention of the time of his appearance.[1] There are two predictions in his slender collection of prophecies, but these are so nearly alike that it is best to treat them together.

II. THE GLORY OF THE NEW TEMPLE.

§ 108. *Haggai predicts that heaven and earth will be shaken, kingdoms overthrown, and the instruments of war destroyed. The nations will bring their choicest treasures into the house of Jahveh, and the latter glory of the house will be greater than the former. Zerubbabel, the servant of Jahveh, will become His signet.*

"For thus saith Jahveh Sabaoth: again once more, it will be after a little; and I am about to shake the heavens, and the earth, and the sea, and the dry land, and shake all nations; and the things desired[2] of all nations will come, and I will fill this house with

---

[1] Ezra v. 1, vi. 14.

[2] חמדת is referred by the Vulgate, Luther, A.V., and most of the older interpreters, to the Messiah as the desire of all nations, and then made the subject of the clause. But it is properly a collective, meaning the desirable things, the riches of the nations, in accordance with the context. So R.V. and most modern interpreters rightly regard it.

glory, saith Jahveh Sabaoth.   Mine is the silver, and mine is the gold, is the utterance of Jahveh Sabaoth.   The latter glory of this [1] house will be greater than the former, saith Jahveh Sabaoth ; and in this place I will give peace, is the utterance of Jahveh Sabaoth." —Hag. ii. 6–9.

This prediction is based upon those of Ezekiel, Jeremiah, and the great unknown.[2]   The temple that the returned exiles have in mind to erect is to be vastly more glorious than the temple of Solomon.   It is to be the shrine of all nations, to which they will bring their choicest treasures, and it will be a place of peace.   This result is to be accomplished by a divine interposition. There is to be an earthquake in physical nature, and in the political and social relations of the nations.   The same prediction is renewed and enlarged by attaching to it the exaltation of Zerubbabel.

"I am about to shake the heavens and the earth, and overturn the throne of kingdoms, and destroy the strength of kingdoms of the nations, and overthrow the chariot and its riders ; and horses and their riders will descend each by the sword of his brother.   In that day is the utterance of Jahveh Sabaoth, I will take thee, Zerubbabel, son of Shealtiel, my servant, is the utterance of Jahveh, and make thee like a signet ; for thee have I chosen, is the utterance of Jahveh Sabaoth."—Hag. ii. 21–23.

The shaking of the nations is now explained as the overthrow of their kingdoms, and the destruction of their warlike strength, in order to the exaltation of Zerubbabel. As in the previous prediction, the temple was to become more glorious than ever before ; so in this prediction, Zerubbabel, the heir of the throne of David, is to become

---

[1] האחרן is taken by the Peshitto, Vulgate, A.V., and the older interpreters as connected with הבית.   But it is better to connect it with כבוד, after the LXX., Ewald, Hitzig, Keil, and most modern scholars.

[2] Jer. iii. 14–18 ; Ezek. xl.–xlix. ; Isa. liv. 11–14, lx.   See pp. 242, 283, 389, and 395.

glorious. He is the servant of Jahveh, who is to become the head of the nation. He is the signet, in that he is the pledge and assurance of the fulfilment of the sure mercies of David. The name of Zerubbabel is used here as the name of David had been in Jeremiah. He is the type of the second Zerubbabel.

ZECHARIAH.

Zechariah is the chief of the prophets of the Restoration. Like Ezekiel, he was a priest as well as a prophet. He resembles Ezekiel also in the symbolic forms of his predictions. There are three sections in the present book. The first section, chaps. i.–viii., is the genuine product of Zechariah's prophetic inspiration; the other two sections differ in such a marked degree, that they are assigned by critics to other authors and other times. Chaps. ix.–xi. have been assigned to an older Zechariah, in the time of Ahaz, who mediated between Hosea and Isaiah. This seems to be clear from the historical situation of the prophecy, which represents the kingdoms of Israel and Judah as existing side by side, and the chief enemies as those of the times of the dissolution of the northern kingdom.[1] Chaps. xii.–xiv. came from a different hand from our Zechariah. It seems to us that they are post-exilic, and that they are later in their origin than the Zechariah of history. We shall first consider the genuine predictions of Zechariah, and then give the later section in an appropriate place.

III. THE GLORY OF THE NEW JERUSALEM.

§ 109. *Jerusalem will be inhabited by a vast multitude.*
and will be without walls, for Jahveh will be a wall of fire

[1] See p. 183.

round about her, a glory in her midst; for He will take possession of it as His royal residence.   Little children and the aged alike will be found in her streets.   All nations will lay hold of the skirt of the Jew, and seek Jahveh in His holy city, and be recognised among His people.

There are two similar predictions relating to the new Jerusalem, the former in chap. ii., and the later in chap. viii.   These may be considered together.

"Jerusalem will abide unwalled villages, because of the multitude
  of men and cattle in her midst,
And I will become for her, is the utterance of Jahveh, a wall of
  fire round about,
And a glory will I be in her midst.
Ho, Ho, and flee from the land of the North, is the utterance of
  Jahveh ;
For as the four winds of heaven have I dispersed you, is the
  utterance of Jahveh.
Ho, Zion, escape dweller with the daughter of Babylon.
For thus saith Jahveh Sabaoth,
After glory hath he sent me unto the nations which spoiled you ;
For the one touching you is touching the apple of his eye.
For lo, I am about to shake mine hand over them, and they will
  become a spoil to those that served them,
And ye shall know that Jahveh Sabaoth hath sent me.
Sing and rejoice, daughter of Zion,
For lo, I am about to come and dwell in your midst, is the utter-
  ance of Jahveh ;
And many nations will assemble unto Jahveh in that day,
And they will become my people, and I will dwell in thy midst,
And thou wilt know that Jahveh Sabaoth hath sent me unto thee;
And Jahveh will inherit Judah as his inheritance upon the holy
  land,
And choose Jerusalem again."   —Zech. ii. 8–17.

This prediction combines features of many previous prophecies, especially of the great unknown.   The vast numbers of the population of the new Jerusalem are in accordance with Jeremiah's book of comfort,[1] and the hexameters of the great unknown.[2] Jahveh a wall of fire round about Jerusalem, is similar to the conception of the great apocalypse, that salvation constituted its walls and ramparts,[3] and the thought of the great unknown, that its walls were called "Salvation" and its gates "Praise."[4] The call to flee from Babylon reminds us of the refrains of the great prophecy of the exile.[5] It shows that the call had to be made again and again, even after many of the exiles had returned to the holy land. The doctrine that Jahveh will dwell in Jerusalem for ever, is the ancient doctrine of the prophets that constantly recurs in their writings.[6] The participation of the nations in the redemption has also become a familiar idea in Messianic prophecy.[7] We cannot see, therefore, that Zechariah has added anything here to the unfolding of the Messianic idea, beyond gathering a considerable number of previous prophecies in one representation.

The latter prediction is found in chap. viii. It also is chiefly a renewal of predictions from the great unknown.

"Thus saith Jahveh—
I have returned to Zion, and will dwell in the midst of Jerusalem,
And Jerusalem will be called 'the city of fidelity;' and the
mountain of Jahveh Sabaoth 'the holy mountain.'
Thus saith Jahveh Sabaoth—
Again old men and old women will dwell in the streets of
Jerusalem,
Each with his staff in his hand because of great age;
And the streets of the city will be filled with boys and girls
playing in the streets thereof.

---

[1] Jer. xxxi. 8. See p. 247.
[2] Isa. xlix. 20–21, liv. 1–3. See pp. 382 and 387.
[3] Isa. xxvi. 1. See p. 300.　　　[4] Isa. lx. 18. See p. 397.
[5] Isa. xlviii. 20, lii. 11, lxii. 10. See pp. 380, 386, and 401.
[6] Joel iv. 21; Zeph. iii. 15; Jer. iii. 17, etc. See pp. 159, 224, and 242.
[7] See especially Isa. lxvi. 18; p. 405.

Thus saith Jahveh Sabaoth—
Lo, I am about to save my people from the land of the sunrise
and from the land of sunset,
And bring them, and they will dwell in the midst of Jerusalem,
and become my people,
And I shall become their God in faithfulness and in righteousness.
Thus saith Jahveh Sabaoth—
Yet will it be that peoples and inhabitants of great cities will come,
And the inhabitants of one will go unto another, saying,
'Let us go on to court the face of Jahveh,'
'And to seek Jahveh Sabaoth, Let me go also.'
And many peoples and strong nations will come
To seek Jahveh Sabaoth in Jerusalem, and to court the face of
Jahveh.
Thus saith Jahveh Sabaoth—
In those days, when ten men of all tongues of the nations shall
lay hold, they will lay hold of the skirts of a Jewish man,
saying,
'Let us go with you, for we have heard that God is with you.'"
—Zech. viii.

The names given to the new Jerusalem, "city of
fidelity" and "holy mountain," resemble the names given
to the city in Zephaniah, Jeremiah, Ezekiel, and the
great unknown.[1] The aged and the children in the streets
of the city remind us of Isa. lxv.[2] The finest scene in
this prophecy is the dramatic representation of the
nations exhorting each other to court Jahveh. When
one says, "Let us go on to court the face of Jahveh," the
other replies, "Let me go also;" and then we see them all
clinging to the skirt of the Jew, and soliciting his guidance to the presence of Jahveh. In these predictions,
Zechariah gathers up the threads of previous prophecies.

[1] Zeph. iii. 16; Jer. xxxiii. 16; Ezek. xlviii. 35; Isa. lx 14, lxii. 4
See pp. 224, 245, 290, 396, and 400.
[2] Isa. lxv. 20. See p. 403.

IV. THE CROWNING OF THE PRIEST-KING.

§ 110. *The servant of Jahveh, named Branch, is to build the temple of Jahveh and be its capstone. He combines the priestly and royal offices in His noble crown. He becomes the perpetual channel of the divine grace.*

Zechariah takes several Messianic terms, especially from Isaiah and Jeremiah, and heaps them upon one person. There are two passages that may be best considered together; the first of these is contained in chaps. iv.-v.

"Hear now, O Joshua the high priest, thou and thy fellows that sit before thee; for they are men which are a sign :[1] for, behold, I will bring forth my servant Branch.[2] For, behold, the stone[3] that I have set before Joshua; upon one stone are seven eyes: behold, I will engrave the graving thereof, saith Jahveh Sabaoth, and I will remove the iniquity of that land in one day. In that day, saith Jahveh Sabaoth, shall ye call every man his neighbour to come

---

[1] אנשי מופת =men of miracle. They are the signs and pledges that Jahveh has in part fulfilled His promises, and therefore will entirely fulfil them.

[2] צמח has here become a proper name of the Messiah, owing to its use in Jer. xxiii. 5, xxxiii. 15. See p. 244. Compare Zech. vi. 12.

[3] האבן. The stone placed before Joshua was regarded by the older interpreters as the Messiah, after Ps. cxviii. 22 and Isa. xxviii. 16. Keil, Chambers, and others refer to the kingdom of God. Henderson, Hitzig, C. H. H. Wright, and others, think of the foundation stone, but this had already been laid long ago. Ewald properly thinks of the capstone, in accordance with Zech. iv. 7. The interpretation of the stone depends upon that of the eyes. These are על אבן. The most natural view is that the eyes were graven on the stone, in accordance with the following context. But Keil, Henderson, and Chambers prefer to supply שים, and think of the eyes as directed upon the stone in loving care and protection. The one stone is compared with the seven eyes. The cherubic chariot of Ezek. i. 18 was full of eyes. The eyes represent the sacred activity of the divine רוח. Comp. Zech. iv. 10; Isa. xi. 2; Rev. v. 6. The capstone of the temple is full of eyes, as was the cherubic chariot. It is full of the energy of the divine life, it is the Messiah Himself.

under [1] the vine and under the fig-tree. And the angel that talked
with me came again, and waked me, as a man that is wakened out
of his sleep. And he said unto me, What seest thou? And I said,
I have seen, and behold, a candlestick all of gold, with its bowl
upon the top of it, and its seven lamps thereon; there are seven
and seven [2] pipes to the lamps which are upon the top thereof: and
two olive trees by it, one upon the right side of the bowl, and the
other upon the left side thereof. And I answered and spake to the
angel that talked with me, saying, What are these, my lord? Then
the angel that talked with me answered and said unto me, Knowest
thou not what these be? And I said, No, my lord. Then he
answered and spake unto me, saying, This is the word of Jahveh
unto Zerubbabel, saying, Not by force, nor by power, but by my
spirit, saith Jahveh Sabaoth. Who art thou, O great mountain?
before Zerubbabel become a plain:[3] and he will bring forth the
head stone with shoutings of 'Grace, grace, unto it.' Moreover, the
word of Jahveh came unto me, saying, The hands of Zerubbabel
have laid the foundation of this house; his hands shall also finish
it; and thou wilt know that Jahveh Sabaoth hath sent me unto
you. For who hath despised the day of small things? for they shall
rejoice, and shall see the plummet in the hand of Zerubbabel, even
these seven,[4] the eyes of Jahveh; searching through and through

---

[1] אל תחת is pregnant, implying the verb בא. This phrase for
peace and prosperity we have seen in Amos ix. 14; Micah iv. 4.
See pp. 163 and 182.

[2] שבעה ושבעה is variously explained. It is generally taken
distributively, seven by seven, that is, seven pipes for each lamp, so
the R.V. But this would be too many. The LXX. and Vulgate
render seven pipes only. Hitzig, Ewald, and Henderson suppose
that there has been a mistake of repetition in the Massoretic text.
Köhler and C. H. H. Wright take the second seven as additional to
the first, making two sets, one set connecting the lamps with the
bowl of the reservoir, the other connecting the lamps with one
another, and regulating the flow of the oil. This is best. For this
is a great self-feeding lamp-stand. The olive trees produce the oil
and discharge it into the reservoir of the lamp-stand, and so the lamps
are ever supplied with an even flow of oil.

[3] למישור is the same as in Isa. xl. 4. It is better to supply an
imperative than an imperfect.

[4] וישמחו. The subject of this verb is שבעה אלה, as Henderson,
Keil, Hitzig, and Chambers, with which עיני יהוה is in apposition.
The rejoicing eyes of the divine spirit are contrasted with the scorn
of the wordlings. The LXX., Targum, Peshitto, Vulgate, Ewald,
and others find the subject in מי בן.

the whole earth. Then answered I and said unto him, What are these two olive trees upon the right side of the candlestick and upon the left side thereof ? And I answered the second time, and said unto him, What be these two olive branches, which by means of the two golden spouts [1] empty the golden oil out of themselves ? And he answered me and said, Knowest thou not what these be ? And I said, No, my lord. Then said he, These are the two sons of new oil,[2] that stand by the Lord of the whole earth."

—Zech. iii. 8–iv. 14.

The divine promise is made to the high priest Joshua, that the divine servant bearing the name of Branch will be brought forth. Branch is here used as a proper name of the Messiah, on the basis of the prophecy of Jeremiah.[3] It is true our prophet does not use the name of David, and does not connect the servant Branch with the son of David, and yet it is clear that to Zechariah Zerubbabel has taken the place of David, and he looks for a second Zerubbabel, as Jeremiah and Isaiah had looked for a second David. The term servant is used here as in the passage in Jeremiah, and has no connection with the Messianic servant of the great unknown. The mention of the servant Branch is only for a moment, for the prophet passes over to a contemplation of a wonderful stone that is placed before Joshua. That stone has seven eyes graven upon it, that represent the sevenfold operations of the divine Spirit as it searches everything through and through. These eyes engraven on the stone show that it could not be the foundation stone upon which the temple was to be erected. It was rather the crowning stone, the gable stone, the capstone, that was to complete the structure. This stone placed before Joshua was the

---

[1] שבלים is only found here. It is essentially the same as שבלת, channels, pipes. צנתרות is only found here, a weaker form of צנער. It is similar to צנור, cataract, waterfall.

[2] בני היצהר are the anointed ones, namely the priest and the king. בן is a noun of relation.

[3] Jer. xxiii. 5–8, xxxiii. 14–22. See p. 244 seq.

assurance to him and to Israel that the temple whose foundation stone had long since been laid, would eventually be completed. The Divine Spirit whose eyes looked forth from the capstone placed before the high priest, would ere long look down from the summit of the completed temple. This stone is another form of the Messianic idea. As we have had a Messianic cornerstone in Isaiah,[1] so we have now a Messianic capstone here. The foundation and the completion of the temple are both to be found in the Messiah at His advent.

The result of this advent of the servant Branch, and the completion of the temple by the raising of the capstone to its final position, will be the removal of sin and the establishment of universal peace.

The prophet now sees a wonderful transformation of the lamp-stand of the temple. By its side, on the right and left, are two olive trees, ever producing olive oil for the lamps. They are connected with the lamp-stand by two spouts, which convey the golden oil from the trees into the bowl, which at the summit of the lamp-stand serves as its reservoir. From this bowl seven pipes convey the oil to the seven lamps, and there are seven other pipes that run around, connecting each lamp with its neighbour, so that there is a constant and an even supply of oil. It needs no ministering priests to supply its lamps with oil and light. The olive trees, ever living and producing golden oil, give it a constant supply. These olive trees are evidently the two anointed ones that stand before God, the anointed priest and the anointed king. Through their ministrations the oil of divine grace ever supplies the lamp-stand of the kingdom of God with the ability to shine. As in Jeremiah the holy city became a great ark of the covenant and throne

[1] Isa. xxviii. 14–18; Ps. cxviii. 22–23. See p. 208 seq.

of Jahveh,[1] so here the new temple becomes a great lamp-stand, a light to Israel and the nations.

It is hardly possible that the prophet designed to pre-dict that Joshua and Zerubbabel would accomplish all this. It is true it is said that Zerubbabel had laid the foundations of the temple, and he would complete it with a festival of rejoicing. But back of this temple of Zerubbabel is the greater temple of Jeremiah, Ezekiel, the great unknown and Haggai.[2] Zechariah and his hearers could not have supposed that the temple of Zerubbabel was the realization of these wonderful ideals, or of his own no less marvellous representation. The temple of Zerubbabel was a pledge of a more glorious temple in the future. So the prophet might think of Joshua as an anointed priest, but he could hardly have thought that Zerubbabel was an anointed king, though he was of the royal line of David. But Joshua and Zerubbabel become to him the types of these great offices which they at the time represented, so far as they were able under the circumstances. These offices will in the latter days transcend their ancient dignity and worth. The Messiah, Branch, will come forth, realize the ideal and become a channel of divine grace, the source of light and joy to the world. Mountains of difficulty are still in the way. But they will become a plain. Not by force or power will these things be accomplished, but by the Spirit of God, whose sacred eyes search the earth through and through for the accomplishment of the divine plan of redemption.

The second prophecy of the servant named Branch is contained in chap. vi., and is in some respects an en-largement of the first.

"And the word of Jahveh came unto me, saying, Take of them of the captivity, even of Heldai, of Tobijah, and of Jedaiah, and

---

[1] Jer. iii. 14–18. See p. 242.   [2] See pp. 242, 285.

come thou the same day, and go into the house of Josiah the son of Zephaniah, whither [1] they are come from Babylon ; yea, take of them silver and gold, and make a noble crown,[2] and set it upon the head of Joshua the son of Jehozadek, the high priest ; and speak unto him, saying, Thus speaketh Jahveh Sabaoth, saying, Behold, the man whose name is Branch ; and he will grow up out of his place, and he will build the temple of Jahveh : even he will build the temple of Jahveh ; and he will bear the glory, and will sit and rule upon his throne ; and he shall be a priest upon his throne :[3] and the counsel of peace[4] will be between them both. And the noble crown shall be to Helem, and to Tobijah, and to Jedaiah, and to Hen[5] the son of Zephaniah, for a memorial in the temple of Jahveh. And they that are far off will come and build in the temple of Jahveh, and ye will know that Jahveh Sabaoth hath sent me unto you. And it will come to pass, if ye will diligently obey the voice of Jahveh your God."—Zech. vi. 9–15.

This prediction enlarges upon the servant named Branch. It is promised that he will grow up out of his place and build the temple of Jahveh. This shows very clearly that the prophet cannot think of Zerubbabel or of his temple ; for Zerubbabel had already arisen, and was engaged in the erection of the new temple. The prophet

---

[1] אשר באו is taken by the Vulgate, Peshitto, Targum, A.V., Henderson, and many others as a relative of person, and is rendered "who came." But it is better with R.V., after Ewald, Hengst., Keil, Chambers, and others, to render it as a relative of place.

[2] עטרות is taken as a real plural by the R.V. and many interpreters, thinking of two crowns, the royal and the priestly. Henderson thinks of a double crown, and compares the triple crown of the papacy. But it is best, with Keil and C. H. H. Wright, to regard it as an intensive plural, as in Job xxxi. 36, and render noble crown or glorious crown. Compare Rev. xix. 12.

[3] והיה כהן It seems most natural to take כהן as predicate, in accordance with Psalm cx. 4, and the repetition of כסאו ; so Keil, Chambers, and most interpreters. But Ewald and Hitzig make it the subject, and so find two persons and two thrones.

[4] עצת שלום is counsel of peace, not in the sense of reconciliation between the two offices, but as having peace as their common design. Compare Isa. ix. 6, Mic. v. 5. See pp. 200 and 218.

[5] It is better to take חן as a proper name in place of Josiah. But Ewald, Keil, and Köhler interpret it as the noun חן with the ordinary meaning, grace, favour, i.e. that of the son of Zephaniah.

causes a noble crown to be made of the gold and silver brought from Babylon by messengers from the Jews still remaining there. This crown was placed upon the head of Joshua, not to crown him as the Messiah, but as a symbol and pledge that the Messiah would arise and be crowned with such a noble crown. And this crown was preserved as a memorial and pledge in the temple of Zerubbabel. The Messiah, named Branch, is to be the builder of that temple of Jahveh of which the temple of Zerubbabel was the preparation. He will be crowned, and will be enthroned. He will unite in his crown the royal and the priestly offices, for he will sit on his royal throne as a priest, and the two offices will combine in him in a ministry of peace. This is the same priest-king that we have seen in Psalm cx.,[1] only here he is enthroned in peaceful dominion ; there he was a great conqueror. The priest-king is the same as the branch of Jeremiah,[2] and the shoot of Isaiah,[3] and the seed of David, the temple builder of Nathan's prophecy.[4] It is in this prediction that Zechariah advances the Messianic idea beyond any of his predecessors. Jesus Christ of Nazareth is the realization of these predictions.

V. JAHVEH THE HOLY KING.

There is a group of psalms, embracing xciii., xcv.-c., and we may add xlvii., that have as their theme, " Jahveh doth reign." They all have the same rhythmical structure. They are trimeters in strophes of twelve lines each, although they have been changed in some places by additions of a liturgical character, and in some places by insertions from the margin. It is probable that the most of them were originally parts of one great hymn,

[1] See p. 132.   [2] See p. 214.   [3] Isa. xi. See p. 201.
[4] 2 Sam. vii. 11–16 ; 2 Chron. xvii. 10–14. See p. 126.

but it was broken up for use in the synagogue and temple, and then the separate parts were modified in the places that can be easily detected. It seems to us that these psalms all express the joy and hopes of that time when the second temple was first completed. They follow naturally the prophecies of Haggai and Zechariah, with which they are in accord.

§ 111. *Jahveh is the holy king enthroned in Zion. His sovereignty extends over the whole earth. All nature rejoices in His advent. His reign is a reign of justice, holiness, and manifold blessings.*

These psalms are full of the thoughts and hopes of the great unknown, and resemble very much those little hymns that constitute the refrains of the original edition.[1]

> "*Jahveh doth reign*, he is clothed with majesty,
> Jahveh is clothed with strength,[2] he hath girded himself,
> Yea the world is sustained, it cannot be moved.
> Thy throne is established from of old, O thou from everlasting;
> The streams have lifted up, Jahveh,
> The streams have lifted up their voice,
> The streams lift up their roaring
> Above the voices of many waters.
> Magnificent are the breakers of the sea,
> Jahveh on high is magnificent.[3]
> Thy testimonies are very sure, at thy house.[4]
> Holiness is becoming, Jahveh, for length of days."—Ps. xciii.

This psalm opens with the words, "Jahveh doth reign." This is the theme of the entire series. Jahveh has

---

[1] See p. 340.

[2] It is best, with Ewald, to attach עז to לבש, in accordance with the parallelism.

[3] אדירים is not in apposition with משברי, but is predicate, as in the next clause.

[4] The R.V. follows Delitzsch, Hupfeld, and Ewald, and makes three lines out of the last two. Perowne makes two lines, but attaches לביתך to the last line, and spoils the rhythm.

2 F

clothed Himself with majesty and strength, and is enthroned upon His everlasting throne. The streams and the breakers of the sea rejoice. Holiness is the chief characteristic of His temple.

I. "O come, let us shout aloud to Jahveh,
　　O let us make a joyful noise to the rock of our salvation;
　　O let us go to meet his face with thanksgiving,
　　With pieces of music we shall make[1] a joyful noise to him.
　　For Jahveh is a great 'El,
　　And a *great king* above all gods,
　　In whose[2] hands are the deep places of the earth,
　　And the heights of the mountains are his;
　　Whose is the sea; and he made it;
　　And the dry land which his hands formed.
　　Come let us worship and let us bow down,
　　Let us kneel before Jahveh our maker.

II. Verily he is our God,
　　And we are the people of his pasture, and flock of his hand.
　　To-day if[3] ye will hearken to his voice,
　　Harden not your heart as at Meribah,
　　As the day of Massa in the wilderness,[4]
　　When your fathers tempted me,
　　Tried me, yea saw my work.
　　Forty years long was I loathing a generation.[5]

---

[1] The cohortatives here give place to the simple indicative. The R.V. ignores the difference.

[2] אֲשֶׁר shows that this is a relative clause. It is improper to make it an independent clause, as the R.V. Hupfeld, Ewald, and others give it correctly.

[3] This clause with אִם may be taken as a wish, "O that ye would," with R.V., Perowne, Delitzsch, and others. But it is better, with Heb. iii. 7, Hupfeld, Ewald, and Reuss, to take it as conditional.

[4] For these historical references, see Ex. xvii. 1–7; Num. xx. 1–13; Deut. xxxiii. 8.

[5] דּוֹר is without the article, and is emphatically indefinite, a generation, that is an entire generation. The imperf. אָקוּט also expresses the oft-repeated loathing of the people on account of their repeated transgression. It lasted during the entire forty years.

> And I said, 'A people of erring heart are they,
> Not knowing my way ;'
> When [1] I sware in my anger,
> 'They shall not enter into my resting-place.'"
>
> —Ps. xcv.

This psalm is a call to praise Jahveh, the great king exalted above all gods ; the creator of all things, and the universal sovereign. Its second strophe is a warning based upon the experience of Israel in the wilderness.

I. "Sing unto Jahveh a new song,[2]
Sing to Jahveh, all the earth,
Sing to Jahveh, bless his name,
From day to day tell the glad tidings of [3] his salvation,
Declare among the nations his glory,
Among all peoples his wonders.
For great is Jahveh, and highly to be praised :
He is to be revered above all gods.
For all the gods of the peoples are idols :
But Jahveh made the heavens.
Honour and majesty are before him :
Strength and beauty are in his sanctuary.

II. Give to Jahveh, ye kindreds of peoples,
Give to Jahveh glory and strength,
Give to Jahveh the glory due unto his name,
Lift up a minchah and come into his courts.
Worship Jahveh in holy array :
Tremble in his presence, all the earth.
Say among the nations, *Jahveh doth reign,*[4]
He judgeth the peoples with equity.
Let heaven rejoice, and let the earth exult ;
Let the sea roar and its fulness ;

[1.] אשר is a relative of time, as Ewald, and not expressive of result, as Hupfeld, Delitzsch, and Perowne; or consequence, "therefore," as R.V., which would require vav consec. of imperf.

[2] See Isa. xlii. 10.   [3] See Isa. xl. 9, lii. 7.

[4] We eliminate אף תכן תבל בל תמוט, which has come in from the marginal reference to xciii. 2.

Let the field exult, and all that is therein.
Then let all the trees of the wood shout for joy."[1]—Ps. xcvi.

This is another summons to praise Jahveh, and to
declare the glad tidings of His salvation and His glory
among the nations. It is in the style of the great
unknown. Jahveh is exalted above all, and is worthy
of reverence and praise, for He alone is the creator.
Honour and majesty, strength and beauty are in His temple.
The second strophe is a universal call. All nations are
to unite in the praise of Jahveh, and in the sacrificial
worship in the courts of His temple. For Jahveh doth
reign over all nations, and universal nature rejoices.

I. "*Jahveh doth reign*, let the earth exult ;
Let the many coasts be glad.
Clouds and darkness are round about him :
Righteousness and justice are the basis of his throne.
Fire goeth before him,
And it burneth up his adversaries round about.
His lightnings light up the world ;
The earth doth see and writhe,
The mountains do melt like wax from before Jahveh,
From before the Lord of the whole earth.
The heavens do declare his righteousness,
And all the peoples do see his glory.[2]

---

[1] We also regard the lines

לפני יהוה כי בא
כי בא לשפט הארץ
ישפט תבל בצדק
ועמים באמונתו

as an added refrain ; comp. Ps. xcviii. 9. It was possibly for a
responsive chorus in the liturgical worship.
[2] The distich of ver. 7 has a different movement. The first line
is a pentameter.

"All they that serve graven images, that boast themselves of idols,
will be ashamed :
Worship him, all ye gods."

It reminds us of similar pentameters in Isa. xli. 11–12, xlii. 17,
xlv. 16, etc. It seems to us that they are a later addition. Possibly
they were for responsive song.

II. Zion heard and rejoiced,
 And the daughter of Judah exulted ;
 Because of thy judgments, Jahveh.
 For thou, Jahveh, art 'Elyon above all the earth :
 Thou art exalted highly above all gods.
 Ye who love Jahveh, hate evil ;
 Keeper of the persons of his favoured ones,
 From the hand of the wicked he delivereth them.
 Light is sown for the righteous,
 And joy for the upright in heart.
 Rejoice, ye righteous, in Jahveh,
 And give thanks to his holy memory."　　　—Ps. xcvii.

This psalm begins in the same way as Ps. xciii.
God is enthroned upon a lofty throne that is founded on
justice and righteousness. His messengers are lightnings.
These execute His judgments. He is sovereign of the
whole earth. The heavens declare His righteousness,
and all nations see His glory. Zion has especial joy
in beholding the divine judgments. They are for her
deliverance and glory. The righteous are called upon to
rejoice, and give thanks in the remembrance of the
holiness of their God.

I. *"Sing to Jahveh a new song, for he hath done wonders;*
 His right hand and holy arm hath gained him victory.
 Jahveh hath made known his salvation, in the eyes of the nations
 　　hath revealed his righteousness;
 Hath remembered his mercy and his faithfulness to the house of
 　　Israel.
 All the ends of earth have seen the salvation of our God.

II. Make a joyful noise to Jahveh, all the earth;
 Break forth and sing for joy, and sing praises ;
 Sing praises unto Jahveh with the harp,
 With the harp and the voice of melody,
 With trumpets and sound of cornet ;
 Make a joyful noise before the king Jahveh.
 Let the sea roar, and its fulness :
 The world, and they that dwell therein ;
 Let the streams clap their hands,

Let the mountains sing for joy together [1]
Before Jahveh, for he cometh to judge the earth.
He will judge the world with righteousness, and the people with
equity.' —Ps. xcviii.

This psalm resembles Psalm xcvi. in the opening call to sing a new song, but the five lines with which it begins are not trimeters, but pentameters. They must either be a later liturgical addition, or else designed to be sung by a different voice. These lines resemble the introduction and the refrains of the great unknown.[2] The psalm closes with two pentameter lines. Thus the psalm, as we have it at present, is a trimeter enclosed in pentameters. The psalm was probably sung by two different voices, with different movement. It is a call to a new song in praise of the wonders of salvation wrought by the holy arm of Jahveh, which have been displayed before the whole earth. In view of this, all mankind are called to praise Him with all kinds of musical instruments, and universal nature breaks in with its chorus.

I. "*Jahveh doth reign*, the peoples tremble,
Enthroned upon the cherubim, the earth moveth.
Jahveh in Zion is great,
And he is high over all peoples ;
Let them praise thy great and terrible name :
Holy is he.
A king's strength loveth justice ;
Thou hast prepared justice in uprightness,
And righteousness in Jacob thou hast made.
Exalt Jahveh our God,
And worship at his footstool,
Holy is he.

II. Moses and Aaron among his priests,
And Samuel among those calling on his name,
Callers unto Jahveh, he used to answer them.

---

[1] Compare Isa. lv. 12.
[2] See Isa. xl. 5, 10, li. 9, lii. 10, lxii. 8.

> In the pillar of cloud he used to speak unto them ;
> They kept his testimonies
> And the ordinance he gave them.
> Jahveh our God, thou didst answer them,
> A forgiving 'El wast thou to them,
> And avenging upon their deeds.
> *Exalt Jahveh our God,*
> *And worship ye at his holy mountain,*
> *For holy is Jahveh our God."*
>   —Ps. xcix.

This psalm begins with the great theme, " Jahveh doth reign." Jahveh is enthroned upon the cherubim in Zion, and exalted above all nations ; above all He is holy. This is the refrain of the psalm, and gives it its chief characteristic. The ancient history is recalled, as in Psalm xcv., as an inducement to worship. Moses and Aaron and Samuel were heard and answered. The pillar of cloud and fire was the form of the theophany from which He spake to them. He forgave them their sins. How much more now on Zion, His holy mountain, will He prove Himself a righteous and holy Saviour !

> " Shout to Jahveh, all the earth ;
> Serve Jahveh with joy ;
> Come before him with singing.
> Know that Jahveh, he is God.
> He made us, and we are his,[1]
> His people and the sheep of his pasture.
> Come to his gates with thanksgiving,
> To his courts with praise.
> Thank him, bless his name,
> For Jahveh is good ;
> His mercy is for ever,
> And unto all generations his faithfulness."   —Ps. c.

---

[1] לֹא, the Kethibh, " and not we ourselves," is sustained by the LXX., Vulgate, Peshitto, and A.V. The Qeri לֹו is supported by Jerome, the Targum, and Saadia, and has been adopted by most modern scholars, and by the R.V. It is better suited to the parallelism.

This psalm is composed of a single strophe, a call to praise. It is based on the thought of Isa. xl. 11, that Jahveh was the shepherd and Israel the flock of his hand. They are therefore exhorted to praise Him in His courts, and render thanks for His goodness, His ever-lasting mercy and His faithfulness.

Psalm xlvii. so much resembles the group just considered, that it seems to belong to the same time.

> I. "Clap the hands, all peoples;
>   Shout unto God with the voice of triumph!
>   For Jahveh 'Elyon is awe-inspiring,
>   A great king over all the earth.
>   He subdueth[1] peoples under us,
>   And nations under our feet!
>   He chooseth for us our inheritance,
>   The excellency of Jacob, whom he loves.[2]
>   God is gone up with a shout,
>   Jahveh with the sound of a trumpet.
>
> II. Play ye to God, play ye;
>   Play ye to our king, play ye;
>   For God is king of all the earth;
>   Play ye a maskil.[3]
>   God reigns over the nations;
>   God is enthroned on his holy throne.
>   The nobles of the peoples have assembled,
>   The people of the God of Abraham:
>   For God's are the shields of earth;
>   He is greatly exalted."

---

[1] ירבר is only found here and in Ps. xviii. 48 in this sense. See p. 145.

[2] Perowne follows the *selah*, and divides here, making the strophes unequal. Delitzsch divides here, and makes a third strophe of the last four lines. But the *selah* is no safe guide to strophical organization. The strophes are exactly equal and symmetrical.

[3] We prefer to leave משכל untranslated, because it is not clear what was the exact meaning of this technical word for a kind of psalm. The R.V. renders in the text "with understanding," ignoring the technical word altogether. In the margin it gives "in a skilful psalm." So Perowne, "in skilful strains," after Ewald. But this can hardly be said to have been established as the meaning appropriate to all passages.

This psalm is likewise a summons to praise Jahveh, the great king over all the earth. It resembles Psalm lxviii. in the reference to the triumphal ascent to Zion with the sound of trumpet.[1] The second strophe is a call to praise with musical instruments. God reigns over all nations from His holy throne, the nobles of all nations are there assembled, and the shields of heroes from all parts of the earth are hung up in His palace. He is the universal king, highly exalted over all.

VI. THE LAND OF THE GLORY OF JAHVEH.

§ 112. *Jahveh will restore the prosperity of His people. His glory will dwell in the land, and the divine attributes meet in sweet communion. Earth and heaven will respond to each other in friendship. The soil will be fruitful, the cattle innumerable, and the children of the land will be full grown and beautiful. There will be universal peace and joy.*

I. " Thou hast been favourable, Jahveh, to thy land,
    Thou hast restored the prosperity of Jacob,
    Thou hast pardoned the iniquity of thy people,
    Thou hast covered all their sins,
    Thou hast withdrawn all thy fury,
    Thou hast turned from the heat of thine anger.
    Restore us, O God of our salvation,
    And cause thine indignation with us to cease.
    For ever wilt thou be angry at us ?
    Wilt thou draw out thine anger to generation after
        generation ?
    Wilt thou not quicken us again,
    That thy people may rejoice in thee ?
    Show us thy mercy, Jahveh,
    And give to us thy salvation.

---

[1] See p. 432.

> II. Let me hear what 'El will speak,
> Jahveh,[1] yea, he speaks peace
> Unto his people, and unto his favoured ones,
> But let them not return to folly.
> Surely his salvation is near to those that fear him,
> That glory may dwell in our land;
> Mercy and faithfulness are met together,
> Righteousness and peace have kissed,
> Faithfulness sprouteth out of the earth,
> And righteousness bendeth down from heaven.
> Yea, Jahveh giveth welfare,
> And our land giveth its produce.
> Righteousness goeth before him,
> That it may direct [2] in the way of his footsteps."—Ps. lxxxv.

The first strophe begins with a thankful recognition of the mercy of God in the past. He has accomplished His promises and restored the exiles to the holy land, and forgiven all their sins.[3] But there is still great need of the divine favour and blessing. What has been accomplished, forms the basis for the plea with which the strophe closes, that prosperity may be restored to the land, and that the divine anger may altogether cease. The blessings have only been realized in part; the entreaty is for the full measure of the divine salvation.

The second strophe gives the divine promise in response to the petition. The divine salvation is near to those that fear him. They are first warned lest they should again commit folly. The prediction then rises to those wondrous heights in which the great unknown moves. The divine glory is to dwell in the holy land. The divine attributes are to meet in it in loving union.

---

[1] יהוה is usually attached to the previous line. But the rhythm requires that we should have three lines here and not two. And the parallelism is more complete with a divine name in the two lines.

[2] יָשֵׂם is jussive. It is best, therefore, to take it as a final clause with weak Vav.

[3] Compare Isa. xliv. 22.

They will descend from heaven and spring up from the earth, coming from all parts to the centre of the land of divine blessing, to Zion the holy place of the restoration. The divine mercy and the divine faithfulness coming from different directions, meet together in Zion. Righteousness and peace have been, as it were, long absent from one another. When they meet they kiss as the dearest friends. Faithfulness springs forth from the earth to meet the divine righteousness that bends down from the heavens. Righteousness becomes the guide of the people to conduct them in the footsteps of Jahveh. The land again becomes wonderfully fruitful, and prosperity is restored.

Ps. cxliv. 12–15 is a little pentameter poem that has in some way been attached to a trimeter psalm. It describes the felicity of the land of Jahveh.

" When [1] our sons are as plants, grown up in their youth,
  Our daughters as corner stones, hewn after the fashion of a palace;
  Our garners are full, affording all manner of store ;
  Our sheep bringing forth thousands, ten thousands in our fields ;
  Our kine are great with young ; there is no breaking in through our thorn-hedges ; [2]
And there is no going forth to war, and no cry of alarm in our streets ;
Happy the people when [3] they have it so ;
Happy the people, when Jahveh is their God."

VII. THE IDEAL MAN TRIUMPHANT OVER EVIL.

The psalms just considered have described the blessedness of the land in which Jahveh dwells, and the people

[1] אשר greatly perplexes interpreters, who try to find a connection with the previous context. It is a relative of time.

[2] We insert the rare word צן of Job v. 5 and Prov. xxii. 5, " thorn hedge," and with the suffix צנינו after פרץ. The LXX. implies some such word in its κατάπτωμα φραγμόν. It was easy for a copyist to leave out צן or צנינו between פרץ and ואין.

[3] The שככה is for an older אשכ ככה, as the rhythm requires.

that enjoy His favour. Ps. xci. gives a picture of the
happy lot of the pious man who is in intimate communion
with God, and is triumphant over all evil.

§ 113. *The pious man who is in intimate communion
with God, will be delivered from perils of every kind. He
will be sustained by angels, and be lord of the animals.*

I. " He who dwells in the secret place of 'Elyon,
Abideth in the shadow of Shadday,
Saying [1] of Jahveh, ' My refuge,
And my fortress, my God in whom I trust ;'
Surely he will deliver thee from the snare of the fowler,
From the noisome pestilence.
With his pinions may he cover thee,[2]
That thou mayest take refuge under his wings.

II. A shield and buckler is his faithfulness.
Thou wilt not be afraid of the terror by night,
Of the arrow that flieth by day,
Of the pestilence that walketh in darkness,
Of the destruction that wasteth at noonday,
Though [3] a thousand fall at thy side,
And ten thousand at thy right hand ;
Unto thee it will not come nigh,
Only with thine eyes thou wilt behold,
And the recompense of the wicked thou wilt see.

---

[1] אֹמֵר of the Massoretic text is first person, imperfect. But this
seems inconsistent with the context, and it troubles interpreters to
give a satisfactory explanation. Ewald makes it in apposition
with the subject of the previous participles. Delitzsch divides the
psalm between three voices, assigning the first and second lines to
the first voice, the third and fourth to a second voice, and then
makes the first voice resume in the fifth line. The third voice closes
the psalm. But the second voice has too little to do, having only
two lines here and one line in ver. 9. It is better to follow the
LXX., Peshitto, and Jerome, with Hupfeld, Perowne, and others,
and read אֹמַר or יֹאמַר.

[2] It is better to give the jussive יָסֶךְ its force.

[3] It is better, with Delitzsch, to take יִפֹּל as hypothetical.

III. Since Jahveh, my refuge,
  'Elyon, thou hast made thy dwelling place,[1]
  Evil will not befall thee,
  And plague will not approach thy tent;
  For he will give his angels charge over thee,
  To keep thee in all thy ways;
  Upon their palms they will bear thee up,
  Lest thou dash thy foot against a stone.
  Upon the roaring lion thou wilt tread,
  And thou wilt trample under foot the young lion and
    serpent.

IV. Because he doth set his love on me,[2]
  I will deliver him, I will set him on high,
  Because he doth know my name.
  When he calleth, I will answer him,
  I will be with him in trouble,
  I will strengthen him, yea, I shall honour him;
  With length of days I will satisfy him,
  And I will show him my salvation."

This beautiful psalm presents the ideal man living in communion with God, and accordingly delivered from all evil. Such an experience could not be found in times of exile and sin, but only in times of prosperity, and in the holy land of Jahveh. The ideal man can appear only in ideal times, and in an ideal land and nation. The land of the divine blessing involves the man of the divine blessing. The ideal man of Ps. viii.[3] and of the Prot-evangelium[4] here reaches the height of its representation. The supremacy over all evil has been achieved. The serpent is trampled under foot, and paradise and the

---

[1] The difficulty of these two lines arises from the emphatic position of אַתָּה, and the fact that its verb is in the second line. The thought of the Psalmist is this: "Jahveh is my refuge;" and since thou hast made him also thy dwelling-place, all these benefits will come to you. Delitzsch takes the first line as the first voice, and the second line as the second. Some insert אָמַרְתָּ.

[2] The remainder of the psalm is a divine promise.

[3] See p. 146.   [4] Gen. iii. 14, 15. See p. 71 seq.

divine communion are regained. It was appropriate that
Satan should cite this passage in the temptation of the
Messiah and apply it to Jesus.[1] It had its application
to Him, but not at the time of the temptation, or during
the period of His humiliation. It is a picture of the
risen and glorified Messiah, who achieved the ideal manhood of our race by His triumph over sin and Satan and
all evil.

The section of Zechariah embraced in chaps. xii.–xiv.
is an apocalypse that stands by itself with its title,
and without indication of author or time of composition.
It was appended to Zechariah, in ancient times, with the
message already considered.[2] It is placed by many
critics in the times of Jeremiah, but the tendency at
present is to regard it as post-exilic. Indeed, it shows
dependence upon the predictions of Ezekiel and the
great unknown. It seems to reflect a situation somewhat later than the governorship of Zerubbabel, when
the bright prospects of the previous predictions had
become somewhat darkened. These chapters constitute
a single piece, and yet there are two Messianic ideas
that should be considered apart, although they are
mingled in the prophecy. The suffering Messiah is
connected with the final distress at Jerusalem, just as
we have seen it to be the case in Daniel.[3] We shall
first examine the predictions of the suffering Messiah,
and then the predictions of the great judgment and its
consequences.

VIII. THE SMITTEN SHEPHERD.

§ 114. *The house of David and the inhabitants of
Jerusalem lament in penitential sorrow the death of their*

---

[1] Matt. iv. 6.   [2] See p. 183.   [3] Dan. ix. 24–27.

rejected shepherd. He has been smitten by the sword of Jahveh for the salvation of the flock. And a fountain is opened to wash away all sin.

There are two passages, the first the lamentation over the rejected shepherd, and the other the smiting of the shepherd by Jahveh. It seems better to treat the latter first.

"Awake, O sword, against my shepherd, and against the man that is my fellow,[1] saith Jahveh Sabaoth : smite the shepherd, and the sheep will be scattered ; and I will turn mine hand upon the little ones. And it will come to pass, that in all the land, is the utterance of Jahveh, two parts therein will be cut off and die ; but the third will be left therein. And I will bring the third part through the fire, and will refine them as silver is refined, and will try them as gold is tried : they will call on my name, and I will hear them : I will say, It is my people ; and they will say, ' Jahveh is my God.' "—Zech. xiii. 7–9.

This shepherd is a ruler of the people, rather than a prophet. The shepherd is smitten to death by the sword. He is engaged in war at the head of his flock, and is defeated by the enemy, as was Josiah on the battle-field at Megiddo. His fall results in the flight of his army, and great suffering. They pass through the furnace of affliction, and two-thirds of them are cut off, and only a third are preserved. These are saved by Jahveh. The little ones of the flock call upon Him, and He turns His hand upon them and delivers them. The shepherd is here the martyr shepherd of his people, like the martyr prince of Daniel,[2] rather than the martyr, servant of the great unknown,[3] although both alike suffer for the sins of the people under the divine infliction

---

[1] עָמִית is only found here and in the priestly document of the Pentateuch, where it has the meaning, neighbour, fellow. It implies companionship and association. This shepherd is indeed the one appointed by Jahveh to have charge of the flock, Israel.

[2] Dan. ix. 26. See p. 422.   [3] Isa. liii. See p. 356 seq.

of judgment. Our Saviour applies this prophecy to
Himself on the night of His betrayal, as the one who
was servant and prince in one.[1]

In the other section we behold the people lamenting
over their smitten shepherd.

> "And I will pour upon the house of David, and upon the inhabit-
> ants of Jerusalem, the spirit of grace and of supplication ; and
> they will look unto me[2] whom they have pierced : and they will
> mourn for him, as one mourneth for his only son ; and will be in
> bitterness for him, as one that is in bitterness for his first-born.
> In that day will there be a great mourning in Jerusalem, as the
> mourning of Hadadrimmon in the valley of Megiddon. And the
> land will mourn, every family apart; the family of the house of
> David apart, and their wives apart; the family of the house of
> Nathan apart, and their wives apart ; the family of the house of
> Levi apart, and their wives apart; the family of the Shimeites
> apart, and their wives apart; all the families that remain, every
> family apart, and their wives apart. In that day there will be a
> fountain opened to the house of David, and to the inhabitants of
> Jerusalem, for sin and for uncleanness."—Zech. xii. 10–xiii. 1.

The prophet here uses the defeat of the army of
Josiah at Megiddo, and the death of the heroic prince
on the battle-field, together with the lamentation for him
that burst forth all over the land,[3] as a symbol of the
greater calamity that will befall the nation in the rejection
and death of their Messiah. Josiah was sustained by
his people, and when he fell the nation fell with him.

---

[1] Matt. xxvi. 31–32 ; Mark xiv. 27.

[2] אֵלַי is difficult. The suffix refers to Jahveh, who is the speaker.
In what sense can it be said that Jahveh was pierced ? This is
explained by Keil as a slaying of the מַלְאַךְ יהוה, but this theophany
was no less divine than Jahveh Himself. It is best, with Hitzig,
Köhler, Umbreit, and C. H. H. Wright, to think of the identification
of Jahveh with His servant. There is insufficient external authority,
and little internal evidence, to justify the reading אֵלָיו, although the
change is an easy one, and it is defended by Ewald, Geiger,
Kennicott, and others. John xix. 37 applies this passage to the
crucified Jesus, as the rejected and pierced Messiah.

[3] See 2 Kings xxiii. 29.

But the martyr prince Zechariah has in view, is not slain by the enemy, but is rejected, and is thrust through by his own people, who refuse to follow him into the struggle with their enemies. In the previous passage the sword of Jahveh smote him; here the people pierce Jahveh when they reject His shepherd. This apparent inconsistency is resolved when we consider that Jahveh is the sovereign who controls the destiny of all. The enemies of His people are the sword of judgment in His hands to chastise them for their sins. Hence, when the martyr shepherd falls by the hands of the enemies, he falls by the divine infliction of judgment. But he falls not because he is displeasing to Jahveh. He is rather His own shepherd, His fellow whom He has given charge of His flock. He falls because of the sins of the people whose shepherd he is. The shepherd gives his life for His flock. But, on the other hand, the flock refuse to follow him, they reject his leadership, and when the crisis of the struggle comes, abandon him and leave him alone to sustain the conflict. Hence, when the enemies of his people thrust him through and slay him, those who rejected him have dealt him the blow, and in slaying him they have pierced Jahveh Himself in His representative. Thus it was when Jesus was left alone to die upon the cross for the sins of men. The Roman soldiers pierced him, but His own people were responsible for his death, and the blow was laid to their charge.

After the death of their Messiah, the people are hard pressed by their enemies, and deeply feel the sad loss they have sustained. They cry unto Jahveh in their distress, and He pours upon them His Spirit. This outpouring of the Spirit in the times of judgment is after the manner of Ezekiel.[1] Ezekiel represents that the

[1] Ezek. xxxix. 29. See p. 281 seq.

2 G

Divine Spirit gives them the knowledge of Jahveh as their Saviour. Zechariah describes the Divine Spirit as a spirit of grace and supplication for grace; it inspires the people to true penitence, and they break forth in a national lamentation for their rejected Messiah. In response to this lamentation of repentance, Jahveh opens up for them a fountain for sins and uncleanness, where all their guilt, ceremonial as well as moral, may be washed away.

Our Saviour recognised Himself as this rejected shepherd. As He sees that rejection in His crucifixion and death, so He sees that great lamentation in the judgment that was impending upon Jerusalem that rejected Him; only that lamentation is no longer of penitence and redemption, but of conviction of sin and condemnation.[1] It is noteworthy that our Saviour never refers to the suffering servant of the great unknown, but lays so much stress upon the suffering prince of Zechariah and Daniel. Indeed, the conception of the suffering Messiah reaches its height in these passages of Zechariah. The darker side of rejection, piercing and death, stands out in all its dreadfulness, without relief. But in the representation of the great unknown it is enclosed in the bright frame of the exaltation of the servant.

IX. THE UNIQUE DAY.

§ 115. *There is to be a final conflict with all nations at the gates of Jerusalem. Jahveh comes with all His saints to deliver His people and destroy their enemies. The mount of Olives is cleft in twain by a great earthquake to provide a refuge, and Jahveh takes His stand above it in judgment. The nations are smitten with leprosy and blindness; the warriors of Jerusalem are endowed with marvellous*

Matt. xxiv. 30; comp. Rev. i. 7.

*strength and heroism; and all enemies are destroyed.
Jahveh becomes king over the earth, and all nations serve Him.
Living waters go forth eastward and westward from Jerusalem. A day that has no night and no winter dawns,
and knows no end. "Holy to Jahveh" is inscribed on everything in Jerusalem, and no unclean person will enter it
any more. All nations come up to keep the feast of Tabernacles.*

There are two representations of the final conflict.
The former describes the conflict itself, and the deliverance
wrought by Jahveh.

" The utterance of Jahveh, who stretcheth forth the heavens, and
layeth the foundation of the earth, and formeth the spirit of man
within him : Behold, I am about to make Jerusalem a cup of reeling
unto all the peoples round about,[1] and against Judah also will it be
in the siege against Jerusalem. And it will come to pass in that
day, that I will make Jerusalem a burdensome stone for all the
peoples ; all that burden themselves with it will be severely
lacerated ; and all the nations of the earth will gather themselves
together against it. In that day, is the utterance of Jahveh, I will
smite every horse with astonishment, and his rider with madness ;
and I will open mine eyes upon the house of Judah, and will smite
every horse of the peoples with blindness. And the chieftains of
Judah will say in their heart, The inhabitants of Jerusalem are my
strength,[2] in Jahveh Sabaoth, their God. In that day will I make the
chieftains of Judah like a pan of fire among wood, and like a torch
of fire among sheaves ; and they will devour all the peoples round
about, on the right hand and on the left : and Jerusalem will yet
again dwell in her own place, even in Jerusalem. Jahveh also will
save the tents of Judah first, that the beauty of the house of David
and the beauty of the inhabitants of Jerusalem be not magnified
above Judah. In that day should Jahveh defend[3] the inhabitants

---

[1] Comp. Isa. li. 17–22 ; Ps. lx. 5.

[2] אמצה is only found here. It is usually taken as equivalent to
אמץ, strength.

[3] יגן is jussive, but it is usually taken as indicative on the ground
that the difference of the form is passing out of mind. It is better
to make it the protasis of a conditional clause.

of Jerusalem, he that stumbleth among them in that day will be as David ; and the house of David will be as God, as the Malakh Jahveh before them. And it will come to pass in that day, that I will seek to destroy all the nations that come against Jerusalem."— Zech. xii. 1-9.

This passage describes a conflict between Jerusalem and the nations that have gathered against it. It is not said that Jerusalem is captured, as in the second passage, but this is really implied. For the nations find Jerusalem more than they can manage to dispose of. It is like a cup of intoxication to them. They drink and become drunken. It is like a heavy stone that they endeavour to lift, but it falls upon them, and lacerates them. Jahveh interposes on behalf of His people in their extremity. He smites the enemies with blindness and madness, and strengthens his people, so that the weakest of them becomes a hero like David, and the princes of David's house become like the theophanic Malakh.[1] Hence they become like a pan of fire in the midst of wood, and, like a torch among sheaves of grain, they consume and destroy all nations that have come up against Jerusalem. The deliverance of Jerusalem is thus accomplished by a divine advent, as in Ezekiel.[2]

The second representation of the last conflict is much fuller as regards the peril, the interposition, and the glorious results. It is indeed the culmination of all the apocalypses of the Old Testament.

"Behold, a day for [3] Jahveh cometh, when thy spoil will be divided in the midst of thee. For I will gather all nations against

---

[1] See p. 88. Zechariah and Malachi revive this technical term of the prophetic historians.

[2] Ezek. xxxviii.-ix. See p. 279.

[3] ליהוה. The ל is taken by R.V., Henderson, Pusey, Chambers, and others, as ל of the genitive. But it could hardly be separated from יום by בא. It is better, with Keil and C. H. H. Wright, to take it as the indirect object "for Jahveh."

Jerusalem to battle; and the city will be taken, and the houses rifled, and the women ravished : and half of the city will go forth into captivity, and the residue of the people will not be cut off from the city. Then will Jahveh go forth, and fight against those nations, as when he fought in the day of battle. And his feet will stand in that day upon the mount of Olives, which is before Jerusalem on the east, and the mount of Olives will cleave in the midst thereof toward the east and toward the west, and there will be a very great valley ; and half of the mountain will remove toward the north, and half of it toward the south. And ye will flee by the valley of my mountains ; for the valley of the mountains will reach unto Azel : yea, ye will flee, like as ye fled from before the earthquake in the days of Uzziah king of Judah : [1] and Jahveh my God will come, and all the holy ones with thee. And it will come to pass in that day, that there will be no light or cold or ice : [2] but it will be a unique [3] day which is known unto Jahveh ; not day and not night : but it will come to pass, that at evening time there will be light. And it will come to pass in that day, that living waters will go out from Jerusalem ; half of them toward the eastern sea and half of them toward the western sea ; in summer and in winter will it be. And Jahveh will be king over all the earth : in that day will Jahveh be one, and His name one. All the land will be turned as the Arabah, from Geba to Rimmon, south of Jerusalem ; and it will be lifted up, and dwell in its place, from Benjamin's gate unto the place of the first gate, unto the corner gate, and from the tower of Hananel unto the king's winepresses. And men will dwell

---

[1] Comp. Amos i. 1.

[2] יקרות יקפאון is difficult. The last word in the Kethibh is a verb from קפא, to contract oneself. Comp. Ex. xv. 8. יקרות is then interpreted as referring to the stars, as the יקר הלך in Job xxxi. 26 refers to the moon. This is the view of Hengst., Keil, Pusey, C. H. H. Wright, Chambers, and others. But the Qeri reads יְקָרוֹת וְקִפָּאוֹן. The ancient versions, LXX., Peshitto, Symmachus, Targum, also take them as nouns. The LXX. renders καὶ ψύχος καὶ πάγος. יקרות is then equivalent to קרות, the plural of קרה, cold (see Job xxiv. 7). קפאון is found nowhere else. Ewald, Umbreit and Bunsen, take the three nouns as united in one chain, rendering, "There will be no light, or cold, or ice," that is, the changes of night and day, or summer and winter, will no more exist in that unique day of Jahveh. We are then to compare Isa. lx. and Rev. xxi. 23.

[3] יום אחד, one day, or rather unique day, that has no mate.

therein, and there will be no more ban ; but Jerusalem will dwell safely. And this will be the plague wherewith Jahveh will smite all the peoples that have warred against Jerusalem : their flesh will consume away while they stand upon their feet, and their eyes will consume away in their sockets, and their tongue will consume away in their mouth.[1] And it will come to pass in that day, that a great tumult from Jahveh will be among them ; and they will lay hold every one on the hand of his neighbour, and his hand will rise up against the hand of his neighbour. And Judah also will fight at Jerusalem ; and the wealth of all the nations round about will be gathered together, gold, and silver, and apparel in great abundance. And so will be the plague of the horse, of the mule, of the camel, and of the ass, and of all the beasts that will be in those camps, as this plague. And it will come to pass, that every one that is left of all the nations which came against Jerusalem, will go up from year to year to worship the king, Jahveh Sabaoth, and to keep the feast of Tabernacles. And it will be, that whoso of all the families of the earth goeth not up unto Jerusalem to worship the king, Jahveh Sabaoth, upon them there will be no rain. And if the family of Egypt go not up and come not, neither will it be upon them ; there will be the plague wherewith Jahveh will smite the nations that go not up to keep the feast of Tabernacles. This will be the sin of Egypt, and the sin of all the nations that go not up to keep the feast of Tabernacles. In that day will there be upon the bells of the horses, ' Holy unto Jahveh ;' and the pots in the house of Jahveh will be like the bowls before the altar. Yea, every pot in Jerusalem and in Judah will be 'holy unto Jahveh Sabaoth ;' and all they that sacrifice will come and take of them, and seethe therein : and in that day there will be no more a Canaanite [2] in the house of Jahveh Sabaoth."—Zech. xiv. 1–21.

The final conflict at the gates of Jerusalem results in the capture of the city. All nations have been gathered together against it, and they have apparently accomplished their will. Half of the people go into captivity, but half of them escape. Jahveh interposes on their behalf in theophany. He takes His stand upon the mount of Olives, and it quakes at His presence, and divides, opening

---

[1] Comp. Isa. xxxv. 8.

[2] בִּנְעַנִי. The Canaanite is the representative of the unclean nations. See Rev. xxi. 27.

up a great valley of refuge for the fugitives from
Jerusalem. Jahveh comes with all His angels.[1]

He smites the hostile armies with the plague, and
they waste away upon their feet like a body of lepers.
A panic comes upon them, as in the days of Jehoshaphat,
and they turn their weapons against each other.[2] The
rich spoils are enjoyed by the redeemed people of
Jerusalem.

A unique day dawns upon the world, the long expected
day of judgment and redemption, a day that has no sun-
light, and no cold or ice, no changes of the seasons, and
no night. Its sun will never set. At evening it will
be as bright as noonday. Jahveh is the light of that
everlasting day.[3]

Jerusalem becomes the source of living waters. We
have seen this wonderful stream of life in Joel, Isaiah,
Ezekiel, and the Psalter;[4] but in all these previous predictions the stream has been but one; here, however, it is
a double stream, breaking forth in two directions, both
toward the Dead Sea, as in Joel and Ezekiel, and also
now, as an additional feature, toward the Mediterranean
Sea. It is a perennial stream, whose waters know no
change. In summer and winter it flows on with the
same inexhaustible supply.

All nations that survive the great judgment come up
to worship Jahveh at Jerusalem. As in the great unknown, they assembled in immense congregations on the
Sabbaths and new moons,[5] so here they assemble to
observe the crowning feast, the great festival of Tabernacles. Jerusalem is pre-eminently holy. As in

[1] Dan. vii. 10. See p. 415.
[2] 2 Chron. xx. 22–24.
[3] Compare Isa. lx. 19–20. See p. 397.
[4] Joel iv. 18; Isa. xxxiii. 21; Ps. xlvi. 5; Ezek. xlvii. 1–12. See
pp. 158, 211, 214, and 290.
[5] Isa. lxvi. 23. See p. 406.

Jeremiah, the entire city is the throne of Jahveh, as
sacred as the ancient ark of the covenant ;[1] so here everything in Jerusalem, even the bells of the horses and the
ordinary cooking utensils, bears the same inscription as
the tiara of the high priest of Israel. " Holy to Jahveh,"
is the character of the entire city and all its contents,
and no Canaanite or unclean person will be able to enter
it any more.

MALACHI.

The prophecy of Malachi closes the canon of the Old
Testament prophets ; but whether the word Malachi is
the name of the prophetic person or of his office, is disputed.[2]   There seem to be no sufficient reasons, however,
for rejecting Malachi as a proper name of the prophet,
and exegetical opinion has turned strongly in favour of
this interpretation.   It is manifest that the prophecy was
delivered some time after the return from exile and the
building of the temple.   It can hardly be placed as late
as Alexander the Great.   The author was probably a
contemporary and an assistant of Nehemiah in his work.

Malachi is variously estimated.   His style is peculiar
and original, especially in his use of the dialogue.   His
language is forcible, not departing far from that of the
classic writers.   Malachi closes the line of prophets of
the old covenant.   · " Although like a late ، evening
closing a long day, he is yet at the same time the grey of
dawn bearing a noble day in its bosom."[3]   The message
of the prophet is divided into three sections, with the

[1] Jer. iii. 14-18.   See p. 242.
[2] The LXX. renders this term by " his angel," and the Targum
regards Ezra as the prophet, and in this respect is followed by
Jerome, Calvin, and Hengstenberg.   Ewald adopts the view of the
LXX., but assigns no author.
[3] Nägelsbach, article *Maleachi*, in Herzog, Realencyklopaedie,
1 Aufl. viii. p. 756.

introduction. The introduction states the peculiar love of God to Israel (chap. i. 1–6). Section 1st rebukes the priests who contemn His name (chap. i. 7–ii. 9). Section 2nd rebukes the people for unfaithfulness in marriage relations (ii. 10–16).[1] Section 3rd describes the Advent of the Lord, and is Messianic (ii. 17–iii.).

X. THE SECOND ELIJAH.

§ 116. *The Malakh of the covenant comes to execute judgment. His advent is heralded by a messenger, a second Elijah. That day is a day of fire, consuming the wicked, and also a day of the Sun of righteousness, giving joy to those who fear God. The Levites are purified by the fires of judgment, and the offerings of the people are again acceptable to Jahveh.*

"Behold, I am about to send my messenger,[2] and he will prepare the way before me;[3] and the Lord, whom ye are seeking, will suddenly come to his temple, and the Malakh of the covenant, whom ye delight in: Behold, he is about to come, saith Jahveh Sabaoth. But who may abide the day of his coming? and who is he who can stand when he appeareth? for he is like a refiner's fire, and like fuller's soap: and he will sit as a refiner and purifier of silver, and he will purify the sons of Levi, and purge them as gold and silver: and they will offer unto Jahveh vegetable-offerings in righteousness. Then will the vegetable-offering of Judah and Jerusalem be pleasant unto Jahveh, as in the days of old, and as in ancient years.

.   .   .   .

For, behold, the day is about to come, burning as a furnace; and all the proud, and all that do wickedness, will be stubble: and the day that cometh will burn them up, saith Jahveh Sabaoth,

---

[1] See Neh. xiii. 23–31.

[2] We have to distinguish the מלאכי of the first clause from the מלאך הברית. The former is the herald of the latter. The latter is the theophanic Malakh of the prophetic historians. See p. 88.

[3] Compare Isa. xl. 3, lvii. 14, lxii. 10.

that it will leave them neither root nor branch. But unto you that fear my name will the sun of righteousness[1] arise, with healing in his wings;[2] and ye will go forth, and gambol as calves of the stall. And ye will tread down the wicked: for they will be ashes under the soles of your feet in the day when I am about to do it, saith Jahveh Sabaoth.

Remember ye the law of Moses, my servant, which I commanded unto him in Horeb for all Israel, even statutes and judgments. Behold, I am about to send you Elijah the prophet, before the coming of the great and terrible day of Jahveh.[3] And he will turn the heart of the fathers to the children, and the heart of the children to their fathers: lest I come and smite the earth with a ban."[4]—Mal. iii.

Malachi is in accord with Zechariah and the psalms of the Restoration in his dependence upon the great unknown. He describes the herald preparing the way of Jahveh, in similar terms to those of the introduction to the prophecy of the restoration of Zion.[5] The herald is first presented as the messenger, and then as Elijah the prophet. The prophet does not imagine that the ancient Elijah, who ascended in a theophanic chariot to heaven will come again to introduce the last times; but he looks for a second Elijah, a great prophet, of whom the ancient Elijah was an appropriate type. The work of this Elijah is the preparatory work of turning the hearts of fathers and children to one another, in reconciling the generations, in bringing back the people to the pure faith and life of their ancestors; indeed, a work of preaching repentance.

[1] שמש צדקה. The construct is not that of apposition, with Keil, as if righteousness were the sun, but the construct of the characteristic. The sun is parallel with the day of the previous context. Jahveh Himself is the sun. Comp. Isa. lx. 19.

[2] בנפיה. The wings are not for the beams of the sun, but involve another figure of speech. The prophet is thinking of the eagle's wings of Ex. xix. 4; Deut. xxxii. and Ps. xci. 4.

[3] Comp. Joel iii. 4.

[4] חרם is the ban, the devotion to destruction. Comp. Zech. xiv. 11.

[5] See p. 375.

The advent is a divine advent, for the Malakh of the covenant is the ancient theophanic angel, who so often appeared in the early history of the nation to guide and deliver them. He comes to judge Israel according to his covenant keeping. He comes suddenly to His temple, when men will not expect Him, although His advent had been heralded. He comes as judge and as redeemer in the day of doom. The day is a day of fire, that will burn like a furnace, and consume the wicked, leaving them neither root nor branch. They will be reduced to ashes, to be trodden under foot by the righteous. This is another form of the river of fire of Daniel, and the flames of Gehenna of the great unknown.[1] The day will also be a day of fire to the corrupt in Israel. The people, and especially the Levitical priests, will pass through the furnace, and be purged of their dross as gold and silver are refined. They will be thoroughly washed from all their impurities, as by the fuller's lye. They need to be refined and purified before their offerings can be accepted by Jahveh as in ancient times. But the day is also a day of light. The Sun of righteousness arises and gives its glorious light to those who fear God. He comes like a great eagle to shelter His people under His healing wings. They will triumph over the wicked, and rejoice with great joy.

The Messianic prophecy of the Old Testament comes to an appropriate conclusion in this day of light and fire, when the recompense of the Old Covenant is given by Jahveh to each one in accordance with his fidelity and purity.

[1] Isa. lxvi. 24; Dan. vii. 10.   See pp. 406 and 415.

CHAPTER XV.

THE MESSIANIC IDEAL.

THE Messianic prophecy of the Old Testament advances through the centuries of the history of redemption, from the simplest germs to the most complex conceptions; and yet there is a unity in the midst of the great variety of representations, and a harmony in the manifold development of the theme, so that the whole constitutes an organism of redemption, the Messianic ideal given by divine revelation to guide the people of God in their advance toward the goal of history.

I. THE IDEAL OF MANKIND.

The ideal of the human race was first given in the divine blessing preserved in the poem of creation.[1] Mankind was created in the divine image, and endowed with dominion over the creatures. His destiny was to assume sovereignty, and take possession of the earth by a numerous posterity. Psalm viii. gives a lyric expression to the same ideal.[2] The ideal man is a little below the heavenly intelligences in dignity, but is exalted to dominion over all creatures.

This ideal was disturbed by the original sin of our first parents, but it was not destroyed. The tragedy of Eden changed the form of the divine blessing and its mode of realization; but its substance remained the same,

[1] Gen. i. 26–30, p. 68.   [2] P. 146.

for the ultimate destiny of mankind could not be different from the original design of the Creator. The divine blessing of fruitfulness and growth was transformed into a covenant of redemption. And so Ps. xvi. represents the ideal man enjoying the favour of God in a happy lot in life, and in communion with God after departing from life;[1] and Ps. xci. describes the pious man in intimate communion with God, delivered from perils of every kind, sustained by angels, and lord of the animals.[2]

This ideal of the human race was the inheritance of the people of God. It is the blessing of the Mosaic codes. The institutions of the old covenant were the means for its realization; but when these failed owing to the sinfulness and perversity of Israel, the prophets presented the same ideal in the new covenant. Hosea sees all nature responding in concert to Israel when she is remarried to Jahveh.[3] Isaiah describes that universal peace, when the little child is the shepherd of the wild animals, and the infant plays with the serpent.[4] Ezekiel points to a second Eden;[5] and the great unknown predicts a transformation of nature in which the garden of Jahveh takes the place of the wilderness, and a new earth and new heavens of righteousness and peace are created, instead of the earth that had been cursed with sin and death.[6] Ps. lxxxv. describes the land of the glory of Jahveh. The divine attributes meet therein in sweet communion. Earth and heaven respond to each other in friendship.[7] Ps. cxliv. 12–15 gives a picture of universal peace and joy. The soil is fruitful, the cattle innumerable, and the children of men are full grown and beautiful.[8]

[1] P. 148.   [2] P. 460.   [3] Hos. ii. 18, p. 172.
[4] Isa. xi. 6–9, p. 205.   [5] Ezek. xxxvi. 35, p. 274.
[6] Isa. li. 3, lv. 12, 13, lxv. 17, pp. 363, 384, 403.
[7] P. 228.   [8] See pp. 457–459.

II. THE CONFLICT WITH EVIL.

The protevangelium [1] is the miniature of the history of humanity, a conflict with evil until the ultimate victory over it. The seed of the woman is the conqueror of the serpent,—the son of man triumphs over the prince of evil. The conflict in this primitive prophecy is with the serpent and his seed. But in subsequent prophecy the combat is between good and evil in families, tribes, nations, the powers of heaven and earth, until it becomes a universal struggle; for evil creates divisions in the human race, and hence the conflict is not merely between humanity and evil, it is a battle in humanity itself between an evil seed and the seed of promise. There is an increasing elimination of the evil seed from the seed of redemption. Abraham and his seed take the place of Eve and her seed. The children of Hagar, Keturah, and Esau are also excluded, so that Israel becomes the holy seed, the heir of all the promises. Isaiah and his successors distinguish between carnal Israel and the righteous remnant. This remnant is still further reduced in the persecutions of the last days of the kingdom of Judah and of the exile, until it culminates in the conception of a unique servant, a second Israel, who suffers for the sins of all and achieves redemption for all; [2] and in a son of man who comes upon the clouds of heaven, to triumph over the Antichrist in whom the hostile powers culminate. [3]

III. THE DIVINE ADVENT.

The blessing of Shem [4] introduces the doctrine of the divine advent. Man needs divine help in order to gain the victory over evil. God comes to dwell in the tents

---

[1] Gen. iii. 14, 15, p. 71.   [2] Isa. liii., p. 356.
[3] Dan. ix. 23, p. 424.   [4] Gen. ix. 26, 27, p. 79.

of Shem as the God of the race. The divine Malakh
assures the patriarchs that He will abide with them and
fulfil the promises of the covenant. At the exodus
the Malakh selects the holy tabernacle as his residence,
and Israel takes the place of the race of Shem in the
unfolding of the promise. God dwells in the tabernacle
until the destruction of Shiloh by the Philistines. In
the covenant with David He promises to abide in the
temple erected by the seed of David.[1] He enters the
temple of Solomon and resides there until the exile. The
divine presence secures Jerusalem from ruin. A corner-
stone is laid in Zion that is worthy of all confidence. It
abides firm in the overwhelming storm.[2] Zion is the
quiet abode of Jahveh, the glorious judge, warrior, and
king, a place of streams where hostile fleets appear only
to be shattered and destroyed.[3] Zion, the city of the
great king, is the safe abode of the people of God ; its
beauty and glory reflect the majesty of God. Jahveh
quiets the commotions of the nations, rebukes the rebellious, and reigns over the earth. The weapons of war
are destroyed in order to the establishment of universal
peace.[4]

Such sublime thoughts as these could not be realized
in the old Jerusalem, or in the old temple, on account of
the sins of the people. The prophets attach them to the
new temple and the new Jerusalem. Ezekiel sees Jahveh
departing from the desecrated temple, and yet granting
His presence to His people during the exile as their
sanctuary.[5] He predicts a new temple of great magnificence and sanctity.[6]

One of the earlier prophets predicted that the temple
mount would be exalted above all the mountains, as the

---

[1] 2 Sam. vii. 11–16, p. 126
[2] Isa. xxviii. 16, p. 208.
[3] Isa. xxxiii. 20–24, p. 210.
[4] Pss. xlvi. and xlviii., p. 213.
[5] Ezek. xi. 16, p. 268.
[6] Ezek. xl.–xlviii., p. 283.

goal of the pilgrimage of the nations, the source of instruction and judgment.[1] Jeremiah sees a new Jerusalem that will be as sacred as the ark of the covenant,[2] that will bear the name "Jahveh is our righteousness,"[3] that will be rebuilt and be holy in all its suburbs, so that there will be no places of uncleanness.[4] A psalmist declares that Jahveh will come and dwell in Zion for ever, and provide abundantly for all its inhabitants.[5] Ezekiel names the holy city, "Jahveh is there."[6]

The great unknown represents that the new temple will be the house of prayer for all nations, and that they will bring their choicest treasures thither. Jerusalem will be rebuilt of precious stones, its gates salvation, its walls praise. It will be the light and glory of the world, and bear the names "Married," and "My delight is in thee." It will be the centre of a new earth and new heavens.[7]

Haggai predicts that the latter glory of the temple will be greater than the former.[8] Zechariah sees that the new Jerusalem will be inhabited by a vast multitude, and that Jahveh will be a wall of fire round about it, and a glory in its midst, and that it will be called "the city of fidelity."[9] A later prophet predicts that the new Jerusalem will be so holy that the bells of the horses and the cooking utensils will bear the same inscription as the tiara of the high priest, "Holy to Jahveh."[10]

---

[1] Micah iv. 1, and Isa. ii. 2, p. 181.
[2] Jer. iii. 17, p. 242.
[3] Jer. xxxiii. 16, p. 244.
[4] Jer. xxxi. 38-40, p. 257.
[5] Ps. cxxxii., p. 263.
[6] Ezek. xlviii. 35, p. 290.
[7] Isa. xlix. 23, liv. 12, lvi. 7, lx., lxii., lxv. 17 seq., pp. 383, 389, 392, 394, 400, 403.
[8] Hag. ii. 9, p. 437.
[9] Zech. ii. 8-17, viii. 3, p. 438.
[10] Zech. xiv. 20, 21, p. 471.

IV. THE HOLY LAND.

The blessing of Abraham[1] introduces the doctrine of the holy land. This land is the inheritance of the holy seed. Jacob divides it among his sons, and appoints Judah as the leader in the march of conquest. The portions of Judah and Ephraim are especially rich and fruitful.[2] The codes of the Pentateuch enlarge upon the blessings of the promised land as the rewards of obedience to the divine instruction.[3] The prophets represent that the failure to realize these blessings was owing to divine chastisement for sin, and they make the holy land a prominent feature of the new covenant. The land of the restoration is to become wonderfully fruitful like the garden of Eden. It will again be divided among the tribes, and especial portions will be given to the priests, the Levites, the holy city, and the prince. A river of life will flow forth from the temple, quicken the barren tracts of the land, and restore the waters of the Dead Sea. It will flow eastward and westward, increasing its waters as it flows in inexhaustible and abounding supply. Upon its banks will be trees of life with monthly fruits and healing leaves.[4] A highway of redemption will be opened up leading to the promised land, the path of the returning exiles will be made easy, and all their wants supplied. The land will be filled with trees of beauty and the choicest flowers; and it will become exceedingly fruitful, and paradise will be regained. There will be new heavens and a new earth, the abode of righteousness and peace. All evils, physical and moral, will be banished. There will be no more sorrow, or tears, or death, but everlasting joy and festivity will everywhere prevail.[5]

[1] Gen. xii. 1–3, p. 84.   [2] Gen. xlix. 11, 12, 22–26, p. 93 seq.
[3] P. 115.   [4] Ezek. xxxvi. 35, xlv.–xlviii., pp. 274, 283.
[5] Isa. xxv. 6–8, xxxv., xli. 18–20, xlix. 9–13, li. 3, lv. 12, 13, lxv. 17, pp. 306, 318, 342, 354, 365, 384, 404.

V. JAHVEH THE FATHER AND HUSBAND.

At the exodus Jahveh adopted Israel as his first-born son, assigned him an inheritance in the midst of the nations, and guided him with paternal care until he took possession of it.[1] The sonship of Israel unfolds into the sonship of David and his seed. But the latter conception does not displace the former, although it renders its use less frequent. Thus Hosea represents that the children of Israel will be recognised in the Messianic time as the sons of the living God.[2] Jahveh will not give up Israel, as He had abandoned other nations to their sins and death. He will raise him from the dead, and deliver him from Sheol.[3] Jeremiah graphically presents Ephraim as the first-born of Jahveh lamenting under divine discipline, and returning in penitence unto Jahveh, who receives him in compassion as a precious and delightful son.[4] The great unknown represents Jahveh as more faithful to Zion than a mother to her babe. He will never forget her, but will restore her to her land and multiply her children.[5]

But the relation of sonship is not so common as that of marriage. This is also a conception of the Pentateuch, but Hosea first introduces it into the Messianic idea. Mother Israel has been guilty of adultery with Baal, and is rejected by her husband Jahveh. But after faithful discipline in the wilderness she is restored to her own land, where she is remarried, the divine attributes being the bonds of union.[6] Zephaniah represents Jahveh renewing his love to Zion, and rejoicing over her with great joy, and singing with exultation.[7] Jeremiah also thinks of a remarriage of Zion to Jahveh.[8]

[1] Ex. iv. 22, 23. See p. 100.   [2] Hosea i. 10. See p. 166.
[3] Hosea xi. 8, 9, xiii. 14. See pp. 174–176.
[4] Jer. xxxi. 18–20. See p. 252.   [5] Isa. xlix. 14–22. See p. 381.
[6] Hos. i.–ii. See p. 165 seq.   [7] Zeph. iii. 17. See p. 224.
[8] Jer. iii. 14. See p. 242.

The great unknown unfolds this conception in its fulness. Zion has been forsaken for a short time, and suffered affliction. But Jahveh is her husband and saviour. He is faithful to her, and will restore her to her own land and bestow upon her His covenant of peace.[1] Zion has been named "Forsaken" and "Desolate," but she is to receive the names "Married" and "My delight is in thee." Jahveh will rejoice over her as His bride, and make her His crown of glory.[2]

The relation of shepherd and flock is less frequent, but it is important to the development of the Messianic idea. It is found in the poetry ascribed to Jacob,[3] but first enters into the Messianic idea in the earlier Zechariah. The good shepherd Jahveh rejects His flock, having been estimated by them at the miserable price of a slave. These poor wages are thrown away, and the shepherd's staves, beauty and concord, are broken as a symbol of the separation.[4] Psalm lxxx. calls upon the shepherd of Israel to come for the salvation of His people.[5] Ezekiel describes the good shepherd searching out and gathering his scattered flock and restoring them to their fold in the land of Israel.[6] The great unknown sees Jahveh leading His flock on the highway of redemption. He is gentle and attentive to the suckling lambs and their mothers.[7] Psalms xcv. and c. represent Israel as the people of Jahveh's pasture and the flock of His hand.[8]

VI. THE KINGDOM OF GOD.

The covenant at Horeb constituted Israel the kingdom of God, a kingdom of priests and a holy nation.[9] The

---

[1] Isa. liv. 1–17. See p. 387. [2] Isa. lxii. See p. 400.
[3] Gen. xlix. 24. [4] Zech. xi. 7–14. See p. 187.
[5] Ps. lxxx. 2. See p. 229. [6] Ezek. xxxiv. 11–31. See p. 272.
[7] Isa. xl. 11. See p. 377. [8] Ps. xcv. 7, c. 3. See pp. 450, 455.
[9] Ex. xix. 6, p. 101.

blessing of Abraham had already promised that the seed
of Abraham should be a blessing to mankind;[1] but the
covenant at Horeb outlined the methods of its accomplishment. Israel is a royal priesthood, and as such has
a ministry of priesthood and a ministry of royalty. Both
of these relations unfold in Messianic prophecy.

In the prophecy of Balaam the kingdom of God is
apart from the nations, is composed of vast numbers, and
is irresistible. It subdues all nations to its sceptre.[2]
Jahveh is the king of this kingdom. He marches at the
head of His people, and subdues all its enemies.

In the covenant with David He installs the seed of
David as a Messianic dynasty to rule over His kingdom,
but does not thereby divest Himself of His royal sway.[3]
Hence the triumphs of the kingdom of God are sometimes
represented as the triumphs of the Messiah and then as
a divine victory. In the earlier days of the Davidic
monarchy the Messianic conqueror is more prominent,
but in the darker days the Messiah retires into the background, and the divine king becomes more prominent.
Psalm xxiv. represents Jahveh Sabaoth entering the holy
city in triumph.[4] Psalms xlvi. and xlviii. describe
Jerusalem as the city of the great king whence He
triumphs over all His enemies.[5]

The kingdom of God was reduced by the follies of the
house of David. It was broken in two by the secession of
the northern tribes, so that thenceforth the reunion of
Israel became a familiar theme for Messianic prophecy.
The kingdom was still further reduced by the invasions
of the Assyrians, so that Jerusalem and Zion take the
place and significance of the larger kingdom. The
corner-stone established there will abide firm amidst all

---

[1] Gen. xii. 1–3, p. 84.
[2] Num. xxiii. 9, 10, xxiv. 17–19, p. 104 seq.
[3] 2 Sam. vii. 11–16, p. 126.   [4] Ps. xxiv., p. 145.   [5] P. 213.

the troubles and confusion.[1] Psalm lxxx. compares the
kingdom to a vine that once enjoyed a marvellous
growth, but is now stripped of its branches and ravaged
by beasts of prey.[2] Ezekiel sees that the kingdom is to
remain in ruins until the advent of the appointed king,[3]
and represents that it will be planted like a little cedar
sprig upon the mountains of the holy land and grow to
be a majestic tree.[4] Daniel sees the kingdom in a little
stone cut out of the mountains without hands that grows
until it dashes all other kingdoms in pieces, and becomes
itself a mountain filling the earth.[5] Jahveh Himself
comes to the front in the predictions of the exile as the
king of Israel. When the time for restoration has come,
He works greater miracles than at the time of the exodus ;
He marches at the head of His people on a highway of
redemption ; all nature is transformed before Him ; He
leads the restored captives in triumphal procession to
Zion ; He takes up His residence in the holy city, and
reigns there for ever as the light and glory of Israel and
the world ; all nature rejoices in His reign of peace ; and
all nations bow to His sceptre, and recognise and obey
Him as the universal king.[6]

The priestly relation is more developed in the later
periods of prophecy. The priestly nation unfolds into a
priestly order in the nation which throws the priestly
relation of the entire nation into the background. Isaiah
is the first of the prophets to unfold this priestly relation
of the nation. He sees Egypt and Assyria united with
Israel as the people of God, speaking the holy language and
serving Jahveh with altar and sacrifice, while Ethiopia and

---

[1] Isa. xxviii. 16–18, p. 208. [2] P. 228.
[3] Ezek. xxi. 31, 32, p. 270. [4] Ezek. xvii. 22-24, p. 269.
[5] Dan. ii. 44, 45, p. 412.
[6] Isa. xli., xlii., xlix. 21-25, lii. 7-12, lvii. 11-21, lx., lxii. 10-12 ;
Ps. lxviii., xciii., xcv.-c., pp. 375, 379, 386, 393, 394, 429, 448.

Tyre consecrate offerings to Him.[1]　Zephaniah sees
the renown of Israel extending to the distant parts of
Africa, and the Ethiopians and the Libyans sending
offerings to the temple.[2]　Psalm lxxxvii. sings of the
adoption of the nations into the city of God, and their
enrolment among the citizens of Zion.[3]

The great unknown dwells upon this as his favourite
theme.　The name of Jacob becomes a title of honour,
all the ends of the earth turn unto Jahveh, and every
tongue swears allegiance to Him; kings and queens
become the foster-fathers and foster-mothers of Zion; a
great invitation is extended to all men to partake freely
of the blessings of the new covenant; the eunuchs and
foreigners are cordially invited to worship in the house
of prayer for all nations; the peoples of the world bring
their choicest treasures to Zion; the people of Israel
become the priests, and the nations their servants;
Egypt, Ethiopia, and all nations unite in the worship of
Jahveh, in the offerings, the feasts, and even in the
priesthood.[4]　Psalm lxviii. represents Ethiopia, Egypt,
and all nations paying tribute and singing the praises of
Jahveh.[5]　Zechariah describes the nations encouraging
one another to seek Jahveh, and catching hold of the
skirts of the Jew to secure his guidance to the holy
place.[6]　The royal psalms describe the whole earth
engaged in the worship of God;[7] and Zech. xiv. represents all nations celebrating the feast of Tabernacles.[8]

---

[1] Isa. xviii. 7, xix. 16–25, xxiii. 18, p. 206.

[2] Zeph. iii. 9, 10, p. 221.　　　　　　[3] P. 226.

[4] Isa. xliv. 5, xlv. 21–25, lv. 1–5, lvi. 6, 7, lx., lxi. 5, 6, lxvi. 20, 21,
pp. 351, 363, 369, 378, 391, 394, 403.

[5] Ps. lxviii. 31, 32, p. 433.　　　　[6] Zech. viii. 22, 23, p. 439.

[7] Ps. xcvi., xcviii., xcix., p. 448 seq.　[8] Zech. xiv. 16, 17, p. 467.

VII. THE DAY OF JAHVEH.

The doctrine of divine judgment springs from the blessings and curses of the Mosaic codes.[1] The blessing of Israel involves the cursing of all his enemies. The blessings of obedience have as their counterpart the curses of disobedience. Hence the doctrine of divine judgment is now a judgment of the enemies of his people; and then a chastisement and purification of Israel himself. The judgment is a heaping up of evils of all kinds upon the enemies of the kingdom of God, whether these are within the kingdom or without. The song of Hannah describes Jahveh as the all-knowing judge, who espouses the cause of the weak and executes justice in the earth.[2] Psalm i. describes a theophany for judgment.[3] The righteous and the wicked alike are warned to make sincere offerings lest they be destroyed.

Joel first introduces the doctrine of the day of Jahveh. There is a great and terrible day when Jahveh will judge the nations in the vale of judgment. All nature will be disturbed. The judgment will be a battle, a harvest, and a treading of the winepress.[4] Zephaniah enlarges upon this great and terrible day, when everything will be consumed.[5] Ezekiel describes a great struggle upon the mountains of the holy land with Gog at the head of all the hostile nations. These will be overthrown by the advent of Jahveh, who will rain fire and brimstone upon them, and utterly destroy them.[6]

The prophets of the exile describe the judgment in various terms. There is to be a great judgment upon Babylon, Egypt, and Moab; the earth staggers like a drunkard and swings like a hammock; it is utterly laid

---

[1] See p. 115.
[2] 1 Sam. ii. 1–10, p. 123.
[3] See p. 237.
[4] Joel iv. 18–21, p. 154.
[5] Zeph. i. 14–18, iii. 1–3, p. 221.
[6] Ezek. xxxviii.–xxxix., p. 279.

waste; the great metropolis is reduced to chaos; the
kings of the earth and the evil powers of heaven are
imprisoned and reserved for punishment; the wicked
oppressors perish for ever.[1] The judgment is a great
slaughter; Jahveh is the conqueror of Edom; His sword
is bathed in the blood of the enemies, and His garments
are stained with it; even the heavens and earth are
contaminated with the blood and carcases of the slain;
the heavens are rolled up like a scroll, and their host fall
as the foliage of a tree.[2] The nations that war against
Jerusalem are smitten with blindness and leprosy, and
are destroyed.[3] Jahveh comes as the Ancient of days
upon a throne of flames, and all His enemies are cast
into the river of fire.[4] The wicked are cast out of the
holy city like a mass of rotting, burning carcases in the
vale of Gehenna.[5] The day of fire consumes the wicked,
and leaves them neither root nor branch.[6]

The day of judgment is also a day of redemption.
The prophet Joel sees the outpouring of the divine Spirit
on all flesh, with the manifold gifts of prophecy as the
counterpart to the universal judgment.[7] Ezekiel also
connects the outpouring of the divine Spirit upon Israel
with the destruction of Gog and the nations.[8] Amos
teaches that Israel will be sifted among all nations, so
that the wicked will be destroyed like the chaff, but not
a grain of the true Israel will be lost.[9] Hosea represents
that mother Israel will be disciplined in the wilderness
and then restored; that Israel will be put to death, and
then raised from the dead.[10] Isaiah predicts that Jahveh

---

[1] Isa. xiii. 1–13, xxiv.–xxvii., p. 295 seq.
[2] Isa. xxxiv., lxiii. 1–6, p. 311 seq.
[3] Zech. xii. 1–9, xiv. 1–21, p. 466 seq.
[4] Dan. vii. 9–12, p. 413.
[5] Isa. lxvi. 24, p. 408.
[6] Mal. iii., p. 473.
[7] Joel iii., p. 155.
[8] Ezek. xxxix.
[9] Amos ix. 9, p. 161.
[10] Hos. ii., iii., xiii. 14, pp. 168 seq., 176.

will refine and purify His people, so that the remnant will become holy and blessed.[1] Jeremiah describes the loving chastisement that brings Israel to repentance.[2] Ezekiel sees Israel lying on the battlefield a mass of dry bones, but also sees Jahveh restoring them to life again.[3] Jahveh will sprinkle His people with clean water, and purify them, so that they will have a new heart and a new spirit.[4] The prophets of the exile enlarge upon this representation. The great apocalypse represents that Israel has been smitten in exact measure for the removal of sin and ultimate redemption; his corpse belongs to Jahveh, and will be quickened by the light of life; all sorrow and death will be banished in the times of restoration; and there will be a great banquet of joy for all the redeemed on Mount Zion.[5]

The great unknown shows that Zion's warfare has been accomplished, her iniquity discharged, and that she will be restored by the victorious arm of Jahveh; she has been forsaken for a short time in a gush of wrath; but will be restored, and will receive the comforting assurance that Jahveh will never be angry with her again; the divine Spirit will be poured out upon the seed of Israel, and they will become fruitful and be increased to vast numbers.[6]

Daniel predicts that there will be a resurrection of the dead, when the righteous will receive their inheritance, but the wicked Israelites will become a reproach and an everlasting abhorrence.[7]

The latest prophets bring this conception to its culmination. The spirit of grace and supplication is poured

---

[1] Isa. iv. 2–6, p. 193.   [2] Jer. xxx. 12–xxxi., p. 246.
[3] Ezek. xxxvii. 7–14, p. 275.   [4] Ezek. xxxvi. 25–35, p. 274.
[5] Isa. xxiv.–xxvii., p. 296.
[6] Isa. xl. 1, 2, xliv. 1–5, liv. 1–17, lxii. 11, 12, pp. 351, 374, 387, 400.
[7] Dan. xii. 1–13, p. 421.

upon Jerusalem, and they turn to Jahveh in sincere repentance, and are cleansed in the fountain for sin and uncleanness.[1] There is a unique day whose sun will never set, whose hours will know no changes of seasons.[2] Malachi sees Jahveh coming as the sun of righteousness to purify by the fires of judgment, which will destroy the wicked, but will refine the righteous and make them acceptable to God. He will heal them with His wings, and will take them to Himself as His chosen inheritance and priceless possession.[3]

VIII. THE HOLY PRIESTHOOD.

The covenant with Israel at Horeb, making Israel a kingdom of priests,[4] is unfolded in the covenants with Phinehas and with David. In the former we have a faithful priesthood for Israel; in the latter, a royal dynasty for Israel. Each of these is a Messianic idea that has its own special development.

Phinehas and his seed secure by covenant an everlasting priesthood;[5] they become the priestly mediators for Israel, as Israel itself was by covenant the priestly mediator for the nations. This covenant was renewed in the prediction that a faithful priesthood would take the place of the unfaithful house of Eli.[6] The Messianic priesthood is thrown into the background by the Messianic king until the time of Jeremiah, when the covenant with David and the covenant with Phinehas are represented as alike eternal and irrevocable, and as certain of fulfilment as the ordinances of heaven. Jeremiah predicts that the Levitical priests will not only be an everlasting priesthood, but that they will be

---

[1] Zech. xii. 10–xiii. 1, p. 464   [2] Zech. xiv. 6–10, p. 466.
[3] Mal. iii., p. 473.   [4] Ex. xix. 3–6, p. 101.
[5] Num. xxv. 12, 13, p. 109.   [6] 1 Sam. ii. 35, 36, p. 122.

composed of vast numbers.[1] Ezekiel assigns the priesthood in the new temple to the line of Zadok on account
of their faithfulness, and lays great stress upon their
sanctity; they alone are admitted to the ministry in the
inner court of the new temple.[2] The great unknown
gives the nations a share in the Levitical priesthood.[3]
Malachi predicts that the Levites will be purified, that
they may offer acceptable sacrifices.[4] Zechariah sees the
priestly and the royal offices in the symbol of living
olive trees producing a perpetual supply of holy oil for
the lampstand that gives the light for the people of God;
and then sees them combined on one throne in one noble
crown and in one holy person.[5]

IX. THE FAITHFUL PROPHET.

Moses predicts a prophet like himself divinely authorized to speak, who will complete the divine instruction,
and demand obedience under the penalty of divine judgment.[6] This Messianic prophet does not reappear in the
Messianic idea until the exile. Then, when priest and
king had disappeared, and the prophet was the only
minister of Jahveh, the Messianic idea gathered about the
office of the prophet. This prophet is a great sufferer.
He is called by Jahveh from the womb and assigned his
high calling. Jahveh is well pleased with him, and
bestows His spirit upon him. He is entirely consecrated
to the divine service, consumed with zeal for the house
of God, and fasts, prays, and preaches to the poor and
the afflicted. He is concealed for a season in a condition
of humiliation. He is surrounded by cruel enemies, who
mock him for his trust in God, and persecute him with

[1] Jer. xxxiii. 17–22, p. 214.
[2] Ezek. xliv., xlv., p. 283 seq.
[3] Isa. lxvi. 21, p. 407.
[4] Mal. ii. 4–9, iii. 3, 4, p. 473.
[5] Zech. vi. 13, p. 442.
[6] Deut. xviii. 16–19, p. 110.

bitter and mocking words; he is unattractive in form, despised and rejected, a man of sorrows and an outcast; he is innocent as a lamb, and yet is pierced, scourged, and crushed for his people; his body is stretched and racked with pain, his frame is feverish, and in his intense thirst his enemies give him vinegar and gall to drink; his hands and feet are pierced; he is plunged in a miry and watery abyss, and is dying of a broken heart; his enemies are dividing his garments among them; he is abandoned by his own kindred; God delivers him over to the will of his enemies for a season; he lays upon him as a trespass-offering the iniquities of all; and the servant suffers as a substitute, and dies a martyr's death. But his heroic patience and self-sacrifice are at last rewarded; Jahveh delivers him, and all the meek rejoice; He highly exalts him, and rewards him with spoils of victory, a prosperous ministry, and great honour; He praises his deliverer in the great congregation; his enemies incur a dreadful doom; but he becomes the great preacher of redemption. He proclaims the year of grace and the day of judgment; he transforms sorrow into joy, and rejoices in the accomplishment of his ministry; he delivers the captives, restores Israel, and becomes the covenant of the people; he is the light of the nations, and the salvation of the ends of the earth; kings and princes honour him, and wonder at the greatness of his exaltation.

X. THE MESSIANIC KING.

The doctrine of the royal Messiah springs from the covenant with David.[2] Jahveh adopts the seed of David

---

[1] Pss xxii., xl., lxix., lxx.; Isa. xlii. 1–13, xlix. 1–13, lii. 13–liii., lxi., pp. 320–373.

[2] 2 Sam. vii. 11–16, p. 126.

as His son, whom He will chastise by human agents, for sin; but will never forsake. He promises to build the house of David into an everlasting dynasty. The seed of David takes the place of the seed of Israel in the development of the relation of divine sonship. The royal Messiah is described in several psalms. Ps. cx. cites a divine utterance and oath to the king enthroning him at His right hand as the priest-king after the order of Melchizedek, and then describes a conflict in which the Messiah is engaged at the head of a priestly army. God stands at his right hand, and gives him the victory over the nations.[1] Ps. ii. represents the Messiah enthroned on Zion at the right hand of Jahveh as His son, citing a divine decree entitling him to the position, with all its prerogatives of universal and everlasting sovereignty.[2] Ps. lxxii. represents the Messianic king ruling in right-eousness, mercy, and peace, receiving the homage of the nations, the source and object of universal blessing.[3] Ps. xlv. describes the king as a bridegroom in God-like majesty; he espouses the nations, and rejoices over them as his brides.[4]

These psalms reflect the Messianic hopes of the Davidic period; but in the prophetic period the decline of the dynasty of David and the humiliation of the kingdom give the predictions of the Messianic king a new form. Amos introduces this new phase of the royal Messiah. The ruined house of David will be restored to its former prosperity; it will take possession of the nations as its inheritance.[5] Hosea predicts that Israel, who had for-saken the house of David and Jahveh at the same time, will eventually return in penitence to Jahveh and the second David.[6]

The earlier Zechariah sees Zion rejoicing at the advent

[1] P. 132. [2] P. 134. [3] P. 137. [4] P. 140.
[5] Amos ix. 11, 12, p. 161. [6] Hos. iii. p. 174.

of her king, who comes meek and victorious, riding upon
the foal of an ass. He has destroyed the weapons of
war, and reigns in peace over the earth.[1] The reign of
peace now becomes the prominent feature of the ideal of
the royal Messiah in Isaiah and Micah. A wonderful
child will be born of a young woman, and be named
Immanuel. He is the sign and pledge that Jahveh is with
His people, and that He will deliver them. Distress
will continue in the land until his maturity.[2] A great
light will shine upon the north-eastern frontier of Israel,
exalting the people as highly as they had been previously
humiliated, as the first of the Israelites to go into exile.
A great deliverance will be wrought, transcending that of
Gideon in the day of Midian. A child of the house of
David will be born, and bear the names Wonderful
Counsellor, Divine Hero, Distributor of Spoils, and Prince
of Peace. He will reign on the throne of David in
righteousness for ever. All military equipments will be
destroyed in order to universal peace.[3] A twig will come
forth from the stump of Jesse, and a shoot from his roots
will be fruitful. The sevenfold gifts of the divine Spirit
will rest upon him, and endow him to fulfil his work
of judging the poor with spiritual discernment, and the
wicked with the rod of his mouth. Girded with righteousness and faithfulness, he establishes peace in the
earth, in which the animal kingdom shares. The knowledge of God becomes universal. He becomes the
standard about which the nations rally, and the strife
of Ephraim and Judah comes to an end.[4] A ruler will
be born in little Bethlehem, who will bear the name of
Peace. He will go forth to fulfil the ancient promises,
and become great unto the ends of the earth.[5]

[1] Zech. ix. 9, 10, p. 184.   [2] Isa. vii. 13–17, p. 195.
[3] Isa. viii. 23–ix. 6, p. 198.   [4] Isa. xi., p. 201.
[5] Micah v. 1–4, p. 217.

The ideal of the Messianic king reached its height in the reign of Hezekiah, and in the predictions of Isaiah and Micah. In the subsequent predictions the royal Messiah retires to the background, and when he appears in the prediction it is in a less brilliant and a more subordinate position. Ps. lxxx. refers to him as the man of the right hand of Jahveh, and entreats Jahveh's favour for him.[1] Jeremiah describes him as the righteous branch, who will bear the name "Jahveh is our righteousness," and declares that the Davidic monarchy will be everlasting.[2] He also predicts that a very great multitude will return from exile and serve Jahveh their God and David their king.[3] Pss. lxxxix. and cxxxii. represent that Jahveh is faithful to His covenant with David notwithstanding the decline of the dynasty. His mercies are everlasting. He will cause prosperity and splendour to sprout forth for David.[4] Ezekiel predicts that the tiara of the priest and the crown of the king will be removed until the advent of the one appointed by Jahveh.[5] This one is the second David, the shepherd of the restoration,[6] under whose sway Israel and Judah will be reunited for ever.[7]

The great unknown and his associates know nothing of the royal Messiah. The divine king and the prophetic servant absorb their attention. The royal Messiah reappears in Zechariah alone of the prophets of the restoration. He bears the name Branch. He is to build the temple of Jahveh, and be its capstone. He combines the priestly and royal offices in his noble crown, and becomes the perpetual channel of the divine grace.

[1] Ps. lxxx. 18, p. 232.   [2] Jer. xxiii. 5–8, xxxiii. 14–22, p. 244.
[3] Jer. xxx. 9, p. 247.   [4] Pp. 258 seq.
[5] Ezek. xxi. 31, 32, p. 270.   [6] Ezek. xxxiv. 23, p. 272.
[7] Ezek. xxxvii. 21–25, p. 277.
[8] Zech. iii. 8–iv. 14 vi. 9–15 p. 442.

Daniel sees a Messianic prince in the last times of affliction, who bears the brunt of the troubles, and is cut off without having accomplished the redemption of his people.[1] The author of Zech. xiii. xiv. also represents the house of David and the inhabitants of Jerusalem, lamenting in penitential sorrow the death of their rejected shepherd. He has been smitten by the sword of Jahveh for the salvation of the flock.[2] The smitten shepherd and slain prince are evidently the same, but there is nothing in these prophets to show that this martyr is to be connected either with the martyr prophet of the great unknown and his associates, or with the royal Messiah. The comprehension of these separate pictures in one person could not be seen until the advent of Jesus Christ, who combined the prophet with the priest and the king, and who suffered and died that He might conquer and reign.

XI. THE NEW COVENANT.

The failure of the old covenant and its institutions to accomplish the work of redemption and to realize the Messianic ideal, showed that the old covenant was not the last word of God to man, but that it was preparatory to a new covenant of the Messianic age. The conception of the new covenant is the product of the prophetic period. Hosea first introduces it into the Messianic idea in the form of a remarriage of Jahveh to Israel. The divine attributes are the bonds of union, and all nature is included in the covenant of universal peace and harmony.[3]

Jeremiah unfolds the doctrine of the new covenant. Its instruction will not be on tables of stone, but on the

---

[1] Dan. ix. 26, p. 421.　　[2] Zech. xii. 10–xiii. 1, xiii. 7–9, p. 462.
[3] Hos. ii. 18–23, p. 171.

heart. There will be no need of teachers, for all will know Jahveh, from the least to the greatest.[1] Ezekiel describes a new covenant of peace that will secure exemption from war, peace with the animals, and fruitfulness of the land. It is an everlasting covenant, in which Judah and Israel will be united under the second David, and which will secure the divine presence in their midst for ever.[2]

The great unknown connects the new covenant with the prophetic servant of Jahveh. This servant is the embodiment of the new covenant. It is a realization of the sure mercies of David, and it is freely offered to all who will partake of it. It is an everlasting covenant, granting security from fear and oppression, and the universal recognition of all who share in it as the seed of divine blessing. They are disciples of Jahveh, are under His divine guidance and instruction; His Spirit is within their hearts; His words are in their mouths; and they enjoy everlasting peace.[3]

We have in the Messianic prophecy of the Old Testament an organic system constantly advancing on the original lines, and expanding into new and more comprehensive phases with the progress of the centuries. Vast and complex that organism is,—so complex that the wisest sages of Israel could not comprehend it,—as vast as the difference between a divine advent and a human advent, as contrasted as a suffering and a reigning Messiah, as an advent of grace and revival, and as an advent of judgment and perdition; and yet there is a unity in all this variety and complexity that no one

[1] Jer. xxxi. 31–37, p. 256.
[2] Ezek. xxxiv. 25–31, xxxvii. 26–28, pp. 272 and 277.
[3] Isa. xlii. 6, liv. 10–17, lv. 3, lix. 21, lxi. 8, 9, pp. 345, 363, 368, 370, and 391.

could discern until Jesus Christ was born, God manifest
in the flesh; until He passed through the experience of
a suffering Messiah, and advanced to His throne as the
reigning Messiah; until the advent of the Holy Spirit at
Pentecost warned of the advent of the great and terrible
day of judgment.

In Jesus of Nazareth the key of the Messianic prophecy of the Old Testament has been found. All its
phases find their realization in His unique personality,
in His unique work, and in His unique kingdom. The
Messiah of prophecy appears in the Messiah of history.
The redemption predicted as the completion of the redemption experienced in greater and richer fulness in the
successive stages of the old covenant is at last completed
in the Messiah of the cross and of the throne, in the
Lamb that was slain for the redemption of men, but who
ever liveth as the fountain of life, and the owner of the
keys of Hades.

Hebrew prophecy vindicates its reality, its accuracy,
its comprehensive ideality as a conception of the divine
mind, as a deliverance of the divine energy, as a system
constructed by holy men who spoke as they were moved
by the Holy Spirit. The Messiah of prophecy and the
Messiah of history, the redemption of Hebrew prediction
and the redemption of Christian possession, are not
diverse, but entirely harmonious in the Lamb, who was
foreordained before the foundation of the world, but was
manifest in these last times of its history.[1] For it was
the same divine Being who devised the redemption of the
world, who revealed it in prophetic prediction, who
prepared for it in the development of history, who
accomplished it in time and eternity. Hebrew prophecy
springs from divinity as its source and ever‑flowing
inspiration, and it points to divinity as its fruition and

1 Pet. i. 20.

complete realization. None but God could give such prophecy; none but God can fulfil such prophecy. The ideal of prophecy and the real of history correspond in Him, who is above the limits of time and space and circumstance, who is the creator, ruler, and saviour of the world, and who alone has the wisdom, the grace, and the power to conceive the idea of redemption, and then accomplish it in reality through the incarnation, crucifixion, resurrection, ascension, and second advent of His only begotten and well-beloved Son, very God of very God, the Light and Life and Saviour of the world.

INDEX OF TEXTS.

GENERAL INDEX.

THE END.